D1226773

ASSESSMENT
AND
TREATMENT
OF
ADDICTIVE
DISORDERS

ASSESSMENT
AND
TREATMENT
OF
ADDICTIVE
DISORDERS

Edited by

Timothy B. Baker

and

Dale S. Cannon

New York
Westport, Connecticut
London

890909

DEC. 29 1989

Library of Congress Cataloging-in-Publication Data

Assessment and treatment of addictive disorders / edited by Timothy B.
  Baker and Dale S. Cannon.
      p. cm.
    Bibliography: p.
    Includes index.
    ISBN 0–275–92388–6 (alk. paper)
    1. Alcoholics—Rehabilitation. 2. Alcoholism—Treatment.
3. Cigarette smokers—Rehabilitation. 4. Cigarette habit—
Treatment. I. Baker, Timothy B. II.Cannon, Dale S.

HV5276.A87 1988
262.2'9—dc 19   87–30537

Copyright © 1988 by Praeger Publishers

Library of Congress Catalog Card Number: 87–30537

ISBN: 0–275–92388–6

First published in 1988

Praeger Publishers, One Madison Avenue, New York, NY 10010
A division of Greenwood Press, Inc.

Printed in the United States of America

The paper used in this book complies with the
Permanent Paper Standard issued by the National
Information Standards Organization (Z39.48–1984).

10 9 8 7 6 5 4 3 2 1

CONTENTS

v

PART II TREATMENT

INTRODUCTION

This book does not constitute a broad review of assessment and treatment approaches to addictive or habitual disorders. Rather, we have solicited contributions that we believe represent promising approaches to addiction assessment and treatment and that report complex data sets on relevant topics. We asked all contributors to incorporate their own data into their chapters. We believe that this promoted a specificity of exposition that should make the chapters more valuable to the reader.

We have divided the offerings into two major sections: assessment and treatment. The treatment section is admittedly parochial in that it contains two chapters on aversion therapy. However, the subjects of one of these chapters (Tiffany and Baker) are smokers, and the subjects of the other are alcoholics (Cannon et al.). Moreover, the Tiffany and Baker chapter also contains material on coping-response counseling. The Brandon, Zelman, and Baker chapter examines the effectiveness of a relapse prevention program, while the Hall, Sorensen, and Loeb chapter describes a job-training program for heroin addicts.

The assessment section contains chapters on self-monitoring (Kirschenbaum), assessment of social/family interaction patterns (Humphrey), assessment of self-efficacy and relapse determinants (Annis and Davis), and assessment of drinking patterns over time (Maisto et al.).

Marlatt and Gordon (1985) proposed a model of relapse that has gained wide acceptance among behavioral psychologists interested in addictive behavior. A central tenet of their model is that a "lapse" is most likely to occur following a high-risk situation for which the addict has no effective coping response. Thus, identification of high-risk situations is an essential task for clinicians using Marlatt and Gordon's model. Marlatt and Gordon proposed eight categories of high-risk situations and determined through interviews the relative frequency with which relapses were preceded by each category for various addictions. Annis and Davis (Chapter 2) developed two questionnaires for alcoholics that attempt to assess the threat posed by each category of high-risk situation. The Inventory of Drinking Situations (IDS) was designed to assess high-risk situations in the year prior to treatment. The Situational Confidence Questionnaire (SCQ) asks about the same situations as the IDS but in the subjunctive mood rather than in the past tense. The SCQ is intended to measure self-efficacy for potential high-risk situations.

The questionnaires offer several advantages over Marlatt and Gordon's interview-based scoring procedure. First, they are self-administered and so are easier to use. The clinician will probably want to supplement the questionnaire results with a patient interview, but the questionnaires may prove to be efficient tools for initial assessment. Second, the IDS may permit a more accurate understanding of multiple antecedents of lapses than does Marlatt and Gordon's interview scoring system, which requires that a lapse be attributed only to one category of high-risk situation according to a hierarchy of categories. For example, in Marlatt and Gordon's scoring system a lapse could be attributed to a physical urge only if the patient had not also experienced a negative emotional state. On the IDS, questions about physical urges and negative emotional states could both be answered affirmatively for the same lapse. It should be noted, though, that Annis and Davis empirically found good agreement between the IDS and Marlatt and Gordon's interview results with respect to how frequently each high-risk category is endorsed as the precipitant of a lapse. A third potential advantage of Annis and Davis's questionnaires is that the SCQ may prove to be a useful measure of self-efficacy on which therapeutic intervention might be based. In the absence of any data, though, one cannot be sure the SCQ measures anything different than does the IDS. Annis and Davis illustrated how these measures can be integrated into a theory-derived treatment for alcoholism.

Annis and Davis's chapter also makes important contributions to treatment. First, they provided an excellent set of guidelines for designing a self-efficacy-based assessment and treatment program. For example, they observed that performance-based treatments appear to be prepotent in producing persistent behavior change, that self-efficacy treatments should provide subjects with mastery experiences graded in difficulty level so as to insure early success, that mastery experiences should be representative of challenges that clients will face, and so forth. These observations introduce a variety of questions; for example, what are the performance-based addiction interventions? How do we provide subjects with helpful feedback? Although Annis and Davis's contribution models some answers to these questions, much research remains to be done. For instance, is it indeed the case that superior outcomes would be produced by a treatment program that comprises drug-refusal practice, practice of coping responding, urge induction, and coping with urges in the treatment context (all with performance feedback) than by a traditional program emphasizing admission of problem, educational/didactic information, and sharing/group support? The fact that we have no clear answer to this question stands as a testament to the primitive state of addiction-treatment research—indeed, as a testament to the primitive nature of all treatment-outcome research (e.g., Smith and Glass 1977).

Annis and Davis's work also introduces the observation that subjects' own efficacy or confidence estimate (their estimates that they will succeed or fail at remaining abstinent) is generally the most accurate single predictor of posttreatment functioning. Thus, although clinicians and researchers may have great difficulty predicting which of their clients will do well after treatment, the clients apparently do not. This is illustrated by the fact that in both the Tiffany and Baker and the Brandon, Zelman, and Baker chapters, subjects' confidence ratings were the single best predictor of posttreatment functioning. On what do clients base their estimates? With what factors are the estimates associated?

Bandura's (1977) self-efficacy theory, of course, predicts that clients' confidence or efficacy estimates have a causal role in determining treatment outcomes. (While efficacy and confidence estimates constitute performance and outcome appraisals, respectively, they are conceptually similar and share substantial variance; e.g., see Tiffany and Baker.) Clients are presumed to appraise their present and past criterion-relevant behavior and arrive at an efficacy estimate. This estimate is, in turn, thought to influence subsequent coping behavior; for example, high efficacy estimates are presumed to mediate persistent coping. The conceptual status of efficacy estimates is important because, if Bandura's theory is correct, increases in efficacy estimates may serve as important process measures and guide future treatment development.

The research by Tiffany and Baker and by Brandon, Zelman, and Baker provides new information about the nature of self-efficacy. First, both studies found that a single, global confidence question afforded a more accurate prediction of outcome than did Condiotte and Lichtenstein's (1981) 48-item questionnaire. This result is compatible with Baer, Holt, and Lichtenstein's (1986) recent finding that the Condiotte and Lichtenstein instrument principally taps a single factor. In addition, Baer, Holt, and Lichtenstein found that pretreatment smoking rate was the psychosocial variable most highly related to posttreatment self-efficacy ratings.

Moreover, once posttreatment smoking status (abstinent versus smoking) was regressed on baseline smoking rate, self-efficacy accounted for no additional variance in follow-up smoking status. Baer, Holt, and Lichtenstein (1986) interpreted this to mean that self-efficacy made no independent contribution to the determination of smoking status.

Data from both Brandon, Zelman, and Baker and Tiffany and Baker suggest that confidence ratings account for variance in numbers of days of abstinence that cannot be accounted for by any single performance variable, such as baseline smoking rate. It is certainly true that confidence estimates are statistically related to performance measures, but this is not theoretically telling. The causal/conceptual status of self-efficacy appraisal remains an important topic for future research.

The contributions by Cannon et al. and Tiffany and Baker provide evidence that pairing the taste and smell of an addictive agent with malaise results in the acquisition of a taste aversion that is indexed by a tachycardiac response. The replication of this finding with two different addictive agents and different populations suggests that this finding is externally valid. While there is growing evidence that taste or chemical aversion therapy produces aversions, there is still relatively little evidence that aversion therapy produces long-term outcomes superior to those achieved with nonaversive approaches. Demonstration of the clinical benefits of aversion therapy seems especially needed in the treatment of alcoholism, as so few experiments have been conducted that have included appropriate controls.

Kirschenbaum's chapter is aimed at characterizing the self-regulatory processes thought to be important to the maintenance and generalization of behavior change. He addressed the challenging question of why treatments aimed at producing enduring behavior change—for example, weight loss—produce results only slightly less evanescent than the treatment itself. Kirschenbaum's review suggests that three factors contribute significantly to self-regulatory failure:

1. depressogenic cognitions—low performance expectations, negative self-appraisals, low rates of self-reward;
2. difficulties in coping with stressors;
3. disengagement from self-monitoring.

Although there is strong evidence that these factors are related to relapse, we do not know the nature of these relationships. For example, disengagement from self-monitoring is definitely linked to relapse, but does such disengagement activate relapse processes or does it instead reflect such processes? Kirschenbaum also pointed to the importance of initial postcessation drug or substance use in precipitating full-blown relapse. Kirschenbaum contended that such a slip may occasion complete relapse because it causes individuals to disengage from coping and self-monitoring. He suggested that disengagement occurs after a slip because coping and self-monitoring cause persons to attend to their failures and may occasion self-punishment.

Kirschenbaum asserted that "some form of systematic attention to the self-regulated target behavior must be sustained to avoid self-regulatory failure." He suggested that a goal of therapy might be to help clients develop an obsessive-compulsive self-regulatory style. In the case of addictions this might involve monitoring exposure to high-risk situations (situations in which there is great danger of relapse), assessing urge frequency and severity, the use of coping strategies to deal with high-risk situations, and self-reinforcement for appropriate coping.

Kirschenbaum's implication of self-monitoring failure in relapse is persuasive. However, his model of relapse does not address a question of paramount importance: What treatments or experiences are sufficient to motivate sustained, repetitive self-monitoring? In the Brandon, Zelman, and Baker study smokers were provided with bound, professionally printed "ex-smoker diaries" to use in self-monitoring their urges, encounters with high-risk situations, and compliance with treatment over a three-month posttreatment maintenance period. Despite having periodic group meetings to check diary completion, despite instruction in how to complete the diary, and despite desperate pleadings and urgings to complete diaries, compliance was abysmal. No subject completed his or her diary for more than a two-week period. This low rate of compliance does not necessarily mean that many individuals will be reluctant to self-monitor on their own, but such reluctance is likely given the reasons that subjects offered for their lack of compliance. Subjects reported that attention to smoking was aversive because it reminded them of cigarettes and the unavailability of cigarettes, and therefore it led to tension, dysphoria, and urges. Among these smokers the most successful ones reported that they typically spent hours or days not even thinking of smoking. These successful subjects claimed that attending either to smoking or abstinence from smoking tended to increase their urges to smoke, even when they attended to positive aspects of their quitting (e.g., a successful coping occasion). While these observations are of dubious epistemological status, they do raise questions about self-monitoring approaches to addiction treatment. How to motivate conscientious self-monitoring? Can self-monitoring be harmful in that it promotes thoughts about substance use? Might the efficacy of self-monitoring vary as a function of stage of the cessation process? Might self-monitoring efficacy be related to individual differences? These questions, plus the issue of whether self-monitoring failure is a cause or consequence of relapse, present important questions for future research.

The impact of alcoholism on family members and the impact of recurring family interaction patterns on the alcoholic are receiving increasing clinical attention. Similar effects may be assumed for other addictive behaviors. Empirical analysis of these effects has been hampered by the absence of a satisfactory instrument for measuring complex family interactions. Humphrey (Chapter 4) described an instrument, the Structural Analysis of Social Behavior (SASB), and showed how it can be useful in studying dysfunctional families. The SASB may be unfamiliar to many in the substance-abuse field and so is presented here even though Humphrey described its use with families of bulimics. The purported advantage of the SASB is that it is a standardized technique for scaling complex, clinically relevant interactions. The complexity of the behaviors measured accounts for a major disadvantage of the technique; that is, it is difficult to learn to use. Humphrey reported that 100 or more hours initially plus ongoing "booster" sessions are required to train a rater. Such training is available in workshops around the country offered by Benjamin, the technique's originator.

How might the SASB approach be used? First, it might be used to determine the relationship between current family communication patterns and the addict's/abuser's present or future problem characteristics. For example, among problem drinkers, do particular family communication patterns predict progression to more abusive drinking? Are some communication patterns related to subclasses of addict populations (e.g., do communication patterns differ between families in which the alcoholic member has a strong genetic/family history as opposed to families in which the alcoholic has no such history)? Second, family interaction might be used as an index of treatment effects. This might be especially useful when the treatment is targeted at family/social interaction patterns, but it possesses broader utility. Interaction patterns might reflect how changed drug-use patterns affect family interaction no matter the nature of the treatment. Complex family-interaction coding schemas might be more sensitive to the consequences of different drug-use patterns than are traditional outcome measures (e.g., Gerard, Saenger, and Wile 1962). Finally, the interaction rating schema that Humphrey described might be useful for coding or characterizing the process of verbal psychotherapy itself. Perhaps this will allow us to identify characteristics of the therapeutic interchange that are associated with treatment success (e.g., Henry, Schacht, and Strupp 1986).

While considerable recent research shows that there is a genetic contribution to some forms of addiction (e.g., alcoholism), there certainly is evidence that family and rearing environment influences the nature and course of addictive disorders. For example, there is evidence that family disturbance or family breakup is associated with early-onset alcohol abuse (e.g., Francis, Timm, and Bucky 1980; Vaillant 1983). Moreover, there is strong evidence that posttreatment functioning among alcoholics is related to family environment (e.g., Finney, Moos, and Mewborn 1980). The

SASB represents a new, and we believe powerful, approach to characterizing the intrafamilial behaviors that encourage or discourage exacerbations of drug use.

What is the best way to characterize an addict's pattern of drug self-administration over time? It is widely appreciated that dichotomizing people into abstinent/nonabstinent categories does not accurately reflect the wide variability in individual patterns of posttreatment drug administration; so researchers doing treatment outcome studies have developed various quantity-frequency indexes to reflect treatment effects (e.g., Armor, Polich, and Stambul 1978). Pretreatment differences in substance-abuse pattern have served as one criterion for substance-abuse typologies thought to have prognostic significance (e.g., Jellinek 1960). Maisto et al. (Chapter 1) proposed a statistical/analytical procedure for the grouping and characterization of drug-use profiles.

Through a technique called modal profile analysis, the authors showed how the drinking patterns of 48 alcoholics can be characterized by a relatively small number of prototypic drinking profiles. Each profile depicts a different pattern of drinking across days. The authors noted the many potential research applications of their profile-matching procedure. For example, research might reveal that different long-term drinking profiles are differentially associated with personality type (e.g., psychopathy), etiological factors (positive family history), or response to treatment. Moreover, modal profile analysis may provide new insights into typical patterns of drug-use careers.

Hall, Sorensen, and Loeb's chapter describes a training program designed to help heroin addicts find and keep jobs. This chapter is important because it underscores that recovery from a drug-abuse career is dependent on more than a change in the motivation to take drugs. Because addictive drug use exerts far-ranging effects, it influences diverse aspects of the addict's life, including vocational, physical, social status, and abilities.

It is a common observation that among addict populations (e.g., alcoholics, opiate addicts) those who enjoy the highest social-vocational status tend to do the best following intervention (e.g., Cannon et al., Chapter 7). Why is this? One obvious answer is that social-vocational status is correlated with physical dependence on drugs and that the addicts without social-vocational resources are likely to do poorly following treatment because of their level of dependence, not because of their social-vocational status. However, another perspective on this is that it is the actual posttreatment social-vocational opportunity that makes a difference. If so, a primary aim of intervention programs in the addictions should be to improve clients' social-vocational status. Changing clients' belief systems about drugs, discussing drug urges, or instilling a fear or repugnance of drugs (e.g., aversion therapy) may be relatively inconsequential over the long term. This perspective is consistent with Gerard,

Saenger, and Wile's (1962) observation that most alcoholics attribute their posttreatment recovery from alcoholism to events and experiences that occurred outside of the treatment context. As Gerard and Saenger noted, "The less the clinic became involved in the intricacies of the determinants of the patients' symptoms, relationships, or defenses, the more likely was the clinic to succeed in supporting change in drinking behavior" (1962, p. 192). More recent research attests to the importance of extratherapeutic social-vocational changes to the long-term functioning of addict populations (Finney, Moos, and Mewborn 1980; Vaillant 1983). Hall, Sorensen, and Loeb's chapter suggests a route to making extratherapeutic social-vocational changes therapeutic.

A notable and important aspect of Hall, Sorensen, and Loeb's research is that they did not merely demonstrate the efficacy of the Job Seeker's Workshop in replicated studies, but also tackled the problem of how to disseminate this intervention. The silver lining in the finding that pragmatically oriented interventions may have more impact than psychologically oriented interventions is that the former may be easier to disseminate widely, as they require less training for their implementation. Yet, as Hall, Sorensen and Loeb noted, dissemination has received relatively scant attention. The research by Hall and her colleagues strongly supports face-to-face contact between disseminators and treatment staff to facilitate treatment implementation. Finally, in their chapter Hall and her colleagues took an extraordinary step toward dissemination of their workshop—they described the workshop procedures well enough so that the reader might implement a similar program.

Modern smoking cessation treatments are very successful in producing high initial cessation rates (e.g., Hall et al. 1984; Tiffany and Baker, this volume). However, inexorable subsequent relapse occurrences have led to calls for effective maintenance treatments that have become an obligatory feature of smoking treatment reviews. The Brandon, Zelman, and Baker chapter reports data on the effectiveness of a maintenance procedure designed to train coping-response execution and to break the association between drug signals and urges through exposure treatment. The results of this research suggest that maintenance intervention results in a reduced relapse rate, but only for that period of the follow-up interval when maintenance sessions are ongoing. Moreover, it is difficult to attribute this transitory success to coping response or exposure training because those treatments should, presumably, result in more durable effects and because subjects were so unwilling to participate in central aspects of treatment (e.g., diary completion, completing exposure assignments). It may be that nonspecific effects of therapy, such as group support, were responsible for whatever benefit the maintenance treatment had.

One purpose of the Brandon, Zelman, and Baker study was to gather information on the specific routes through which maintenance procedures reduce or delay relapse. This research yielded hints regarding this topic. In particular, maintenance treatments may have delayed or prevented relapse among subjects who were not confident of their success or who were prone to psychological disturbance. Maintenance subjects were more likely than nonmaintenance subjects to relapse in response to stressors. It is important to note that this latter result does not indicate that maintenance sessions render individuals more susceptible to stressors. Rather, it is likely that maintenance sessions kept some proportion of relapse-susceptible subjects abstinent long enough so that they could encounter significant stressors.

Finally, we shall close with an observation made by one of the editors (T.B.B.) who served as a therapist in the Brandon, Zelman, and Baker study. Halfway through the maintenance study I became convinced that the orientation or goals of the maintenance treatment were all wrong. We were training people to anticipate urge-eliciting situations to cope with cognitive precursors to relapse, to expose themselves to drug signals, and so forth. However, it quickly became apparent that this was not what our subjects wanted. They wanted instead to talk about incidents or specific problems that troubled them (e.g., "what to do about my job"), to find out what was happening in the lives of other group members, and to discuss their moods. While the therapists asked about problems in the subjects' lives, they did so to the extent that the problems seemed directly related to smoking.

I would now recommend that maintenance treatments emphasize that smoking (or perhaps other types of addictive behaviors) is no longer the subject's problem. The problem is depression, or a divorce, or a dead-end job, or a lack of friends. The best type of coping-response training for maintenance subjects may not be urge coping but, instead, life coping. An implicit message of this approach is that smoking is irrelevant to the subjects' problems—it certainly does not constitute a solution. This approach would emphasize what Marlatt and Gordon labeled as "lifestyle modification" and in many ways would resemble traditional therapy. The preceding suggestion is exceedingly speculative, but I believe some clinical hunches are permitted, even in a research-oriented volume such as this.

REFERENCES

Armor, D. J.; J. M. Polich; and H. B. Stambul. (1978). *Alcoholism and treatment.* New York: Wiley.

Baer, J. S.; C. S. Holt; and E. Lichtenstein. (1986). Self-efficacy and smoking reexamined: Construct validity and clinical utility. *Journal of Consulting and Clinical Psychology,* 54:846–52.

Bandura, A. (1977). Self-efficacy: Toward a unifying theory of behavioral change. *Psychological Review,* 84:191–215.

Condiotte, M. M, and E. Lichtenstein. (1981). Self-efficacy and relapse in smoking cessation programs. *Journal of Consulting and Clinical Psychology*, 49:648–58.

Finney, J. W.; R. H. Moos; and C.R. Mewborn. (1980). Post-treatment experiences and treatment outcome of alcoholic patients six months and two years after hospitalization. *Journal of Consulting and Clinical Psychology*, 48:17–29.

Francis, R. J.; S. Timm; and S. Bucky. (1980). Studies of familial and nonfamilial alcoholism. *Archives of General Psychiatry*, 37:564–66.

Gerard, D. L.; G. Saenger; and R. Wile. (1962). The abstinent alcoholic. *Archives of General Psychiatry*, 6:83–95.

Hall, S. M.; D. Rugg; C. Tunstall; and R. T. Jones. (1984). Preventing relapse to cigarette smoking by behavioral skill training. *Journal of Consulting and Clinical Psychology*, 52:372–82.

Henry, W. P.; T. E. Schacht; and H. H. Strupp. (1986). Structural analysis of social behavior: Application to a study of interpersonal process in differential psychotherapeutic outcome. *Journal of Consulting and Clinical Psychology*, 54:27–31.

Jellinek, E. M. (1960). *The disease concept of alcoholism*. New Brunswick, N.J.: Hillhouse Press.

Marlatt, G. A., and J. R. Gordon. (1985). *Relapse prevention: Maintenance strategies in the treatment of addictive behaviors*. New York: Guilford Press.

Smith, M. L., and G. V. Glass. (1977). Meta-analysis of psychotherapy outcome studies. *American Psychologist*, 32:752–60.

Vaillant, G. E. (1983). *The natural history of alcoholism*. Cambridge, MA: Harvard University Press.

ASSESSMENT
AND
TREATMENT
OF
ADDICTIVE
DISORDERS

Part I

Assessment and Theory

1

PROFILES OF DRINKING PATTERNS BEFORE AND AFTER OUTPATIENT TREATMENT FOR ALCOHOL ABUSE

Stephen A. Maisto, Linda C. Sobell,
Mark B. Sobell, Hau Lei, and
Kathy Sykora

Traditionally, alcoholism treatment outcome evaluations have been limited to comparisons of independent group means at a given time or examinations of within group changes over time (usually six months or more). Although these types of analyses are useful for determining the relative efficacy of different treatment approaches and changes in group results over time, they can only provide limited information about the course of alcohol problems and the nature of recovery processes. Limiting outcome analyses to the comparison of group means can mask patterns of outcomes that have theoretical and practical importance. Other types of outcome analyses are needed to study such topics as the relationships among different dimensions of outcome over time, the testing of predictive models (e.g., by path analysis) of recovery and relapse, and the identification of shared patterns of outcome. This chapter presents the results of an exploratory analysis of patterns of drinking outcome based on a recently developed method of classification—Modal Profile Analysis.

The study on which the analyses reported in this chapter were based was supported, in part, by a research contract from the Tennessee Department of Mental Health and Mental Retardation, Alcohol and Drug Section, with L. C. Sobell. The views expressed in this publication are those of the authors and do not necessarily reflect those of the Addiction Research Foundation.

3

Evidence from both clinical and nonclinical studies shows that drinking behavior, as represented by a broad array of measures, often fluctuates over time. In studies of nonclinical, general population samples, for instance, Cahalan and his colleagues found that patterns of alcohol consumption and problems associated with drinking tended to vary even over intervals as long as four years (Cahalan 1970; Cahalan, Cisin, and Crossley 1969; Cahalan and Room 1974). More pertinent to this chapter are clinical studies of drinking patterns among alcohol abusers that suggest that drinking behavior following treatment is characterized by variability rather than stability. For example, in a four-year treatment outcome study, Polich, Armor, and Braiker (1981) concluded:

As the previous studies of this sample have shown, there can be considerable fluctuation from one status to another over a 1- or 2-year period. Some alcoholics who were abstaining at the 18-month followup may be engaging in alcoholic drinking at 4 years, whereas alcoholics who were unimproved at the 18-month followup may be abstaining at the 4-year point (p. 159).

Annis and Ogborne (1981) argued that instability in drinking behavior following alcoholism treatment is an important but neglected topic. By reanalyzing the data from eight published outcome studies, these authors demonstrated that grouped outcome results were stable over varying intervals when the drinking variable was nominally measured and had few categories. However, when more precise outcome measures were used (i.e., scaled variables rather than categories), group averages showed considerably greater fluctuation. Finally, when individual subject changes in drinking were examined, a substantial degree of instability in outcome was apparent.

The previously mentioned studies demonstrate that the use of group averages to summarize drinking over time tends to obscure changes in drinking patterns among individuals, as well as individual differences in drinking patterns over time. Such fluctuations have important theoretical and clinical implications. For example, Vaillant (1983), in his discussion of longitudinal studies showing "oscillations" in alcoholics' patterns of use and abuse of alcohol, seriously questioned the popular model of alcoholism as a progressive disease (also see Roizen, Cahalan, and Shanks 1978). From a practical perspective, reports of group drinking data averaged over long intervals of time also have limited value for clinicians. Of greater value would be an understanding of individual differences in drinking patterns over time that might allow clinicians to predict likely outcomes and to prevent relapses in their patients. It may be, for example, that patients who show a particular pretreatment drinking pattern have a much greater likelihood of posttreatment relapse than other patients (e.g., Eckardt et al. 1982).

One of the few studies to examine patterns in alcoholics' drinking (Litman, Eiser, and Taylor 1979) involved a further analysis of Orford, Oppenheimer, and Edwards's (1976) outcome data from male alcoholics and their spouses. Available data for 79 of the 100 patients over 12 months of follow-up showed the typical negatively accelerated group cumulative relapse (defined as the first day of heavy drinking) function, but there were considerable individual differences in alcohol consumption following the relapse. To probe further these individual differences, Litman, Eiser, and Taylor derived five scores for each patient—month of first heavy drinking, postrelapse frequency of heavy drinking, uptrend (in drinking over three successive months), erratic variation (an increase from the first to the second month, followed by a decrease from the second to the third month, or vice versa), and downtrend (over three successive months). The latter three variables were computed for 3-month blocks within the 12-month follow-up interval. A component analysis of the five variables showed two principal components in the data. The first component was dominated by month of first heavy drinking, which was not correlated with any of the other variables except for a strong negative relationship with downtrend. The second component was based on the moderate to high positive interrelationships among the other variables, excluding month of first heavy drinking. These results suggest a relationship between erratic drinking patterns (with three months as the unit of analysis) and frequency of heavy drinking. Moreover, they suggest that the time of initial relapse (as defined by Litman, Eiser, and Taylor) may not be the best variable for predicting longitudinal patterns of drinking among alcoholics following treatment. This study illustrates the limitations of the conventional "time to relapse" measure of treatment outcome. For example, other variables, such as level of drinking, vocational status, or medical complications of drinking, might be found to be more highly related to the second component than the first.

Before individual differences in drinking patterns can be evaluated, data must be gathered with some level of precision and quantification (e.g., daily drinking behavior, weekly summaries) for periods of time (preferably continuous) before, during, and following treatment (e.g., O'Farrell, Cutter, and Floyd 1985). Unfortunately, few outcome researchers use such procedures (see Riley et al. in press, for a review). Additionally, there is a serious lack of statistical techniques by which such data can be meaningfully analyzed.

The purpose of this chapter is to present some exploratory analyses that address the question of subtypes of drinking patterns among problem drinkers before and after treatment. Modal profile analysis (MPA; Skinner and Lei 1980) was used to derive the drinking pattern subtypes. The data were obtained in a study of problem drinkers in outpatient treatment (Maisto et al. 1985) that included assessment of daily drinking behavior for

12 months prior to treatment (retrospective) and 18 months following the initiation of treatment.

METHOD

The method, procedures, and major findings of the treatment outcome study from which the present data were obtained have been described elsewhere (Maisto et al. 1985). Thus, only information relevant to the present analysis will be presented here.

Subjects

The subjects were 48 male patients in an outpatient alcohol treatment program who volunteered to participate in the study and who met several screening criteria. They were randomly assigned to four treatment conditions created by the factorial combination of variations in length of treatment and style of follow-up data collection. Since the focus of MPA is on individual patterns, data from all subjects were used in the present analyses with no distinctions among treatment groups. (In any case, the various conditions had little effect on outcome—see Maisto et al. 1985.)

Subjects reported a mean age of 37.8 years (range: 18–65 years), a mean education of 10.0 years (range: 3–16 years), and the majority (83.3%) were white. They reported a mean drinking problem history of 7.6 years (range: 0–45 years), with means of 0.8 alcohol-related hospitalizations (range: 0–17), 3.3 drunk driving arrests (range: 0–13), and 13.1 public drunkenness arrests (range: 0–300; median = 1; two subjects had an extreme number of arrests, 150 and 300, respectively). Few subjects reported ever having experienced major alcohol withdrawal symptoms; delirium tremens—8.3%; hallucinations—20.8%; and seizures—4.2%. The large majority of subjects also reported no prior treatment for alcohol problems: 16.8% had attended at least one Alcoholics Anonymous (AA) meeting, 6.4% had used disulfiram at least once, and 6.4% had received some type of outpatient treatment. The majority of subjects were diagnosed (American Psychiatric Association 1980) as continuous alcohol abusers (52.1%), and the remainder were either episodic alcohol abusers (25.0%) or alcohol dependent (22.9%). Nearly one quarter of the subjects (23.4%, 11 of the 47 tested) had elevated serum glutamic oxaloacetic transaminase (SGOT) levels when admitted to the study; such levels are frequently associated with acute liver dysfunction due to recent heavy drinking (e.g., Wiseman and Spencer-Peet 1977).

Table 1.1 presents the mean percentage of days during the pretreatment year that subjects reported they spent in different daily drinking dispositions and the percentage of days that they were employed full or

Table 1.1.
Mean Percentage of Days Spent in Different Daily Drinking Dispositions[a] and Employed for All (*N* = 48) Subjects 12 Months Pretreatment

Variables	
% days abstinent	28.56
% days ≤ 3 oz absolute ethanol consumed	22.52
% days > 3 oz absolute ethanol consumed	46.86
% days jailed, alcohol-related	1.69
% days hospitalized, alcohol-related	0.37
% days employed (full-time or part-time)[b,c]	88.19

[a]No subjects reported being in a residential treatment program or being jailed or hospitalized for nonalcohol-related reasons during the pretreatment year.

[b]Maximum of 260 days in the pretreatment year; based on 52 weeks and a maximum of a five-day work week.

[c]Subjects who were students, disabled, or retired were excluded from this statistic, which reduced the *N* to 45.

Source: Compiled by the authors.

part time. As might be expected with this outpatient population, many of the subjects reported a substantial number (mean: 22.52% of all days) of low ethanol consumption (≤ 3 ounces absolute ethanol) days during the pretreatment year.

Procedure

After volunteering to participate in the study, subjects were individually interviewed at the treatment facility to gather pretreatment background and social and drinking history information. Data on subjects' daily drinking behavior during the 12 months before treatment were obtained using the time-line technique; this technique has been described elsewhere, and its reliability for patients from the treatment program that provided the subjects for the present study has been established (Sobell et al. 1979). Daily drinking behavior data obtained through this method were coded into six mutually exclusive categories: (1) no drinking (no alcohol consumed); (2) low ethanol consumption [≤ 3 ounces (≤ 37.8 grams) of absolute ethanol, which is approximately the equivalent of 6 ounces of 86- to 100-proof spirits or six 12-ounce cans of 3.6% beer]; (3) heavy ethanol consumption (> 3 ounces of absolute ethanol); (4) jailed for alcohol-related reasons; (5) hospitalized for alcohol-related reasons; or (6) in a residential alcohol treatment program. These six categories, as well as "incarcerated, non-alcohol related," were also used to assess subjects' postadmission drinking behavior. Subjects signed release-of-information forms to allow record verification of their self-reports of pretreatment events and incarcerations (e.g., arrests,hospitalizations, stays in residential treatment facilities, driving infractions). Similar releases were obtained to verify all reported incarcerations and events during the postadmission period.

The follow-up interval began with the day of the first treatment session, with the first follow-up interview scheduled for one month after the first treatment session. For outpatient treatment programs this follow-up design allows a more standardized comparison of outcomes than does having follow-up commence with treatment completion, since the length of outpatient treatment tends to vary widely across patients. Thus, the present follow-up data reflect functioning both during and after treatment.

Outcome data comparable to the pretreatment data were collected from subjects and their respective collateral informants for a total of 18 months.[1] Followup interviews were conducted in person, when possible, or by telephone. Interviews with subjects were scheduled monthly, although sometimes it took longer to contact subjects. In such cases, when the subject was contacted, he was asked about the total amount of time that had passed since the last interview. For example, if 67 days had elapsed between follow-up contacts for a subject, the interviewer collected data covering that 67-day period. Overall, 51.5% of all scheduled interviews were conducted within plus or minus seven days of the scheduled monthly contact.

Interviews with collaterals were scheduled to occur at bimonthly (60-day) intervals. As with the subject interviews, if contact was not made within the scheduled time period, then the interview covered the elapsed time between sequential collateral interviews. Collaterals were asked the same questions as those asked the subjects in their monthly interviews, except that the interview period covered a longer time interval. Collaterals were also asked how often and in what manner they had been in contact with the subject during the preceding interval. Analyses of the subject–collateral concordance data suggested that subjects' self-reports of their postadmission drinking were highly valid (Maisto et al. 1985).

Two interviewers, both with equivalent experience, conducted the follow-up. The first collected all of the pretreatment data and the first nine months of follow-up data before leaving to enter graduate school. The second interviewer joined the project before the first interviewer left, and the change of interviewers was accomplished without any problems or loss of subjects.

Modal Profile Analysis

The pretreatment and postadmission daily drinking data were analyzed using a technique called Modal Profile Analysis (MPA). The technical details and computer program of MPA have been published elsewhere (e.g., Skinner 1977, 1978, 1979; Skinner and Lei 1980). In this chapter MPA will be described conceptually, with emphasis on its application to the type of data represented by the daily drinking disposition measure.

Modal Profile Analysis is essentially a Q-type component analysis, that is, component analysis on subjects rather than on variables (see, e.g., Nunnally 1967). In other words, MPA uses a dimensional approach to classification. The focus of MPA is on the identification of a small number of dimensions that best capture the variation in the data. This is different from the usual clustering approach adopted by many clustering procedures, in which the focus is on grouping the subjects based on the distance among the data points representing them.

The first step in MPA is to remove the elevation and scatter components from each individual profile (these terms are defined in a later section of this chapter). What remains for each profile is a set of standardized scores that relate only to the shape of the profile. The cross-products of the individual profiles are correlation coefficients and reflect the similarity between profile shapes. Q-type component analysis is then applied to the correlation matrix of the profiles to derive a number of "modal" profiles. Thus, MPA derives modal profiles by using only the correlation coefficient, a similarity measure. This is in contrast to many clustering methods that use either similarity or dissimilarity (or distance) to derive clusters.

The choice between similarity and dissimilarity measures has remained an unsettled issue in the classification literature. Skinner (1978) showed that euclidean distance measures may be expressed as a function of elevation, scatter, and a scatter-by-shape interaction. It is often useful and desirable to differentiate the contribution of these three components of profile similarity (or dissimilarity), and MPA may be used to achieve this. For more information on cluster analysis, see, for example, Everitt (1980).

Two additional considerations are particularly important when using MPA: (1) Level of measurement: MPA assumes that the variables have been measured by at least a quasi-interval scale. To analyze rank order or categorical data, a simple transformation may be applied (Skinner and Sheu 1982). (2) Scale compatibility: If measures (for different attributes or occasions) vary considerably in means and variances, standardization of each measure may be needed to avoid a large "species factor" (Cattell 1952, p. 99).

More specifically, as the name suggests, MPA is a method of analyzing profiles. In this study, a profile refers to a plot of scores on a single attribute measured repeatedly at a fixed set of points in time. Usually, trend analysis is used to analyze this type of data. However, trend analysis is based on group averages, and its focus is on the fluctuations of mean scores over time. In contrast, MPA directs attention to the scores of each individual, and its focus is on the degree of resemblance of individual profiles.

A profile may be decomposed into the components of elevation, scatter, and shape (Cronbach and Gleser 1953). Elevation is the mean score of a profile, scatter is the standard deviation of the profile, and shape refers to its pattern of "ups and downs." To assess profile similarity, it is often desirable to separate the contribution of the three components. This is particularly the case for such attributes as alcohol use, since each of the three parameters has its own substantive significance. Specifically, elevation reflects a person's mean level of alcohol use (or abstinence) in a given time period, scatter indicates extent of variability in use, and shape describes the pattern of use.

After calculating each subject's elevation and scatter, each individual profile is standardized to have a mean of zero and a standard deviation of one. These standard scores of a profile reflect only its shape. Profile dissimilarity with respect to elevation and scatter is assessed by the magnitude of profile differences in elevation and scatter parameters, respectively. Similarity among profile shapes is assessed by correlations between profiles.

For a group of N individuals, similarities among profile shapes can be represented by an N-by-N correlation matrix. Usually, there is interest in grouping the N profiles into a few types. One of the primary objectives of MPA is to assist investigators in determining how many statistically independent types are required to capture the essential information in the correlation matrix. These orthogonal types are called Modal Profiles. Each modal profile is a distinct pattern of "ups and downs" of scores over a set of time points.

Similarities between individual profiles and modal profiles can be found in an N-by-M (the number of modal profiles) factor loading matrix. A large loading on a modal profile for an individual profile signifies that the modal profile has significant weight in reproducing the particular individual profile. Thus, these loadings are used to classify individual profiles. When a profile has equivalent loadings on more than one modal profile, the profile cannot be classified as belonging to a particular type.

There are three stages of MPA. Stage I involves the identification of modal profiles based on a sample of individuals. Stage II validates the modal profiles found in Stage I by investigating whether the modal profiles derived from several independent samples are equivalent to one another. The techniques used in Stage-II analysis are essentially the same as in Stage I, except that the input is a collection of modal profiles derived in Stage I, rather than individual profiles. The cross-validated modal profiles may then be used to classify individual profiles through the use of Stage III of MPA. This classification is based on the size of the correlations between an individual's profile and the cross-validated profiles.

In summary, MPA serves three major functions: (1) data reduction—it identifies modal profiles that underlie a group of individual profiles; (2) cross-validation—it determines if the modal profiles can be replicated across samples; and (3) classification—it classifies individual profiles into one of a few types, according to their correlations with the modal profiles. The overall objective is to assess individual profile similarity with respect to profile elevation, scatter, and shape parameters, separately.

Monthly Drinking Profiles

Since the study focused on the profile over months (rather than over days), subjects' daily drinking behaviors were aggregated into 30-day periods for each of the seven drinking behavior categories (see Procedure section). Three monthly drinking variables were then derived for each subject from these aggregates: (1) the proportion of days abstinent of days not incarcerated—this was the ratio of the number of abstinent days to the number of nonincarcerated days in the 30-day "month"; (2) the proportion of all drinking days that involved low ethanol consumption (LEC)—this was the ratio of LEC days to the sum of LEC days and heavy ethanol consumption (HEC) days; and (3) the proportion of days functioning well of days not incarcerated—this was the ratio of the sum of abstinent days and LEC days to the number of nonincarcerated days.

A logit transformation was applied to the monthly proportions to avoid their undesirable measurement properties (Cohen and Cohen 1975). This transformation changes the monthly proportion into the natural logarithm of the ratio of the proportion (or days) of having a given drinking behavior (say, abstinence) to the proportion (or days) of not having it. In other words, logit (p) = $\log[p/(1 - p)]$. For example, the logit of the proportion of abstinent days is the log of the ratio of abstinent days to nonabstinent days; the logit of the proportion of LEC days is the log of the ratio of LEC to HEC days; and the logit of functioning well is the log of the ratio of "abstinent or LEC" days to HEC days. Table 1.2 gives some anchor points between the logit and the proportion. Notice that one unit of change on the logit scale corresponds to a change of about 3% on the two ends of the proportion scale but about 23% in its center. That is to say, with the logit scale, percentage changes around the ends of the proportion scale are weighted more than those around its center. Since the logarithm of zero is undefined, a constant (known as a start) of 0.5 was added to each monthly aggregate so that none of the proportions could be zero.

Modal Profile Analysis was conducted on the monthly profiles of the logit of the three drinking variables: abstinence, LEC, and functioning

Table 1.2.
Some Examples of the Relationships Between Logit Transformed and Proportion Data

logit	equivalent proportion	logit	equivalent proportion
4.0	0.98	-4.0	0.02
3.0	0.95	-3.0	0.05
2.0	0.88	-2.0	0.12
1.0	0.73	-1.0	0.27
0.0	0.50		

Source: Compiled by the authors.

well. The unit of analysis was the subject, and each subject's profile consisted of 30 data points, 12 for the preadmission months and 18 for the postadmission months. A subject could have been excluded from the analysis for a given variable either because some data were missing or because all of the subject's data points were the same. All the analyses reported here coincidentally included 39 of the 48 subjects.

The minimum loading for classifying individual profiles into a modal profile was 0.5. The decision on the number of modal profiles hinges on a number of things, such as the distribution of eigenvalues, the interpretability and usefulness of the profiles, and the reproducibility of the profiles across samples. In our analysis, the number of profiles was based on the number of eigenvalues greater than 1 if we had conducted a component analysis on the variables. To arrive at that number, we rescaled the eigenvalues by the ratio of subjects to variables. For two of the three variables studied, abstinence and functioning well, there were five rescaled eigenvalues greater than one. (For LEC, there were seven.) Thus, we chose five profiles as our starting point.

RESULTS

For this study only Stage I of MPA was applied to the subjects' monthly drinking profiles. The results of the analyses on the three drinking variables are summarized in Table 1.3. This table lists the estimates of the elevation, scatter, and shape parameters of the individual profiles.

Subjects classified under the same profile for a variable share a similar pattern on that variable, even though their elevation (mean) or scatter (standard deviation) may differ. The magnitude of the loading indicates how closely the shape of the individual profile resembles the modal profile.

Table 1.3.
Estimates of MPA Parameters for Each Subject on Abstinence, LEC, and Functioning Well

Subject Number	MPA Parameter		
	Elevation	Scatter	Shape[a]
Abstinence Profiles			
1	1.628	1.640	1 (0.75)
2	-1.830	2.202	1 (0.68)
3	1.971	1.697	1 (0.98)
4	0.078	3.194	1 (0.98)
5	0.666	3.404	1 (0.94)
7	-0.489	1.357	1 (0.86)
8	2.115	1.173	1 (0.77)
9	-1.919	3.084	3 (0.68)
10	3.146	0.444	-2 (-0.78)
12	0.271	2.320	3 (0.70)
13	1.756	2.025	1 (0.87)
14	2.548	1.611	1 (0.74)
15	2.718	0.964	1 (0.80)
16	0.377	1.993	1 (0.82)
17	0.673	3.005	1 (0.93)
20	-1.115	3.040	-1 (-0.91)
21	2.266	0.572	-4 (-0.79)
22	0.116	1.898	1 (0.89)
23	-3.012	1.185	5 (0.81)
24	-0.494	2.638	1 (0.92)
25	0.953	1.222	2 (0.74)
27	-3.111	1.973	2 (0.58)
28	-0.164	2.157	1 (0.95)
29	-0.192	1.817	1 (0.94)
30	-1.741	2.148	1 (0.68)
32	-1.956	2.208	2 (0.50)
33	0.312	3.448	1 (0.99)
36	0.218	3.765	1 (0.96)
37	-1.116	2.135	1 (0.93)
38	0.738	2.587	4 (0.73)
40	-0.629	2.829	1 (0.73)
41	-2.265	1.321	3 (0.69)
42	-0.068	2.826	1 (0.91)
43	-1.179	1.640	1 (0.89)
44	0.240	2.318	5 (0.57)
45	0.930	3.281	1 (0.94)
46	0.639	3.298	1 (0.95)
47	2.166	1.748	1 (0.93)
48	0.949	0.542	3 (0.69)

Table 1.3
(continued)

Subject Number	MPA Parameter		
	Elevation	Scatter	Shape[a]
Low Ethanol Consumption Profiles			
1	0.343	1.077	2 (0.58)
2	-1.510	2.247	N.C.[b]
3	-1.398	1.607	1 (0.98)
4	-0.867	2.514	1 (0.93)
5	-1.480	1.964	1 (0.95)
7	1.749	1.198	2 (0.79)
8	-0.320	0.750	1 (0.80)
9	-2.281	2.685	-2 (-0.75)
10	-0.392	0.623	-3 (-0.63)
12	1.272	1.793	1 (0.73)
13	0.477	0.631	-1 (-0.91)
14	-0.037	0.084	1 (0.58)
15	-0.741	1.218	1 (0.85)
16	-0.128	1.276	N.C.[b]
17	0.487	2.153	-4 (-0.70)
20	-1.962	2.285	-2 (-0.71)
21	1.240	0.913	4 (0.75)
22	-0.746	1.890	5 (0.78)
23	1.806	1.732	1 (0.83)
24	-1.731	2.444	1 (0.79)
25	-0.563	1.615	1 (0.53)
27	0.053	2.061	-5 (-0.58)
28	-1.655	1.641	2 (0.50)
29	0.140	1.602	5 (0.87)
30	-2.150	1.704	1 (0.81)
32	-0.648	2.430	1 (0.86)
33	-1.454	2.194	1 (0.95)
36	0.819	0.590	N.C.[b]
37	1.163	1.021	-2 (-0.66)
38	0.297	2.141	1 (0.65)
40	-2.004	1.713	3 (0.54)
41	3.143	1.040	1 (0.81)
42	-1.955	1.732	1 (0.64)
43	-1.062	1.530	4 (0.72)
44	-1.751	2.017	1 (0.57)
45	-0.151	1.150	-3 (-0.75)
46	-0.526	1.711	3 (0.74)
47	-0.564	1.308	-4 (-0.71)
48	0.112	2.557	1 (0.95)

[a]Entries under shape indicate the modal profile (see Figure 1.2) to which the individual profile was classified and the loading (in parentheses) of the individual profile on the modal profile. A minus sign preceding the profile type indicates that the individual profile had a shape similar to the opposite pattern of the modal profile (see text).

Table 1.3
(continued)

Subject Number	MPA Parameter		
	Elevation	Scatter	Shape[a]
	Functioning Well Profiles		
1	2.844	1.542	1 (0.91)
2	-0.421	2.411	1 (0.75)
3	2.401	1.990	1 (0.86)
4	1.269	3.514	1 (0.89)
5	1.426	3.359	1 (0.89)
7	2.553	1.288	-3 (-0.77)
8	2.799	1.308	1 (0.70)
9	-0.796	3.522	3 (0.68)
10	3.724	0.647	-2 (-0.60)
12	2.957	1.589	4 (0.80)
13	3.153	1.172	4 (0.66)
14	3.360	1.418	1 (0.69)
15	3.269	1.246	4 (0.64)
16	1.678	1.909	1 (0.72)
17	2.732	2.641	1 (0.74)
20	0.000	3.069	-1 (-0.60)
21	3.929	0.467	2 (0.67)
22	1.275	2.141	4 (0.62)
23	1.988	1.541	4 (0.64)
24	0.439	2.928	1 (0.80)
25	1.889	1.294	1 (0.56)
27	0.528	2.050	3 (0.54)
28	0.539	2.155	1 (0.89)
29	1.692	1.376	4 (0.63)
30	-0.797	1.984	1 (0.88)
32	0.264	2.467	1 (0.71)
33	1.135	3.546	1 (0.87)
36	2.824	1.613	1 (0.86)
37	1.956	1.216	1 (0.58)
38	2.437	2.582	2 (0.65)
40	0.063	2.770	1 (0.71)
41	3.328	1.019	1 (0.88)
42	0.527	2.788	1 (0.82)
43	0.110	1.385	2 (0.71)
44	0.908	2.466	5 (0.76)
45	2.524	2.253	1 (0.77)
46	2.002	2.812	1 (0.81)
47	2.958	1.542	1 (0.91)
48	2.542	1.475	1 (0.66)

[b]N.C. = Not classified because the factor loadings of the individual profile on the modal profiles were below 0.5.

Note: Only those 39 subjects who had a profile loading of at least 0.5 on at least one modal profile are included.

Source: Compiled by the authors.

A negative loading signifies that the subject's profile is opposite to the modal profile. Figure 1.1, for example, shows abstinence profiles of three subjects whose pattern was classified as Profile 1 with large (in magnitude) loading, but different elevations, scatters, and signs of loading.

As can be seen in Table 1.3, about half of the 39 subjects had a positive mean logit over the 30 months. That is to say, over the 30 months, about half of the subjects were, on average, abstinent at least half of the nonincarcerated days. The table also shows that about one third of the subjects, on average, engaged in low ethanol consumption on at least half of their drinking days. However, all subjects except three were, on average, functioning well at least half of the nonincarcerated days. Many subjects had a large profile scatter. This suggests that these subjects had substantial variation in their drinking behavior over the 30 months.

Figure 1.2 shows the plots of the five modal profiles derived for each of the three drinking variables. Interpreting profile patterns, as interpreting factors in factor analysis, is an art rather than a science. Interpretation is especially difficult in our context, since we must rely only on the "ups and downs" of the same variable across time. Therefore, the following interpretations of the modal profiles are only tentative. Note that the zero point on a modal profile corresponds to an individual's elevation, and one unit along the vertical axis corresponds to an individual's scatter. Elevation and scatter differences among individuals (see Table 1.3) do not appear in Figure 1.2. This is because the modal profiles were derived after the individuals' profiles were standardized.

For abstinence, Profile 1 is characterized by stability and a lack of extremes within each of the preadmission (months 1 to 12 on the graphs) and postadmission (months 13 to 30) phases, coupled with an improvement in the level of abstinence a month before and a month after admission to treatment. Profile 2 is characterized by a peak level of abstinence in the month prior to treatment admission; the level of abstinence is generally increasing in the preadmission months and decreasing in the postadmission months. In Profile 3 the level of abstinence gradually declines in the preadmission months; after an abrupt increase in the month just after admission, it starts the gradual decline again. In Profile 4, during the preadmission months, the level of abstinence initially increases and then decreases back to its initial level; after admission the level of abstinence rises to the subject's overall elevation level, remains steady for about half a year, and then starts to fluctuate around that level. Profile 5 presents a pattern of hazardous fluctuations in the level of abstinence over the entire 30 months.

Profile 1 of low ethanol consumption, similar to that of abstinence, is characterized by an improvement in the level of low ethanol consumption both the month before and the month after admission; otherwise the level of low ethanol consumption is stable within the preadmission and

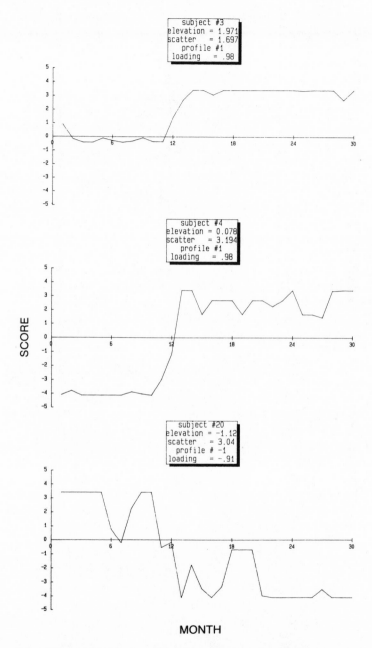

Figure 1.1. Three individual profiles for subjects who loaded high on modal Profile 1 (abstinence), illustrating individual variation in elevation, scatter, and sign of profile. *Source*: Compiled by the authors.

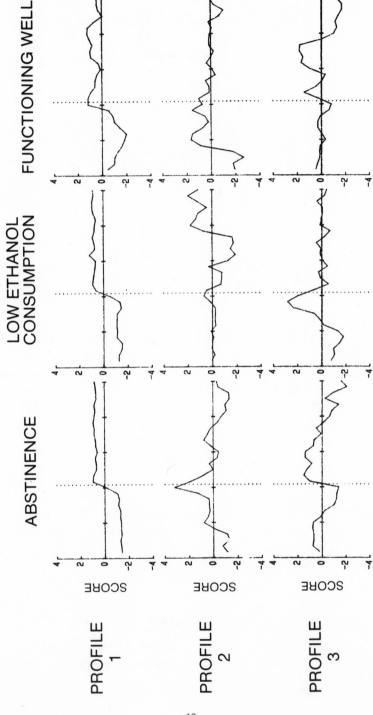

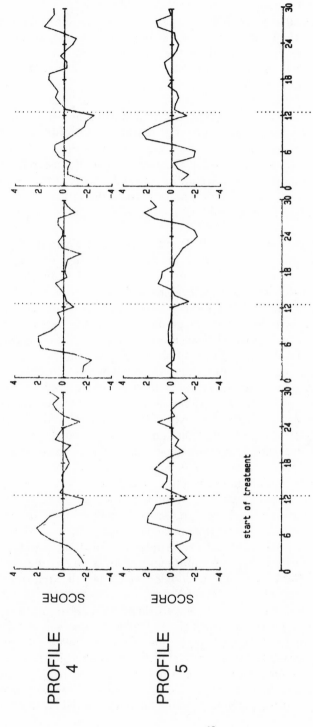

Figure 1.2. Five modal profiles obtained for each of the three drinking behavior variables (abstinence, low ethanol consumption, functioning well) and plotted using logit scores (see text). *Source:* Compiled by the authors.

postadmission months. In Profile 2 low ethanol consumption stays at the subject's mean level in the preadmission months; after admission low ethanol consumption initially declines, then rises to a level above the mean in the last seven to eight months of follow-up. Profile 3 is marked by an increase in low ethanol consumption in the preadmission months, with a peak a couple of months before admission; the level in low ethanol consumption starts to drop a month prior to admission and stays around the elevation level in the postadmission months. In Profile 4, in the preadmission months, the level of low ethanol consumption rises to a peak level, then drops to the mean level; it fluctuates around the mean level in the postadmission months. Profile 5 indicates a stable level of low ethanol consumption in the preadmission months and alternating phases of increases and decreases in low ethanol consumption in the postadmission months.

For the variable functioning well, Profile 1 is one in which during the preadmission months the level of desirable drinking behavior initially decreases and then increases but remains below the elevation level; it generally stays above the elevation level in the postadmission months. In Profile 2 desirable drinking behavior increases and peaks about half a year prior to admission; it then shows a gradual decline for the remaining months to around the subject's mean level. Profile 3 shows a relatively stable pattern in the preadmission months; in the postadmission months, the pattern shows large fluctuations and drops below the subject's mean level a year after admission. In Profile 4 the level of desirable drinking behavior first increases and then decreases in the preadmission months; after admission the level rises to the level of subject's mean and fluctuates wildly around it over the postadmission months. Profile 5 is characterized by a pattern of fluctuations around the mean level; the magnitude of fluctuations is reduced, however, after admission to treatment.

Although it appears that all the profiles have their idiosyncrasies, they can be decomposed, within each of the preadmission and postadmission phases, into five common element patterns: steady, rising, dropping, alternating phases of rising and dropping, and hazardous "ups and downs." In addition, it is notable that the five profiles for functioning well bear considerable similarity to those for abstinence. This is largely due to the heavy influence of abstinence on functioning well, since the frequency of LEC days in this sample was relatively low.

In Table 1.3 the column that is labeled shape lists, for each drinking variable, the modal profile to which the individual profile was classified and the loading of the individual profile on the modal profile. In these columns a negative sign before the modal profile number signifies that the individual profile is similar to the opposite pattern of the modal profile; that is, when the loading is negative (see Figure 1.1 for example). When the factor loadings of the individual profile on all the modal profiles were

Table 1.4.
Number of Subjects Classified Under Each Profile for Abstinence, Low Ethanol
Consumption, and Functioning Well

	Profile					
Variable	1	2	3	4	5	Proportion Classified
Abstinence	27	4	4	2	2	39/39
Low Ethanol Consumption	19	6	4	4	3	36/39
Functioning Well	25	4	3	6	1	39/39

Note: N = 39.
Source: Compiled by the authors.

below 0.5, the profile was not classified. All the individual profiles were classified except three on the variable of LEC.

Table 1.4 presents the number of subjects who were classified under each profile for each of the three drinking variables. For abstinence, all of the subjects included were classified into one of the five modal profiles. These subtypes accounted for 82.9% of the variance in this variable. For LEC, 92.3% (36/39) of the subjects were classified, and 72.2% of the variance was accounted for. For functioning well, 100.0% (39/39) of the subjects were classified, and 82.9% of the variance was accounted for. It is clear from Table 1.4 that the majority of subjects (49% to 69%) were classified as Profile 1 for each of the variables. This indicates that Profile 1 is the dominant profile for all the drinking variables studied. Although only a few individual profiles were classified into each of the remaining profiles, the four remaining profiles together accounted for a sizable number of individual profiles.

DISCUSSION

Several aspects of these results should be emphasized. First, a large number of individual profiles can be presented by a few basic modal profiles through the use of MPA. Second, as shown in Figure 1.2, the dominant profiles (Profile 1) identified in this study share a similar shape and are characterized by stability, with an improvement in outcome at admission to treatment that generally was maintained for the subsequent

18 months. Third, the remaining modal profiles show considerable fluctuations over the time period studied. These profile patterns confirm previous studies, reviewed earlier, showing that there are major individual differences in long-term patterns of drinking after treatment admission and indicate that such variability characterizes the period prior to entry to treatment as well. Finally, although stability was the dominant profile pattern, a sizable number of individual profiles could not be classified to that pattern and were marked by fluctuations rather than stability. These findings underscore that the use of group averages to describe the drinking patterns of individuals constituting a sample may not convey an accurate representation of the diverse array of actual patterns of outcome. It is also important to note that profiles with a similar shape may differ greatly in their elevation and scatter.

It is crucial to emphasize that the findings presented in this chapter are preliminary. The modal profiles identified and described here are based only on one outpatient sample and have yet to be cross-validated. Such cross-validation with similar outpatient samples is essential for determining the reproducibility of the drinking pattern typologies that were derived. Furthermore, the values specified in the MPA program (such as the number of modal profiles derived) under which those profiles were obtained are only tentative. Changing the values of these MPA parameters may yield different solutions. Some possible major variations for MPA are as follows:

1. The three drinking variables used in the study were all functions of the categories of a daily drinking variable originally collected and were analyzed separately. This is appropriate when the primary concern is these functions of the original categories. Alternatively, it is possible to analyze each category of the original variable (see the Procedure section), if the profiles of each category are of interest. If there is interest in the profiles of the original drinking variable as a whole (as contrasted to abstinence or LEC alone), then one may either apply the transformation as suggested by Skinner and Sheu (1982) or simply delete one of the categories and include all of the remaining categories in a single MPA analysis. In the latter case there is no loss of information, because the information for the deleted category is redundant. The interpretation for the modal profiles, however, will be more difficult than when analyzing categories separately.

2. In this study, data points before and after admission were treated as an integral part of the profile. It may also have value to analyze the preadmission phase separately from the postadmission phase. While a combined analysis facilitates the inspection of the drinking pattern and its change over the entire period, a separate analysis distinguishes between within-phase change and between-phase change.

3. The minimum loading for classifying individual profiles, as mentioned, was set as 0.5 in these initial analyses. The size of the minimum loading affects the homogeneity of the subtypes and their coverage. A higher minimum loading yields

a lower percentage of classification but a more homogeneous subtype. Therefore, there is a trade-off between the coverage and the homogeneity of the subgrouping. It is useful to examine closely the results of the analysis in evaluating the appropriateness of the cutoff point.

The finding that the dominant profile for each of the drinking variables (reflecting better functioning) was characterized by stability and lack of extreme values for the drinking behavior variables before treatment, followed by a similarly stable pattern but with improved functioning after treatment admission, suggests that stable, nonextreme pretreatment drinking patterns, at least as measured in this study, might be associated with postadmission stable improvement in drinking (Profile 1; see also Eckardt et al. 1982). This is particularly true of the abstinence variable, for which the only profile showing stable pretreatment behavior is the dominant profile (Profile 1). The remaining profiles, however, suggest that for individuals not matching the Profile 1 subtype it would be more difficult to make prognostic hypotheses about postadmission drinking based solely on pretreatment drinking. This latter conclusion reflects the previously cited variation in drinking behaviors over time that has been found to characterize nonclinical as well as clinical samples.

While there are several intriguing features of the results presented here, it must be kept in mind that we have presented only the product of a Stage I analysis of modal profiles. Although it is tempting to examine the relationship between the profiles obtained in this analysis and other factors—such as subjects' drinking histories, levels of dependence, reasons for entering treatment, compliance with treatment, and types of drinking-related problems—we have chosen not to do so for two reasons. First, the sample size is simply too small to justify a large set of such analyses. Second, and most important, it would be inappropriate to conduct such analyses based only on Stage I findings. Until the findings are cross-replicated with an independent sample, it will remain unknown whether they represent common patterns of drinking behavior or are simply idiosyncratic findings from a single study. As an alternative, we will discuss a few of the hypothetical, possible implications of the present findings that would obtain if our results were to be independently cross-replicated.

Perhaps the most striking aspect of the present findings is that the dominant pattern (Profile 1) for all variables shows a marked positive change in drinking behavior that ocurs during the month prior to entering treatment, with the change then maintained for the duration of follow-up. This suggests that factors other than treatment were responsible for the change and that the impact of treatment, if any, was on the maintenance of change. Such individuals might profit from a treatment specifically designed to enhance maintenance, such as the relapse prevention approach

(Marlatt and Gordon 1985). What factors might have produced the initial change is a matter for speculation. For example, the change might have been the result of cognitive processes, such as contemplation, as hypothesized to occur by Prochaska and DiClemente (1982). However, if subjects had experienced a drinking-related traumatic event shortly before entering treatment (e.g., arrest for drunk driving, marital separation), that could also have produced both an abrupt change in behavior and the decision to enter treatment. It is also possible that several different processes of these sorts yielded a common pattern—behavior change shortly before entering treatment. These examples serve to illustrate how MPA can be a useful tool in furthering knowledge about the natural history of alcohol problems and the treatment process.

There are several other ways in which MPA could be of value. Thus, it might be found that a Profile 1 type pattern applies mainly to those with lower levels of alcohol dependence or particular patterns of consumption (e.g., episodic heavy drinking). Identifying a cluster of variables, of which pretreatment drinking profile was one, might strengthen our ability to predict outcomes and to target interventions (e.g., place greater emphasis on maintenance processes for some persons). It also would be possible to use MPA as a dependent measure in an experimental comparison of different treatments. Marlatt (1983), for example, suggested that aversion therapy used in isolation will have an initial positive, but short-lived, effect on drinking behavior, whereas a relapse prevention approach might have a snowballing effect with subjects improving over time and maintaining that improvement. Naturally, the extent to which patterns of drinking behavior following treatment are determined by the specific treatment received or, alternatively, represent phenomena not specific to treatment type can only be evaluated by further research.

A final possibility that will be discussed here is that the analysis of outcome profiles might be useful in planning aftercare. Consider the possibility that cases could be identified in which a particular early pattern of outcome, plus perhaps additional characteristics (e.g., level of dependence, vocational problems), led to a prognosis of continuing deterioration. Such findings could form the basis for recommending reinvolvement in treatment, or for the experimental evaluation of after-care interventions specifically designed to alter the expected pattern of outcomes. A particularly promising potential line of research would be to examine patterns of outcome for a variety of populations of alcohol abusers (e.g., different levels of dependence) and for a variety of treatment approaches. Based on such work, crucial aspects of patient-treatment matching (Glaser 1980) might be empirically identified.

Finally, the methods described in this chapter could also be used to study relationships between pretreatment and postadmission drinking clusters (i.e., pattern types) and factors related to the etiology of drinking problems (e.g., family history), types of problems experienced (consequences), and the course of recovery (e.g., relapse precipitants, coping skills). Of course, such research would require larger samples of patients than used in the present study.

In summary, this descriptive study exemplified the value of Modal Profile Analysis for studying alcohol problems. The present findings are consistent with past research in revealing important individual differences among alcohol abusers in their drinking patterns before and following admission to treatment, and temporal fluctuations in drinking behavior in general. These findings have implications for developing more refined theories of alcohol abuse, enhancing the meaning of treatment outcome evaluations, and clinical practice. Advances in all of these areas would result from further research on long-term drinking patterns in clinical samples.

ACKNOWLEDGMENTS

We would like to thank Barbara Sanders and Terri Cooper for their assistance in collecting the data on which this chapter is based.

NOTES

1. Originally, all 48 subjects consented to participate in the follow-up study for 12 months. Later, it was decided that 18 months would be a more adequate postadmission evaluation interval. Therefore, all subjects were approached and asked to consent to continue the follow-up for a total of 18 months. Three subjects refused to consent to the additional six months of follow-up.

REFERENCES

American Psychiatric Association (1980). *Diagnostic and Statistical Manual of Mental Disorders*. 3d ed. Washington, D.C.: American Psychiatric Association.

Annis, H. M., and A. C. Ogborne. (1981). The temporal stability of alcoholism treatment outcome results. Unpublished manuscript, Addiction Research Foundation.

Cahalan, D. (1970). *Problem drinkers: A national survey*. San Francisco: Jossey-Bass.

Cahalan, D.; I. H. Cisin; and H. M. Crossley. (1969). *American drinking practices: A national survey of behavior and attitudes*. Monograph no. 6. New Brunswick, N.J.: Rutgers Center for Alcohol Studies.

Cahalan, D., and R. Room. (1974). *Problem drinking among American men*. New Brunswick, N.J.: Rutgers Center for Alcohol Studies.

Cattell, R. B. (1952). *Factor analysis*. New York: Harper and Brothers.

Cohen, J., and P. Cohen. (1975). *Applied multiple regression/correlation analysis for the behavioral sciences*. Hillsdale, N.J.: Lawrence Erlbaum.

Cronbach, L. J., and G.C. Gleser. (1953). Assessing similarity between profiles. *Psychological Bulletin*, 50:456–73.

Eckardt, M. J.; B. I. Graubard; R. S.Ryback; and L. A. Gottschalk. (1982). Pretreatment consumption as a predictor of posttreatment consumption in male alcoholics. *Psychiatry Research*, 7:337–44.

Everitt, B. (1980). *Cluster analysis*. 2d ed. London: Heineman Educational Books, Ltd.

Glaser, F. B. (1980). Anybody got a match? Treatment research and the matching hypothesis. In *Alcoholism treatment in transition*, eds. G. Edwards and M. Grant. London, England: Croom Helm, pp. 178–96.

Litman, G. K.; J. R. Eiser; and C. Taylor. (1979). Dependence, relapse and extinction: A theoretical critique and a behavioral examination. *Journal of Clinical Psychology*, 35:192–99.

Maisto, S. A.; L. C. Sobell; M. B. Sobell; and B. Sanders. (1985). Effects of outpatient treatment for problem drinkers. *American Journal of Drug and Alcohol Abuse*, 11:131–49.

Marlatt, G. A. (1983). The controlled-drinking controversy; A commentary. *American Psychologist*, 38:1097–10.

Marlatt, G. A., and J. R. Gordon, eds. (1985). *Relapse prevention: Maintenance strategies in the treatment of addictive behaviors*. New York: The Guilford Press.

Nunnally, J. C. (1967). *Psychometric theory*. New York: McGraw-Hill.

O'Farrell, T. J.; H. S. G. Cutter; and F. J.Floyd. (1985). Evaluating behavioral marital therapy for male alcoholics: Effects on marital adjustment and communication from before to after treatment. *Behavior Therapy*, 16:147–67.

Orford, J.; E. Oppenheimer; and G. Edwards. (1976). Abstinence or control: The outcome for excessive drinkers two years after consultation. *Behavior Research and Therapy*, 14:409–18.

Polich, J. M.; D. J. Armor; and H. B. Braiker. (1981). *The course of alcoholism: Four years after treatment*. New York: John Wiley & Sons.

Prochaska, J. O., and C. C. DiClemente. (1982). Transtheoretical therapy: Toward a more integrative model of change. *Psychotherapy: Theory, Research and Practice*, 19:276–88.

Riley, D. R.; L.C. Sobell; G. I. Leo; M. B. Sobell; and F. Klajner. (in press). Behavioral treatment of alcohol problems: A review and a comparison of behavioral and nonbehavioral studies. In *A resource manual on alcohol problems: How to treat and prevent them*, ed. W. M. Cox. New York: Academic Press.

Roizen, R.; D. Cahalan; and P. Shanks. (1978). Spontaneous remission among untreated problem drinkers. In *Longitudinal research in drug use: Empirical findings and methodological issues*, ed. D. B. Kandel, pp. 197–226. New York: Wiley.

Skinner, H. A. (1977). The eyes that fix you: A model for classification research. *Canadian Psychological Review*, 18:142–51.

Skinner, H. A. (1978). Differentiating the contribution of elevation, scatter and shape in profile similarity. *Educational and Psychological Measurement*, 38:297–308.

Skinner, H. A. (1979). Dimensions and clusters: A hybrid approach to classification. *Applied Psychological Measurement*, 3:327–41.

Skinner, H. A., and H. Lei. (1980). Modal profile analysis: A computer program for classification research. *Educational and Psychological Measurement*, 40:769–72.

Skinner, H. A., and W. J. Sheu. (1982). Dimensional analysis of rank-order and categorical data. *Applied Psychological Measurement*, 6:41–45.

Sobell, L.C.; S. A. Maisto; M. B. Sobell; and A. M. Cooper. (1979). Reliability of alcohol abusers' self-reports of drinking behavior. *Behavior Research and Therapy*, 17:157–60.

Vaillant, G. E. (1983). *The natural history of alcoholism.* Cambridge, Mass.: Harvard University Press.

Wiseman, S. M., and J. Spencer-Peet. (1977). The effects of drinking patterns on enzyme screening tests for alcoholism. *Practitioner*, pp. 243–45.

2

SELF-REGULATORY FAILURE

Daniel S. Kirschenbaum

Self-regulation refers to the processes by which people manage their own goal-directed behavior in the relative absence of immediate external constraints (Bandura 1977a; Carver and Scheier 1981; Kanfer and Karoly 1972; Mischel 1973, 1981). Thus, self-regulation involves interactions between cognitions, behaviors, physiology, and environmental constraints. For the purpose of parsimony, however, these complex relationships are often simplified by casting presumably central elements in a cybernetic model in which a negative feedback loop serves as a basic unit of functioning (see Carver and Scheier 1981; Kanfer 1971; Leventhal, Nerenz, and Straus 1980). This information processing unit is considered "negative" because its function is to negate, or reduce, perceived deviation from a standard of comparison or goal. Accordingly, from this perspective self-regulation involves establishing goals and related processes, such as expectancies and plans, monitoring one's behavior ("self-monitoring"), and evaluating observed performance relative to the goals ("self-evaluation"). According to some theorists (e.g., Bandura 1977a; Kanfer and Karoly 1972), but not others (e.g., Carver and Scheier 1981; Kuhl 1984), the final link in the closed loop of self-regulation involves administering consequences to oneself depending on the outcome of the self-evaluation (i.e., self-reward contingent on favorable self-evaluation; self-punishment contingent on unfavorable evaluation). The process of establishing and using goals (plans, expectancies), self-monitoring, and self-evaluation (with or without self-reinforcement) should result in reducing discrepancies between ongoing behaviors and goals or standards under most conditions, according to self-regulation theorists.

In the early 1970s behavioral self-regulation was heralded as a means of giving "power to the person" (Mahoney and Thoresen 1974). It was argued very persuasively that helping people maximize their abilities to self-regulate should promote maintenance of the behavior changes that were initiated in therapy, despite fluctuations in physical and social environments (Bandura 1969; Kanfer and Phillips 1970; Mischel 1973; Thoresen and Mahoney 1974). This conceptualization generated a great deal of enthusiasm because it not only promised to solve the seemingly intractable problem of achieving long-lasting behavior change, but it meshed with the zeitgeist of the times (Kanfer and Karoly 1972).Interest in self-regulation also swelled in response to a series of remarkable successes obtained through training in self-regulatory skills with such diverse populations as obese adults (Stuart 1967), cigarette smokers (Lando 1977), children in classroom settings (Lovitt and Curtis 1969; Meichenbaum and Goodman 1971), and schizophrenics (Meichenbaum 1969).

Unfortunately, despite the concerted efforts of many researchers and practitioners during the past decade, self-regulatory training has not fulfilled its promise as a means to promote generalized behavior change (see, for detailed documentation, Kirschenbaum and Tomarken 1982). Some may still argue that the interventions failed either because they were too brief or because they focused on the wrong components of self-regulation (e.g., Stuart 1980). This viewpoint, however, appears inconsistent with findings obtained in programs that included many months of training skills that appear readily mastered according to anecdotal and more formal assessments. For example, self-regulatory training programs for weight control have been conducted for 26 weeks (Mahoney et al. 1977) and 52 weeks (Harris et al. 1980; Kindy 1981). Each of these intensive programs resulted in unimpressive weight losses, despite evidence showing that obese people readily improve their abilities to self-regulate eating habits in such programs (e.g., Stalonas and Kirschenbaum 1980). Analogous results, which were again far from ideal, have been reported frequently even in intensive programs designed to improve the self-regulation of less physiologically mediated target behaviors (cf. Peterson 1983), including study skills (see reviews by Kirschenbaum and Perri 1982; Richards 1981) and children's classroom performance (see reviews by O'Leary and Dubey 1979; Rosenbaum and Drabman 1979). In a parallel fashion, studies focused on components of self-regulation thought to be especially important for improving generalization of behavior change (e.g., problem-solving; magnitude and type of self-reinforcement) have yielded inconsistent and generally disappointing results, even when supplemented with booster sessions or other procedures believed to maximize long-term effects (see Kirschenbaum and Tomarken 1982).

Several current models of self-regulation provide potential explanatory mechanisms for the inadequacies of self-regulatory training (Bandura 1977b; Carver and Scheier 1981, 1982b; Kanfer and Busemeyer 1982; Kanfer and Hagerman 1981; Kuhl 1984; Leventhal, Nerenz, and Straus 1980; Marlatt 1982; Marlatt and Gordon 1980). These models generally emphasize the importance of certain thought processes for the maintenance of self-regulated behavior change. It could be suggested that self-regulatory training per se does not necessarily facilitate the kind of thinking required to promote generalization. For example, several models suggest that failing to develop strong, generalized, and positive expectancies may contribute to failures in generalization (e.g., Bandura 1977b; Carver and Scheier 1981). Some theorists also argue that attributions may cause difficulties in generalizing behavior change, particularly internal attributions for failure experiences (e.g., Kanfer and Hagerman 1981). An even greater level of abstraction and complexity is seen in models in which cognitive representations of problem behaviors are considered focal (e.g., Kanfer and Busemeyer 1982; Kuhl 1984; Leventhal, Nerenz, and Straus 1980). Finally, some models posit specific and rather intricate sets of cognitive-behavioral steps that produce failures to maintain self-regulated behavior change (e.g., Kuhl 1984; Leventhal, Nerenz, and Straus 1980; Marlatt 1982; Marlatt and Gordon 1980).

Each of these models has an empirical foundation. Several of the models have also proven remarkably heuristic (see volumes by Carver and Scheier 1981; Karoly and Kanfer 1982). Unfortunately, as it will be shown in this chapter, their specific suggestions about failures in self-regulation have received either very minimal or no direct empirical tests. Moreover, as noted by Nisbett and Wilson (1977), Wortman and Dintzer (1978), and others (e.g., Lang 1978; Rachman 1981; Zajonc 1980), it is becoming increasingly clear that people often behave without invoking some of the complex cognitions proposed in these and related models. Or, at least, the relationship between extant measures of these hypothesized cognitive constructs and behavior often appears more subtle and much more complex than anticipated. For example, proposed attributional mediators (e.g., Denker-Brown and Baucom 1982; Devins et al. 1981; Diener and Dweck 1978, 1980; Harvey 1981), expectancies (McDonald 1980; Kernis et al. 1982), and health belief systems (Evans and Lane 1981; Rapoff and Christophersen 1982) have failed to account for self-regulated affective and overt behavioral responses under many conditions.

The outcomes of self-regulatory training studies and the empirical foundations of current models of self-regulation apparently leave many questions unanswered about how and why people actually fail to generalize behavior change. Perhaps the primary cause for this is the lack of an adequate data base about the active ingredients in failure to generalize behavior change (Kirschenbaum 1976). Self-regulatory training and models of self-regulation make assumptions about what people actually do in extra-therapy settings to interfere with generalization of the changes they initiated in therapy. But what do we really know about the variables that become activated during generalization of self-regulated behavior change? Are we remedying a problem before we understand its nature? The numerous failures in self-regulatory training and the difficulties of establishing links between complex cognitive processes and behavior clearly indicate that more fine-grained empirical scrutiny is warranted.

The purpose of this chapter is to demonstrate that a fine-grained analysis of failure in self-regulation is both feasible and fruitful. To do this, first a conceptualization of the problem will be presented that directs attention to the active elements of self-regulatory dysfunctioning, the study of "self-regulatory failure." Three relevant domains of research will then be examined to identify these active elements: successful versus unsuccessful self-regulation, the relapse process, and attention in self-regulation. Finally, a general means to prevent self-regulatory failure that appropriately reflects the thrust of the proposed description of the components of the problem will be considered—the development of obsessive-compulsive self-regulation.

THE STUDY OF SELF-REGULATORY FAILURE

The study of self-regulatory failure directs attention to "what people actually do to fail at self-regulation" (Kirschenbaum 1976, p. 3). It uses diverse literatures and self-regulatory models to formulate hypotheses and accumulate pertinent information about "self-regulatory failure," that is, "the processes by which individuals fail to generalize desired behavior changes over time and across settings in the relative absence of immediate external constraints" (Kirschenbaum and Tomarken 1982, p. 137). As such, the study of self-regulatory failure retains the emphasis on active processes in generalization embodied by all approaches to training and conceptualizing self-regulation. However, it calls for more direct exploration of the components or elements of self-regulation that interact with social-environment and physiological elements to prevent or inhibit generalization of behavior change.

A graphic illustration may clarify where this search begins. Figure 2.1 presents a hypothetical curve that closely resembles the long term follow-up data available for many treatments of addictive disorders (see Marlatt and Gordon 1980; McFall and Hammen 1971). As shown in the figure, baseline often precedes substantial behavior change during intervention (e.g., weight reduction, smoking cessation) followed by some generalization over

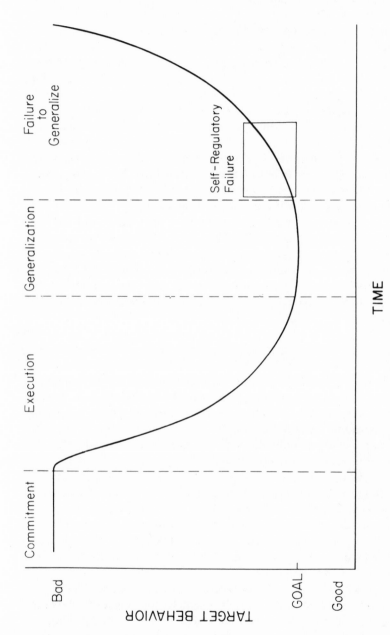

Figure 2.1. Hypothetical depiction of change in self-regulated behavior over time—from the commitment phase through failure to generalize. *Source:* Reprinted with permission from Kirschenbaum, D. S., and A. J. Tomarken [1982]. On facing the generalization problem: The study of self-regulatory failure. In *Advances in cognitive-behavioral research and therapy*, vol. 1, ed. P. C. Kendall. New York: Academic Press.

time. The box labeled "self-regulatory failure" suggests that at some identifiable point following termination of therapy, the failure process often begins. Unfortunately, then it typically proceeds with "inexorable force" (Leventhal and Cleary 1980). The components of that inexorable force may well include certain key changes in dispositional variables regulated by the individuals as proposed in current self-regulation models (e.g., changes in attention, self-evaluation, attribution) as well as social-environmental and physiological influences. By studying what people do and think about within the self-regulatory failure box depicted in Figure 2.1, we may learn a great deal about which elements are vital and when and how these elements interact. Thereby, we may become better able to understand the generalization process. This understanding, in turn, should lead to more precise models of self-regulation and to more effective proposals for helping people prevent self-regulatory failure.

The basic similarity among procedures used to improve self-regulatory skills over the past decade might suggest that little is known about self-regulatory failure (see Hall 1980; Peterson 1983). Actually, relevant information has been accumulating steadily since the mid-1970s, with a noticeable acceleration witnessed in the past few years. In the next section, research on successful versus unsuccessful self-regulation, the relapse process, and attention in self-regulation is examined to identify potentially active elements of self-regulatory failure.

The three literatures about to be reviewed vary considerably in focus and context, with the latter including more laboratory experiments using manipulations of components of self-regulation and the former literatures including more evaluations of treatment outcomes, follow-ups, and questionnaires in field settings. Although issues about external validity of the laboratory studies must be considered and issues about internal validity become more germane for the field studies, it is important to note that all of these studies share at least three important defining features. First, people emitted the behaviors under investigation to reach clearly established goals. Second, the subjects or clients involved were capable of executing the motoric and cognitive components of the to-be-controlled responses (cf. Skinner 1953) with minimal or no training (e.g., restricting caloric intake; eating more slowly; counting cigarettes, calories, study time, or time on task). Finally, the target behaviors consisted largely of "nondominant" (Kuhl 1984) or, equivalently, self-controlling responses (Skinner 1953) performed in the relative absence of immediate external control (see also Kanfer and Karoly 1972). These included primarily responses used to resist temptations (i.e., foregoing short-term positive consequences to avoid negative consequences in the long run, as when the dieter resists dessert to avoid weight gain) or responses emitted to tolerate noxious stimulation (i.e., incurring short-term negative consequences to attain long-term positive effects, as when the student memorizes lists of formulas to achieve a high grade). Thus, performing these target behaviors at a desired level, and particularly generalizing such performances over time and across situations, would not have been expected based on traditional expectancy-value analyses of motivation (Kuhl 1984).

SUCCESSFUL VERSUS UNSUCCESSFUL SELF-REGULATION

Since most people fail to generalize behavior change, self-regulated or otherwise, clinical researchers first examined this issue by searching for dispositional variables associated with failure and success. This approach is consistent with the fundamental attributional bias (Ross 1977) and with the belief that we can increase the efficiency and effectiveness of our therapies by finding ideal matches between interventions and persons. In at least one application of this strategy, studies on self-reinforcement style, the approach has already begun paying off (Bellack, Glanz, and Simon 1976; Carroll, Yates, and Gray 1980). Although the self-reinforcement style studies will be described in more detail shortly, for the present purposes the clinical benefits for which these studies were undertaken are less focal than the theoretical information they yield about self-regulatory failure.

Before analyzing the elements of self-regulatory failure suggested by this body of research, three methodological issues must be considered. First, success and failure in changing several different self-regulated behaviors have been studied. Since the present focus is on self-regulation more generally, I will place greatest emphasis on studies that examined success-failure across several target behaviors. Second, the research strategies used in this literature vary widely in methodological rigor. Some researchers, for example, conducted follow-ups a year or more after an intervention using questionnaires to generate post-hoc scores on various dimensions to determine why people failed or succeeded. Researchers also frequently failed to obtain corroboration of the subjects' responses; neither were other precautions taken nor assessments reported that ensured the reliability of scoring procedures. In contrast, other researchers conducted prospective studies using one or more structured interviews over a period of many months postintervention, taking steps to maximize and/or demonstrate the reliability of scoring procedures (e.g., Dubbert and Wilson 1983; Gormally, Rardin and Black 1980). Unfortunately, much of the success–failure literature contains methodological shortcomings, such as reliance on questionnaires completed anonymously (cf. Braginsky, Braginsky, and Ring 1969), uncorroborated self-report (cf. Nisbett and Wilson 1977), measures of unknown reliability (cf. Nunnaly 1978), and reports of actions and habits engaged in months or years prior to assessment (cf. Anzai and Simon 1979; Heinold et al. 1982). Thus, in this analysis I will focus on findings that have been replicated several times and on studies that evidenced greatest methodological sophistication. Finally, the differences found between successful and unsuccessful self-regulators, identified either correlationally or by comparing extreme groups, must be considered correlates, not causes, of self-regulatory failure. One cannot assume that even the differences found between extreme groups are the essential or active agents that caused them to be different (Heinold et al. 1982; McFall 1976). Differences observed may correlate with other unassessed variables, or they may be limited to the types of assessments utilized (cf. Hopper and Kirschenbaum 1985).

Depressogenic Cognitions

The aforementioned methodological issues mandate a generally cautious analysis of the success–failure literature and a specific focus on some of the more carefully conducted studies. Taking this perspective, one can still find some striking possibilities for active elements of self-regulatory failure by examining the commonalities among the four studies that compared successful with unsuccessful self-regulators assessed across several problem behaviors (Heppner et al. 1982; Marlatt and Kaplan 1972; Perri and Richards 1977; Rozensky and Bellack 1974). In all of these studies, some aspect of the commitment phase of self-regulation (Kanfer and Karoly 1972) appeared to play a role in self-regulatory failure. In particular, unsuccessful subjects generally evidenced weak efficacy and outcome expectations (cf. Bandura 1977a; Rotter 1954). For example, Heppner et al. (1982) found that their extreme groups of generally ineffective problem solvers reported relatively low expectancies for success and depressogenic attributions (Abramson, Seligman, and Teasdale 1978) on a psychometrically sound questionnaire that was corroborated with interview data. Similarly, Perri and Richards (1977) reliably scored structured interviews and showed that their unsuccessful self-regulators (people who attempted, but failed, to change one of four self-regulated problem behaviors) evidenced lower initial commitments to change than their more successful peers.

The nature of the differences between successful and unsuccessful self-regulators in commitment phase cognitions (or orientation to the change process) is perhaps most interestingly revealed in the laboratory study conducted by Rozensky and Bellack (1974). Using a subject selection procedure that was later adopted by Perri and Richards (1977) and Heppner et al. (1982), these researchers identified a small group of successful and unsuccessful self-regulators from a large pool of college students based on their responses to a screening questionnaire. The 12 successful self-regulators reported either self-directed weight losses of at least 15 pounds or smoking cessation within a year of the experiment. Unsuccessful subjects reported trying but failing to change these problems. Rozensky and Bellack used a verbal recognition task in which subjects first memorized 30 nonsense syllables and then attempted to identify those syllables during a subsequent presentation of 30 sets of syllables. Subjects also pressed one button to light a lamp if they believed that they accurately identified a syllable during the test phase ("positive self-reinforcement") or they pressed a second button denoting a perceived error ("self-punishment") or they did not press a button if they felt unsure about the accuracy of their performance.

Rozensky and Bellack found that the unsuccessful self-regulators self-rewarded less and self-punished more than their successful peers, despite nonsignificant differences between groups in accuracy of perform-ance. Although the authors did not report information about the appropriateness of the differential self-reinforcement patterns observed, it appears from their Table 1 that the unsuccessful group more appropriately consequated their performance. In other words, the relatively low self-reinforcement and high self-punishment exhibited by the unsuccessful self-regulators more closely resembled the relatively poor performance shown by these subjects ($M = 44\%$ accuracy).

Rozensky and Bellack's results coincide with findings of several of the other researchers in this grouping (especially Heppner et al. 1982) by showing a parallel between unsuccessful self-regulation and depression. Heppner et al. and Perri and Richards described patterns of expectancies and attributions quite typical of depressed individuals (see Lewinsohn, Larson, and Munoz 1982; Norman, Miller, and Klee 1983). Rozensky and Bellack found evidence for the "depressive realism" recently documented by researchers in depression (Alloy and Abramson 1979; Lewinsohn et al. 1980). That is, depressives, like the Rozensky–Bellack unsuccessful self-regulators, often accurately estimate the relatively low level of performance they achieve on a variety of tasks. Therefore, they fail to self-evaluate and self-reward to the same favorable extent as nondepres-sives who exaggerate the quality of their performance. Thus, the first element of self-regulatory failure suggested by this review is the converse to Rehm's (1977; 1982) self-control model of depression: *depressogenic cognitions (expectancies, attributions, and self-evaluation, and self-consequation patterns) may contribute to self-regulatory failure* (cf. Kanfer and Hagerman 1981).

The active role of depressogenic cognitions in self-regulatory failure is clearly supported by several other studies in the present literature that focused on individual target behaviors rather than on a more global analysis of self-regulation. Regarding weight control, Bellack and his associates extended their previous findings using clinical studies. Bellack, Glanz, and Simon (1976) used a priori assessments of self-reinforcement style (on a time estimation task) and found that low self-reinforcers compared to high self-reinforcers failed to lose as much weight or maintain as much weight loss over a five-month follow-up subsequent to a self-regulatory treatment (see similar findings in treatment studies reported by Rozensky and Bellack 1976; Carroll, Yates, and Gray 1980). Mahoney et al. (1977) also found that persons who tended to use excessive amounts of discouraging self-talk achieved less success in weight control compared to their more positively self-encouraging peers. In a related vein, Richards and his associates have repeatedly obtained evidence indicating that students who tried, but failed, to overcome a study problem reported using self-reward less frequently than their more successful counterparts (Perri and Richards 1977; Heffernan and Richards 1981).

Aside from astringency in self-reinforcement style, other studies of individual target behaviors support the potential importance of depress-ogenic cognitions by documenting the role of unfavorable expectancies and related constructs. Three of these studies tested interventions intended to improve expectancies for success. Blittner, Goldberg, and Merbaum (1978) provided bogus feedback following extensive personality testing to a group of smokers who also received a treatment based on instructions to modify stimulus control of smoking behavior. During 28 biweekly individual meetings, therapists provided these subjects with information that should have increased the strength of their efficacy and outcome expectancies. Specifically, therapists repeatedly told them that they were specially selected for the treatment because the battery of psychological tests (including group Rorschachs administered twice) consistently showed that "they had strong willpower and great potential to control and conquer their desires and behavior. Thus, it was quite clear that during the course of treatment they would completely stop smoking" (p. 555). Although the authors did not assess expectancies, this intervention should have enhanced efficacy and outcome expectancies via verbal persuasion. As self-efficacy theory would predict (Bandura 1977a), this "efficacy enhance-ment" group effectively generalized behavior change (i.e., reduced smoking) over time compared to a stimulus control group that did not receive the persuasive communications about expectancies and compared to a control group. Two analogous studies on weight control also showed that induction procedures designed to enhance favorableness of expectan-cies (e.g., showing clients that they can use self-monitoring and self-reinforcement to increase their tolerance of hand immersion in ice water) similarly led to modest improvements in maintenance of weight reduction at three-month follow-ups (Kirschenbaum, Zastowy, Stalonas, and Tomarken 1985; Steffen and Myszak 1978).

In addition to studies that ostensibly manipulated favorableness of initial expectancies, a number of investigations examined the role of depressoge-nic expectancies and attributions as correlates or predictors of self-regulatory failure. Use of maladaptive attributions (e.g., ascribing failure to internal causes) has been implicated as an element of self-regulatory failure in some studies (e.g., Fisher et al. 1982; Flanery and Kirschenbaum

1986; Nentwig 1978; Saltzer 1981). But the evidence seems at least somewhat mixed on this point (e.g., Tobias and MacDonald 1977; see the review by Cooke and Meyers 1980). Somewhat clearer support emerges for the role of unfavorable or weak efficacy expectations, as predicted by Bandura (1977a) (e.g., Condiotte and Lichtenstein 1981; Gormally, Rardin, and Black 1980; Hartigan, Baker-Strauch, and Morris 1982). Particularly impressive was the outcome obtained recently by Condiotte and Lichtenstein in their study of the predictors of relapse among 78 smokers. Prior to, during, and subsequent to the administration of several different treatments, subjects completed lengthy questionnaires that provided an index of the strength of their efficacy expectations. Both microanalyses for individual data and multiple regression analyses for group data revealed very clear correspondence between strength of efficacy expectations at termination of treatment and relapse during the first three months following treatment. For example, the shrunken Rs were .57 for the regression of whether subjects relapsed on efficacy state ($p <$ .001) and .69 for amount of time taken before relapse on efficacy state ($p <$ .0001). However, a recent, longer term (one year) follow-up failed to replicate the predictive power of efficacy expectations (McIntyre, Lichtenstein, and Mermelstein 1983).

Difficulties Coping with Emotional Stressors

Few studies have investigated the contribution of coping skills used to manage stressful life events as elements of self-regulatory failure. This is surprising in view of the provocative findings reported by Leon and Chamberlain more than a decade ago (1973a). Leon and Chamberlain (1973a) sent questionnaires to members of a weight reduction club who had reached their weight loss goals one year prior to completing the questionnaires. Their successful group had regained less than 20% of the weight they had lost, while the failure group had regained more than 20% of their weight losses. These researchers also included a group of controls, matched for sociodemographic characteristics, who had never had a weight control problem. The unsuccessful subjects reported eating in response to emotional states 50% of the time, whereas successful subjects and controls reported about half that frequency of emotionally based eating. However, both successful and unsuccessful subjects reported more emotional eating than controls in response to a related question. Perhaps most importantly, these researchers conducted a second study to attempt to replicate their findings (Leon and Chamberlain 1973b). In the latter study, they used a more sophisticated research strategy, involving corroboration from significant others. Unfortunately, they failed to replicate any differences in eating in response to emotional stimuli for similar groups of successful versus unsuccessful maintainers of weight loss.

Stronger support for the emotional stress/coping skills hypothesis has appeared in a variety of other related investigations, including research on weight control (Gormally and Rardin 1981; Gormally, Rardin, and Black 1980; Nash 1976), smoking reduction (Pomerleau, Adkins, and Pertschuk 1978), and alcoholism (Chaney, O'Leary, and Marlatt 1978; Litman et al. 1979). For example, Gormally and his associates, on the basis of their structured interviews and some questionnaire data, found that unsuccessful weight maintainers viewed life events as having a negative impact on their weight control efforts, whereas maintainers viewed life events as having a positive impact on weight control (Gormally, Rardin, and Black 1980). In a subsequent study, Gormally and Rardin (1981) found that 82% of their unsuccessful weight maintainers reported eating in response to emotional upsets compared to 0% of their successful subjects.

Chaney, O'Leary and Marlatt (1978) also showed very clearly how failure to use coping responses in emotionally charged situations can contribute to self-regulatory failure. These researchers conducted a one-year follow-up subsequent to a treatment study for alcoholism. They gathered demographic data as well as several indexes of coping response skill when confronting high-risk situations. Latency of response to problematic situations, assessed posttreatment, predicted one-year outcomes as well or better than any other variable. For example, this measure of coping skill accounted for 53% of the variance in number of days abstinent at the one-year assessment. Similarly, Litman et al. (1979) found that their alcoholic "survivors" (six months posttreatment) were most clearly differentiated from "relapsers" by the former group's more frequent use of coping behaviors, such as self-talk strategies (e.g., "stopping to examine motives").

Decreased Use of Habit-Change Techniques, Especially Self-monitoring

The prototypical unsuccessful self-regulator revealed by the literature considered thus far would be expected to fail to engage in coping responses in the face of emotionally upsetting stimuli and, instead, emit depressogenic expectancies, attributions, and self-reinforcement patterns. The literature actually provides even more concrete clues about the behavior that may accompany failure to cope and depressogenic cognitions. In most studies that have examined the use of habit-change techniques by successful and unsuccessful self-regulators, regardless of the self-regulatory problem under investigation, at least one clear pattern has emerged: unsuccessful self-regulators evidence less consistent self-monitoring of target behaviors than successful self-regulators (Carroll, Yates, and Gray 1980; Cohen et al. 1980; Dubbert and Wilson 1983; Fisher et al. 1976; Flanery and Kirschenbaum 1986; Gormally, Rardin, and Black 1980;

Gormally and Rardin 1981; Heffernan and Richards 1981; Jeffrey, Vender, and Wing 1978; Leon and Chamberlain 1973b; Perri and Richards 1977; Rosenthal, Allen, and Winters 1980; Stalonas and Kirschenbaum 1980; Stuart and Guire 1978).

The consistency and degree of difference noted between successful and unsuccessful self-regulators in self-monitoring is quite remarkable. Consider the following three examples. Fisher et al. (1976) found that their weight reducers who stopped self-monitoring during a holiday season gained 50 times as much weight as those who maintained their self-monitoring! In a study of long-term success in weight reduction by children, Flanery and Kirschenbaum (1984) found that both child and parent reports of self-monitoring (and/or the similar construct referred to as "use of a weight chart") was the only eating habit change of the ten assessed that significantly correlated with maintenance of weight losses one and a half years posttreatment. Across the various weight-related dependent measures, the significant zero-order Pearson correlations (all ps < .005) ranged from .59 to .87 (i.e., accounting for between 35% and 76% of the variance). Sampling from a different domain of self-regulatory problems, Heffernan and Richards (1981) noted that 67% of their sample of students who successfully overcame a study problem, compared to 0% of students who failed to overcome a study problem, reported planning their study schedules and then checking to see whether they matched their plans ("a specialized version of self-monitoring").

Disengagement of a variety of other changes in behavioral patterns, often decreases in newly acquired habits to counter problem behaviors, also seems strongly associated with self-regulatory failure (Baer, Foreyt, and Wright 1977; Gormally, Rardin, and Black 1980; Heffernan and Richards 1981; Litman et al. 1979; Perri and Richards 1977; Perri, Richards, and Schultheis 1977; Rosenthal, Allen and Winters 1980; Sjoberg and Persson 1979; Stalonas and Kirschenbaum 1980). For example, Stalonas and Kirschenbaum (1980) found that reports of changes in various eating habits provided by weight reducers coincided clearly with weekly ratings of habit change provided independently by both therapists and spouses; all of these correlated significantly with weight control outcomes posttreatment. A more recent study that also included multimodal assessments of habit change found similarly strong associations between habit change and weight loss (Sandifer and Buchanan 1983). However, it should be noted that other investigations have not consistently showed similar patterns of correlations between changes in various behavioral patterns and self-regulation (e.g., Carroll, Yates, and Gray 1980; Evans and Lane 1981). These latter findings must be viewed with caution because many of these studies either failed to use multimodal assessments of adequate psychometric integrity or used populations that did not include high percentages of truly successful self-regulators (i.e., those most likely to change behavioral patterns).

In sum, the successful–unsuccessful self-regulation literature suggests at least three potentially active elements in self-regulatory failure: (1) depressogenic cognitions; (2) difficulties coping with emotional stressors; and (3) disengagement from self-monitoring and other behaviors associated with habit change. Although it is clear that these elements are related to each other, according to both theoretical formulations and empirical evidence (e.g., Kanfer and Hagerman 1981; Kirschenbaum and Karoly 1977; Rehm 1977, 1982), exactly how they interact in self-regulatory failure remains unknown to date. The current evidence merely indicates that each of the elements may become activated in self-regulatory failure. One cannot assert with any degree of certainty, for example, whether emotional stress usually leads to depressogenic cognitions culminating in disengagement from self-monitoring or whether depressogenic conditions exacerbate stress, which, in turn, disengages self-monitoring. Situational and dispositional parameters undoubtedly determine likely interactions between these elements for particular self-regulatory problems—and further research is obviously needed in this regard.

THE RELAPSE PROCESS

Some of the differences observed between groups of successful and unsuccessful self-regulators in the studies reviewed in the preceding section could have resulted from, rather than caused, their differential success in self-regulation (e.g., Heinold et al. 1982). Also, some of the differences may not represent the "essence" of self-regulatory failure. Rather, these differences may merely correlate with more fundamental, but unassessed, causes (McFall 1976). One could argue persuasively that some of these methodological pitfalls could be circumvented if we move closer in time and focus on actual instances of failing to generalize (cf. Anzai and Simon 1979; Bentler and Speckart 1979). The studies in this and in the following subsections begin taking that next step.

Marlatt and Gordon (1980) defined a relapse as a violation of rules governing the rate or pattern of consumption behaviors. Thus, studies of the *process* of violating behavioral rules (i.e., the relapse process) can describe self-regulatory failure. This occurs when the rule violation pertains to the failure to generalize nondominant goal-directed behaviors performed in the relative absence of external constraints. Since many relapses occur within the context of self-regulated behavior change, the study of the relapse process can provide a fine-grained analysis of potentially vital elements of self-regulatory failure. In this section, I will consider in some detail the literature that has accumulated recently in this important area (Condiotte and Lichtenstein 1981; Chaney, O'Leary and Marlatt 1978; Dubbert and Wilson 1983; Lichtenstein, Antonuccio, and Rainwater 1982; Marlatt 1978; Marlatt and Gordon 1980; Shiffman 1982; Sjoberg and Johnson 1978; Sjoberg and Persson 1979; Sjoberg and

Samsonowitz 1978; Sjoberg, Samsonowitz, and Olsson 1978). This review will show that the study of the relapse process adds to the hypotheses generated in the success–failure literature by more completely describing the situations and emotional reactions that can contribute to self-regulatory failure. In other words, this literature suggests some situations and emotional reactions that may precipitate, or co-occur with, depress-ogenic cognitions, disengagement from self-monitoring, and abandonment of other coping strategies, including habit-change procedures, culminating in failure to generalize behavior change.

Initial Relapse Episode, Social Pressure, and Physiological Pressure

Marlatt and his associates established the foundation to the study of the relapse process in a series of important studies (Chaney, O'Leary, and Marlatt 1978; Cummings, Gordon, and Marlatt 1980; Marlatt 1973, 1978; Marlatt and Gordon 1980). These researchers conducted structured interviews with several hundred alcoholics, smokers, heroin addicts, compulsive gamblers, and dieters during follow-ups subsequent to a variety of treatment programs. They subjected these interviews to a content analysis and showed that they could reliably categorize the relapse episodes into specific sets of situational and emotional precipitants. Although some dissimilarities across studies (Kirschenbaum and Tomar-ken 1982) and across behaviors emerged, several striking commonalities also appeared (Marlatt 1982). In particular, as shown in Table 2.1, five factors were consistently associated with full-blown relapses: (1) an initial relapse episode (e.g., Marlatt and Gordon's [1980] data indicated that the vast majority of their "ex"-smokers and "ex"-alcoholics followed either their first or second relapse episode with full resumption of their former habits); (2) negative emotional states (including frustration, anger, guilt, depression, grief, worry, and boredom); (3) social pressure (e.g., direct encouragement from others to relapse; observation of others engaged in the to-be-controlled behaviors); (4) interpersonal conflict; and (5) physiologically oriented factors (Table 2.1: negative physical states, "urges and temptations").

The findings of Marlatt and his colleagues complement the conclusions reached based on the successful–unsuccessful literature. The former research domain suggested that difficulties coping with emotional upsets seemed central in self-regulatory failure. The data of Marlatt and his colleagues suggest a more specific account of the nature of those emotional upsets. *Initial relapse episodes, social conflicts and pressures, and physiological pressures may well contribute to the creation of a "relapse crisis."* Unsuccessful management of such highly stressful circumstances may well include the use of depressogenic cognitions that could further exacerbate the stressfulness of the situation, resulting in abandonment of

Table 2.1.
Analysis of Relapse Situations with Alcoholics, Smokers, Heroin Addicts, Compulsive Gamblers, and Overeaters

Relapse Situation	Alcoholics (N = 70)	Smokers (N = 64)	Heroin Addicts (N = 129)	Gamblers (N = 29)	Overeaters (N = 311)	Total
Intrapersonal determinants						
Negative emotional states	38%	37%	19%	47%	33%	35%
Negative physical states	3%	2%	9%	–	–	3%
Positive emotional states	–	6%	10%	–	3%	4%
Testing personal control	9%	–	2%	16%	–	5%
Urges and temptations	11%	5%	5%	16%	10%	9%
Total	61%	50%	45%	79%	46%	56%
Interpersonal determinants						
Interpersonal conflict	18%	15%	14%	16%	14%	16%
Social pressure	18%	32%	36%	5%	10%	20%
Positive emotional states	3%	3%	5%	–	28%	8%
Total	39%	50%	55%	21%	52%	44%

Source: Reprinted with permission from Marlatt, G. A. (1982). Relapse prevention: A self-control program for the treatment of addictive behaviors. In *Adherence, compliance, and generalization in behavioral medicine*, ed. R. B. Stuart, p. 339. New York: Brunner/Mazel.

adaptive behavioral regimens (e.g., self-monitoring, other coping strategies) and failure to generalize. However, many other interactions between these elements are possible. Disengagement of habit change may lead to the initial relapse episode, resulting in increased stress, and so on.

Based on largely anecdotal data, Marlatt and associates also suggested that irrational thinking, lowering of efficacy expectations, and related cognitive styles (i.e., reminiscent of depressogenic cognitions) contribute to the relapse process (see Marlatt 1982; Marlatt and Gordon 1980). A group of Swedish researchers also viewed their anecdotal evidence as supporting the importance of maladaptive cognitions in the relapse process. Sjoberg and his associates based this view on a series of unstructured interviews conducted with smokers (Sjoberg and Johnson 1978; Sjoberg and Samsonowitz 1978), alcoholics (Sjoberg, Samsonowitz and Olsson 1978), and obese individuals (Sjoberg and Persson 1979). Although the terminology differs considerably from that of Marlatt and his associates, like the U.S. researchers, Sjoberg and Persson also consider conflicts (including social conflicts) problematic cognitions, and emotional distress as vital in self-regulatory failure:

Conflicts may create demands on mental energy which in turn is taken from the resources available to the cognitive system. When the cognitive system is drained of these resources, it becomes much weaker and more primitive, thus giving rise to distorted and low quality reasoning and judgments. This narrow perspective, typically found in volitional breakdowns ... stem(s) from properties of wish content due to strong needs. The theory thus predicts that breakdowns will occur under emotional stress and that they will be preceded by distorted reasonings and a narrow perspective (Sjoberg and Persson 1979, p. 349).

Two additional studies with obese individuals (Dubbert and Wilson 1983; Rosenthal, Allen, and Winter 1980) and three additional studies with smokers (Condiotte and Lichtenstein 1981; Lichtenstein, Antonuccio, and Rainwater 1982; Shiffman 1982) further underscore many of the same variables as suggested by the two series of studies conducted by Marlatt and Sjoberg and their associates. The obesity researchers conducted structured interviews and scored them as did the group of Marlatt and associates. They again found that negative emotional states and interpersonal conflicts and pressures featured prominently in the accounts of the situations in which clients relapsed. Positive emotional states, however, were equally important factors. These findings, in conjunction with the differential significance of positive states for obese subjects in the research of Marlatt and his colleagues (see overeaters compared to other subject groupings in Table 2.1), may indicate that a greater range of emotional events may contribute to self-regulatory failure for obese individuals in particular. It should also be noted that physiological factors seemed somewhat less central to the obese subjects relative to the other groups of subjects studied by Marlatt and colleagues (see Table 2.1). In view of the topographic, behavioral, and physiological differences between various self-regulatory problems (see also Peterson 1983), it is not surprising to find some notable differences in probable elements of self-regulatory failure across these target behaviors. Nonetheless, the similarities remain of central interest because they seem to account for most of the variance in these studies (Marlatt 1982). Examining them may also broaden our understanding of the generalization problem. This may eventually lead to more constructive research, intervention, and theorizing (Kirschenbaum and Tomarken 1982).

The details of the final studies to be considered in this section, the three recent studies of relapse among smokers, deserve explication because of the unusually high quality of the research, including some innovations in design and assessment. In the previously noted study by Condiotte and Lichtenstein (1981), a subgrouping of the subjects (n = 24) agreed to participate in five weeks of intensive data gathering following treatment. Of the 12 subjects in this group who relapsed within five weeks posttreatment, 11 declined to continue their self-monitoring of cigarette-smoking behavior, mood, and self-efficacy. Interestingly, these 11 subjects stopped self-monitoring "either just prior to or at the same time as they experienced their relapse episode" (p. 655). Furthermore, during subsequent phone calls with experimenters, "many of these subjects indicated that the data collection had become extremely aversive and they couldn't handle it anymore!" This discontinuation of self-monitoring subsequent to relapse strongly supports our earlier assertion about the commonality of this step in self-regulatory failure.

Condiotte and Lichtenstein's careful analysis of the relapse data for all 44 of their subjects who eventually relapsed coincides remarkably well with other elements of self-regulatory failure previously suggested by the various literatures reviewed to this point. Depressogenic cognitions became apparent in that relapsers had reported lower posttreatment self-efficacy responses on a questionnaire prior to their relapses and lowered "confidence" following their first relapse episode. In addition, 49% of the relapsers reported making no coping responses following their first cigarette, whereas 100% of the people who smoked at least once but then remained abstinent (n = 8) reported using some coping response following their smoking episode.

Lichtenstein, Antonuccio, and Rainwater (1982) used structured interviews and reliable coding using the system of Marlatt and his colleagues to investigate relapse among 84 smokers who had quit for a median of five weeks. Their findings provided yet another replication of the basic results of Marlatt and his colleagues. The initial relapse episode, negative emotional states, and social pressures and conflicts again featured prominently as contributors to relapse. In addition, subjects abandoned self-monitoring and related coping procedures; that is, almost half of the relapsers reported not thinking about smoking or failing to use any coping response subsequent to the first cigarette. Finally, although most relapse investigators tend to deemphasize the physiological component of self-regulatory failure, Lichtenstein, Antonuccio, and Rainwater found that 95.5% of their subjects reported continued cravings in at least some circumstances. Nearly half of these people also reported relatively constant or strong cravings prior to relapse. Of course, some aspects of these cravings are undoubtedly influenced by cognitive variables (see Leventhal, Nerenz, and Straus 1980), but physiological factors are also implicated by these and related findings.

The final study relied on an innovative procedure to evaluate relapse "crises." Shiffman (1982) established a well publicized "Stay-Quit Line" in Los Angeles, California, a telephone counseling service for ex smokers undergoing relapse urges and episodes. He gathered data, of the sort collected by the other relapse researchers, by having telephone counselors ask a series of specific questions. Of the 183 interviews tabulated in this creative study, 15 were recorded and scored reliably (77 to 100% agreement) by all three of the telephone counselors. This procedure yielded a sample of people who had been abstinent for a median of ten days, 39% of whom had smoked approximately one cigarette the same day as the call or within a few days of the call. Thus, this procedure may have provided an unusually sensitive means of assessing elements of self-regulatory failure, because initial relapses often precede full-blown failures to maintain abstinence (e.g., Lichtenstein et al. 1982; Marlatt and Gordon 1980) and since data gathered proximal to the behavior of interest is likely to yield more accurate information (Anzai and Simon 1979).

Shiffman's data generally coincide with the other reports describing the relapse process. Affective states again appeared to play a major role, with negative states accounting for more than twice as many crises as positive states. Situational precipitants again appeared to feature social factors, particularly the presence of others engaging in smoking and concurrent consumptive behaviors (including consumption of alcohol). In addition and in accord with the results of Lichtenstein, Antonuccio, and Rainwater (1982), but somewhat contrary to the emphasis by other relapse investigators, Shiffman found that more than half of the callers reported a variety of physical symptoms associated with the relapse crises, including achiness, nausea, headaches, and irritability. Furthermore, Shiffman explicitly excluded tallies of "cravings," which he seemed to have assumed occurred in all of the crises. Finally, he found that failure to use coping responses significantly and substantially increased the probability of relapsing. Twice as many callers who reported not using coping responses were among the 39% of the sample who had actually smoked a cigarette prior to calling compared to the callers who used some coping responses (e.g., reviewing reasons for quitting, leaving the high risk situation).

Summary

Research on the relapse process again underscores the potentially vital roles in self-regulatory failure of depressogenic cognitions, difficulties coping with emotional stressors, and disengagement from self-monitoring and habit change. It also suggests that the stress that arises from interpersonal conflicts may represent a particularly difficult challenge to coping skills. When interpersonal conflicts involve significant people in the life of the self-regulator, social support that can facilitate coping decreases. This may greatly increase the probability of self-regulatory failure.

The three new elements of self-regulatory failure suggested by this literature are social pressure, initial relapse episode, and physiological pressure. It is clear from several of these studies that people often relapse in the presence of others who model the to-be-controlled behaviors or who more actively encourage relapse (e.g., Lichtenstein, Antonuccio and Rainwater 1982; Shiffman 1982). It is also apparent that for addictive disorders (and other behaviors that have strong physiological involvement) initial relapse episodes are often followed by full-blown relapses and that physiological cravings often seem to precipitate relapses (e.g., Lichtenstein, Antonuccio, and Rainwater 1982). This is one example of how type of target behavior can importantly determine likely elements of self-regulatory failure (cf. Peterson 1983). It is clear that the degree of physiological involvement for addictive disorders (alcoholism, smoking, eating problems) and exercise adherence is much more substantial than for target behaviors like classroom participation and studying.

ATTENTION IN SELF-REGULATION

In the preceding analysis, attentional phenomena were implicated in self-regulatory failure. This implication becomes more apparent when one considers the underlying processes of two of the proposed elements of self-regulatory failure: depressogenic cognitions and disengagement of self-monitoring. Some empirical evidence (Dykman and Volpicelli 1983) and several cognitive theories of depression (e.g., Beck et al. 1979; Janoff-Bulman 1979; Rehm 1977, 1982) stress that people become depressed, at least in part, by selectively attending to unpleasant or negative information about themselves and their behaviors. Thus, the assertion that unsuccessful self-regulators may differentially use depressogenic cognitions invoked an attentional mechanism as an active underlying ingredient in self-regulatory failure. In a related vein, disengaging self-monitoring means, by definition and observation (as will be discussed in more detail later in this subsection), diverting attention away from the systematic gathering of information about target behaviors. Thus, when proposing that unsuccessful self-regulators and those who relapse disengage self-monitoring, an attentional mechanism is being proposed in self-regulatory failure.

Definitions and Parameters of Attention

Attention has defied attempts at clear unambiguous definitions (Carver and Scheier 1981). Cognitive psychologists have sidestepped the definitional dilemma by suggesting that attention consists of two major parameters: *intensity* and *selectivity* (Bourne, Dominowski, and Loftus 1979). Intensity refers to the " 'fullness' of the person's awareness of whatever is being noticed" (Carver and Scheier 1981, p. 34). In other words, saying that a person is intensely or fully attending to something means that the individual is in a very alert or vigilant state. Selectivity refers to the focus of attention on particular stimuli or their properties. Since we must filter some aspects of our experience from cognitive processing at all times (see Norman 1969), this means that only certain stimuli are attended to at any given time; conversely, other stimuli are attended to more perfunctorily at that time.

The research considered in the following section did not purport to compare intensity and selectivity dimensions of attention. Much of it pertains largely to selectivity, but it remains unclear the extent to which intensity and perhaps other aspects of attention were confounded with ostensible manipulations of selectivity (Carver and Scheier 1981, p. 35) or vice versa (cf. Kirschenbaum, Tomarken and Humphrey 1985). For the present purposes, let us merely accept the assumption of the usefulness of the construct of attention and consider the studies to be discussed here as pertaining to the intensity and/or selectivity dimensions of this construct.

Self-monitoring

Self-monitoring is defined as the systematic gathering of information about target behaviors. In other words, self-monitoring means discriminating the occurrence of target behaviors and explicitly or cognitively recording them (Kanfer 1970; McFall 1977; Nelson and Hayes 1981). The research already reviewed pertaining to successful–unsuccessful self-regulation and the relapse process suggests that active self-monitoring may be a necessary condition for generalized self-regulated behavior change (Kirschenbaum 1976). The following review of research supports and elaborates that assertion by focusing on the nature and effects of self-monitoring.

Self-regulated behavior change occurred when self-monitoring was activated and failed to occur when self-monitoring was deactivated in a study of the academic behavior of children (Broden, Hall, and Mitts 1971), a study on classroom participation by adolescents (Gottman and McFall 1972), and research on the effects of self-monitoring on the classroom behaviors of teachers (Hendricks, Thoresen, and Hubbard 1974). Several clinical observations supply further corroborative evidence (e.g., Christensen 1976; Maletzky 1974). For example, Maletzky (1974) gave nondemand instructions to five clients by informing them, prior to their use of wrist counters to self-monitor, that "counting their behavior would assist therapists in understanding their problems, but that counting would not necessarily decrease unwanted behaviors" (p. 108). Frequency of skin scratching, fingernail biting, disruptive handraising in class, facial tics, and inappropriate standing in class declined dramatically during self-monitoring. Maletzky's clients also reported that self-monitoring importantly cued their active alteration of problem behaviors. Recall the converse, well illustrated by the 11 of 12 of Condiotte and Lichtenstein's (1981) smoking relapsers who discontinued self-monitoring just as they began relapsing.

Although self-monitoring is probably necessary for self-regulation, it is often insufficient (Kirschenbaum 1976). Many studies reveal little or no effects attributable to self-monitoring (see reviews by McFall 1977; Nelson 1977). Studies on the conditions under which self-monitoring does change behavior, however, again underscore the vital role of this attentional process in effective self-regulation. Self-monitoring more reactively changes behavior when it provides salient information (e.g., Abrams and Wilson 1979; Pennebaker and Skelton 1981; Richards, Anderson, and Baker 1978) about target behaviors that are considered important (e.g., Cavior and Marrabotto 1976; Kazdin 1974)—important enough to express a strong desire to change (e.g., Komaki and Dore-Boyce 1978; McFall and Hammen 1971). Consistent with the view of self-monitoring as a process that directs attentional focus, the reactivity of self-monitoring also depends on preventing an overload of the information processing system (McFall 1977; Peterson 1983). In other words, self-monitoring salient aspects of important target behaviors can prove quite unreactive when the person attempts to monitor concurrently too many aspects of the target behavior (Epstein, Webster, and Miller 1975; Hayes and Cavior 1977, 1980; Kanfer and Busemeyer 1982; Kirschenbaum, Wittrock, Smith, and Monson 1984).

Given the seemingly vital role of sustained self-monitoring in the generalization of self-regulated behavior change, we must discover the conditions under which self-monitoring decreases or ceases. A process related to sustained self-monitoring has been studied by several researchers (Duval and Wicklund 1972; Horan et al. 1975; Mischel, Ebbesen, and Zeiss 1973; Roth and Rehm 1980). These investigators examined factors that influenced selective attention to information about oneself. Selectively attending to certain self-aspects or target behaviors is the initial stage of self-monitoring, the process of discriminating occurrences of target behaviors and related events (Kanfer 1970; Nelson and Hayes 1981). Thus, factors that decrease attention to important self-aspects may predict reductions in sustained self-monitoring. This literature reveals two such factors that may become active in self-regulatory failure: experiencing failure (Mischel, Ebbesen, and Zeiss 1973; see also Condiotte and Lichtenstein 1981; Lichtenstein, Antonuccio, and Rainwater 1982) and accentuating the aversive aspects of failure (Duval and Wicklund 1972; Horan et al. 1975; Mischel, Ebbesen, and Zeiss 1973; Roth and Rehm 1980). The latter accentuation process may occur due to dispositional qualities that make failure especially focal (Mischel, Ebbesen, and Zeiss 1973; Roth and Rehm 1980) or to situational or behavioral manipulations that direct attention to personal liabilities (Duval and Wicklund 1972; Horan et al. 1975; Roth and Rehm 1980).

Studies of self-monitoring show that factors that accentuate negative self-aspects do not always decrease self-monitoring; furthermore, the mechanisms that determine why accentuation of personal failures affects self-regulatory failure are more complex than those originally proposed (Kirschenbaum and Karoly 1977; Kirschenbaum, Tomarken, and Humphrey 1985; Tomarken and Kirschenbaum 1982). As the following review of this research program will show, it has become clear that (1) degree of task mastery interacts with the self-monitoring procedures that differentially direct attention to failures; and (2) affective mechanisms may contribute to this interaction when tasks are poorly mastered, whereas attentional mechanisms seem focal when tasks are well mastered.

Kirschenbaum and Karoly used a paradigm (Mahoney et al. 1973) in which volunteer subjects were invited to work on mathematics problems in preparation for graduate school admissions tests. Ninety-six students were assigned to groups in which they either focused on their failures by self-monitoring their inaccurate problem solving (negative self-monitoring), self-recorded accurate problem solving (positive self-monitoring), did not self-record but received the same kind of immediate performance feedback as the self-monitors (performance feedback), or did not self-record or receive immediate feedback (control). Stratified random assignment, based on performance on a math pretest, controlled for variance attributable to ability. Subjects received either difficult (35% accuracy level) or relatively simple (65% accuracy level) math problems to work on during three 15-minute problem-solving periods. During ten-minute free time periods between problem-solving periods, subjects were encouraged to observe their problem-solving activities on a videotape monitor (problem cards and scratch work, with no feedback in any group).

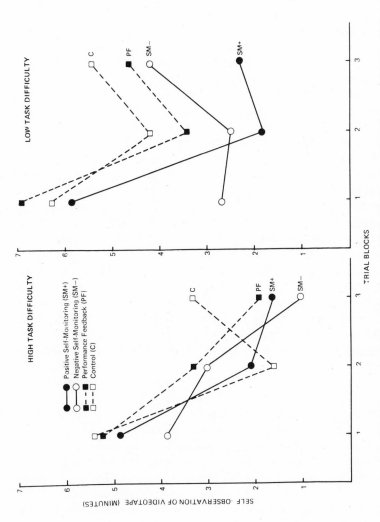

Figure 2.2. Mean self-observation of videotape across trial blocks for the four groups within the high-task difficulty condition (left panel) and the low-task difficulty condition (right panel). *Source:* Reprinted with permission from Kirschenbaum, D. S., and P. Karoly [1977]. When self-regulation fails: Tests of some preliminary hypotheses. *Journal of Consulting and Clinical Psychology, 45*:1116–25.

Based on prior research and theorizing, negative self-monitoring was expected to cause self-regulatory failure (e.g., lower performance, decrease self-observation during free time periods) when the task was difficult, but positive self-monitoring was expected to produce self-regulatory failure when the task was relatively simple. Negative self-monitoring actually lowered performance compared to performance feedback and control groups under both levels of task difficulty. However, negative self-monitors also increased self-observation over time when the task was simple, whereas positive self-monitors showed the predicted decline in self-observation—even when compared to the equally accurate problem solvers in the performance feedback group (see Figure 2.2, right panel). On the other hand, all groups in the high-difficulty condition evidenced self-regulatory failure to a considerable extent (see Figure 2.2, left panel). Compared to low-task difficulty subjects, high-task difficulty subjects self-evaluated less favorably, self-rewarded less favorably, reported higher anxiety, and self-observed somewhat less ($p < .10$).

The results of the Kirschenbaum and Karoly study reinforce the earlier assertion that failure experience (i.e., initial relapse) and accentuated reaction to failure (i.e., a type of depressogenic cognition) may precipitate self-regulatory failure. The repeated experience with very difficult problems (i.e., failure to perform) resulted in negative self-reactions and disengagement from the task (highly significant declines in self-observation over trails for all groups). "The course of this disengagement process was unaltered even when subjects were fitted with experimental 'rose-colored glasses' (i.e., instructed to positively self-monitor)" (p. 1124). In addition, however, focusing on positive aspects of behavior also produced self-regulatory dysfunctioning in the low-difficulty condition. Perhaps when self-regulated tasks become highly overlearned, routine, or automatic (e.g., during extended self-regulation or in the habit-reorganization phases), positive self-focusing may actively contribute to self-regulatory failure.

To examine the role of both positive and negative self-monitoring in self-regulatory failure more completely, Tomarken and Kirschenbaum (1982) replicated and extended certain aspects of the previous study. To assess sustained self-regulatory behavior more naturalistically, we encouraged the volunteer subjects (n = 66) to return for two additional sessions over a two-week interval (the final session included work with a math tutor). In addition, we used a lower level of math difficulty (from 71 to 85% accuracy) to approximate more closely the state of overlearning or task mastery required by activation-arousal theories of motivation. In accord with predictions, positive self-monitoring again produced self-regulatory failure. Relative to negative self-monitors, positive self-monitors performed less accurately, spent somewhat less time in self

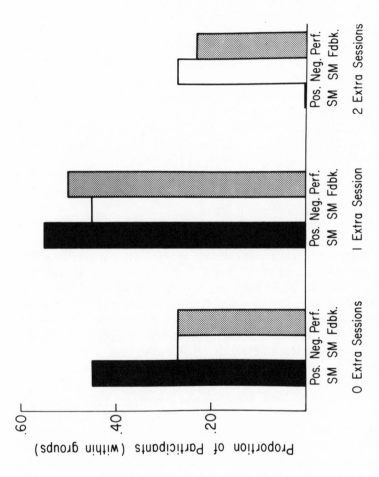

Figure 2.3. Proportions of groups in attendance at extra sessions. Pos SM = positive self-monitoring; Neg SM = negative self-monitoring; Perf Fdbk = performance feedback (no self-monitoring). *Source:* Reprinted with permission from Tomarken, A. J., and D. S. Kirschenbaum [1982]. Self-regulatory failure: Accentuate the positive. *Journal of Personality and Social Psychology,* 43:576–85.

observation (p < .10), wrote fewer notes to themselves during self-observation, and failed to attend as many extra sessions (see Figure 2.3). In addition, when compared to performance feedback subjects, positive self-monitors (but not negative self-monitors) self-observed less.

The results of these two studies accord well with several other findings in the self-monitoring literature by indicating that differential self-monitoring interacts with level of task mastery to affect performance and persistence (e.g., Gottman and McFall 1972; Johnston-O'Connor and Kirschenbaum 1986; Kirschenbaum et al. 1982; Wade 1974). The mediating events responsible for this pattern of results appear to vary as a function of level of task mastery. In the most recent of the three studies in this series by my coworkers and me (Kirschenbaum, Tomarken, and Humphrey 1985), affective state or emotionality more clearly impacted self-regulation when task mastery was low (consistent with the Kirschenbaum and Karoly 1977 results). When tasks were well mastered—in this latter study (1984) and in Tomarken and Kirschenbaum (1982)—we found that affect appeared relatively uninfluential. As I will show in my discussion of the self-focused attention and related literatures in this subsection, it seems that selectivity in attentional focus, rather than affect, may become vital in self-regulatory failure when task mastery is quite high.

There is further support for the claim that self-monitoring produces its effects due to the manner in which it directs attentional focus. Since positive self-monitors selectively attend to positive outcomes, while negative self-monitors attend to negative outcomes or failures, the differential self-monitoring findings can also be compared to those from studies assessing the effects of success and failure on performance. Indeed, the parallels are striking. Just as negative self-monitoring compared unfavorably to positive self-monitoring in a low-mastery high-anxiety context, the actual experience of failure, relative to success, has sometimes impaired the performance of individuals who had a previous history of failure (Lazarus and Ericksen 1952), low expectancies for success (e.g., Diener and Dweck 1978, 1980; Shrauger and Rosenberg 1970), and high levels of anxiety (e.g., Mandler and Sarason 1952; Weiner and Schneider 1971). Similarly, the finding that positive self-monitoring produced self-regulatory dysfunctioning in a high-mastery context corresponds to the evidence that success, relative to failure, may impair the performance of those with a prior history of success (Lazarus and Ericksen 1952), expectations for continued success (e.g., Halisch and Heckhausen 1977; Rijsmon 1974), and low levels of negative affect (e.g., Weiner 1966; Weiner and Schneider 1971). (See also Wortman and Brehm 1975.) These parallels strongly suggest that self-monitoring successes or failures produce effects quite analogous to actual experiences of success. These parallels lend support to the argument that the observed impact of differential self-monitoring derives from the way it selectively focuses attention on successes or failures (see also Mahoney 1974).

Research on the effects of task mastery on naturally occurring forms of selective attention leads to a similar conclusion. The evidence indicates that individuals often selectively attend to negative information about the self and/or evaluate themselves more negatively than is objectively warranted. This occurs when they have previously failed (e.g., Moore et al. 1979; Postman and Brown 1952), negative expectancies for success (e.g., Diener and Dweck 1980; Silverman 1964), and heightened negative affect (e.g., Clark and Arkowitz 1975; Holroyd et al. 1978). This literature has also shown that success experience, positive expectancies, and low levels of anxiety can result in a selective focus on positive self-aspects and overly favorable self-evaluations (for reviews, see Bower 1981; Shrauger 1975; Wine 1980). In short, it appears that low-mastery contexts often elicit covert negative self-monitoring, while high-mastery contexts can, under some conditions, produce covert positive self-monitoring (cf., however, Tomarken and Kirschenbaum 1982). Consider these data in light of the evidence that negative self-monitoring debilitates performance in low-mastery contexts and that positive self-monitoring results in impairments in high-mastery situations. These findings clearly suggest that selective attentional focusing may debilitate self-regulation whether that focusing is induced experimentally (differential self-monitoring or actual success/failure experience) or whether it occurs naturally.

In sum, research on self-monitoring underscores the importance of attentional variables in self-regulatory failure. In particular, the evidence supports the earlier assertion that self-monitoring is necessary for self-regulation and that *selectively self-monitoring (i.e., attending to) either success or failure may serve as an active element of self-regulatory failure depending on conditions of task mastery.* Selectively self-monitoring successes when tasks are very well mastered and selectively self-monitoring failures when tasks are poorly mastered can contribute to self-regulatory failure by disengaging sustained self-monitoring of target behaviors.

Self-focused Attention

Duval and Wicklund (1972) proposed that we attend to either the external environment or ourselves. They argued that attention to the self increases when stimuli (e.g., mirrors, review of our personal history) remind us of our object-like nature. Self-evaluation is then posited as the natural reaction to self-attention. Unfortunately, since self-evaluation often proves unfavorable and, therefore, aversive, withdrawal from the self-attentive state typically follows self-attention and self-evaluation, according to Duval and Wicklund. They further suggested that we adjust our behavior to the standard used in self-evaluation only when escape from self-attention becomes impossible.

Carver (1979) reformulated Duval and Wicklund's theory of objective self-awareness by suggesting an alternative reaction to self-attention. Carver argued that self-attention in the presence of a salient standard, rather than causing withdrawal from continued self-attention, typically initiates a test-operate-test negative feedback loop (cf. Bandura 1977b; Kanfer 1971; Kanfer and Karoly 1972). Carver posited that if the test or self-attentive phase reveals an incongruity between current behavior and a standard, an operate phase ensues during which the individual alters behavior to match the standard. In most cases, self-attention (test) is expected to alternate with behavioral adjustments (operate) until the behavior conforms to the standard. When the desired match occurs, individuals disengage (exit) the self-regulatory feedback loop. However, expectancies, affect, and other factors may interfere with this self-regulatory loop. For example, Carver (1979) indicated that negative "outcome expectancies" (i.e., beliefs that one cannot appropriately alter the behavior; see page 1273) disengage the process whereas positive outcome expectancies maintain it.

Carver's model, like Kanfer's (1971), suggests that a process of orienting to the self triggers a feedback loop of self-regulation when people notice discrepancies between their standards and behaviors. As described in an earlier section, a variety of studies support the assertion that self-monitoring is a necessary condition for self-regulation. Considerable evidence from the self-attention literature also corroborates this vital assumption.

In a particularly convincing demonstration, Diener and Wallbom (1976) found that mirror-induced self-attention reduced the proportion of college students who cheated on an achievement test from 71 to 7% ($p < .001$). Self-attention in the presence of a salient standard also reduced cheating in children (Beaman et al. 1979); decreased physical aggression (e.g., Carver 1975; Scheier, Fenigstein, and Buss 1974); increased prosocial behavior (e.g., Wegner and Schaefer 1978; Gotay 1977); heightened conformity to an equity norm (e.g., Greenberg 1980; Gibbons, Wicklund and Rosenfield 1979); and improved performance and persistence on a variety of tasks (Carver, Blaney, and Scheier 1979b; McDonald 1980; Slapion and Carver 1981; Wicklund and Duval 1971; Carver and Scheier 1979). Additional findings show that self-attention generally cues more careful and complete introspection. Specifically, self-attentive subjects more actively assessed their abilities in several studies (e.g., Carver and Blaney 1977a, 1977b; Carver, Blaney and Scheier 1979a) and more frequently compared their behavior to salient standards in a recent experiment (Carver and Scheier 1979). Other studies have found that expectancy manipulations only significantly affected behavior when subjects were self-attentive (e.g., Carver, Blaney, and Scheier 1979a, 1979b; Kuhl 1981; Steenbarger and Aderman 1979). Furthermore, individuals made self-attentive via mirrors and those who were dispositionally high in "private self-consciousness" (Fenigstein, Scheier and Buss 1975) produced longer (Turner 1978b) and more accurate self-reports (e.g., Pryor et al. 1977; Turner 1978a; Borden and Pryor 1981). Also, they were more cognizant of their transient affective (e.g., Scheier 1976; Scheier and Carver 1977) and physiological states (Pennebaker and Skelton 1978; Scheier, Carver and Gibbons 1979) and they were more likely to read first-person content into incomplete or ambiguous verbal material (e.g., Carver and Scheier 1978; Wegner and Giuliano 1980).

Self-attention apparently increases self-evaluative processes and stimulates self-regulated behavior change under many circumstances. These findings again suggest that some form of self-attention may be a necessary condition for self-regulation (cf. Broden, Hall, and Mitts 1971; Gottman and McFall 1972; Kanfer 1971). Thus, factors that reduce sustained self-attention may become activated in self-regulatory failure. In addition, just as positive self-monitoring increased self-regulatory failure (Kirschenbaum and Karoly 1977; Tomarken and Kirschenbaum 1982), under some conditions self-attention may well contribute to self-regulatory failure (cf. Carver 1979; Duval and Wicklund 1972). Therefore, to explore further potential elements of self-regulatory failure suggested by self-attention research, let us examine factors in this literature that have been shown to decrease self-attention and persistence.

At least two conditions appear to cause individuals to avoid sustained self-attention. First, failure followed by the perception that the failure cannot be changed through subsequent behavioral adjustments appears to motivate escape from sustained self-attention (Duval, Wicklund, and Fine 1972; Gibbons and Wicklund 1976; Gur and Sackeim 1979; Steenbarger and Aderman 1979). For example, in the Steenbarger and Aderman study, subjects were told that they performed very poorly on an initial test of "intelligence and creativity." Those subjects who were led to believe that they should not improve on a subsequent test left a waiting room that contained a self-attentional stimulus (mirror) after a short period of time compared to subjects who were led to expect improvements in performance on the subsequent test (cf. Duval et al. 1972). Second, directing one's attention to things other than oneself also diminished self-attention in several studies. Specifically, explicit redirection of attention to stimuli in the immediate environment produced effects directly opposite to those associated with increased self-attention in studies of dissonance reduction (Allen 1965), attribution of blame for negative outcomes (Duval and Wicklund 1972, Experiments 1, 2, and 3), self-esteem (Ferris and

Wicklund, cited in Wicklund 1975), and disinhibition of behaviors in social contexts (Diener 1978, 1979). For example, in three experiments Duval and Wicklund (1972) asked subjects to apportion responsibility for a negative outcome between themselves and another possible perpetrator. Some subjects squeezed a handgrip (Experiment 1) or rotated a turntable (Experiments 2 and 3), while controls did not engage in physical activities when apportioning blame. In each experiment, attribution of blame to the self was diminished with physical activity.

Regarding persistence, the evidence suggests that self-attention can decrease persistence when people (1) expect to fail; (2) experience excessive negative affect; and (3) expect to continue succeeding at tasks directly relevant to those that they already mastered. Concerning the first of these three conclusions, many studies, in fact 18 of 20 in a review by Tomarken and Kirschenbaum (1984), support the assertion that self-attention debilitates performance and persistence in individuals who expect to fail (e.g., Brockner 1979; Carver, Blaney, and Scheier 1979b; Scheier, Carver, and Gibbons 1981). For example, Carver, Blaney, and Scheier (1979b) exposed subjects to an initial failure experience. Subjects then undertook a second task that ostensibly measured the same intellectual skills as "assessed" by the first task and were either told to expect to do quite well or quite poorly on the second task. As anticipated, negative expectancies plus self-attention reduced persistence on the second task. Similar debilitation of persistence and performance accompanied self-attention in studies that used subjects with chronic negative expectancies (e.g., Carver, Blaney, and Scheier 1979a), exposed subjects to extensive prior failure (e.g., Kuhl 1981), or used a very difficult task (e.g., Duval and Friedan 1979).

Some of the detrimental effects of expecting to fail on persistence may be attributable to a heightened and excessive negative state induced by self-attention. Self-attention clearly increases negative affect for those with negative expectancies (e.g., Carver, Blaney, and Scheier 1979b; Steenbarger and Aderman 1979). More generally, self-attention has intensified the experience of emotion. For example, self-attention has intensified feelings of anxiety (Carver, Blaney, and Scheier 1979b; Scheier, Carver, and Gibbons 1981), anger (Scheier 1976), and sympathy (Scheier et al. 1978). Since affective states and cognitive processes may be somewhat independent (e.g., Kirschenbaum, Tomarken, and Humphrey 1985; Zajonc 1980, 1984), it seems plausible to suggest that negative expectancies and negative affective states may function both independently and interactively to disrupt self-regulation when people are self-attentive. The study of Scheier, Carver, and Gibbons (1981) most clearly illustrates how negative affect, exacerbated by self-attention, may function in self-regulatory failure. These investigators found that very fearful snake phobics who were made self-attentive not only experienced more anxiety but also withdrew earlier from their approach attempts compared to a similar group of non-self-attentive snake phobics (see also Carver and Blaney 1977a, 1977b; Carver, Blaney, and Scheier 1979b).

It should be added that the two conditions promoting debilitation enumerated above are highly consistent with the evidence that negative self-monitoring results in self-regulatory dysfunctioning under low-mastery conditions (e.g., Gottman and McFall 1972; Kirschenbaum and Karoly 1977). As noted earlier, both negative expectancies (e.g., Diener and Dweck 1980) and negative affect (e.g., Holroyd et al. 1978) often result in selective attention to negative self-aspects. Since self-attention heightens awareness of whatever dimensions of the self are most salient at the time (Carver 1979), it may actively promote negative self-monitoring in low-mastery contexts; that is, contexts that are often associated with negative expectancies and negative affect. Thus, perhaps similar mechanisms account for the performance debilitation incurred by both negative self-monitoring and heightened self-attention under low-mastery conditions.

The final conclusion about the conditions under which self-attention decreases persistence contradicts Carver's (1979) assertion about the beneficial effects of combining self-attention and positive expectancies. Some evidence suggests that when people self-attend after succeeding and expecting to continue succeeding on well mastered tasks, decreased persistence may follow (Brockner 1979; McDonald 1980). Brockner's subjects first received either success or failure feedback on a "social insight test" (top tenth versus bottom twentieth percentile) and then completed a simple concept formation task (e.g., M performance for "success" subjects = 81% accuracy). Both tasks were described as parts of one experiment on "problem solving," thereby presumably increasing the relevance of the false success/failure feedback to the second task. The data generally indicated that following the success feedback, subjects who were dispositionally high in self-attention and those who were made self-attentive through experimental manipulation made more errors in the second task. Unfortunately, the specific statistical comparisons needed to test these effects were not reported.

Similar findings were obtained by McDonald (1980). McDonald's subjects also first received either success or failure feedback (top or bottom tenth percentile) on a creativity test. Then subjects were made either self-aware or not while they completed a "similar but not identical" creativity test that merely required writing as much as they wanted to in response to the Thematic Apperception Test card (i.e., an easily mastered task very similar to those used by Liebling and Shaver [1973], Carver and Scheier [1979], and others in the self-attention literature). McDonald, unlike Brockner (1979), actually assessed the perceived relevance of the two tasks. McDonald's subjects, as would be expected for Brockner's subjects also, believed that the two tasks were highly related. Thus, their prior feedback should have induced a highly relevant expectancy for performance in the second task. Most importantly, the subjects who had received the (relevant) success feedback and then became self-aware in the second task persisted significantly less in the second task than participants in the other groups.

If Brockner's and McDonald's subjects had not previously succeeded at a relevant and easily mastered task, several findings suggest that self-attention may have increased, not decreased, persistence on the second task (Liebling and Shaver 1973; Slapion and Carver 1981; Wicklund and Duval 1971; Carver and Scheier 1979). The evidence concerning the effects of success and positive expectancies on attention (e.g., Postman and Brown 1952; Moore et al. 1979) further indicates that self-attention may impair high-mastery task performance after positive feedback because individuals selectively attend to positive self-aspects under the circumstances. If so, the evidence that positive self-monitoring similarly impairs performance in high-mastery circumstances once again provides a direct correspondence between the self-attention and self-monitoring literatures.

Although it is presently unclear why selective attention to favorable outcomes promotes debilitation under high-mastery circumstances, Tomarken and Kirschenbaum (1982) have suggested that its effects may be mediated by an illusion of control (e.g., Alloy and Abramson 1979; Langer 1975). This proposal is based on two sources of evidence. First, high-mastery contexts promote overly high expectancies and perceptions of control. Second, covert positive self-monitoring appears to encourage overconfidence. In support of these assertions, Alloy and Abramson (1979) found that nondepressed people overestimated their degree of control of the outcomes in a task when they received a high frequency of successful trials (see also Koriat, Lichtenstein, and Fischoff 1980; Langer and Roth 1975). Additionally, individuals susceptible to this illusion made contingency estimates that were uncorrelated with their actual degree of control, but highly correlated with the number of successful trials experienced (see also Nisbett and Ross 1980). This later finding suggests that subjects were selectively attending to positive outcomes. If in fact positive self-monitoring promotes the development of this illusion, overconfidence may occasion self-regulatory dysfunctioning by leading individuals to reduce inappropriately effort expenditure below the level necessary for successful performance. Overconfidence may also decrease the individual's effortful responding because it results in lowered positive affect after success (e.g., Atkinson and Raynor 1974; Kukla 1978) and a preference for other, more difficult tasks (e.g., Buckert, Meyer, and Schmalt 1979; Sigall and Gould 1977; Trope 1979).

In sum, research on self-attention clearly highlights the importance of the interaction between attentional focuses, expectancies, affect, and perhaps other dimensions in self-regulatory failure. *Focusing attention on oneself when anticipating failure or when experiencing negative affect or after experiencing repeated successes may actively contribute to self-regulatory failure under certain conditions.* Research on deindividuation and task mastery provides additional information about attentional focusing and expectancies concerning performance that will further clarify how these elements may become activated.

Deindividuation

Several authors (e.g., Diener 1977; Ziller 1964; Zimbardo 1970) have conceptualized deindividuation as a state of non-self-attention, that is, an internal psychological phenomenon characterized by the absence of self-consciousness and self-evaluation. Diener (1977, 1979, 1980) proposed a model of deindividuation consisting of three major premises:

1. Self-awareness is prevented when the group, not individuals, become the focus of attention and is perceived as a whole unit. . . .

2. Lack of attention to one's own behavior and lack of awareness of one's self as a distinct entity are the crucial cognitive factors comprising deindividuation.

3. A lack of self-regulation results from deindividuation and is comprised of several facets: (a) lack of self-monitoring and retrieval of norms; (b) lack of self-reinforcement; and (c) lack of foresight, planning, and other types of linear sequential processing. Since self-regulation is minimal or eliminated, the deindividuated person is more susceptible to the influence of immediate stimuli, emotions, and motivations (Diener 1980).

Although two studies in the deindividuation literature failed to support strongly Diener's model (Diener 1976; Diener et al. 1975), four more recent investigations provided corroborative evidence (Diener 1979; Diener et al. 1980; Prentice-Dunn and Rogers 1980; Diener 1978). In all of the latter studies, attention to membership within a group was correlated with decreased self-attentiveness and increased antinormative behavior. For example, Diener (1979) compared "deindividuated," "non-self-aware," and "self-aware" groups. Pairs of deindividuated subjects participated with six confederates in a creative series of warm-up activities that were designed to increase group cohesion greatly (e.g., the group was called by a name; the group sang, danced, and engaged in nonverbal activities together). Pairs of non-self-aware subjects also participated in group activities with six confederates, but their groups did not have names and the activities were not oriented to developing group cohesion but merely to have a group of people doing the same things at the same times (e.g., listen to music and rating its qualities, writing essays on abstract topics). The groups that included the pairs of self-aware subjects engaged in activities that emphasized the uniqueness of each participant (e.g., rating how music matched their personalities, writing essays about their uniqueness). As expected, in "creativity tests" following the group activities, the deindividuated group engaged in significantly more disinhibited behavior than the other groups (e.g, "finger painting" with their noses, sucking liquids from baby bottles, listing obscenities). A self-report measure of "self-consciousness" summed for all subjects also correlated negatively with disinhibited behavior consistent with Diener's proposal that lack of self-awareness (attentiveness) results in antinormative behavior.

Diener's model and research suggests that within a social context, attending to oneself as part of a group may decrease self-attention and contribute to self-regulatory failure. This notion coincides with the self-attentional proposition that we typically direct our attention in an essentially dichotomous fashion: to ourselves or to other things. It also supports findings indicating that attending to other people or to the external environment can decrease self-attention and, thereby, affect self-regulatory failure under some conditions (e.g., Duval and Wicklund 1972).

The preceding review of research on the relapse process suggests another mechanism of self-regulatory failure described in Diener's model and related research. Most studies of relapse situations (e.g., Pomerleau, Adkins, and Pertschuk 1978; Shiffman 1982), like the deindividuation work, featured social factors in high-risk situations (e.g., parties, drinking with others, restaurants, being around others who exhibit the problematic behavior). It seems very plausible to suggest that directing attention to one's membership in these "high-risk" groups accentuates social pressure for relapsing, resulting in decreased monitoring of the target behavior and, ultimately, self-regulatory failure.

Well Mastered Tasks

At several points I have referred to findings showing that people often selectively attend to favorable outcomes when performing well mastered behaviors (e.g., Diener and Dweck 1980; Moore et al. 1979). Interestingly, some evidence actually suggests that people pay very little attention to any aspect of their behavior when they engage in extremely easy or overlearned tasks. Kimble and Perlmuter's (1970) integration of findings on the development of skillful motor behavior provides evidence consistent with this notion. According to these authors, when first learning to perform unfamiliar motor acts, individuals must continually monitor their responses and compare them to an "image" that has initiated them (see Grant 1968). At this initial stage the image functions very much like a behavioral standard in the cybernetic models of self-regulation proposed by Carver (1979) and Kanfer (1971). Specifically, it is said to guide responses and to provide a stop or "exit" mechanism allowing individuals to proceed to other behaviors once their current responses match it. However, as Kimble and Perlmuter (1970) note, evidence suggests that after mastering the motor act, there ensues an opposite trend toward decreased monitoring of responses and less frequent comparisons of behavior to the image.

Schneider and Shiffrin's work (1977; Shiffrin and Schneider 1977) parallels that of Kimble and Perlmuter (1970) in showing that attentiveness to ongoing behavior varies inversely with degree of task mastery. These authors found that individuals forced to detect complex or novel stimuli engage in controlled processing. This search strategy is a terminating comparison process in which individuals compare external stimuli to a prototype stored in memory. In contrast, when individuals master detection tasks through the consistent mapping of stimuli to responses, they engage in automatic processing. This method of search demands neither conscious attention nor voluntary control and, once initiated, tends to run to completion automatically.

Schank and Abelson (1977) similarly suggested that high levels of competency or familiarity result in lowered self-attention for individuals performing more complex social behaviors. According to these authors, when individuals are acquiring a skill, they engage in plan processing. At these times, after dividing a complex behavioral sequence into its constituent parts, individuals actively monitor and regulate their performance on each component. In contrast, script processing ensues once individuals have attained a high level of task proficiency. In these cases, formerly small units of behavior are chunked together to form coherent scripts, which individuals can perform freed of the necessity of conscious attention.

The notion that increased mastery results in decreased self-attention also is a central tenet of Langer's (1978, 1979) theory of human mindlessness. According to Langer, mindlessness occurs when individuals think that they have been actively monitoring and regulating their behavior, when in fact they have been performing automatically according to well learned and highly general scripts. Langer further speculated that individuals are most likely to be mindless when engaged in highly familiar routinized activities.

In several studies, Langer and her associates have shown that individuals become mindlessly inattentive to their behaviors in high-mastery situations (Langer, Blank, and Chanowitz 1978; Langer and Newman 1979; Miransky and Langer 1978). In Langer and Imber's research, for instance, individuals who had earlier received no practice, moderate practice, or extensive practice with a task were asked to list the task components necessary for successful performance. As predicted, the overpracticed group listed fewer elements than the moderately practiced group and as many components as the no-practice group. Several experiments also suggest that information seeking, as well as the kind of information processing assessed in Langer, Blank, and Chanowitz's mindlessness studies, declines dramatically with increases in the familiarity of the stimuli in the environment (e.g., Berlyne 1960, 1965; Pyszczynski and Greenberg 1981; cf. also Smith and Miller 1978).

While decreased self-attention associated with performing well mastered tasks may be adaptive in some contexts (Kimble and Perlmuter 1970; Langer and Weinman 1981), the evidence reviewed earlier clearly indicates that such inattention to one's behavior may play an active role in self-regulatory failure. Cybernetic models of self-regulation suggest that such inattention to self precipitates disengagement from sustained self-regulation by decreasing self-evaluative other processes. Langer (1978, 1979) suggested another mechanism by which inattention to well mastered behaviors may prove detrimental to sustained behavior change. Specifically, she argued that such inattention may result in an "illusion of incompetence":

Expertise is attained by successfully ignoring more and more of the particulars of the task in question. With repeated experience, the components of the task drop out. The result of complete mastery, then, is that individuals are often in the position of knowing that they can perform the task without knowing the steps required to accomplish its performance. When circumstances lead these people to question their ability to perform that task successfully (e.g., perhaps even a single question from someone, "Are you sure you can do it?") they may be unsure that they can, because they cannot supply as evidence the steps involved that are necessary to do it. Thus, for tasks over which people should feel most confident, they may be most unconfident (Langer 1978, p. 307).

The illusion of incompetence, that is, the unconfident belief in one's ability to perform a well mastered task when questioned about it, appeared to affect behavior in several studies (Langer and Benevento 1978, Experiments 1, 2; Langer and Imber 1980, Experiments 1, 2). In each study, after attaining a high level of mastery on an initial task, subjects performed a different task together with another subject. On this second task, either one of the pair was the "assistant," and the other was the "boss," or neither subject was so labeled. In the final phase, subjects once again worked on the initial task. In each case, subjects given the pejorative label, "assistant," subsequently performed worse on the original task than those in other conditions, and only about half as well as they did earlier. These performance decrements were not obtained with "moderate" instead of high-mastery subjects or with high-mastery subjects who were also directed to attend to task components.

Summary

Research and theorizing on self-attention, deindividuation, and task mastery underscore the importance of several elements in self-regulation. In particular, the evidence from these studies indicates that some form of self-attentive process (like self-monitoring) appears necessary for effective self-regulation. When people direct their attention away from their target behaviors and standards of performance, decrements in performance and persistence often ensue (e.g., Diener 1979; Duval and Wicklund 1972). Depressogenic cognitions also appear influential in self-regulatory failure according to some studies in this literature. For example, perceiving failure as unavoidable (e.g., Steenbarger and Aderman 1979) and developing negative expectancies for success (e.g., Carver et al. 1979a, b) has decreased effective self-regulation. Finally, difficulties coping with emotional states seemed related to self-regulatory failure in several studies (e.g., Scheier et al. 1981).

Research on attentional phenomena not only underscores the importance of several elements of self-regulatory failure suggested by other literatures, but these studies provide an empirical basis for adding a seventh element to the six previously noted: "problematic attentional focusing." The attentional literature provides many examples of how selectively focusing attention on certain aspects of one's environment or self can affect self-regulatory failure. For example, focusing attention on oneself when failure experiences are accentuated (e.g., via negative self-monitoring [Kirschenbaum and Karoly 1977]; via negative expectancies [Carver, Blaney, and Scheier 1979a, b]; via negative affect [Scheier and Carver 1982]) often results in self-regulatory failure. On the other hand, focusing attention away from the self can also adversely affect self-regulation when social conditions encourage such behavior (e.g., Diener 1979; Duval and Wicklund 1972). Yet another key element of problematic attentional focusing pertains to the performance of well mastered tasks. Performing such tasks generally reduces the tendency to focus attention on them (e.g., Kimble and Perlmuter 1970; Schneider and Shiffrin 1977). Unfortunately, this tendency can produce self-regulatory dysfunctioning, according to research that has been reviewed previously on self-monitoring and self-attention. Positive self-monitoring (Tomarken and Kirschenbaum 1982) and the development of positive expectancies (McDonald 1980) may direct attention away from key elements of the task and thereby contribute to self-regulatory failure when tasks are well mastered (see also Kuhl 1984).

The literature on attentional processes in self-regulation makes it especially clear that knowing a good deal about the circumstances in which self-regulation occurs determines which potential elements of self-regulatory failure are likely to become operational. Degree of task mastery, affective state, and valence of expectancy are among the key parameters in this regard. Some of the literature considered earlier made it apparent that degree of physiological involvement is another major parameter. Across all of these parameters, however, at least one common link emerges from the preceding literatures: *It appears that some form of systematic attention to the self-regulated target behavior must be sustained to avoid self-regulatory failure.* The reemergence of this conclusion in all three of the diverse literatures considered in this paper is quite remarkable. This consistency suggests the primacy of the subelement referred to in this chapter as "disengagement from self-monitoring" (and functionally equivalent forms of *systematic* attention over time and across situations). It seems likely that disengaging this kind of sustained self-monitoring may be a proximal precipitant of self-regulatory failure.

Figure 2.4 depicts the proposed relationship between disengagement from self-monitoring and self-regulatory failure. Note that the remaining seven elements are shown as precipitants to disengagement from self-monitoring. (Disengagement from self-monitoring had been included as a subelement along with disengagement from habit change prior to this section.) This conceptualization describes one temporal pattern of

DEPRESSOGENIC COGNITIONS

DIFFICULTIES COPING WITH
   EMOTIONAL STRESSORS

DISENGAGEMENT FROM HABIT
   CHANGE

SOCIAL PRESSURE   →   DISENGAGEMENT FROM
                                   SELF-MONITORING

INITIAL RELAPSE EPISODE

PHYSIOLOGICAL PRESSURE*

PROBLEMATIC ATTENTIONAL
   FOCUSING

TIME

Figure 2.4. Eight elements of self-regulatory failure and one proposed temporal relationship between them.

*Physiological pressure is presumed to play a much more substantial role in the self-regulation of clearly physiologically mediated target behaviors (e.g., addictive behaviors versus academic behaviors).

Source: Compiled by the authors.

interaction between the elements of self-regulatory failure that have been identified in this review. The seven elements on the left side of Table 2.2 are presumed capable of acting independently or interactively to produce disengagement from self-monitoring. Once that occurs, failure to generalize self-regulated behavior change is presumed to be very likely to ensue.

Of course, this view does not specify precise patterns of interactions between the seven elements shown on the left side of Figure 2.4. The data base required for such proposals are simply inadequate at this juncture. We do not know, for example, very much about the circumstances and dispositional styles that determine when people are likely to make depressogenic cognitions (e.g., Danker-Brown and Baucom 1982; Diener and Dweck 1978, 1980; Harvey 1981). The conditions under which emotional stressors become activated in self-regulation also remain largely unknown (Kirschenbaum, Tomarken, and Humphrey 1985; Scheier and Carver 1982). This review, and the relationship proposed in Figure 2.4, merely suggest that close scrutiny of the extant empirical literature can yield important information about potentially vital elements of self regulatory failure, including one proposed temporal sequence for their interaction.

TOWARD PREVENTING SELF-REGULATORY FAILURE: OBSESSIVE-COMPULSIVE SELF-REGULATION

The present conceptualization of self-regulatory failure describes a great many ways to fail to reach long-term goals. The very pervasiveness of these impediments suggests that counterbalancing them may require a radical solution. Consider the nature of successful self-regulation according to this view. The successful self-regulator will have to maintain self-monitoring despite distractions and stressors, such as social pressures and conflicts, difficulties coping with various emotional states, and potentially powerful antagonistic physiological pressures. Certain cognitive styles or focuses may help ensure this sustained effort. These probably include attending to favorable aspects of performance and developing positive expectations when regulating poorly mastered behaviors; conversely, attending to unfavorable aspects of performance can improve self-regulation when engaged in highly overlearned or very well-mastered behavior (Kirschenbaum and Karoly 1977; Tomarken and Kirschenbaum 1982; see also McDonald 1980; Masters and Santrock 1976).

Kirschenbaum and Tomarken (1982) suggested the term "obsessive-compulsive self-regulation" to describe this complex process of maintaining effective self-regulation or preventing self-regulatory failure. Obsessions are defined as repetitive thoughts, images, or impulses that are unwanted and difficult to control; compulsions are similarly defined as stereotyped, persistent, unwanted overt behaviors (McFall and Wollersheim 1979; Rachman and Hodgson 1980). Unlike the usual clinical picture of obsessive-compulsive disorders, obsessive-compulsive self-regulation is not pathological or unmanageable. Although this view strays from the classic portrayal of the obsessive-compulsive cleaner or checker, the nature and intensity of the involvement with a target behavior seemingly required to circumvent self-regulatory failure justifies the usage of the term in this regard. The present review further accentuates this point by pointing to the pivotal role of sustained self-monitoring.

The following passages present an example of someone who maintained effective self-regulation for a long period of time. This case is offered to clarify, somewhat more dramatically, why the term "obsessive-compulsive" most appropriately describes an effective approach to preventing self-regulatory failure. The case is a composite of several of the most successful clients with whom the author has worked during the past several years. This hypothetical client demonstrates the use of cognitions and overt actions that seem to counter or prevent many of the specific elements of self-regulatory failure identified in the present conceptualization. Therefore, the preceding sections of this chapter have established an empirical basis for asserting that the description of this client may illustrate, albeit in an idealized fashion, a useful approach to preventing self-regulatory failure. (Elements of the previously described conceptualization of self-regulatory failure are in *italics*.)

Alice had gained and lost 20 or more pounds many times in her life. She had been overweight as a child, and two years ago, at the age of 39, she decided that her health (she had high blood pressure), her desire to serve as a good model to her children (of someone who could set and reach goals), and her desire to look more attractive, justified trying to lose weight and keep it off this time. Alice had actually developed bulimia over the past year or so prior to starting the most recent attempt at weight reduction. This involved four to ten binges per week (consumptions of large quantities of food in a matter of a few minutes to one hour) and it contributed to her recent weight gain of 45 pounds (to a weight approximately 60 pounds above goal weight).

Alice began the usual self-control training approach to weight reduction in the context of individual therapy. This involved substantial modification of her eating behavior, exercise patterns, and her thinking about weight-related aspects of her life. Thus, Alice began planning meals and exercise sessions (swimming), monitoring her progress in these areas, and self-rewarding accordingly. She constructed charts, cut out photographs to remind her of her goals (e.g., people in bathing suits; grossly obese women), wrote out sayings to encourage herself (e.g., "One Day at a Time!" "Get Thinner, Get Healthier!"), and posted these things around her house (Horan et al. 1975). She slowed down her eating by taking two-minute time-outs during every meal; she ate on small distinctive plates; she ate only in the kitchen and without any nonsocial distractors (such as television) during meals; she weighed almost all of her food and made sure she looked up and then recorded all of the calories she consumed; she weighed herself every three days, charted her weight, and followed similar procedures for exercising (e.g., recording calories consumed on a chart).

Alice clearly worked hard to maintain her *self-monitoring*-related *habit-change* strategies, as clients are instructed to do in all self-control training programs. Her exercise program was also intended to reduce some of the *physiological pressures* associated with weight reduction (see Donahoe et al. 1984; Thompson et al. 1982). The sayings she posted around her house represented one of the ways in which she attempted to maintain favorable expectancies and an appropriate amount of positive *attentional focusing*. In addition, she and her therapist spent several sessions analyzing and attempting various interventions to help her replace some of her *depressogenic cognitions* with a more rational and action-oriented coping style. These efforts, in addition to assertiveness training, discussion of some family issues, and other interventions helped her *cope with emotional stressors* reasonably well. Perhaps the most important intervention along these lines, however, was several sessions of family therapy in which her three children and her husband learned about the stresses associated with weight reduction and how they could help Alice cope with them. This resulted in the family agreeing to exercise together; find ways to enjoy each other's company without going to get ice cream cones or going to restaurants (e.g., going to parks instead); and encourage each other, in very positive concrete ways, regarding various goals that each of them wished to pursue. Clearly, these sessions helped to reduce the *social pressures* Alice experienced. This was demonstrated by the family's adoption of a much more active, positive, and less food-oriented life style over the course of several months. Finally, some of the time in therapy was also devoted to managing Alice's binge eating. These episodes were examined as *initial relapses*, and some of Marlatt's suggestions (e.g., 1982) were followed to help Alice avoid the "abstinence violation effect" and other adverse reactions to these occasional lapses.

During the course of therapy, every effort was made to ensure that these changes in Alice's covert and overt behaviors, as well as in her social environment, became permanent parts of her life. Thus, Alice continued to self-monitor by writing out the calories she consumed and expended in her "Week-at-a-Glance" office calendar over a period of several years. She also continued swimming several times a week, maintaining her weight chart at home, changing her posted signs and photographs, working with the family, and so forth. All of these activities obviously consumed a good deal of time and required Alice to think about her program of weight reduction many times during every day. Many of Alice's coworkers and friends commented about all of the "rituals" in which she engaged, often laughing about it while admiring her apparent degree of commitment. Interestingly, after more than three years of working at these changes and achieving her weight-loss goal (60 pounds) and maintaining the low weight for more than a year, Alice reported feeling that she *needed* to do several of the things associated with her program or she would become somewhat distressed. For example, her swimming became very important to her as a means of relaxing, coping with stress, and doing "something for me." She actually seemed to develop a mild addiction to her exercise routine (see Thaxton 1982) and other habit changes (e.g., maintenance of weight chart). Not incidentally, she felt extremely proud of her successful weight reduction and equally pleased with the changes she had achieved in her own coping skills and in her family's new life style and patterns of interaction.

The case of Alice clearly illustrates how the pursuit of sustained self-regulated behavior change can coincide with the view of self-regulatory failure suggested in this review. As such, effective long-term self-regulation in this case followed a pattern most simply described as obsessive-compulsive self-regulation. Alice modified many aspects of her life and had to work at the changes she achieved on a daily basis to maintain them over time. In addition, many ostensibly subtle aspects of the behavior changes Alice practiced clearly resemble several features of clinical obsessive-compulsive behaviors. For example, she *continually* focused on the necessary behaviors, often using rather stereotyped rituals to assist her. She also felt uncomfortable if she failed to engage in several of her usual routines. On the other hand, it is clear that the thoughts and actions used by Alice were not "unwanted," as is the case for persons who evidence clinical obsessive-compulsive disorders (see Rachman and Hodgson 1980). Nevertheless, the general style and intensity of the pattern evidenced by this hypothetical client certainly mirror many of the central features of obsessions and compulsions.

The pervasiveness of self-regulatory failure (Kirschenbaum and Tomarken 1982) and the elements of self-regulatory failure incorporated into the present conceptualization suggest that the kind of effort displayed by Alice is required frequently to ensure generalized behavior change. This is particularly true for modifying notoriously refractory target behaviors that include strong and antagonistic physiological pressures. However, it should be emphasized that the present analysis probably applies even for such seemingly mundane and "nonphysiological" target behaviors, such as the relatively permanent improvement of study skills by college students. The evidence indicates that people often need to follow a pattern of behavior change quite similar in style and intensity to the approach used by Alice to modify her eating and exercising habits (reviewed by Kirschenbaum and Perri 1982; Richards 1981; see, for examples, Heffernan and Richards 1981). It also seems probable, however, that target behaviors that pertain to more circumscribed aspects of living—for example, the complete elimination of a specific behavior (such as fingernail biting or cigarette smoking)—may require less involving and less permanent obsessive-compulsive self-regulation. For example, after several years, the ex-cigarette smoker may not need to maintain the same self-controlling responses as required to quit the habit and maintain abstinence for the first year or two.

There are several additional sources of information that support the present characterization of successful self-regulation. First, in contrast to the rather pathological connotation of the descriptor "obsessive-compulsive," some evidence supports the contention that this style of behavior is quite common and nonpathological under some conditions. For example, Rachman and de Silva (1978) found that 84% of a large and diverse nonpatient group of people reported experiencing some obsessive thoughts and impulses. These obsessions did not seem terribly disturbing despite the fact that they mirrored those reported by a small clinical sample in many important respects (e.g., content, relationship to mood, meaningfulness, ability of neutralizing behavior to reduce discomfort). Moreover, Pollak (1979) reviewed the literature on obsessive-compulsive personality and concluded that obsessive-compulsive characteristics are both relatively common and quite easily distinguished from obsessive-compulsive disorders. Finally, research on sport psychology illustrates that not only can obsessive-compulsive behaviors be nonpathological, they can actually prove quite adaptive. Studies with gymnasts (Mahoney and Avener 1977), racketball players (Meyers et al. 1979), golfers (Kirschenbaum and Bale 1980), wrestlers (Gould, Weiss and Weinberg 1981; Highlen and Bennett 1983) and divers (Highlen and Bennett 1983 in press) indicate that a variety of ritualistic behaviors and thoughts are associated with favorable performance outcomes. Mahoney and Avener, for example, found that the frequency of thoughts about their sport in "everyday situations" correlated significantly with performance among elite gymnasts (those invited to compete at the tryouts for the 1976 Olympic games). Kirschenbaum and Bale established an even more direct connection in that better golf scores obtained by university-level golfers were positively correlated with the "obsessive" factor of Nideffer's (1976) **Test of Attentional and Interpersonal Style**. In a more recent and larger-scale study, Highlen and Bennett found that qualifiers for Canadian national diving and wrestling teams reported relatively high frequencies of compulsive-like behaviors. These included withdrawal from others, frequent self-talk, and generally living a highly structured life style during training, compared to similarly skilled athletes who failed to qualify for the national teams.

CONCLUSION

It is important to conclude by reemphasizing that the present account of self-regulatory failure, and how to prevent it, is offered primarily as a means of organizing existing information and suggesting directions for further research. Many situational and dispositional parameters require study to determine how and when the proposed elements of self-regulatory failure interact, as well as to discover more about the nature and nurture of obsessive-compulsive self-regulation. Perhaps the promise of this analysis and, concurrently, the need for further development of it, is best illustrated by suggesting some of its clinical implications.

The primary clinical implication of the present view is that therapists may find it helpful to devise and test various means to help their clients develop obsessive-compulsive self-regulation, if self-regulatory problems become focal. Many clients would probably benefit from learning how to attend to their target behaviors continually, systematically, and comfortably, without letting depressogenic cognitions and problematic attentional focusing deter them. This should be augmented by efforts to improve coping skills, including means to avoid and otherwise manage initial relapse episodes, powerful emotional states, and social and physiological pressures.

Not only do these suggestions present a major challenge to interventionists (see also Marlatt 1982), but they call for increasingly sophisticated assessment strategies to afford measures of the process and outcome of these interventions. For example, I know of no method to assess the sort of sustained attentional focusing recommended here. Although some developments in assessments of relevant processes are emerging (Kendall and Hollon 1981; Merluzzi, Glass, and Genest 1981), we have far fewer measures than are needed to determine for which clients, under which conditions, do which interventions produce the greatest dividends in developing obsessive-compulsive self-regulation and otherwise preventing self-regulatory failure.

ACKNOWLEDGMENTS

The author gratefully acknowledges the contributions of Andrew J. Tomarken to the research that serves as a foundation to parts of this manuscript. The helpful comments on an earlier draft provided by Joseph P. Newman and Andrew J. Tomarken are also sincerely appreciated.

REFERENCES

Abrams, D. B., and G.T. Wilson. (1979). Self-monitoring and reactivity in the modification of cigarette smoking. *Journal of Consulting and Clinical Psychology*, 47:243–51.

Abramson, L. Y.; M. E. P. Seligman; and J. Teasdale. (1978). Learned helplessness in humans: Critique and reformulation. *Journal of Abnormal Psychology*, 87:49–74.

Allen, V. L. (1965). Situational factors in conformity. In *Advances in experimental social psychology*, 1, ed. L. Berkowitz. New York: Academic Press.

Alloy, L. B., and L. Y. Abramson. (1979). Judgment of contingency in depressed and nondepressed students: Sadder but wiser? *Journal of Experimental Psychology: General*, 108:441–85.

Anzai, Y., and H. Simon. (1979). The theory of learning by doing. *Psychological Review*, 86:124–41.

Atkinson, J. W., and J. O. Raynor. (1974) *Motivation and achievement*. New York: Wiley.

Baer, P. E.; J. P. Foreyt; and S. Wright. (1977). Self-directed termination of excessive cigarette use among untreated smokers. *Journal of Behavior Therapy and Experimental Psychiatry*, 8:71–74.

Bandura, A. (1969). *Principles of behavior modification*. New York: Holt.

Bandura, A. (1977a). Self-efficacy: Toward a unifying theory of behavioral change. *Psychological Review*, 84:191–215.

Bandura, A. (1977b). *Social learning theory*. New York: Prentice-Hall.

Beaman, A. L.; B. Klentz; E. Diener; and S. Svanum. (1979). Self-awareness and transgression in children: Two field studies. *Journal of Personality and Social Psychology*, 37:1835–46.

Beck, A. T.; J. A. Rush; B.F. Shaw; and G. Emery. (1979). *Cognitive therapy of depression*. New York: Guilford.

Bellack, A. S.; L. M. Glanz; and R. Simon. (1976). Self-reinforcement style and covert imagery in the treatment of obesity. *Journal of Consulting and Clinical Psychology*, 44:490–91.

Bentler, P. M., and G. Speckart. (1979). Models of attitude-behavior relations. *Psychological Review*, 86:452–64.

Berlyne, D. E. (1960). *Conflict, arousal and curiosity*. New York: McGraw-Hill.

Berlyne, D.E. (1965). *Structure and direction in thinking*. New York: Wiley.

Blittner, M.; J. Goldberg; and M. Merbaum. (1978). Cognitive self-control factors in the reduction of smoking behavior. *Behavior Therapy*, 9:553–61.

Borden, M. A., and J. B. Pryor. (1981). *Decreasing and increasing self-report validity by response shaping and self-focusing*. Paper presented at the meeting of the Midwestern Psychological Association, Detroit.

Bourne, L.E., Jr.; R. L. Dominowski; and E. F. Loftus. (1979). *Cognitive processes*. Englewood Cliffs, N.J.: Prentice-Hall.

Bower, G. H. (1981). Mood and memory. *American Psychologist*, 36:129–48.

Braginsky, B. M.; D. D. Braginsky; and K. Ring. (1969). *Methods of madness: The mental hospital as a last resort*. New York: Holt, Rinehart, & Winston.

Brockner, J. (1979). The effects of self-esteem, success-failure, and self-consciousness on task performance. *Journal of Personality and Social Psychology*, 37:1732–41.

Broden, M.; R. V. Hall; and B. Mitts. (1971). The effect of self-recording on the classroom behavior of two eighth grade students. *Journal of Applied Behavior Analysis*, 4:191–99.

Buckert, U.; W. Meyer; and H. Schmalt. (1979). Effects of difficulty and diagnosticity on choice among tasks in relation to achievement motivation and perceived ability. *Journal of Personality and Social Psychology*, 37:1172–78.

Carroll, L. J.; B. T. Yates; and J. Gray. (1980). Predicting obesity reduction in behavioral and nonbehavioral therapy from client characteristics: The self-evaluation measure. *Behavior Therapy*, 11:189–97.

Carver, C.S. (1975). Physical aggression as a function of objective self-awareness and attitudes toward punishment. *Journal of Experimental Social Psychology*, 11:510–19.

Carver, C.S. (1979). A cybernetic model of self-attention processes. *Journal of Personality and Social Psychology*, 37:1251–81.

Carver, C. S., and P. H. Blaney. (1977a). Avoidance behavior and perceived arousal. *Motivation and Emotion*, 1:61–73.

Carver, C. S., and P. H. Blaney. (1977b). Perceived arousal, focus of attention, and avoidance behavior. *Journal of Abnormal Psychology*, 86:154–62.

Carver, C. S.; P. H. Blaney; and M. F. Scheier. (1979a). Focus of attention, chronic expectancy, and responses to a feared stimulus. *Journal of Personality and Social Psychology*, 37:1186–95.

Carver, C. S.; P. H. Blaney; and M. F. Scheier. (1979b). Reassertion and giving up: The interactive role of self-directed attention and outcome expectancy. *Journal of Personality and Social Psychology*, 37:1859–70.

Carver, C. S., and M. F. Scheier. (1978). Self-focusing effects of dispositional self-consciousness, mirror presence, and audience presence. *Journal of Personality and Social Psychology*, 36:324–32.

Carver, C. S., and M. F.Scheier. (1979). The self-attention-induced feedback loop and human motivation: A control-systems analysis of social facilitation. Unpublished manuscript, University of Miami-Coral Gables.

Carver, C. S., and M. F. Scheier. (1981). *Attention and self-regulation: A control-theory approach to human behavior*. New York: Springer-Verlag.

Carver, C. S., and M. F. Scheier. (1982). An information processing perspective on self-management. In *Self-management and behavior change: From theory to practice*, eds. P. Karoly and F. H. Kanfer, pp. 93–128. New York: Pergamon.

Cavior, N., and C. M. Marabotto. (1976). Monitoring verbal behaviors in a dyadic interaction. *Journal of Consulting and Clinical Psychology*, 44:68–76.

Chaney, E. F.; M. R. O'Leary; and G. A. Marlatt. (1978). Skill training with alcoholics. *Journal of Consulting and Clinical Psychology*, 46:1092–1104.

Christensen, A. (1976). Measuring and maintaining weight losses. *Behavior Therapy*, 5:707–08.

Clark, J. V., and H. Arkowitz. (1975). Social anxiety and self-evaluation of interpersonal performance. *Psychological Reports*, 13:321–31.

Cohen, E. A.; D. M. Gelfand; D. K. Dodd; J. Jensen; and C. Turner. (1980). Self-control practices associated with weight loss maintenance in children and adolescents. *Behavior Therapy*, 11:26–37.

Condiotte, M. M., and E. Lichtenstein. (1981). Self-efficacy and relapse in smoking cessation programs. *Journal of Consulting and Clinical Psychology*, 49:648–58.

Cooke, C. J., and A. Meyers. (1980). Assessment of subject characteristics on the behavioral treatment of obesity. *Behavioral Assessment*, 2:59–70.

Cummings, C.; J. R. Gordon; and G. A. Marlatt. (1980). Relapse: Prevention and prediction. In *The addictive behaviors: Treatment of alcoholism, drug abuse, smoking, and obesity*, ed. W. R. Miller. Oxford, England: Pergamon.

Danker-Brown, P., and D. H. Baucom. (1982). Cognitive influences on the development of learned helplessness. *Journal of Personality and Social Psychology*, 43:793–801.

Devins, G. M.; Y. M. Binik; D. J. Hollomby; P. E. Barre; and R. D. Guttmann. (1981). Helplessness and depression in end-stage renal disease. *Journal of Abnormal Psychology*, 90:531–45.

Diener, C. I., and C. S. Dweck. (1978). An analysis of learned helplessness: Continuous changes in performance strategies and achievement cognitions following failure. *Journal of Personality and Social Psychology*, 36:451–63.

Diener, C. I., and C. S. Dweck. (1980). An analysis of learned helplessness. II. The processing of success. *Journal of Personality and Social Psychology*, 39:940–52.

Diener, E. (1976). Effects of prior destructive behavior, anonymity, and group presence on deindividuation and aggression. *Journal of Personality and Social Psychology*, 33:497–507.

Diener, E. (1977). Deindividuation: Causes and consequences. *Social Behavior and Personality*, 5:143–55.

Diener, E. (1978). Causal factors in disinhibition by deindividuation. Unpublished manuscript, University of Illinois.

Diener, E. (1979). Deindividuation, self-awareness, and disinhibition. *Journal of Personality and Social Psychology*, 37:1160–71.

Diener, E. (1980). Deindividuation: The absence of self-awareness and self-regulation in group members. In *The psychology of group influence*, ed. P.B. Paulus. Hillsdale, N.J.: Erlbaum.

Diener, E.; J. Dineen; K. Endresen; A. L. Beaman; and S. C. Fraser. (1975). Effects of altered responsiblity, cognitive set, and modeling on physical aggression and deindividuation. *Journal of Personality and Social Psychology*, 31:328–37.

Diener, E.; R. Lusk; D. DeFleur; and R. Flax. (1980). Deindividuation: Effects of group size, density, number of observers, and group member similarity on self-consciousness and disinhibited behavior. *Journal of Personality and Social Psychology*, 39:449–59.

Diener, E., and M. Wallbom. (1976). Effects of self-awareness on antinormative behavior. *Journal of Research in Personality*, 10:107–11.

Donahoe, C. P.; D. Lin; D.S. Kirschenbaum; and R.E. Keesey. (1984). Metabolic consequences of dieting and exercise in the treatment of obesity. *Journal of Consulting and Clinical Psychology*, 52:827–36.

Dubbert, P. M., and G.T. Wilson. (1983). Failures in behavior therapy for obesity: Causes, correlates, and consequences. In *Failures in behavior therapy*, eds. E. B. Foa and P. M. G. Emmelkamp. New York: Wiley.

Duval, S., and G. Friedan. (1979). Objective self-awareness, task complexity and performance. Unpublished manuscript, University of Southern California.

Duval, S., and R. A. Wicklund. (1972). *A theory of objective self-awareness*. New York: Academic Press.

Duval, S.; R. A. Wicklund; and R. L. Fine. (1972). Avoidance of objective self-awareness under conditions of high and low intra-self discrepancy. In *A theory of objective self-awareness*, eds. S. Duval and R. A. Wicklund. New York: Academic Press.

Dykman, B. M., and J. R. Volpicelli. (1983). Depression and negative processing of evaluative feedback. *Cognitive Therapy and Research*, 7:485–98.

Elliott, C. H., and D. R. Denny. (1978). A multiple-component treatment approach to smoking reduction. *Journal of Consulting and Clinical Psychology*, 46:1330–38.

Epstein, L. H.; J. S. Webster; and P. M. Miller. (1975). Accuracy and controlling effects of self-monitoring as a function of concurrent responding and reinforcement. *Behavior Therapy*, 6:654–66.

Evans, D., and D. S. Lane. (1981). Smoking cessation follow-up: A look at post-workshop behavior. *Addictive Behaviors*, 6:325–29.

Fenigstein, A.; M. F. Scheier; and A. H. Buss. (1975). Public and private self-consciousness: Assessment and theory. *Journal of Consulting and Clinical Psychology*, 43:522–27.

Fisher, E. B., Jr.; L. Green; C. Friedling; J. C. Levenkron; and F. L. Porter. (1976). Self-monitoring of progress in weight reduction: A preliminary report. *Journal of Behavior Therapy and Experimental Psychiatry*, 7:363–65.

Fisher, E. B., Jr.; J. C. Levenkron; M. R. Lowe; A. D. Loro; and L. Green. (1982). Self-initiated self-control in risk reduction. In *Adherence, compliance and generalization in behavioral medicine*, ed. R. B. Stuart. New York: Brunner/Mazel.

Flanery, R. C., and D. S. Kirschenbaum. (1986). Dispositional and situational correlates of long-term success at weight reduction by children. *Addictive Behaviors*, 11:249–61.

Gibbons, F. X., and R. A. Wicklund. (1976). Selective exposure to the self. *Journal of Research in Personality*, 10:98–106.

Gibbons, F. X.; R. A. Wicklund; and D. Rosenfield. (1979). Self-focused attention and prosocial behavior. Unpublished manuscript, University of Texas, Austin.

Gormally, J., and D. Rardin. (1981). Weight loss maintenance and changes in diet and exercise for behavioral counseling and nutrition education. *Journal of Counseling Psychology*, 28:295–304.

Gormally, J.; D. Rardin; and S. Black. (1980). Correlates of successful response to a behavioral weight control clinic. *Journal of Counseling Psychology* 27:179–91.

Gotay, C. C. (1977). Helping behavior as a function of objective self-awareness and salience of the norm of helping. Unpublished doctoral dissertation, University of Maryland.

Gottman, J. M., and R. M. McFall. (1972). Self-monitoring effects in a program for potential high school dropouts: A time series analysis. *Journal of Consulting and Clinical Psychology*, 39:273–81.

Gould, D.; M. Weiss; and R. S. Weinberg. (1981). Psychological characteristics of successful and nonsuccessful big ten wrestlers. *Journal of Sport Psychology*, 3:69–81.

Grant, D. A. (1968). Adding communication to the signaling property of the CS in classical conditioning. *Journal of General Psychology*, 79:147–75.

Greenberg, J. (1980). Attentional focus and locus of performance causality as determinants of equity behavior. *Journal of Personality and Social Psychology*, 38:579–85.

Gur, R.C., and H. A. Sackeim. (1979). Self-deception: A concept in search of phenomenon. *Journal of Personality and Social Psychology*, 37:147–69.

Halisch, F., and H. Heckhausen. (1977). Search for feedback information and effort regulation during task performance. *Journal of Personality and Social Psychology*, 35:724–33.

Hall, S. M. (1980). Self-management and therapeutic maintenance: Theory and research. In *Improving the long-term effects of psychotherapy: Models of durable outcome*, eds. P. Karoly and J. J. Steffen. New York: Gardner.

Harris, M. B.; M. Sutton; E. M. Kaufman; and C. W. Carmichael. (1980). Correlates of success and retention in a multifaceted, long-term behavior modification program for obese adolescent girls. *Addictive Behaviors*, 5:25–34.

Hartigan, K. J.: D. Baker-Strauch; and G. W. Morris. (1982). Perceptions of the causes of obesity and responsiveness to treatment. *Journal of Counseling Psychology*, 29:478–85.

Harvey, D. M. (1981). Depression and attributional style: Interpretations of important personal events. *Journal of Abnormal Psychology*, 90:134–42.

Hayes, S. C., and N. Cavior. (1977). Multiple tracking and the reactivity of self-monitoring: I. Negative behaviors. *Behavior Therapy*, 8:819–31.

Hayes, S. C., and N. Cavior. (1980). Multiple tracking and the reactivity of self-monitoring: II. Positive behaviors. *Behavior Therapy*, 2:283–96.

Heffernan, T., and C. S. Richards. (1981). Self-control of study behavior: Identification and evaluation of natural methods. *Journal of Counseling Psychology*, 28:361–64.

Heinold, J. W.; A. J. Garvey; C. Goldie; and R. Bosse. (1982). Retrospective analysis in smoking cessation research. *Addictive Behaviors*, 7:347–53.

Hendricks, C. G.; C. E. Thoresen; and D. R. Hubbard. (1974). Effects of behavioral self-observation on elementary teachers and students. Memorandum no. 121, Stanford Center for Research and Development.

Heppner, P. P.; J. Hibel; G.W. Neal; C. L. Weinstein; and F.E. Rabinowitz. (1982). Personal problem solving; A descriptive study of individual differences. *Journal of Counseling Psychology*, 29:580–90.

Highlen, P.S., and B.B. Bennett. 1983. Elite divers and wrestlers: A comparison between open- and closed-skill athletes. *Journal of Sport Psychology*, 5:390–409.

Holroyd, K. A.; T. Westbrook; M. Wolf; and E. Badhorn. (1978). Performance, cognition, and physiological responding in test anxiety. *Journal of Abnormal Psychology*, 87:442–51.

Hopper, R. B., and D. S. Kirschenbaum. (1985). Social problem-solving and social competence in preadolescents: Is inconsistency the hobgoblin of little minds? *Cognitive Therapy and Research*, 9:685–701.

Horan, J. J.; S. B. Baker; A. B. Hoffman; and R. E. Shute. (1975). Weight loss through variations in the coverant control paradigm. *Journal of Consulting and Clinical Psychology*, 43:68–72.

Janoff-Bulman, R. (1979). Characterological versus behavioral self-blame: Inquiries into depression and rape. *Journal of Personality and Social Psychology*, 37:1798–1809.

Jeffrey, R. W.; M. Vender; and R. R. Wing. (1978). Weight loss and behavior change one year after behavioral treatment for obesity. *Journal of Consulting and Clinical Psychology*, 46:368–69.

Johnston-O'Connor, E. J., and D. S. Kirschenbaum. (1986). Something succeeds like success: Positive self-monitoring for unskilled golfers. *Cognitive Therapy and Research*, 10:123–36.

Kanfer, F. H. (1970). Self-monitoring: Methodological limitations and clinical applications. *Journal of Consulting and Clinical Psychology*, 35:148–52.

Kanfer, F. H. (1971). The maintenance of behavior by self-generated stimuli and reinforcement. In *The psychology of private events*, eds. A. Jacobs and L. B. Jachs. New York: Academic Press.

Kanfer, F. H., and J. R. Busemeyer. (1982). The use of problem solving and decision making in behavior therapy. *Clinical Psychology Review*, 2:239–66.

Kanfer, F. H., and S. Hagerman. (1981). The role of self-regulation. In *Behavior therapy for depression: Present status and future directions*, ed. L. P. Rehm. New York: Academic Press.

Kanfer, F. H., and P. Karoly. (1972). Self-control: A behavioristic excursion into the lion's den. *Behavior Therapy*, 3:398–416.

Kanfer, F. H., and J.S. Phillips (1970). *Learning foundations of behavior therapy.* New York: Wiley.

Karoly, P., and F. H. Kanfer. (1982). *Self-management and behavior change: From theory to practice.* New York: Pergamon.

Kazdin, A. E. (1974). Reactive self-monitorings: The effects of response desirability, goal-setting, and feedback. *Journal of Consulting and Clinical Psychology*, 42:704–16.

Kendall, P. C., and S. D. Hollon. (1981). *Assessment strategies for cognitive-behavioral interventions.* New York: Academic Press.

Kernis, M. H.; M. Zuckerman; A. Cohen; and S. Spadafora. (1982). Persistence following failure: The interactive role of self-awareness and the attributional basis for negative expectancies. *Journal of Personality and Social Psychology*, 43:1184–91.

Kimble, G.A., and L. C. Perlmuter. (1970). The problem of volition. *Psychological Review*, 77:361–84.

Kindy, S. (1981). Behavioral treatment of morbid obesity through extended contact. Unpublished data, University of Wisconsin School of Medicine, Madison, Wisconsin.

Kirschenbaum, D.S. (1976). When self-regulation fails: Tests of some preliminary hypotheses. (Doctoral dissertation, University of Cincinnati, 1975). *Dissertation Abstracts International*, 36 (9-B), 4692.

Kirschenbaum, D. S., and R. M. Bale. (1980). Cognitive-behavioral skills in golf; Brain power golf. In *Psychology in sports: Methods and applications*, ed. R. M. Suinn, pp. 334–43. Minneapolis, Minn.: Burgess.

Kirschenbaum, D. S., and P. Karoly. (1977). When self-regulation fails: Tests of some preliminary hypotheses. *Journal of Consulting and Clinical Psychology* 45:1116–25.

Kirschenbaum, D.S.; A. M. Ordman; A. J. Tomarken; and R. Holtzbauer. (1982). Effects of differential self-monitoring and level of mastery on sports performance: Brain power bowling. *Cognitive Therapy and Research*, 6:335–42.

Kirschenbaum, D. S., and M. G. Perri. (1982). Improving academic competence in adults: A review of recent research. *Journal of Counseling Psychology*, 29:76–94.

Kirschenbaum, D. S.; P. M. Stalonas; T. R. Zastowy; and A. J. Tomarken. (1985).

Behavioral treatment of adult obesity: attentional controls and a two-year follow-up. *Behaviour Research and Therapy*, 23:675–82.

Kirschenbaum, D. S., and A. J.Tomarken. (1982). On facing the generalization problem: The study of self-regulatory failure. In *Advances in cognitive-behavioral research and therapy*, vol. 1, ed. P. C. Kendall. New York: Academic Press.

Kirschenbaum, D. S.; A. J. Tomarken; and L. L. Humphrey. (1985). Affect and adult self-regulation. *Journal of Personality and Social Psychology*, 48:509–23.

Kirschenbaum, D. S.; A. J. Tomarken; and A. M. Ordman. (1982). Specificity of planning and choice applied to adult self-control. *Journal of Personality and Social Psychology*, 41:576–85.

Kirschenbaum, D. S.; D. A. Wittrock; R. J. Smith; and W. Monson. 1984. Criticism inoculation training: Concept in search of strategy. *Journal of Sport Psychology*, 6:77–93.

Komaki, J., and K. Dore-Boyce. (1978). Self-recording: Its effects on individuals high and low in motivation. *Behavior Therapy*, 9:65–72.

Koriat, A.; S. Lichtenstein; and B. Fischoff. (1980). Reasons for confidence. *Journal of Experimental Psychology: Human Learning and Memory*, 6:107–18.

Kuhl, J. (1981). Motivational and functional helplessness: The moderating effect of state versus action orientation. *Journal of Personality and Social Psychology*, 40:155–70.

Kuhl, J. (1984). Volitional aspects of achievement motivation and learned helplessness: Toward a comprehensive theory of action control. In *Progress in experimental personality research*, vol. 13, ed. B. A. Maher. New York: Academic Press.

Kukla, A. (1978). An attributional theory of choice. In *Advances in experimental social psychology*, vol. 11, ed. L. Berkowitz. New York: Academic Press.

Lando, H. A. (1977). Successful treatment of smokers with a broad-spectrum behavioral approach. *Journal of Consulting and Clinical Psychology*, 45:361–66.

Lang, P. J. (1978). Self-efficacy theory: Thoughts on cognition and unification. *Advances in Behaviour Research and Therapy*, 1:187–92.

Langer, E. J. (1975). The illusion of control. *Journal of Personality and Social Psychology*, 32:311–28.

Langer, E. J. (1978). Rethinking the role of thought in social interaction. In *New directions in attribution research*, vol. 2, eds. J. H. Harvey, W. Ickes, and R. F. Kidd. Hillsdale, N. J.: Erlbaum.

Langer, E. J. (1979). The illusion of incompetence. In *Choice and perceived control*, eds. L. Perlmutter and R. Monty. Hillsdale, N.J.: Erlbaum.

Langer, E. J., and A. Benevento. (1978). Self-induced dependence. *Journal of Personality and Social Psychology*, 36:886–93.

Langer, E. J.; A. Blank; and B. Chanowitz. (1978). The mindlessness of ostensibly thoughtful action: The role of placebic information in interpersonal interaction. *Journal of Personality and Social Psychology*, 36:635–42.

Langer, E. J., and L. G. Imber. (1979). When practice makes imperfect:

Debilitating effects of overlearning. *Journal of Personality and Social Psychology*, 37:2014–24.

Langer, E. J., and H. Newman. (1979). The role of mindlessness in a typical social psychological experiment. *Personality and Social Psychology Bulletin*, 5:295–98.

Langer, E. J., and J. Roth. (1975). Heads I win, tails it's chance: The illusion of control as a function of the sequence of outcomes in a purely chance task. *Journal of Personality and Social Psychology*, 32:951–55.

Langer, E. J., and C. Weinman. (1981). When thinking disrupts intellectual performance: Mindfulness on an overlearned task. *Personality and Social Psychology Bulletin*, 7:240–43.

Lazarus, R. S., and C. W. Ericksen. (1952). Effects of failure stress upon skilled performance. *Journal of Experimental Psychology*, 43:100–5.

Leon, G. R., and K. Chamberlain. (1973a). Comparison of daily eating habits and emotional states of overweight persons successful or unsuccessful in maintaining a weight loss. *Journal of Consulting and Clinical Psychology*, 41:108–15.

Leon, G. R., and K. Chamberlain. (1973b). Emotional arousal, eating patterns, and body image as differential factors associated with varying success in maintaining a weight loss. *Journal of Abnormal Psychology*, 40:474–80.

Leventhal, H. (1980). Toward a comprehensive theory of emotion. In *Advances in experimental social psychology*, vol. 13, ed. L. Berkowitz. New York: Academic Press.

Leventhal, H., and P. D. Cleary. (1980). The smoking problem: A review of the research and theory in behavioral risk modification. *Psychological Bulletin*, 88:370–405.

Leventhal, H.; D. Nerenz; and A. Straus. (1980). Self-regulation and the mechanisms for symptom appraisal. In *Psychosocial epidemiology*, ed. D. Mechanic. New York: Neale Watson.

Lewinsohn, P. M.; D. W. Larson; and R. F. Munoz. (1982). The measurement of expectancies and other cognitions in depressed individuals. *Cognitive Therapy and Research*, 6:437–46.

Lewinsohn, P. M.; W. Mischel; W. Chaplin; and R. Barton. (1980). Social competence and depression: The role of illusory self-perceptions. *Journal of Abnormal Psychology*, 89:203–12.

Lichtenstein, E.; D. O. Antonuccio; and G. Rainwater. (1982). The resumption of cigarette smoking: A situational analysis of retrospective reports. Unpublished manuscript, University of Oregon.

Liebling, B. A., and P. Shaver. (1973). Evaluation, self-awareness, and task performance. *Journal of Experimental Social Psychology*, 9:298–306.

Litman, G. K.; J. R. Eisler; N. S. B. Rawson; and A. N. Oppenheim. (1979). Differences in relapse precipitants and coping behavior between alcohol relapsers and survivors. *Behavior Research and Therapy*, 17:89–94.

Lovitt, T. C., and K. Curtis. (1969). Academic response rate as a function of teacher- and self-imposed contingencies. *Journal of Applied Behavior Analysis*, 2:49–53.

Mahoney, B. K.; T. Rogers; M. K. Straw; and M. J. Mahoney. (1977). Results and implications of a problem solving treatment program for obesity. Paper presented at the annual meeting of the Association for Advancement of Behavior Therapy, Atlanta, December.

Mahoney, M. J. (1974). *Cognition and behavior modification.* Cambridge, Mass.: Ballinger.

Mahoney, M. J. M., and M. Avener. (1977). Psychology of the elite athlete: An exploratory study. *Cognitive Therapy and Research,* 1:135–41.

Mahoney, M. J.: B. E. Moore; T. C. Wade; and N. G. M. Moura. (1973). The effects of continuous and intermittent self-monitoring on academic behavior. *Journal of Consulting and Clinical Psychology,* 41:65–69.

Mahoney, M. J., and C. E. Thoresen. (1974). *Self-control: Power to the person.* San Francisco: Brooks Cole.

Maletzky, B. M. (1974). Behavior recording as treatment: A brief note. *Behavior Therapy,* 5:107–12.

Mandler, G., and S. Sarason. (1952). A study of anxiety and learning. *Journal of Abnormal and Social Psychology,* 47:166–73.

Marlatt, G. A. (1973). A comparison of aversive conditioning procedures in the treatment of alcoholism. Paper presented at the meeting of the Western Psychological Association, Anaheim, Calif. Reported in G. A. Marlatt, Craving for alcohol, loss of control, and relapse: A cognitive-behavioral analysis. In *Alcoholism: New directions in behavioral research and treatment,* eds. P. E. Nathan, G. A. Marlatt, and T. Loberg. New York: Plenum, 1978.

Marlatt, G. A. (1978). Craving for alcohol, loss of control, and relapse: A cognitive-behavioral analysis. In *Alcoholism: New directions in behavioral research and treatment,* eds. P. E. Nathan, G. A., Marlatt, and T. Loberg. New York: Plenum.

Marlatt, G. A. (1982). Relapse prevention: A self-control program for the treatment of addictive behaviors. In *Adherence, compliance and generalization in behavioral medicine,* eds. R. B. Stuart, pp. 329–78. New York: Brunner/Mazel.

Marlatt, G. A., and J. R. Gordon. (1980). Determinants of relapse: Implications for the maintenance of behavior change. In *Behavioral medicine: Changing health lifestyles,* eds. P. O. Davidson and S. M. Davidson. New York: Brunner/Mazel.

Marlatt, G. A., and B. Kaplan. (1972). Self-initiated attempts to change behavior: A study of New Year's resolutions. *Psychological Reports,* 30:123–31.

Masters, J. C., and J. W. Santrock. (1976). Studies in the self-regulation of behavior: Effects of cognitive and affective events. *Developmental Psychology,* 12:334–48.

McDonald, P. J. (1980). Reactions to objective self-awareness. *Journal of Research in Personality,* 14:250–60.

McFall, M. E., and J. P. Wollersheim. (1979). Obsessive-compulsive neurosis: A cognitive-behavioral formulation and approach to treatment. *Cognitive Therapy and Research,* 3:333–48.

McFall, R. M. (1976). *Behavioral training: A skill-acquisition approach to clinical problems.* Morristown, N.J.: General Learning Press.

McFall, R. M. (1977). Parameters of self-monitoring. In *Behavioral self-management: Strategies, techniques, and outcomes,* ed. R. B. Stuart. New York: Brunner/Mazel.

McFall, R. M., and C. L. Hammen. (1971). Motivation, structure, and self-monitoring: The role of nonspecific factors in smoking reduction. *Journal of Consulting and Clinical Psychology*, 37:80–86.

McIntyre, K. O.; E. Lichtenstein; and R. J. Mermelstein. (1983). Self-efficacy and relapse in smoking cessation: A replication and extension. *Journal of Consulting and Clinical Psychology*, 51:632–33.

Meichenbaum, D. (1969). The effects of instructions and reinforcement on thinking and language behaviors of schizophrenics. *Behaviour Research and Therapy*, 7:101–14.

Meichenbaum, D. H., and J. Goodman. (1971). Training impulsive children to talk to themselves: A means of developing self-control. *Journal of Abnormal Psychology*, 77:115–26.

Merluzzi, T. V.; C. R. Glass; and M. Genest, eds. (1981). *Cognitive assessment.* New York: Guilford.

Meyers, A. W.; C. J. Cooke; J. Cullen; and L. Liles. (1979). Psychological aspects of athletic competitors: A replication across sports. *Cognitive Therapy and Research*, 3:361–66.

Miransky, J., and E.J. Langer. (1978). Burglary (non)prevention: An instance of relinquishing control. *Personality and Social Psychology Bulletin*, 4:399–405.

Mischel, W. (1973). Toward a cognitive social learning reconceptualization of personality. *Psychological Review*, 80:252–83.

Mischel, W. (1981). A cognitive-social learning approach to assessment. In *Cognitive assessment*, eds. T. V. Merluzzi, C. R. Glass, and M. Genest. New York: Guilford.

Mischel, W.; E. B. Ebbesen; and A. R. Zeiss. (1973). Selective attention to the self: Situational and dispositional determinants. *Journal of Personality and Social Psychology*, 27:129–42.

Moore, B.; B. Underwood; P. Heberlein; L. Doyle; and K. Litzkie. (1979). Generalization of feedback about performance. *Cognitive Therapy and Research*, 3:371–80.

Nash, J. D. (1976). Curbing dropout from treatment for obesity. Paper presented at the meeting of the Association for Advancement of Behavior Therapy, New York, December.

Nelson, R. O. (1977). Assessment and therapeutic functions of self-monitoring. In *Progress in behavior modification*, vol. 5, eds. M. Hersen, R. M. Eisler, and P. M. Miller. New York: Academic Press.

Nelson, R. O., and S. C. Hayes. (1981). Theoretical explanations for reactivity in self-monitoring. *Behavior Modification*, 5:3–14.

Nentwig, C. G. (1978). Attribution of cause and long-term effects of the modification of smoking behavior. *Behavioural Analysis and Modification*, 2:285–95.

Nideffer, R. M. (1976). Test of attentional and interpersonal style. *Journal of Personality and Social Psychology*, 34:394–404.

Nisbett, R. E., and L. Ross. (1980). *Human inference: Strategies and shortcomings in social judgement.* Englewood Cliffs, N.J.: Prentice-Hall.

Nisbett, R. E., and T. D. Wilson. (1977). Telling more than we know: Verbal reports on mental processes. *Psychological Review*, 84:231–59.

Norman, D. A. (1969). *Memory and attention: An introduction to human information processing.* New York: Wiley.

Norman, W. H.; I. W. Miller III; and S. H. Klee. (1983). Assessment of cognitive distortion in a clinically depressed population. *Cognitive Therapy and Research*, 7:133–40.

Nunnally, J. C. (1978). *Psychometric theory.* 2d ed. New York: McGraw-Hill.

O'Leary, S. G., and D. R. Dubey. (1979). Applications of self-control procedures by children: A review. *Journal of Applied Behavior Analysis*, 12:449–65.

Pennebaker, J. W., and J. A. Skelton. (1978). Psychological parameters of physical symptoms. *Personality and Social Psychology Bulletin*, 4:524–30.

Pennebaker, J. W., and J. A. Skelton. (1981). Selective monitoring of bodily sensations. *Journal of Personality and Social Psychology*, 41:213–23.

Perri, M. G., and C. S. Richards. (1977). An investigation of naturally occurring episodes of self-controlled behaviors. *Journal of Counseling Psychology*, 24:178–83.

Perri, M. G.; C. S. Richards, and K. R. Schultheis. (1977). Behavioral self-control and smoking reduction: A study of self-initiated attempts to reduce smoking. *Behavior Therapy*, 8:360–65.

Peterson, L. (1983). Failures in self-control. In *Failures in behavior therapy*, eds. E. B. Foa and P. M. G. Emmelkamp. New York: Wiley.

Pollak, J. M. (1979). Obsessive-compulsive personality: A review. *Psychological Bulletin*, 36:225–41.

Pomerleau, O.; D. Adkins; and M. Pertschuk. (1978). Predictors of outcome and recidivism in smoking cessation treatment. *Addictive Behaviors*, 3:64–70.

Postman, L., and D. R. Brown. (1952). The perceptual consequences of success and failure. *Journal of Abnormal and Social Psychology*, 47:213–21.

Prentice-Dunn, S., and R. W. Rogers. (1980). Effects of deindividuating situational cues and aggressive models on subjective deindividuation and aggression. *Journal of Personality and Social Psychology*, 39:104–13.

Pryor, J. B.; F. X. Gibbons; R. A. Wicklund; R. H. Fazio; and R. Hood. (1977). Self-focused attention and self-report validity. *Journal of Personality*, 45:514–27.

Pyszczynski, T. A., and J. Greenberg. (1981). Role of disconfirmed expectancies in the instigation of attributional processing. *Journal of Personality and Social Psychology*, 40:31–38.

Rachman, S. J. (1981). Emotional processing. *Behaviour Research and Therapy*, 18:51–60.

Rachman, S. J., and P. de Silva. (1978). Abnormal and normal obsessions. *Behaviour Research and Therapy*, 16:233–48.

Rachman, S. J., and R. J. Hodgson. (1980). *Obsessions and compulsions.* Englewood Cliffs, N.J.: Prentice-Hall.

Rapoff, M. A., and E. R. Christophersen. (1982). Compliance of pediatric patients with medical regimens: A review and evaluation. In *Adherence, compliance and generalization in behavioral medicine*, ed. R. B. Stuart. New York: Brunner/Mazel.

Rehm, L. P. (1977). A self-control model of depression. *Behavior Therapy*, 8:787–804.

Rehm, L. P. (1982). Self-management in depression. In *Self-management and behavior change: From theory to practice*, eds. P. Karoly and F. H. Kanfer. New York: Pergamon.

Richards, C. S. (1981). Improving college students' study behaviors through self-control techniques. A brief review. *Behavioral Counseling Quarterly*, 1:159–75.

Richards, C. S.; D. C. Anderson; and R. B. Baker. (1978). The role of information feedback on the relative reactivity of self-monitoring and external observations. *Behavior Therapy*, 9:687.

Rijsmon, J. B. (1974). Factors in social comparison of performance influencing actual performance. *European Journal of Social Psychology*, 4:279–311.

Rosenbaum, M. S., and R. S. Drabman. (1979). Self-control training in the classroom: A review and critique. *Journal of Applied Behavior Analysis*, 12:467–85.

Rosenthal, B. S.; G. J. Allen; and C. Winters. (1980). Husband involvement in the behavioral treatment of overweight women: Initial effects and long-term follow-up. *International Journal of Obesity*, 4:165–73.

Ross, L. (1977). The intuitive psychologist and his shortcomings: Distortions in the attribution process. In *Advances in experimental social psychology*, vol. 10, ed. L. Berkowitz. New York: Academic Press.

Roth, D., and L. P. Rehm. (1980). Relationships among self-monitoring processes, memory, and depression. *Cognitive Therapy and Research*, 4:149–58.

Rotter, J. B. (1954). *Social learning and clinical psychology*. Englewood Cliffs, N.J.: Prentice Hall.

Rozensky, R. H., and A. S. Bellack. (1974). Behavior change and individual differences in self-control. *Behavior Research and Therapy*, 12:267–68.

Rozensky, R. H., and A. S. Bellack. (1976). Individual differences in self-reinforcement style and performance in self- and therapist-controlled weight reduction programs. *Behavior Research and Therapy*, 14:357–64.

Saltzer, E. B. (1981). Cognitive moderators of the relationship between behavioral intentions and behavior. *Journal of Personality and Social Psychology*, **41:260–71.**

Sandifer, B. A., and W. L. Buchanan. (1983). Relationship between adherence and weight loss in a behavioral weight reduction program. *Behavior Therapy*, 14:682–88.

Schank, R.C. and R. P. Abelson. (1977). *Scripts, plans, goals, and understanding*. Hillsdale, N.J.: Erlbaum.

Scheier, M. F. (1976). Self-awareness, self-consciousness, and angry aggression. *Journal of Personality*, 44:627–44.

Scheier, M. F., and C. S. Carver. (1977). Self-focused attention and the experience of emotion: Attraction, repulsion, elation, and depression. *Journal of Personality and Social Psychology*, 35:625–36.

Scheier, M. F., and C. S. Carver. (1982). Cognition, affect, and self-regulation. In *Affect and cognition: The 17th annual Carnegie symposium on cognition*, eds. M. S. Clark and S. T. Fiske. Hillsdale, N.J.: Erlbaum.

Scheier, M. F.; C. S. Carver; and F. X. Gibbons. (1979). Self-directed attention, awareness of bodily states, and suggestability. *Journal of Personality and Social Psychology*, 37:1576–88.

Scheier, M. F.; C. S. Carver; and F. X. Gibbons. (1981). Self-focused attention and reactions to fear. *Journal of Research in Personality*, 15:1–15.

Scheier, M. F.; C. S. Carver; R. Schulz; D. C. Glass; and I. Katz. (1978). Sympathy, self-consciousness, and reactions to the stigmatized. *Journal of Applied Social Psychology*, 8:270–82.

Scheier, M. F.; A. Fenigstein; and A. H. Buss. (1974). Self-awareness and physical aggression. *Journal of Experimental Social Psychology*, 10:264–73.

Schneider, W., and R. M. Shiffrin. (1977). Controlled and automatic human information processing: I. Detection, search, and attention. *Psychological Review*, 84:1–66.

Shiffman, S. (1982). Relapse following smoking cessation: A situational analysis. *Journal of Consulting and Clinical Psychology*, 50:71–86.

Shriffrin, R. M., and W. Schneider. (1977). Controlled and automatic human information processing. II. Perceptual learning, automatic attending, and a general theory. *Psychological Review*, 84:127–90.

Shrauger, J. S. (1975). Responses to evaluation as a function of initial self-perceptions. *Psychological Bulletin*, 82:581–96.

Shrauger, J. S., and S. E. Rosenberg. (1970). Self-esteem and the effects of success and failure feedback on performance. *Journal of Personality*, 38:404–17.

Sigall, H., and R. Gould. (1977). The effects of self-esteem and evaluator demandingness on effort expenditure. *Journal of Personality and Social Psychology*, 35:12–20.

Silverman, I. (1964). Self-esteem and differential responsiveness to success and failure. *Journal of Abnormal and Social Psychology*, 69:115–19.

Sjoberg, L., and T. Johnson. (1978). Trying to give up smoking: A study of volitional breakdowns. *Addictive Behaviors*, 3:149–64.

Sjoberg, L., and L. Persson. (1979). A study of attempts by obese patients to regulate eating. *Addictive Behaviors*, 4:349–59.

Sjoberg, L., and V. Samsonowitz. (1978). Success and failure in trying to quit smoking. *Scandinavian Journal of Psychology*, 19:205–12.

Sjoberg, L.; V. Samsonowitz; and G. Olsson. (1978). Volitional problems in alcohol abuse. *Goteberg Psychological Reports*, 8, no. 5.

Skinner, B. F. (1953). *Science and human behavior*. New York: Macmillan.

Slapion, M. J., and C. S. Carver. (1981). Self-directed attention and facilitation of intellectual performance among persons high in test anxiety. *Cognitive Therapy and Research*, 5:115–21.

Smith, E., and F. Miller. (1978). Limits on perception of cognitive processes: A reply to Nisbett and Wilson. *Psychological Review*, 85:355–62.

Stalonas, P. M., Jr., and D. S. Kirschenbaum. (1980, November). Are eating habits associated with weight loss? Paper presented at the meeting of the Association for Advancement of Behavior Therapy, New York. Manuscript under review, 1987.

Steenbarger, B. N., and D. Aderman. (1979). Objective self-awareness as a nonaversive state: Effect of anticipating discrepancy reduction. *Journal of Personality*, 47:330–39.

Steffan, J. J., and K. A. Myszak. (1978). Influence of pretherapy induction upon the outcome of a self-control weight reduction program. *Behavior Therapy*, 9:404–90.

Stuart, R. B. (1967). Behavioral control of overeating. *Behavior Research and Therapy*, 5:357–65.

Stuart, R.B. (1980). Weight loss and beyond: Are they taking it off and keeping it off? In *Behavioral medicine: Changing health lifestyles*, eds. P. O. Davidson and S. M. Davidson. New York: Brunner/Mazel.

Stuart, R. B., and K. Guire. (1978). Some correlates of weight lost through behavior modification. *International Journal of Obesity*, 2:127–37.

Thaxton, L. (1982). Physiological and psychological effects of short-term exercise addiction on habitual runners. *Journal of Sport Psychology*, 4:73–80.

Thompson, J. K.; G. J. Jarvie; B. B. Lahey; and K. J. Cureton. (1982). Exercise and obesity: Etiology, physiology, and intervention. *Psychological Bulletin*, 91:55–79.

Thoresen, C. E., and M. J. Mahoney. (1974). *Behavioral self-control*. New York: Holt.

Tobias, L. L., and M. L. MacDonald. (1977). Internal locus of control and weight loss: An insufficient condition. *Journal of Consulting and Clinical Psychology*, 45:647–53.

Tomarken, A. J., and D. S. Kirschenbaum. (1982). Self-regulatory failure: Accentuate the positive? *Journal of Personality and Social Psychology*, 43:584–97.

Tomarken, A. J., and D. S. Kirschenbaum. (1984). Self-awareness and self-regulation. Unpublished manuscript, University of Wisconsin, Madison.

Trope, Y. (1979). Uncertainty-reducing properties of achievement tasks. *Journal of Personality and Social Psychology*, 37:1505–18.

Turner, R. G. (1978a). Consistency, self-consciousness and the predictive validity of typical and maximal personality measures. *Journal of Research in Personality*, 12:117–32.

Turner, R. G. (1978b). Effects of differential request procedures and self-consciousness on trait attributions. *Journal of Research in Personality*, 12:431–38.

Wade, T. C. (1974). Relative effects on performance and motivation of self-monitoring correct and incorrect responses. *Journal of Experimental Psychology*, 77:245–48.

Wegner, D. M., and T. Giuliano. (1980). Arousal-induced attention to the self. *Journal of Personality and Social Psychology*, 38:719–26.

Wegner, D. M., and D. Schaefer. (1978). The concentration of responsibility: An objective self-awareness analysis of group size effects in helping situations. *Journal of Personality and Social Psychology*, 36:147–55.

Weiner, B. (1966). The role of success and failure in the learning of easy and complex tasks. *Journal of Personality and Social Psychology*, 3:339–44.

Weiner, B., and K. Schneider. (1971). Drive versus cognitive theory: A reply to Boor and Harmon. *Journal of Personality and Social Psychology*, 18:258–62.

Wicklund, R. A. (1975). Objective self-awareness. In *Advances in experimental social psychology*, vol. 8, ed. L. Berkowitz. New York: Academic Press.

Wicklund, R. A., and S. Duval. (1971). Opinion change and performance facilitation as a result of objective self-awareness. *Journal of Experimental Social Psychology*, 1:319–42.

Wine, J. D. (1980). Cognitive-attentional theory of test anxiety. In *Test anxiety: Theory, research, and applications*, ed. I. G. Sarason. Hillsdale, N.J.: Erlbaum.

Wortman, C. B., and J. W. Brehm. (1975). Responses to uncontrollable outcomes: An integration of reactance theory and the learned helplessness model. In *Advances in experimental social psychology*, vol. 8, ed. L. Berkowitz. New York: Academic Press.

Wortman, C. B., and L. Dintzer. (1978). Is an attributional analysis of the learned helplessness phenomena viable?: A critique of the Abramson-Seligman-Teasdale reformulation. *Journal of Abnormal Psychology*, 87:75–82.

Zajonc, R. B. (1980). Feeling and thinking: Preferences need no inferences. *American Psychologist*, 35:151–75.

Zajonc, R. B. (1984). On the primary of affect. *American Psychologist*, 39:117–23.

Ziller, R. C. (1964). Individuation and socialization: A theory of assimilation in large organizations. *Human Relations*, 17:341–60.

Zimbardo, P.G. (1970). The human choice: Individuation, reason, and order versus deindividuation, impulse, and chaos. In *Nebraska Symposium on Motivation*, eds. W. J. Arnold and D. Levine. Lincoln, Nebr.: University of Nebraska Press.

3

SELF-EFFICACY AND THE PREVENTION OF ALCOHOLIC RELAPSE: INITIAL FINDINGS FROM A TREATMENT TRIAL

Helen M. Annis and
Christine S. Davis

It has been recognized for some time that treatment intervention strategies that are effective in initiating behavior change frequently fail to maintain this change over time and across different situations. This failure to maintain behavior change is a major concern in the alcoholism field in which programs have reported relapse rates as high as 80% or more by six months posttreatment discharge (Armor, Polich, and Stambul 1978; Gottheil et al. 1979; Orford and Edwards 1977), and the instability of treatment outcome status for alcoholic clients has been found to be extremely high (Polich, Armor, and Braiker 1980).

Hunt, Barnett, and Branch (1971) provided evidence that the temporal pattern of relapse is strikingly similar for a number of addictive behaviors. In their study of heroin addicts, smokers, and alcoholics, two thirds of the relapses in each group occurred within the first three months following treatment, suggesting the possibility that common elements may underlie the relapse process. Based on interview data on the determinants of relapse, Marlatt and his associates have been able to identify common antecedent events associated with relapse among alcoholics, smokers, and heroin addicts (Marlatt and Gordon 1980). For each group about three

The views expressed in this chapter are those of the authors and do not necessarily reflect those of the Addiction Research Foundation.

quarters of all relapse episodes fell into just three categories of antecedent events: coping with negative emotional states, social pressure, and coping with interpersonal conflict. Their work suggests that common behavioral and cognitive components may be associated with the relapse process regardless of the particular addictive substance involved.

How are we to account for the fact that treatment strategies that are successful in effecting a change in drinking behavior frequently fail to sustain that change over time in the natural environment? What may explain the presence of common behavioral and cognitive components that appear to underlie the relapse process? What theoretical framework can be drawn on to develop treatment strategies for alcoholics that may lead to greater generalization of treatment effects?

Relapse, by definition, involves a failure to maintain behavior change, rather than a failure to initiate change. We speak of an alcoholic relapsing from a period of abstinence (or, alternatively, from moderate drinking). In the case of an abstinence goal, the period of abstinence was successfully embarked on—that is, the client stopped drinking. The problem became one of maintaining that abstinence over time—that is, the client began to drink. Traditional alcoholism programming has enjoyed considerable success in initiating a change in drinking behavior in clients. At the same time, reports of alcoholics in the community suggest that many alcoholics successfully initiate periods of abstinence on their own. A critical problem in alcoholism, as in other addictive behaviors, is one of maintaining the change in behavior over time.

The translation of the relapse problem into these terms (i.e., initiation versus maintenance) is important from a learning theory analysis of what has gone wrong. From the perspective of social learning theory, the treatment implications of a failure to initiate change are very different from the treatment implications of a failure to maintain change. The type of treatment strategies called for differ in each case.

The distinction between initiation and maintenance was of central importance in our choice of Bandura's theory of self-efficacy as a framework to guide the development of new relapse prevention procedures for treatment of alcoholics. To date in the alcoholism field, empirical study has been restricted largely to demonstrations of the predictive power of self-efficacy ratings in relation to posttreatment drinking behavior (e.g., Condra 1982; Stiemerling 1983; Rist and Watzl 1983). Although the relevance of self-efficacy theory to an explanation of the alcoholic relapse process (Wilson 1978a, b, 1979, 1980) and to the design of treatment strategies (Marlatt 1985a, b; Marlatt and George 1984; Marlatt and Gordon 1980) has received some attention in the literature, no empirical work has been reported.

At the Clinical Institute of the Addiction Research Foundation in Toronto, the treatment implications of self-efficacy theory have been integrated into a relapse prevention model for alcoholics (Annis 1985; Annis and Davis 1985; Peachey and Annis 1985). In this chapter we provide an overview of the treatment implications of self-efficacy theory for the design of maintenance strategies, describe the development and implementation of a relapse prevention program for alcoholics, and present initial findings from a treatment outcome trial.

SELF-EFFICACY THEORY

Self-efficacy theory (Bandura 1977) is a general cognitive-behavioral theory of the development and modification of human behavior. An efficacy expectation is defined as a judgement that one has the ability to execute a certain behavior pattern. (This is distinguished from an outcome expectation that involves a judgement of the likely consequences such a behavior will produce.) Extrapolating to the area of alcoholism, it would be predicted that durable treatment effects (i.e., effects that will generalize across time and settings) will be a function of the development of strong efficacy expectations with respect to coping with alcohol-related situations in the natural environment. Thus, a critical element in treatment entails the development of a strong sense of personal capability or confidence on the part of the client in being able to cope with drinking situations. Furthermore, self-efficacy theory would predict that in the eventuality that the client should take a drink, the behavior, per se, of ingesting alcohol would not necessarily lead to a full-blown relapse. The outcome would depend on the meaning that the act of drinking had for the client, the coping strategies available, and the persistence with which the client engaged in coping behavior, which in turn would be determined by the strength of the client's efficacy expectations.

Empirical work related to social learning theory in general, and self-efficacy theory in particular, supports a number of principles that can provide guidelines for the design of treatment strategies aimed at the enhancement of client self-efficacy and the maintenance of behavior change. An overview of these principles and supporting evidence is presented in the following sections.

A Focus on Performance-Based Procedures

A distinction must be drawn between the theoretical *process* of behavior change and treatment *procedure*. Although cognitive mechanisms are hypothesized to mediate the acquisition and regulation of behavior, there is evidence that the most powerful methods of lasting behavior change are performance based. Behavioral procedures, therefore, are typically best employed to alter cognitive processes. Treatment methods based on actual performance accomplishments (i.e., personal mastery experiences) have been shown to be significantly more effective in producing change on multiple subjective and objective measures of psychological functioning than methods that rely on verbal, imaginal, or vicarious procedures. This has been demonstrated for phobic behaviors (Bandura et al. 1980; Bandura, Blanchard, and Ritter 1969; Blanchard 1970), obsessive-compulsive disorders (Rachman and Hodgson 1979), and sexual dysfunction (Kockott, Dittmar, and Nusselt 1975; Mathews et al. 1976). However, to date, no similar demonstration of the superiority of actual performance accomplishments has been reported for alcoholic clients.

Supplementary Use of Cognitive Procedures

Although the most powerful methods of durable behavior change are based on behavioral performance, efficacy expectations can also be enhanced through vicarious experience (e.g., live modeling, symbolic modeling), verbal persuasion (e.g., suggestion, self-instruction), and emotional arousal (e.g., relaxation, symbolic desensitization, attribution, biofeedback). Treatment techniques relying on each of these sources of information have been shown to increase efficacy expectations (Bandura, Adams, and Beyer 1977). Most importantly, it has been found that there are certain clinical situations (e.g., self-defeating ideation on the part of the client) for which direct cognitive manipulations may be necessary to foster gains in self-efficacy (cf. Bandura et al. 1980; Kopel and Arkowitz 1975). Therefore, in working with a client, the therapist should be vigilant for evidence that supplementary use of direct cognitive strategies may be indicated. This is discussed further under the monitoring of self-efficacy and the cognitive processing of efficacy information in the following section.

The Predictive Value of Self-Efficacy Ratings

A distinction must be drawn between outcome expectations and efficacy expectations. An outcome expectancy is an individual's belief that a specific behavior (e.g., exerting control over one's consumption of alcohol) will result in a certain outcome (e.g., acceptance by boss, peers, wife); whereas an efficacy expectancy is an individual's belief that he/she is capable of executing the behavior required to produce that outcome. It is the strength of efficacy expectations that determines the initiation and persistence of coping behavior over time and in the face of difficult situations. It has been shown that the degree of change in behavior and the generalization of behavior change to new stimulus situations is closely related to an increase in efficacy expectations (Bandura, Adams, and Beyer 1977). The strength of efficacy expectations has been found to be a better predictor of behavior in the posttreatment period than actual behavioral performance during treatment. The predictive superiority of efficacy expectations over simple overt past behavior has been demonstrated for phobics in relation to encounter with novel situational cues (Bandura, Adams, and Beyer 1977). Although enhanced self-efficacy has been found to generalize most predictably to activities that are similar to those in which self-efficacy was restored in treatment (Bandura, Blanchard, and Ritter 1969), generalization effects may also occur to activities substantially different from those on which treatment focused (Bandura, Adams, and Beyer 1977; Bandura, Jeffery, and Gajdos 1975). In the smoking field, low client ratings of self-efficacy for specific smoking situations at the end of treatment have been found to be predictive of the actual circumstances under which individual clients relapse (Condiotte and Lichtenstein 1981; McIntyre, Lichtenstein, and Mermelstein 1983). Evidence has begun to accumulate in the alcoholism field as well, indicating that clients' efficacy expectations with respect to coping with drinking situations are predictive of future drinking behavior (Condra 1982; Stiemerling 1983; Rist and Watzl 1983).

A Microanalysis of the Problematic Behavior

In analyzing the covariation between cognitions and behavior, a microanalytic procedure results in the most powerful predictive equations. This approach involves a detailed, situation-specific assessment of cognitive events in close proximity to the behavior they supposedly regulate (cf. Bandura 1977). It has been repeatedly demonstrated that global measures of personality and/or cognitive functioning do not have the same predictive power in relation to designated behaviors as do situation-specific person measures (e.g., Endler 1975). For this reason, efficacy judgments should be made with respect to highly specific behavioral performances.

Development of a Hierarchy of Risk Situations

In the scheduling of performance tasks in treatment, the client's risk situations with regard to the problematic behavior should be ordered from low to higher risk with treatment focusing initially on the easier situations. It is particularly important early in treatment that the client experience mastery in performance assignments. Tasks based on behaviors with relatively high self-efficacy ratings have been shown to be more likely to result in success experiences (Bandura 1978).

The Use of a Two-Phase Treatment Plan

It is critical that conditions be arranged throughout treatment so that clients can perform successfully despite their incapacities (cf. Bandura

1977). This may be facilitated by the use of a two-phase treatment plan in which phase one concentrates on "initiation strategies" and phase two on "maintenance strategies." Powerful procedures for the initiation of change include induction aids, such as the modeling and rehearsal of difficult activities, the judicious use of graduated tasks, joint performance with the therapist, protective aids to reduce the likelihood of negative outcomes, and variation in the difficulty level of the task (Bandura, Jeffery, and Wright 1974). However, it is important that such aids be gradually withdrawn in phase two in which the emphasis shifts to "maintenance strategies" designed to foster client self-inferences from mastery experiences that are consistent with those known to enhance self-efficacy and produce strong maintenance of behavior change. The nature of such self-inferences is discussed in the following sections.

Monitoring Self-Efficacy
and the Cognitive Processing of Efficacy Information

Because successful behavioral peformances do not always create strong expectations of personal efficacy, it is necessary to monitor a client's perceived self-efficacy over the course of treatment. In instances in which success with performance tasks is not associated with improved efficacy expectations, the client's self-inferences in relation to the successful performances should be explored. Bandura et al. (1980) have pointed out that "Judgement of personal efficacy . . . involves an inferential process in which the relative contribution of various personal and situational factors to performance successes and failures must be weighted" (p. 42). Efficacy information must be interpreted to form a judgment of personal capability. Unfortunately, research on factors influencing the formation of efficacy judgments is in its infancy. Bandura (1978) commented on four factors that appear to play a role in an individual's cognitive appraisal of risk situations and resulting efficacy expectations. These are (1) the perceived difficulty of the situation; (2) the amount of effort expended in coping in the situation; (3) the perceived degree of external aid provided; and (4) the temporal patterning of success and failure experiences. Additional factors derived from the social psychology literature on self-perception and attribution theory that have been found to affect the formation of self-inferences include (5) the perceived degree of control over the situation and (6) the perceived degree of situational generality of the performance. Each of these dimensions of cognitive appraisal of efficacy information is discussed as follows:

1. *Perceived difficulty of the situation.* Success on an easy task (e.g., to control one's drinking in a situation that has presented few difficulties in the past) provides no new information for altering one's sense of self-efficacy. On the other hand, mastery of a challenging task (e.g., to control one's drinking in a situation that has

frequently resulted in excessive drinking in the past) usually conveys evidence of enhanced competence. Therefore, in the design of performance tasks to increase self-efficacy, tasks should be graded to permit a series of mastery experiences over formerly difficult situations that will be appraised by the clients as salient evidence of increased competency.

2. *Amount of effort expended.* Given that a situation is perceived by the client as difficult, a success achieved with a moderate effort is likely to be interpreted as evidence of improved ability and competence; a success achieved through high expenditure of effort conveys more doubtful information to clients about their abilities and thus is likely to have a weaker effect on perceived self-efficacy. Therefore, in therapy tasks should be ordered so that they will result in appraisal by clients that only a moderate degree of effort was required for successful performance leading to an inference of improved coping ability. Some support for this prediction exists in the literature on attribution theory in what is referred to as the "stability dimension" of self-attribution (Weiner 1980). In this framework effort is usually regarded as an unstable cause. Demonstrations to date that changes in clients' attributions of the cause of their behavior can result in changes in performance have dealt mainly with depressed patients (Miller and Norman 1981). The attribution by clients of a "stable" reason for a success (e.g., improved coping ability) is more likely to result in improvement in their future performance than attribution of an "unstable" cause (e.g., degree of effort made).

3. *Perceived degree of external aid.* Success achieved only under conditions of extensive external aid (e.g., drugs, presence of therapist, and so forth) is unlikely to result in a major gain in one's sense of personal competency. When clients appraise their performance success as due to external factors rather than to improvement in their own capabilities, self-efficacy is not enhanced (Bandura, Jeffery, and Gajdos 1975). Therefore, although external therapy supports can be powerful methods for inducing behavior change, it is critical that these external aids be gradually withdrawn so that clients appraise the cause of their success as increased personal competency. To further foster an appraisal that "internal" rather than "external" factors are responsible for performance gains, therapist fading techniques are useful in placing increasing responsibility on the client to design therapy tasks and engage in self-directed mastery experiences. The internal–external dimension of causality has been extensively investigated in the literature on attribution theory. This research strongly supports the conclusion that self-attributed change is maintained to a greater extent than behavior change attributed to an external agent or circumstance. Demonstrations have involved experimental analogue studies of drug therapy (Davison and Valins 1969) and hypnosis (Bowers 1971), as well as a clinical trial on the treatment of insomnia (Davison, Tsujimoto, and Glaros 1973). An external attribution for the cause of a performance success would not be expected to produce an increase in perceived self-efficacy since it would likely be appraised as due to unusual situational circumstances. On the other hand, self-attributed change permits new self-inferences regarding one's improved competency.

4. *Temporal pattern of successes and failures.* Repeated failure experiences lower efficacy expectations, particularly if they occur early in the course of events. After strong efficacy expectations are developed through repeated success, the negative impact of an occasional failure is reduced. What seems to be of greatest importance

in this regard in raising clients' levels of perceived efficacy is that they should appraise the pattern of performance achievements as showing a steady rate of progress (cf. Bandura 1977). This can be approached in therapy through a careful monitoring of clients' perceptions of their rates of improvement. If perceived progress should falter, an attempt can be made to modify performance tasks to increase significant mastery experiences.

5. *Perceived control over the situation.* The issue of perceived control would seem to be particularly critical in the case of an alcoholic population (cf. Donovan and O'Leary 1979; Wilson 1979). Until recently, there has been wide acceptance in the alcoholism treatment field of the "loss of control" construct and the notion of a physiological addiction process responsible for triggering a full-blown relapse after a single drink. More recently, "loss of control" has been reinterpreted as a psychological phenomenon arising out of a belief system fostered among alcoholics by traditional treatment programs (Marlatt 1978; Ogborne and Bornet 1982; Wilson 1978a). This belief system deliberately minimizes the alcoholics' efficacy expectations about their ability to control alcohol after a single drink and in so doing contributes to a full-blown relapse. Intervention strategies designed to increase an alcoholic's sense of self-efficacy should instill a sense of personal responsibility and control over drinking behavior. It has been suggested that this may include "programmed relapse" trials involving the actual consumption of alcohol within training situations in which alcoholics are instructed in alternative coping behaviors and cognitions emphasizing personal control (Marlatt 1978). In any case, it is important in treatment that success experiences be appraised by clients as evidence of increased personal control over drinking. It would be expected that clients' conviction of their personal control would be strengthened by the inclusion of some situations involving the consumption of alcohol. It should be noted that the importance of perceived control in behavior change has played a prominent role in the work of Weiner (1979, 1980) on attributional factors in school achievement. Causes that are appraised by students as controllable, rather than uncontrollable, lead to greater planning of constructive coping behavior (Wong and Weiner 1981). Some clinical evidence of the importance of perceived control has also been reported. Stuart and Guire (1972) found a positive correlation between measures of client's perceived control over coping with food and weight loss.

6. *Perceived situational generality of performance.* Success experiences that are appraised as occurring under atypical or unusual circumstances provide little new information for altering one's sense of competency in dealing with everyday events. On the other hand, successes regarded by the client as highly relevant or representative of normally-encountered circumstances would be expected to raise perceived self-efficacy. Therefore, in the design of performance tasks care should be taken to draw on frequently encountered problematic situations to ensure perceived generality of a mastery experience. Some support for this prediction arises from studies on the "generality" dimension of attribution theory and the learned helplessness model of depression (Abramson, Seligman, and Teasdale 1978). It has been found that more global (general) attributions result in greater persistence in performance.

In summary, monitoring by the therapist of changes in client self-efficacy over the course of treatment allows detection of any instances in which the successful completion of performance tasks has failed to enhance the client's efficacy expectations. In such cases, long-term maintenance of performance gains can be expected to be poor. Probing on the part of the therapist, along the six cognitive appraisal dimensions just listed, should identify the nature of the impediment that is interfering with the enhancement of client self-efficacy. Once the responsible factor has been identified, a direct cognitive manipulation and/or a modification in performance assignments may facilitate the formation of more positive self-inferences from mastery experiences. Examples of these are given in the following section with regard to work with alcoholic clients.

A RELAPSE PREVENTION PROGRAM FOR ALCOHOLICS

Based on the treatment implications of self-efficacy theory, a relapse prevention model for alcoholics has been developed at the Clinical Institute of the Addiction Research Foundation in Toronto (Annis 1985; Annis and Davis 1985; Peachey and Annis 1985). In this section, we describe the clinical assessment and treatment procedures employed in this program. Treatment process data are presented from a clinical trial in which 41 alcoholic clients in an employed problem drinker program at the foundation received the relapse prevention procedures.

Assessment of High-Risk Drinking Situations

Following the principles of self-efficacy theory, clinical work with a client begins with a situational diagnosis of the drinking problem. A microanalysis is made of the client's past drinking behavior and current efficacy expectations with regard to high-risk situations for relapse. To facilitate this microanalysis, two 100-item self-report questionnaires have been developed. The Inventory of Drinking Situations (IDS; Annis 1982a) is designed to assess situations in which the client drank heavily over the past year.[1] The Situational Confidence Questionnaire (SCQ; Annis 1982b) is designed as a measure of Bandura's concept of self-efficacy for alcohol-related situations. Following the work of Marlatt and his associates in categorizing alcoholic relapse episodes (Marlatt 1978, 1979a, b; Marlatt and Gordon 1980), both questionnaires assess the following eight categories of drinking situations: negative emotional states, positive emotional states, negative physical states, testing personal control, urges and temptations, interpersonal conflict, social pressure to drink, and interpersonal positive emotional states. From this assessment, an individual profile of drinking risk situations is developed that forms the basis for discussion with the client of the types of situations that have resulted in heavy drinking over the past year and the client's efficacy expectations (or relative confidence level) in being able to cope with each of these situations in the future.

Design and Ordering of Performance Tasks

Therapy focuses on having the client engage in performance-based homework assignments in areas that have been identified as high-risk drinking situations. Homework assignments are graded in terms of increasing difficulty (as reflected in lower ratings of self-efficacy) over the course of treatment and are designed to help promote successful performance (i.e., abstinence or moderation) in high-risk drinking situations as the primary vehicle of behavior change. The aim of treatment is to effect a rise in self-efficacy across all areas of perceived drinking risk.

A two-phase treatment plan is employed, with phase one concentrating on strategies known to be powerful for the initiation of a change in drinking behavior and phase two focusing on strategies with greater potential for the long-term maintenance of this change. Liberal use is made in phase one of a variety of response-induction aids such as the modeling and rehearsal of activities during counseling sessions (Chaney, O'Leary, and Marlatt 1978), joint performance of assignments with a spouse or a responsible collateral (Bandura et al. 1980), and the use of protective conditions, such as antialcohol drugs (Peachey and Annis 1985). In phase two such external aids are gradually withdrawn as the emphasis shifts to promoting client self-inferences from performance tasks that are consistent with those known to facilitate strong, generalized behavior change.

A blueprint for the design of phase two maintenance strategies is presented in Table 3.1. The successful completion of a homework assignment in a high-risk drinking situation is most likely to result in improved self-efficacy and long-term maintenance of a change in drinking behavior if the client interprets the experience as one in which (1) the task was challenging; (2) only a moderate degree of effort was extended to control the drinking; (3) little external aid was involved; (4) the success was part of an overall pattern of improved performance; (5) an increase in personal control over alcohol was demonstrated; and (6) the successful performance was highly relevant to problematic drinking situations frequently encountered. Treatment intervention procedures that facilitate the formation of such self-inferences can be expected to have a powerful effect on client self-efficacy in the drinking area and on the long-term maintenance of a change in drinking behavior. Therapeutic strategies that may engender these cognitions and thereby create strong maintenance of behavior change include the creation of conditions that challenge clients to succeed in controlling drinking behavior in situations that were formerly problematic; the use of a graduated series of performance tasks with gradual fading of involvement of any external aids; the assignment of

Table 3.1.
Client Self-inferences that Enhance Self-efficacy and the Maintenance of Behavior Change

Self-inference	Therapeutic Strategy for Maintenance
The task was challenging (i.e., in the past the situation would likely have resulted in heavy drinking).	• Design assignments involving entry by the client into high-risk drinking situations.
Only a moderate degree of effort was needed to experience success (i.e., the degree of effort expended to control the drinking was not highly aversive).	• Use a series of graduated assignments (based on self-efficacy scores) ranging from easier to more difficult.
Little external aid was involved in the success (i.e., the success was attributed to the client, not to the therapist, spouse, significant other, a drug, and so forth).	• Gradually remove the use of external aids to performance. • Gradually shift the responsibility for the design of homework assignments to the client.
The success was part of an overall pattern of improved performance (i.e., the client perceives a steady improvement in the drinking problem).	• Use multiple assignments in a variety of drinking risk areas, taking care that the client can experience mastery. (Note: Success in initial homework assignments is particularly critical.) • Review progress, eliciting from the client reports of improved competency.
An increase in personal control was demonstrated	• Structure assignments so that the client will be willing to infer improved personal control.
The successful performance was highly relevant to problematic drinking situations frequently encountered.	• Arrange assignments in areas critical to clients' perceptions of their drinking problems.

Source: Compiled by the authors.

multiple performance tasks across a variety of drinking risk situations so that a self-perception is fostered of the incremental achievement of improved competency; and the transfer of responsibility for the anticipation of drinking risk and the planning of coping strategies to the clients so that clients assume control of their own therapy and progress.

During the initiation stage (phase one) and the maintenance stage (phase two), as many drinking risk situations as possible are covered by homework assignments. Before treatment is terminated, improvement in perceived self-efficacy across each of the eight categories of drinking situations should be reported by the client.

Monitoring Progress in Treatment

Because client self-efficacy is not always enhanced following a successful experience in controlling drinking behavior, it is important for the therapist to monitor the client's cognitions following the completion of homework tasks. If the client reports improved confidence (i.e., an increase in self-efficacy) in coping with similar situations in the future, no further exploration of client self-inferences is necessary. However, in instances in which the client successfully executes a performance task but fails to perceive an improvement in coping ability, probing by the therapist along the six dimensions of self-inference outlined in Table 3.1 should reveal the cause of the difficulty. For example, the clients may not perceive the homework experience as being sufficiently relevant to their drinking problems. This may be because the drinking situation involved is evaluated by the clients as too easy in that it does not entail significant risk, or as not being representative of typically encountered problematic drinking situations, or as being too artificial or contrived to provide a realistic test of coping ability. In other instances, exploration of clients' appraisals of the experience may reveal that the clients are attributing the successful performance to the involvement of a spouse or significant other in the homework assignment, or to the role played by the therapist. In still other instances, clients may report expending such an aversive level of effort in successfully controlling the drinking behavior during the assigned task that they despair of the overall prognosis on a long-term basis.

Once the therapist has determined the nature of the self-defeating ideation that is interfering with the enhancement of self-efficacy, remedial action can be taken. As noted above, in some cases direct cognitive strategies may be appropriate. Most frequently, however, an adjustment in homework assignments, along the lines outlined in Table 3.1, will result in growth in clients' efficacy expectations.

Treatment Process and Outcome Findings from a Clinical Trial

Forty-one clients presenting for treatment in an employed problem drinker program at the Addiction Research Foundation participated in a clinical trial in which they received the previously mentioned relapse prevention procedures. Detailed documentation was kept of each client's drinking risk areas and associated self-efficacy ratings, the source, type, and outcome of all homework assignments undertaken during the course of treatment, and the situational determinants of any drinking that occurred.

Following treatment, clients were followed up at three months (telephone interview) and at six months (face-to-face interview) posttreatment discharge. Client descriptive information and treatment process and outcome data from this clinical trial are presented in the following section.

Description of Client Population

Thirty-eight of the 41 clients were male. The great majority (85%) had completed at least some high school education. Their ages ranged from 24 to 64 years with a mean of 45.1 years. About half (49%) were married or living common-law at the time of treatment. All were employed. Their average yearly income was $19,500 (SD = $5,800). The majority of clients (61%) reported seeking treatment because they felt that they had a drinking problem, although a substantial minority (39%) reported that their major motivation was coercion from others, such as employers or family members. Twenty-two percent admitted to drinking while on the job; 50% said they had worked under the influence of alcohol; and 61% reported that they had missed time from work due to drinking. The mean number of years of problem drinking was 6.0 (SD = 6.7). Over 80% of the clients reported a heavy drinking pattern over the year prior to intake; 46% reported consuming five to nine drinks on a drinking day, and 36% reported a level of ten or more drinks on a drinking day. Only a minority of the clients (27%) had received treatment before for an alcohol problem.

The Relapse Prevention Program

The program consisted of six hours of intake assessment followed by eight outpatient counseling sessions over a three-month period. During the initial assessment, a psychosocial and drug use history were taken and the client completed the Inventory of Drinking Situations (IDS) and the Situational Confidence Questionnaire (SCQ). The therapist discussed the results of the IDS and SCQ with the client, constructed an individual hierarchy of drinking risk situations, and developed with the client an initial treatment plan. It was emphasized that the focus of treatment would be on having the client perform homework assignments in these risk situations. By learning to enter and successfully cope with increasingly more problematic drinking situations during the course of treatment, the client would gain control over the drinking problem. All clients were given a pocket-sized booklet containing a number of self-monitoring forms on drinking behavior, which they were instructed to complete on a daily basis. At each treatment appointment, homework assignments were entered into this booklet by the therapist.

Each of the eight outpatient counseling sessions consisted of one hour of group participation (with four to seven clients in attendance) and 15 to 20 minutes of individual counseling. General problems being experienced in trying to control drinking behavior were discussed in group sessions.

Clients also met individually with the therapist to review in greater detail the previous session's homework assignments and to plan new performance tasks. Attendance at the eight scheduled appointments was high (over 80%). In the case of missed appointments, the therapist maintained contact by phone.

High-Risk Drinking Situations

Over two thirds of initial relapse episodes reported by Marlatt and Gordon (1980) in their interview study of clients following discharge from treatment fell into just three categories: negative emotional states (38%), interpersonal conflict (18%), and social pressure to drink (18%). As described previously, this same eight category classification system was used to design the intake questionnaires (IDS and SCQ), which formed the basis for the therapist's construction of the client's hierarchy of drinking risk situations. It was found that the highest-ranked risk situations for clients agreed well with the frequency of relapses within categories reported by Marlatt. Over two thirds of the clients had their highest-ranked risk situation for drinking in response to negative emotional states (39%), interpersonal conflict (17%), or social pressure to drink (12%).

Types of Homework Assignments

Details on the nature of all performance tasks assigned to a client during the course of treatment were documented on a therapist recording form. A coding system was subsequently developed to describe the types of homework assignments that had been involved in the implementation of the new relapse prevention procedures. This coding system is outlined in Table 3.2.

The coding system for homework assignments was found to have adequate inter-rater reliability. A random sample was drawn of 14 therapy sessions across the three therapists who had been involved in implementing the relapse prevention program. Homework assignments within these sessions were independently coded by two raters. The nine-category coding system achieved an inter-rater agreement of 90%.

The types and frequency of homework assignments performed by the 41 clients are given in Table 3.3. Clients performed a mean of 42 assignments each over the course of the three-month program, for an average of 3.5 assignments a week. Homework assignments were designed in relation to each client's hierarchy of high-risk situations for drinking identified during the intake assessment. It was found that half of the assignments involved planning and employing alternative coping responses in high-risk drinking situations, and increasing an awareness of drinking urges. The next most frequent performance tasks involved increasing alternative activities to drinking, such as leisure pursuits, and the deliberate noting by the client of areas of improved competency. The remaining five categories of

Table 3.2.
Coding System for Categorization of Homework Assignments

1. *Testing interpersonal competency*
   - 101   deliberate noting of circumstances and cognitions associated with interpersonal difficulty
   - 102   planning/rehearsal of behavioral strategies for testing competency
   - 103   practice in behavioral strategies
   - 104   practice in sharing feelings/concerns with others
   - 105   practice in assertive responses
2. *Increasing social interaction*
   - 201   spending more time with others
   - 202   improvement of communication skills
3. *Coping with habitual drinking situations*
   - 301   avoiding habitual drinking settings
   - 302   exposure to setting without drinking
   - 303   slip rehearsal
4. *Increasing alternative activities*
   - 401   planning or structuring of leisure time
   - 402   increase in activities/interests:
     taking courses or lessons/engaging in sports/making improvements in living environment
   - 403   increase in job responsibilities
5. *Employing alternative coping responses*
   - 501   deliberate noting of negative thoughts/feelings and associated circumstances
   - 502   planning/rehearsal of cognitive/behavioral coping strategies
   - 503   practice in cognitive interventions for negative thoughts/feelings/urges
   - 504   practice in behavioral interventions for negative thoughts/feelings/urges
   - 505   avoiding people/places associated with previous drinking
   - 506   eliciting support or aid from other people
   - 507   practice/rehearsal of strategies for refusing a drink
   - 508   having a nonalcoholic drink/serving drinks to others
   - 509   use of antialcohol drug
   - 510   use of other drugs (not antialcohol)
6. *Attempting to resolve relationship problems*
   - 601   increase in activities with family or close friends
   - 602   improving communications/sharing feelings or concerns
   - 603   working on sexual problems
   - 604   anticipating problem situations
7. *Testing personal control*
   - 701   increasing awareness of situations and cognitions associated with testing control
   - 702   rehearsal, in less problematic situations, of strategies for not drinking
   - 703   slip rehearsal
   - 704   planning cognitive/behavioral strategies for nonproblematic drinking
   - 705   practice in nonproblematic drinking

Table 3.2 (continued)

8.	*Increasing awareness of urges*	
	801	deliberate noting of circumstances and cognitions associated with temptations to drink
	802	noting of competency regarding drinking/abstinence
	803	anticipating problem situations
	804	noting of negative consequences of drinking
9.	*Noting improved competency*	
	901	noting of improved physical condition
	902	noting of improved attitude, mental set, emotional state
	903	noting of improved work performance
	904	noting of improved interpersonal relationships

Source: Compiled by the authors.

Table 3.3.
Frequency of Major Categories of Homework Assignments

Type of Homework Assignment	Total Assignments		Frequency per Patient	
	N	*%*	*Median*	*Mean (SD)*
Employing alternative coping responses	503	29.0	13	12.3 (6.2)
Increasing awareness of urges	366	21.1	9	8.9 (3.8)
Increasing alternative activities	230	13.3	5	5.6 (3.4)
Noting improved competency	149	8.6	3	3.6 (2.8)
Testing interpersonal competency	116	6.7	1	2.8 (3.4)
Increasing social interaction	96	5.5	1	2.3 (3.0)
Testing personal control	94	5.4	1	2.3 (2.9)
Attempting to resolve relationship problems	92	5.3	0	2.2 (4.0)
Coping with habitual drinking situations	89	5.1	2	2.2 (2.3)
Total	1735	100.0	42	42.3 (13.4)

Source: Compiled by the authors.

homework assignments (testing interpersonal competency, increasing social interaction, testing personal control, attempting to resolve relationship problems, and coping with habitual drinking situations) were used somewhat less frequently but still had a mean frequency of two to three times per patient. All homework assignments were individualized and designed to improve client self-efficacy in areas of identified high drinking risk.

Source and Outcome of Homework Assignments

One of the maintenance strategies employed in the relapse prevention program required clients to become their own therapists by assuming increasing responsibility for the planning and design of their own performance tasks. At the same time, it was of central importance in the behavior change model that most assignments result in mastery experiences for clients so that self-efficacy in dealing with drinking situations would be enhanced. In order to evaluate the extent to which these objectives had been realized, all homework assignments were coded for source (i.e., patient generated, therapist generated, therapist/patient generated, spontaneous/other) and outcome (i.e., completed successfully, completed unsuccessfully, not completed), and change in client self-efficacy over the course of treatment was assessed. Overall, it was found that more homework assignments were patient generated (46%) than therapist generated (40%) and that the great majority of assignments were completed successfully (83%). Patient-generated tasks were somewhat more likely to be completed successfully (90%) than were therapist-generated tasks (73%). As predicted, there was a marked improvement in reported self-efficacy in dealing with drinking-related situations (see next section).

Drinking Episodes During Treatment

Client daily self-monitoring forms indicated that the percentage of abstinent days for all clients over the three-month program was high (mean = 91%, SD = 20). Eighteen of the 41 clients in the study group, including 4 clients who were on a controlled drinking goal, reported at least one drinking episode during treatment. Almost two thirds (64%) of the 55 drinking episodes reported by these clients involved light consumption of one to four drinks, 16% involved consumption of five to nine drinks, and 20% involved consumption of ten or more drinks. For the majority of clients who drank during treatment (13 out of 18), the initial drinking occasion involved light consumption (one to four drinks). Five clients drank heavily (five or more drinks) on their first drinking occasion, while in the case of 5 other clients, a heavy drinking episode was preceded by one or more light drinking occasions. Because the program encouraged the daily self-monitoring and recording of any drinking that occurred and

Table 3.4.
Situational Context of Heavy Drinking and Light Drinking Episodes During Treatment

Situation	Heavy Drinking Episodes (5+ Drinks)		Light Drinking Episodes (1–4 Drinks)	
	N^1	%	N^2	%
Negative emotional states	7	35.0	1	2.9
Testing personal control	6	30.0	14	40.0
Interpersonal conflict	3	15.0	6	17.1
Interpersonal positive emotional states	2	10.0	9	25.7
Urges and temptations	1	5.0	2	5.7
Social pressure to drink	1	5.0	1	2.9
Positive emotional states	0	0.0	2	5.7
Negative physical states	0	0.0	0	0.0

[1]The 20 episodes of heavy drinking were reported by 10 clients
[2]The 35 episodes of light drinking were reported by 16 clients.
Source: Compiled by the authors.

emphasized that drinking slips during treatment should be used constructively in learning to control the use of alcohol, it was felt that most clients complied in reporting drinking episodes.

Table 3.4 presents the situational context of the heavy drinking episodes (five or more drinks) and light drinking episodes (one to four drinks) during treatment. Heavy drinking episodes were much more likely to occur in response to negative emotional states, and light drinking episodes were much more likely to occur in response to intra- and interpersonal positive emotional states. These findings suggest that situations involving negative emotional states may be more likely to result in serious relapse.

The four clients on a controlled drinking goal had some drinking assignments in phase two as part of their treatment plan. Of the 19 drinking occasions reported by these clients, 15 (79%) involved moderate use of alcohol (one to four drinks). The 4 heavy drinking occasions (five or more drinks) all took place in response to either a negative emotional state or the testing of personal control. Two of the 4 heavy drinking occasions of these clients were associated with the execution of a planned homework task.

An important issue relates to whether self-efficacy ratings taken at intake to treatment allow the therapist to identify the client's weakest areas—that is, the areas in which the client is most likely to relapse. Theoretically, one would expect that relapse would most likely occur in situations in which clients reported the least confidence in being able to

Table 3.5

Drinking, Adverse Consequences, and Self-efficacy Scores at Intake and Posttreatment Discharge

Variable	Intake (1 year prior)		3-Month Follow-up[a]		6-Month Follow-up[a]	
			Alcohol Use			
Drinking rates	X	(SD)	X	(SD)	X	(SD)
Weekly quantity (mean number of drinks per week)	46.14	(22.94)	1.73[b]	(3.10)	5.96[b]	(17.85)
Frequency (mean days drinking per week)	5.47	(1.52)	0.40[b]	(0.71)	0.85[b]	(1.37)
Quantity (mean number of drinks per drinking day)	8.69	(4.36)	2.50[b]	(3.49)	3.93[b]	(4.52)
Longest interval without a drink in past month (days)	10.03	(9.02)	—	—	20.41[b]	(11.27)
Drinking styles	% Clients		% Clients		% Clients	
Drinking pattern						
Total abstinence	0.0		47.4		28.6	
Weekend	4.9		28.9		14.3	
Occasional	0.0		23.7		40.0	
Binge	9.8		0.0		5.7	
Steady	85.3		0.0		11.4	
Typical drinking level						
Total abstinence	0.0		47.4		28.6	
1–4 drinks/drinking day	17.1		34.2		42.8	
5–9 drinks/drinking day	46.3		10.5		20.0	
10+ drinks/drinking day	36.6		7.9		8.6	
Modal beverage						
Beer drinkers	39.0		—		32.0	
Wine drinkers	2.4		—		8.0	
Liquor drinkers	41.5		—		40.0	
Drinks more than one above	17.1		—		20.0	

Table 3.5 (continued)

Variable	Intake (1 year prior)		3-Month Follow-up[a]		6-Month Follow-up[a]	
Self-efficacy	X	(SD)	X	(SD)	X	(SD)
SCQ score	62.42	(27.88)	—	—	89.66[b]	(14.87)
Self-ratings	Adverse Consequences					
	% Clients		% Clients		% Clients	
Impaired physical health	63.3		—		12.0	
Cognitive impairment	63.5		—		20.0	
Affective impairment	51.2		—		28.0	
Interpersonal problems	68.3		—		32.0	
Vocational problems	85.4		—		24.0	
Legal problems	43.9		—		0.0	
Financial problems	56.1		—		12.0	

[a]Comparisons between intake ($N = 41$) and three-month follow-up ($N = 38$), and between intake and six-month follow-up ($N = 35$) are based on paired t-tests (two-tailed).
[b]$p < .001$
Source: Compiled by the authors.

control their drinking. This question was explored by comparing clients' eight subcategory scores on the SCQ at intake to the actual situation during treatment in which relapse occurred. For the 10 clients who reported a heavy drinking episode (five or more drinks), the situation in which the heavy drinking initially occurred was ranked lowest or next lowest in self-efficacy at intake by 6 of the clients (60%). Episodes of light drinking were much less likely to show a relationship to self-efficacy scores; only 3 of 16 clients (19%) ranked the situation in which the light drinking initially occurred as lowest or next lowest in self-efficacy at intake. Hence, self-efficacy scores at intake were successful in predicting the specific nature of the situation in which relapse would occur in instances of heavy drinking but not in instances of relatively light drinking.

Outcome at Three and Six Months

The work of Hunt and his associates (Hunt, Barnett, and Branch 1971) suggests that relapse rates for alcoholics are highest in the first three months following discharge from treatment. Clients were followed up at three months and at six months posttreatment discharge. The three-month follow-up was conducted primarily by telephone interview and the six-month follow-up by face-to-face interview. Thirty-eight of the 41 clients (93%) cooperated in providing three-month follow-up information, and 35 clients (85%) provided six-month outcome data. Measures of client functioning at intake to treatment and at three and six months posttreatment are presented in Table 3.5.

Dramatic decreases in drinking from intake to follow-up were evident on all measures of alcohol use. From a mean weekly quantity of 46 drinks per week at intake, the average reported consumption of clients decreased to fewer than two drinks per week at three months posttreatment and fewer than six drinks per week at six months. This was accomplished by a decrease in both the frequency of drinking days per week (from a mean intake level of five and a half days per week to less than one drinking day per week), and the number of drinks consumed on a drinking day (from a mean intake level of eight and a half drinks per drinking day to fewer than four drinks per drinking day). Forty-seven percent of the clients reported total abstinence over the three-month follow-up period, and 29% reported total abstinence over the entire six-month follow-up period. There was a marked decrease in steady and binge drinking patterns and an increase in occasional and weekend use of alcohol. Little change was evident in the choice of alcoholic beverage.

The relapse prevention model predicted that improvement in control over drinking behavior would be associated with enhanced drinking-related self-efficacy. As shown in Table 3.5, clients' ratings of self-efficacy (as measured by scores on the Situational Confidence Questionnaire) improved substantially from intake to six months follow-up ($t = 5.42$; $p < .001$). Marked improvement was also seen in adverse consequences due to drinking (see Table 3.5). Fewer clients reported impaired physical health, cognitive or affective impairment, or problems of an interpersonal, vocational, legal, or financial nature. Although showing a substantial decrease, interpersonal and vocational problems and affective/mood complaints continued to be reported by a quarter or more of the clients. These three areas of functioning continued to be most problematic for a sizable minority of the clients. Nevertheless, in addition to the dramatic changes in alcohol consumption, the majority of clients also reported improvement across a wide range of areas of personal and social functioning.

NOTE

1. Details on the development, item content, and scoring for the IDS are available in Annis (1985). Reliability, normative data, and factor structure are given in Annis and Kelly (1984).

REFERENCES

Abramson, L. Y.; M. E. P. Seligman; and J. D. Teasdale. (1978). Learned helplessness in humans: Critique and reformulation. *Journal of Abnormal Psychology*, 87:49–74.

Annis, H. M. (1982a). *Inventory of drinking situations*. Toronto: Addiction Research Foundation of Ontario.

Annis, H. M. (1982b). *Situational confidence questionnaire*. Toronto: Addiction Research Foundation of Ontario.

Annis, H. M. (1985). A relapse prevention model for treatment of alcoholics. In *Processes of change*, eds. W. R. Miller and N. Heather. The Addictive Behaviors, vol. 2. New York: Pergamon Press.

Annis, H. M., and C. S. Davis. (1985). Alcohol dependence: Cognitive assessment procedures. In *Assessment of addictive behaviors*, eds. G.A. Marlatt and D. Donovan. New York: Guilford Press.

Annis, H. M., and P. Kelly. (1984). Analysis of the inventory of drinking situations. Paper presented at the American Psychological Association Convention, Toronto, Ontario.

Armor, D. J.; J. M. Polich; and H. B. Stambul. (1978). *Alcoholism and treatment* (R-1729-NIAAA). Rand Corporation.

Bandura, A. (1977). Self-efficacy: Toward a unifying theory of behavioral change. *Psychological Review*, 84:191–215.

Bandura, A. (1978). Reflections on self-efficacy. *Advances in Behavioral Research and Therapy*, 1:237–69.

Bandura, A.; N. E. Adams; and J. Beyer. (1977). Cognitive processes mediating behavioral change. *Journal of Personality and Social Psychology*, 35:125–39.

Bandura, A.; N. E. Adams; A. B. Hardy; and G. N. Howells. (1980). Tests of the generality of self-efficacy theory. *Cognitive Therapy and Research*, 4:39–66.

Bandura, A.; E. B. Blanchard; and B. Ritter. (1969). Relative efficacy of desensitization and modeling approaches for inducing behavioral, affective, and attitudinal changes. *Journal of Personality and Social Psychology*, 13:173–99.

Bandura, A.; R. W. Jeffery; and E. Gajdos. (1975). Generalizing change through participant modeling with self-directed mastery. *Behavior Research and Therapy*, 13:141–52.

Bandura, A.; R. W. Jeffery; and C. L. Wright. (1974). Efficacy of participant modeling as a function of response induction aids. *Journal of Abnormal Psychology*, 83:56–64.

Blanchard, E. B. (1970). Relative contributions of modeling, informational influences, and physical contact in extinction of phobic behavior. *Journal of Abnormal Psychology*, 76:55–61.

Bowers, K.S. (1971). Attributional analysis of operant conditioning: Paradoxical effects of reinforcement on the endurance of behavior change. *Proceedings of the 79th Annual Convention of the American Psychological Association*, 6:287–88.

Chaney, E. F.; M. R. O'Leary; and G. A. Marlatt. (1978). Skill training with alcoholics. *Journal of Consulting and Clinical Psychology*, 46:1092–1104.

Condiotte, M. M., and E. Lichtenstein. (1981). Self-efficacy and relapse in smoking cessation programs. *Journal of Consulting and Clinical Psychology*, 49:648–58.

Condra, M. St. John (1982). The effectiveness of relapse-prevention training in the treatment of alcohol problems. Doctoral dissertation, Queen's University, Canada.

Davison, G. C.; R. N. Tsujimoto; and A. G. Glaros. (1973). Attribution and the maintenance of behavior change in falling asleep. *Journal of Abnormal Psychology*, 82:124–33.

Davison, G. C., and S. Valins. (1969). Maintenance of self-attributed and drug-attributed behavior change. *Journal of Personality and Social Psychology*, 11:25–33.

Donovan, D. M., and M. R. O'Leary. (1979). Control orientation among alcoholics: A cognitive social learning perspective. *American Journal of Drug and Alcohol Abuse*, 6:487–99.

Endler, N. S. (1975). A person-situation interaction model of anxiety. In *Stress and anxiety*, vol. 1, eds. C. D. Spielberger and I. G. Sarason. Washington, D.C.: Hemisphere Publishing Corporation (J. Wiley).

Gottheil, E.; C.Thornton; T. Skolada; and A. Alterman. (1979). Follow-up study of alcoholics at 6, 12, and 24 months. In *Treatment, rehabilitation and epidemiology*, ed. M. Galanter. *Currents in Alcoholism*, vol. 4. Toronto: Grune and Stratton.

Hunt, W. A.; L. W.Barnett; and L. G. Branch. (1971). Relapse rates in addiction programs. *Journal of Clinical Psychology*, 27:455–56.

Kockott, G.; F. Dittmar; and L. Nusselt. (1975). Systematic desensitization of erectile impotence: A controlled study. *Archives of Sexual Behavior*, 4:493–500.

Kopel, S., and H. Arkowitz. (1975). The role of attribution and self-perception in behavior change: Implications for behavior therapy. *Genetic Psychology Monographs*, 92:175–212.

Marlatt, G. A. (1978). Craving for alcohol, loss of control, and relapse: A cognitive-behavioral analysis. In *Alcoholism: New directions in behavioral research and treatment*, eds. P. E. Nathan, G. A. Marlatt, and T. Loberg. New York: Plenum Press.

Marlatt, G. A. (1979a). Alcohol use and problem drinking: A cognitive-behavioral analysis. In *Cognitive behavioral interventions: Theory, research and procedures*, eds. P. C. Kendell and S. D. Hollon. New York: Academic Press.

Marlatt, G. A. (1979b). A cognitive-behavioral model of the relapse process. In *Behavioral analysis and treatment of substance abuse*, ed. N. A. Krasnegor. Research Monograph, vol. 25. Rockville, Md.: National Institute on Drug Abuse.

Marlatt, G. A. (1985a). Relapse prevention: Theoretical and overview of the model. In *Relapse prevention: Maintenance strategies in the treatment of addictive behaviors*, eds. G. A. Marlatt and J. R. Gordan. New York: Guilford Press.

Marlatt, G.A. (1985b). Cognitive assessment and intervention procedures for relapse prevention. In *Relapse prevention: Maintenance strategies in the treatment of addictive behaviors*, eds. G. A. Marlatt and J. R. Gordan. New York: Guilford Press.

Marlatt, G.A., and W. H. George. (1984). Relapse prevention: Introduction and overview of the model. *British Journal of Addiction*, 79:261–75.

Marlatt, G. A., and J. R. Gordon. (1980). Determinants of relapse: Implications for the maintenance of behavior change. In *Behavioral medicine: Changing health lifestyles*, eds. P. Davidson and S. Davidson. New York: Brunner/ Mazel.

Mathews, A.; J. Bancroft; A. Whitehead; A. Hackmann; D. Julier; J. Bancroft; D. Garth; and P.Shaw. (1976). The behavioral treatment of sexual inadequacy: A comparative study. *Behavior Research and Therapy*, 14:427–36.

McIntyre, K. O.; E. Lichtenstein; and R. J. Mermelstein. (1983). Self-efficacy and relapse in smoking cessation: A replication and extension. *Journal of Consulting and Clinical Psychology*, 51:632–33.

Miller, I. W., and W. H. Norman. (1981). Effects of attributions for success on the alleviation of learned helplessness and depression. *Journal of Abnormal Psychology*, 90:113–24.

Ogborne, A. C., and A. Bornet. (1982). Abstinence and abusive drinking among affiliates of Alcoholics Anonymous: Are these the only alternatives? *Addictive Behaviors*, 7:199–202.

Orford, J., and G. Edwards. (1977). *Alcoholism: A comparison of treatment and advice, with a study of the influence of marriage*. Maudsley Monographs, vol. 26. New York: Oxford University Press.

Peachey, J. E., and H. M. Annis. (1985). New strategies for using the alcohol-sensitizing drugs. In *Research advances in new psychopharmacological treatments for alcoholism*, eds. C. A. Naranjo and E. M. Sellers. New York: Elsevier Science Publishers.

Polich, M. J.; D. J. Armor; and H. B. Braiker. (1980). *The course of alcoholism: Four years after treatment* (ADM 281-76-0006). Santa Monica, Calif.: Rand Corporation.

Rachman, S., and R. Hodgson. (1979). *Obsessions and compulsions*. Englewood Cliffs, N.J.: Prentice-Hall.

Rist, F., and H. Watzl. (1983). Self assessment of relapse risk and assertiveness in relation to treatment outcome of female alcoholics. *Addictive Behaviors*, 8:121–27.

Stiemerling, N. (1983). Relapse in alcohol abusers: A short term longitudinal study. Doctoral dissertation, Queen's University, Canada.

Stuart, R.B., and K. Guire. (1972). Some correlates of the maintenance of weight lost through behavior modification. *International Journal of Obesity*, 2:225–36.

Weiner, B. (1979). A theory of motivation for some classroom experiences. *Journal of Educational Psychology*, 71:3–25.

Weiner, B. (1980). *Human motivation*. New York: Holt, Rinehart & Winston.

Wilson, G. T. (1978a). Booze, beliefs and behavior: Cognitive processes in alcohol use and abuse. In *Alcoholism: New directions in behavioral research and treatment*, eds. P.E. Nathan, G. A. Marlatt, and T. Loberg. New York: Plenum Press.

Wilson, G. T. (1978b). The importance of being theoretical: A commentary on Bandura's "Self-efficacy: Towards a unifying theory of behavioral change." *Advances in Behavior Research and Therapy*, 1:217–30.

Wilson, G. T. (1979). Perceived control and the theory and practice of behavior therapy. In *Choice and perceived control*, eds. L. C. Perlmuter and R. A. Monty. N.J.: Hillsdale.

Wilson, G. T. (1980). Cognitive factors in lifestyle changes: A social learning perspective. In *Behavioral medicine: Changing health lifestyles*, eds. P. O. Davidson and S. M. Davidson. New York: Brunner/Mazel.

Wong, P. T., and B. Weiner. (1981). When people ask "Why" questions and the heuristics of attributional search. *Journal of Personality and Social Psychology*, 40:650–63.

4

FAMILY-WIDE DISTRESS IN BULIMIA

Laura Lynn Humphrey

Recent epidemiological studies suggest that 1 out of every 12 high school and college age females has bulimia, a vicious cycle of gorging and purging (cf. Halmi, Falk, and Schwartz 1981; Pyle, Mitchell, and Eckert 1981; Johnson et al. 1982). Most clinicians and researchers agree that bulimia is a complex and pervasive disorder involving poor self-regulation of eating habits and weight, but also of emotions, self-esteem, work and school performance, and interpersonal relationships (see, for example, reviews by Johnson, Lewis, and Hagman 1984; Mitchell and Pyle 1982; Schlesier-Stropp 1984). New findings are also emerging that implicate a family-wide, transgenerational problem of dysregulation in bulimia (e.g., Humphrey 1986a; Strober et al. 1981). The present chapter will examine this family-wide distress and dysregulation, as well as the parallels between such family processes and the psychopathology of the bulimic herself. In addition, it will highlight some compelling similarities between these deficits in bulimia and related patterns in chemical addictions. First, however, there will be a brief discussion of the nature and possible origins of this potentially dangerous and intractable disorder.

DESCRIPTION AND OVERVIEW

The Diagnostic and Statistical Manual (DSM) III (American Psychiatric Association 1980) criteria for bulimia include episodic binge eating, awareness that such an eating pattern is abnormal, and depressed mood and self-deprecating thoughts following a binge. They also specify that at least three of the following must apply: (1) consumption of high caloric, easily ingested food during a binge; (2) inconspicuous eating during a binge; (3) termination of a binge through self-inflicted vomiting, social interruption, sleep, or abdominal pain; (4) repeated attempts to lose weight by severely restrictive diets, self-induced vomiting, or use of cathartics or diuretics; or (5) frequent weight fluctuations greater than ten pounds due to alternating binges and fasts. According to the DSM III criteria, bulimia can only occur at normal or obese body weights; binge eating can, however, also be a component of anorexia nervosa.

As suggested earlier, estimates of the prevalence of bulimia range from 5% (Johnson et al. 1982) to 19% (Halmi, Falk, and Schwartz 1981) among adolescent and young adult females, with most studies converging on figures between 5 and 10% (e.g., Pyle, Mitchell, and Eckert 1981; Strangler and Printz 1980) of that population. The demographic profile of the typical bulimic is a single, white, female college student in her early twenties, who has been secretly struggling with her problem for about five years prior to seeking help (Johnson et al. 1982; Schlesier-Stropp 1984).

For most bulimics, their entire day revolves around when and what to eat, how much they weigh, and whether others will think that they are fat. Typically, bulimics binge and self-induce vomiting about once a day, but some may do so continuously for a day or more at a time (Mitchell, Pyle, and Eckert 1981). Binges usually last about one to one and a half hours (Mitchell, Pyle, and Eckert 1981) and consist of 2,000 to 5,000 calories (Johnson et al. 1982) of sweets and starches, particularly in easily prepared foods (Mitchell et al. 1981). Feelings of dysphoria, agitation, and emotional lability will often precipitate a binge, as will being alone in the evening (Johnson and Larson 1982).

The clinical profile of the bulimic includes significant problems with anxiety and, especially, with depression (Hudson et al. 1983; Pyle, Mitchell and Eckert 1981). More specifically, Katzman and Wolchik (1984) found that compared to controls, bulimics were more depressed, had lower self-esteem, higher self-expectations, higher needs for approval, and poorer body images. They are also likely to have problems with impulse control, including chemical dependency (Carroll and Leon 1981; Pyle, Mitchell, and Eckert 1981).

Thus, the syndrome of bulimia is a deeper, more extensive problem than merely binge eating and purging to control weight gain. It is a pervasive problem of dysregulation and distress throughout the bulimics's emotional, behavioral, and interpersonal experience. In light of its complex and multifaceted nature, Johnson developed a bio-psychosocial model of the etiology and maintenance of bulimia (see Johnson and Maddi 1986).

Johnson's model proposes that young women who are at risk for developing bulimia are biologically vulnerable to affective instability. This biological instability is exacerbated by a family environment that is also disorganized and conflictive and by a society in transition regarding the role of women. These factors together contribute to the bulimic's poor self-regulation and self-esteem. The bulimic's solution to the problem is to gain social acceptance, the appearance of self-control, and improved self-worth through the achievement of thinness. Her bulimia allows her to relieve temporarily both her biological and psychological pressures to let go and dysregulate (i.e., binge), almost instantly, but also to enhance her self esteem by approaching thinness (i.e., dieting and purging).

Johnson's bio-psychosocial model is comprehensive enough to address the multiplicity of causes of this all-too-common and complex disorder. His model also underscores the critical role of the family in the psychogenesis of bulimia. The remainder of this chapter will delineate the role of family relationships and interaction patterns in bulimia, with an emphasis on the parallels in dysregulation between the bulimic herself and more family-wide processes.

BULIMIA AS A METAPHOR FOR THE SELF AND FAMILY

There are a number of striking parallels between the binge–purge cycle and both the psychological and familial patterns of distress and dysregulation found in bulimia. A host of studies, for example, has suggested that in addition to her eating disorder, the bulimic also has other broader deficits in affective and behavioral self-regulation, such as mood lability and chemical dependency (Carroll and Leon 1981; Hudson et al. 1983; Johnson and Larson 1982; Pyle, Mitchell, and Eckert 1981; Schlesier-Stropp 1984). Similarly, the families of bulimics also have difficulty modulating and regulating negative affects and impulses, as well as interpersonal conflict and hostility (Garner, Garfinkel, and O'Shaughnessy 1983; Humphrey 1986a; Strober et al. 1982).

Thus, the bulimia itself may mirror concurrent psychological and familial deficits and distress. In an earlier paper I proposed that the binge–purge cycle is an apt metaphor for the bulimics's deeper problems in regulating and expressing dysphoric affects and behavior, both within herself and her family relationships (Humphrey 1986a). Table 4.1 presents the similarities between the four primary components of the binge–purge cycle and the bulimic's self and family experiences. This metaphor is not intended to be exact in every respect; it is only meant to highlight some interesting parallels. As the table summarizes, the bulimic and her family have chronic, unfulfilled needs for nurturance, soothing, and autonomy both intra- and interpersonally (food). This insatiable "hunger" drives the

Table 4.1

The Binge-Purge Cycle as a Metaphor for the Bulimic's Self and Family

Bulimic's cycle	Diet	Binge	Purge
Bulimic's self	Food cravings Unmet developmental needs for nurturance, individuation, self-regulation, and self-esteem	Strict and oppressive self-restraint and expectations	Loss of self-control, structure, and affective stability in gratifying needs	Expulsion of hostility, tension, and frustration
Bulimic's family	Family-wide needs for affection, autonomy, and organization	Interpersonal control and intrusion	Chaotic, unmodulated relations and poor regulation and structure	Expression of conflict and negative affect without focus, structure, or resolution

Source: Compiled by the author.

family to try to deny and overcome these deficits by controlling and constricting themselves and each other (diet). Such efforts, however, fail to modulate such intense needs; so family members will, at times, abandon all structure, boundaries, and controls. Instead, they become impulsive, demanding, and chaotic (binge) in their attempts to gratify these needs. Bulimic families will also expel their frustration and aggression toward one another in an unfocused, unstructured manner (purge). In the pages that follow, I will describe the bulimic metaphor in more detail and use it to conceptualize and integrate the results of diverse clinical and research studies. First, clinical observations will be considered; then any existing research support for these hypotheses will be summarized.

The "Food" or Nurturance Hypothesis

Much as the bulimic craves food, so she also has unmet developmental needs for nurturance and affection, a solid identity separate from her family (i.e., individuation), effective self-regulation, and resilient self-esteem (cf. Goodsitt 1983; Mahler 1968; Winnicott 1965). Similarly, there are unfulfilled family-wide needs for affection, autonomy, and for an effective structure and organization. In bulimia, family members are unable to respond to one another's requests for support and affirmation, for external structure, or for acceptance of their separate identities, feelings, and experiences (cf. Minuchin, Rosman, and Baker 1978). Often the parents are very well intentioned and strive to give the affection, firmness, and understanding to their own children that they never had. Unfortunately, though, the parents too were deprived of this "good enough mothering" (Winnicott 1965) when they tried to individuate from their families. Thus, they cannot provide a family environment that nurtures their own children's emerging identities and effective self-regulation.

There are preliminary data to support this nurturance hypothesis. Ordman and Kirschenbaum (1986) compared the respnses of 25 bulimic women to those of 36 normal controls on the Family Environment Scale (FES; Moos and Moos 1980) and on the Family Adaptibility and Cohesion Evaluation Scale (FACES; Olson, Bell, and Portner 1978). They found that bulimics reported significantly less cohesion in their families, on both scales, and less expressiveness on the FES. Similarly, Humphrey (1986a) compared responses in the families of 14 bulimics, 16 bulimic-anorexics, and 24 normal controls. Mothers, fathers, and daughters completed the FES and FACES. Based on a factor-analyzed version of each of the same two rating scales, the results showed that all three family members in both the bulimic groups reported less involvement and support in their families than did controls. Fathers and daughters also agreed that bulimic family members were more isolated and emotionally detached than were their normal counterparts.

In a related study, Humphrey (1986b) examined the "nurturance hypothesis" more directly. This study compared the perceived family relationships among bulimics, bulimic-anorexics, classical anorexics, and normal controls ($n = 20$ each). It utilized an assessment methodology developed by Benjamin (1974) and based on her model of Structural Analysis of Social Behavior (SASB). A more detailed description of the SASB model and methods will be presented in a subsequent section of this chapter. The results of this study showed that only the two bulimic subtypes, as compared to controls, experienced less nurturing, comforting, affirming, and understanding in their relationships with both their mothers and their fathers. In addition, they felt that their fathers were also less helpful and protective toward them than were the controls' fathers. Further, patients with all three types of eating disorders reported that they were less self-nourishing, cherishing, self-accepting, and exploring than were normal women. Only the two bulimic subgroups were also less self-protecting and enhancing. In sum, the accumulated findings from this series of studies suggest that bulimics feel *more* detached and isolated and *less* well loved, understood, and supported by their parents than normal women. Similarly, they in turn are unable to nourish, accept, or help themselves.

The "Diet" or Interpersonal Restriction Hypothesis

Just as the dieting bulimic restricts and ignores her need for food, so also do she and her family restrict and deny their mutual needs for nurturance and individuation. They operate as though they do not want what they cannot have together, that is, emotional "food." Internally, family members constrict and deny their emotional experiences and expression. Interpersonally, they exert rigid controls over one another and isolate and withdraw themselves from such unsatisfying relationships. In these families there is both emotional intrusion and also neglect. Parents watch over and control their daughters on the one hand and are oblivious to their needs for a loving separation on the other. Usually, there is also a pattern of enmeshment, such as that described by Minuchin, Rosman, and Baker (1978) in anorexic families. In bulimic families, though, the enmeshment is always hostile. Parents control and blame, while daughters surrender or resentfully appease, or vice versa. Parents also expect superior achievement without providing the necessary guidance or support. Intergenerational boundaries can also be too rigid and impenetrable at times.

Support for this hypothesized interpersonal restriction and deprivation in bulimic families comes from an observational study of bulimic-anorexic and normal families (Humphrey, 1987). This study utilized Benjamin's SASB observational coding schema (Benjamin et al. 1987) to examine differences in interpersonal interactions among bulimic-anorexic versus normal family triads (i.e., father, mother, and daughter). Parents and their daughter were videotaped while discussing a typical adolescent separation issue. These tapes were coded by highly trained and reliable judges according to the SASB model. The results revealed that both parents of the bulimic-anorexics were significantly more intrusive and controlling, and also neglectful, toward their daughter than were normal parents. The bulimic-anorexics, in turn, were more resentfully submissive toward their parents than were controls, although ambivalently so. In terms of high expectations in the family's diet, Johnson and Flach (1985) found that their sample of bulimics had higher achievement orientation on the FES than did normal women. This set of findings, then, offers some support for the hypothesized interpersonal restriction in bulimics and their families, especially in their rigid controls and high expectations.

The "Binge" or Loss of Control Hypothesis

Like the bulimic herself who at times abandons all self-restraint and binge eats, both she and her family will also cycle between emotional and interpersonal restriction (i.e., diet) and utter chaos and dysregulation (i.e., binge). In attempting to satisfy their emotional needs, the bulimic and her family will demand immediate gratification and become impulsive, labile, and isolative. What is overly structured at one time dissolves into virtual chaos at another. Perhaps most notably, affective expression between family members, including anxiety, frustration, and depression, can be unmodulated and overwhelming. Family boundaries can also shift from hierarchical rigidity to being loose and ineffectual. Thus, the family's "binge," like the bulimic's, consists of a loss of self-regulation, effective relating, and a solid organizational structure to more basic needs, affects, and impulses.

A study by Garner and his colleagues (Garner, Garfinkel and O'Shaughnessy 1983) comparing 42 bulimics to the same numbers of bulimic-anorexics and classical anorexics offers some evidence for the concept of a family-wide psychological binge. They administered the Family Assessment Measure (FAM; Skinner, Santa-Barbara, and Steinhauer 1983) and found that both bulimic groups were significantly more disturbed in affective involvement and expression as compared to classical anorexics and a normative group. Further, data from several studies also suggest that alcohol abuse and obesity, both signs of dysregulation, are more frequent in the families of bulimics than in the general population (Carroll and Leon 1981; Hudson et al. 1983; Pyle, Mitchell, and Eckert 1981; Strober 1981).

Findings from a study by Strober and his associates (Strober et al. 1982) are relevant to this family-wide binge hypothesis. They used MMPI profiles and SADS interviews to compare the psychiatric status of parents of bulimic-anorexics versus classical, restricting anorexics. As they expected, a higher prevalence of affective and impulse disorders in the parents of bulimic-anorexics distinguished them from the parents of restrictors. Fathers of bulimic-anorexics were more impulsive, excitable, dissatisfied with family relations, and showed poorer frustration tolerance than did the fathers of classical anorexics. Similarly, mothers of bulimic-anorexics had greater depression, hostility, and dissatisfaction with familial relations. Strober et al. also performed a multiple regression analysis that showed that maternal depression and paternal impulse disturbance and depression were predictive of more severe bulimia. These findings, then, are clearly supportive of the family-wide dysregulation in affect and behavior that is seen in bulimia and bulimia-anorexia.

The "Purge" or Expelling of Hostility Hypothesis

The bulimic and her family "purge" themselves emotionally through their overt expulsion of hostile affects, especially anger and criticism. However, as with the bulimic herself, the family's expression is indirect, masked, and provides only temporary relief. Their aggression is rarely explosive or rageful, but instead is a constant, unresolved bickering, belittling, and sulking. Unlike the families of classical anorexics, conflict in these families is more overt and can be vicious and manipulative. The conflict often has no structure, no focus, no boundaries, and no end.

In an argument old injuries are considered fair game and then later denied. This leaves the "defendent" feeling accused, resentful, and helpless. Family members cannot seem to accept their own or one another's feelings or to negotiate about them openly. It may sometimes be primitive conflict, but most often it is insidious, strategic, and enduring. Another mechanism for expressing hostility, but indirectly, in these families is through joking and teasing, followed by, "I was only kidding. ... Can't you take a joke?" This style of hostile joking vents the affect for the speaker but precludes any effective discussion or resolution of the problem. The bulimic is a key figure in the family's well rehearsed drama. Sometimes she becomes an ally of her father's against her mother or sister; other times she offers herself as a focus to divert the deeper conflict over father's drinking or mother's coldness.

Several sources of data offer empirical support for this familial purge hypothesis. Three prior studies have reported greater conflict among bulimics' families, as compared to controls, on the FES (Humphrey 1986a; Johnson and Flach 1985; Ordman and Kirschenbaum 1986). In addition, my observational study (Humphrey 1987) of bulimic-anorexic and normal families showed much greater hostility in the bulimics' families, both in their own perceptions and in observed family interactions. More specifically, families of bulimic-anorexics were significantly more blaming, sulking, neglectful, and double-binding in their relationships with one another than were controls. Thus, there is greater hostility and conflict, both overt and covert, in the relationships between bulimics and their families.

To summarize, these families mirror the same pattern of dysregulation and poor modulation of affect and impulses seen in the bulimic herself. All family members seem to need greater independence and nurturance (food) than they can find within the family. This hunger leads them to react with overcontrol and interpersonal restriction and deprivation (diet). Since this solution does not really enable them to master such emotional deficits, periodically they abandon all controls and structure. The family will become impulsive, labile, and chaotic in its efforts to gratify basic affectional and autonomy needs (binge). Family members also expel their hostility (purge) toward one another in an unfocused, unstructured manner. The bulimic daughter internalizes these patterns of poor self-regulation and self-care and treats herself in the same ways.

My intention in proposing the binge–purge metaphor is not to explain the psychogenesis of this complex disorder; instead, the bulimia metaphor is suggested as an organizing conceptual framework. As such, it can, perhaps, improve our understanding of some of the intriguing parallels between the bulimic behavior, the bulimic personality, and the bulimic family. Another striking parallel exists between these bulimic patterns and those observed among alcoholics and drug abusers and their families. There are important similarities between bulimia and chemical dependence both in the nature of the disorders themselves and in their proposed familial origins (cf. Brisman and Siegel 1984). Both types of habitual disorders consist of the chronic, habitual intake of a substance that becomes an all-consuming focus of individuals' thoughts, behavior, feelings, and eventually their whole lives. In fact, bulimics themselves are sometimes also alcoholic, as are their fathers (Hudson et al. 1983; Pyle, Mitchell and Eckert 1981).

As we observed previously with bulimics, alcohol and drug abusers also have other severe psychological deficits. They too have serious limitations in their capacity for self-soothing and self-care, as well as in their ability to contain and regulate dysphoric affects, such as depression, anxiety, frustration, and overstimulation (see, for example, reviews by Blatt et al. 1984; Stimmel 1983). Also similarly, the addict's self-esteem and overall sense of self are very tenuous and fragile (Khantzian 1981; Kohut 1977). Just as in bulimics' families, the families of drug addicts and alcoholics also lack the "maternal" functions of nurturance and caring and the "paternal" capacities of control and organization (Blatt et al. 1984; Stimmel 1983). Weidman (1983) also identified a parallel problem of the young addict's parents being unable to help their child separate and individuate from them without sacrificing affection and intimacy.

There seem to be a number of significant common features in bulimia and chemical addictions that warrant further scrutiny. Although such a project seems important and intriguing, it is not within the boundaries of the present chapter to pursue such parallels any further. The interested reader is referred to an article on this topic by Brisman and Siegel (1984) for more detail. Despite such converging clinical and theoretical findings, however, neither area has generated much substantive research on the nature of these disturbed family relations. Such work seems critical in order to test the clinical–theoretical hypothesis that these disorders emerge, in part, because of disturbed family relations.

The primary reasons for this paucity of empirical family studies are that such studies are extremely difficult to do and current methodologies are quite limited. In the remainder of this chapter, I will present a promising, alternative method for family assessment based on Benjamin's (1974) SASB model. This new, multimethod approach was applied to the study of three subtypes of eating disorders: bulimia, bulimia-anorexia, and classical anorexia, as compared to normal families. The study was recently completed as part of a large-scale project on differentiating family processes among subtypes of eating disorders. Some of the data are described elsewhere (Humphrey in press), but they will be summarized here, in some detail, with an emphasis on the new methodology employed.

USING SASB TO DIFFERENTIATE FAMILY PROCESSES AMONG SUBTYPES OF EATING DISORDERS

Probably the greatest challenge in doing family research is finding an assessment methodology that is both rich and complex enough to capture elusive interpersonal processes but also rigorous enough to provide reliable and valid measurement. In fact, Gurman and Kniskern (1981), in their review of the current state of family assessment, concluded that the field is still limited by "serious deficiencies" in measuring "core theoretical constructs" that have "already had a tremendous influence on thousands of clinicians." Thus, Benjamin's SASB model and methodology seem relatively unique because they are conceptually relevant and capable of operationalizing important family constructs (Humphrey and Benjamin in press) while also being sound psychometrically (Benjamin 1974). A description of the SASB model and methods will be presented first; then their application to the study of eating disordered families will follow.

Overview of SASB

The SASB model evolved from the interpersonal theory of Sullivan (1953) and Murray's (1938) hierarchy of needs, as they were translated into circumplex models by Leary's (1959) interpersonal circle and Schaefer's

(1965) conceptualization of parent–child interactions. A more thorough explanation of the relationship of SASB to prior theories and models of interpersonal behavior can be found elsewhere (Benjamin 1974, in press).

SASB was developed as a circumplex model of interpersonal relations and their intrapsychic counterparts. The model consists of three circumplex surfaces, two of which focus on interpersonal transactions while the third characterizes intrapsychic experiences. The latter is conceptualized as the introjection, or internalizing, of interpersonal relationships with significant other people, such as parents or spouses. The SASB model proposes that the three focuses of attention, represented by the three circumplexes (other, self, and intrapsychic), and two orthogonal dimensions of affiliation and interdependence are all that are needed to describe a range of systemic, interpersonal, and intrapsychic events. Benjamin developed a set of rating scales and an observational coding schema based on the model (Benjamin 1974; Benjamin et al. 1987). These measures assess self and other perceptions, as well as direct observations, of a wide range of interpersonal and intrapsychic processes.

Focus

The full version of the SASB model is presented in Figure 4.1 and consists of three diamond-shaped, or circumplex, surfaces. Each of these surfaces corresponds to a unique attentional focus: (1) focus on other (top surface); (2) focus on self (middle); and (3) intrapsychic (bottom). "Focus on other" consists of a transitive action directed toward another person, such as nurturing or blaming them. "Focus on self" reflects an intransitive state or reaction to another person, for example, enjoying or submitting to the other person. Both focuses describe interpersonal transactions. Intrapsychic experiences, on the other hand, involve the turning inward or introjection of the way one has been treated by important other people, such as parents. An example of this interpersonal conceptualization of introjection would be feeling self-destructive after being abused by a spouse, or turning an attack from mother against the self.

Central Axes

Two central dimensions of affiliation and interdependence comprise all three surfaces of the SASB model. Affiliation is on the horizontal axis, and it extends from friendly and loving on the right-hand side to hostile and attacking on the left-hand side. Interdependence is on the vertical axis, and it ranges from independent or differentiated behavior at the top to dependent, undifferentiated behavior at the bottom.

The poles of each axis correspond to pure extremes or "primitive basics" on each dimension, as they are termed in SASB. For example, on the

INTERPERSONAL

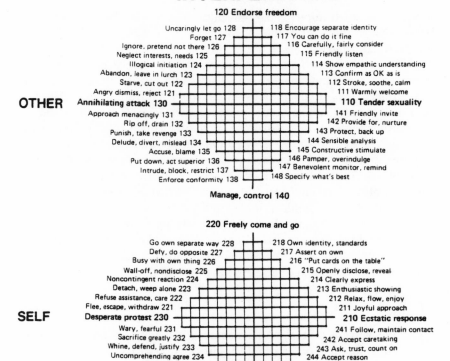

120 Endorse freedom

Uncaringly let go 128
Forget 127
Ignore, pretend not there 126
Neglect interests, needs 125
Illogical initiation 124
Abandon, leave in lurch 123
Starve, cut out 122
Angry dismiss, reject 121

118 Encourage separate identity
117 You can do it fine
116 Carefully, fairly consider
115 Friendly listen
114 Show empathic understanding
113 Confirm as OK as is
112 Stroke, soothe, calm
111 Warmly welcome

OTHER   **Annihilating attack 130**

110 Tender sexuality

Approach menacingly 131
Rip off, drain 132
Punish, take revenge 133
Delude, divert, mislead 134
Accuse, blame 135
Put down, act superior 136
Intrude, block, restrict 137
Enforce conformity 138

141 Friendly invite
142 Provide for, nurture
143 Protect, back up
144 Sensible analysis
145 Constructive stimulate
146 Pamper, overindulge
147 Benevolent monitor, remind
148 Specify what's best

Manage, control 140

220 Freely come and go

Go own separate way 228
Defy, do opposite 227
Busy with own thing 226
Wall-off, nondisclose 225
Noncontingent reaction 224
Detach, weep alone 223
Refuse assistance, care 222
Flee, escape, withdraw 221

218 Own identity, standards
217 Assert on own
216 "Put cards on the table"
215 Openly disclose, reveal
214 Clearly express
213 Enthusiastic showing
212 Relax, flow, enjoy
211 Joyful approach

SELF   **Desperate protest 230**

210 Ecstatic response

Wary, fearful 231
Sacrifice greatly 232
Whine, defend, justify 233
Uncomprehending agree 234
Appease, scurry 235
Sulk, act put upon 236
Apathetic compliance 237
Follow rules, proper 238

241 Follow, maintain contact
242 Accept caretaking
243 Ask, trust, count on
244 Accept reason
245 Take in, learn from
246 Cling, depend
247 Defer, overconform
248 Submerge into role

Yield, submit, give in 240

INTRAPSYCHIC

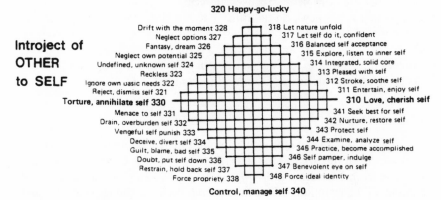

320 Happy-go-lucky

Drift with the moment 328
Neglect options 327
Fantasy, dream 326
Neglect own potential 325
Undefined, unknown self 324
Reckless 323
Ignore own basic needs 322
Reject, dismiss self 321

318 Let nature unfold
317 Let self do it, confident
316 Balanced self acceptance
315 Explore, listen to inner self
314 Integrated, solid core
313 Pleased with self
312 Stroke, soothe self
311 Entertain, enjoy self

**Introject of
OTHER
to SELF**   **Torture, annihilate self 330**

310 Love, cherish self

Menace to self 331
Drain, overburden self 332
Vengeful self punish 333
Deceive, divert self 334
Guilt, blame, bad self 335
Doubt, put self down 336
Restrain, hold back self 337
Force propriety 338

341 Seek best for self
342 Nurture, restore self
343 Protect self
344 Examine, analyze self
345 Practice, become accomplished
346 Self pamper, indulge
347 Benevolent eye on self
348 Force ideal identity

Control, manage self 340

Figure 4.1. Full version of L. S. Benjamin's Structural Analysis of Social Behavior (SASB) model. *Source*: Reprinted with permission from Intrex Interpersonal Institute, 1979. Benjamin, L. S. [1979a]. Structural analysis of social behavior. *Psychiatry*, 42:1–23.

surface reflecting focus on other, the primitive basics would be endorsing freedom (12 o'clock), sexuality (3 o'clock), power (6 o'clock), and murder (9 o'clock), respectively, if you move clockwise from the top of the diamond. All the points in between the four poles consist of varying degrees of affiliation and interdependence.

Full and Cluster Versions

The SASB model consists of varying levels of complexity, including both the full-item (Figure 4.1) and cluster versions (Figure 4.2) of the model. Each version of SASB, however, has the same three focuses and is based on the same central axes of affiliation and interdependence. The full version of the model has 36 points on each of three surfaces for a total of 108 points. Each of these points corresponds to a unique combination of different degrees of affiliation and interdependence, ranging from −9 to +9. Groupings of four to five adjacent points on each surface comprise the cluster version of the SASB model (see Figure 4.2).

SASB Rating Scales

Benjamin developed a set of rating scales and an observational coding system based on her SASB model. Together these ratings of self and others in their relationships, and direct observations of their interpersonal transactions, permit the use of a multitrait–multimethod assessment technology (Campbell and Fiske 1959). These measures also enable the clinician or researcher to assess multiple levels of experience, from intrapsychic conflicts to their (assumed) family systems origins. Since both the rating scales and the observational schema are based on exactly the same model points, comparisons across methods are also possible with SASB. Thus far, Benjamin has applied her model and methodology to a variety of clinical and research problems, including, for example, describing psychotherapy process (Benjamin 1979 a), differentiating psychodynamics among diagnostic groups (Benjamin and Wunderlich 1986), and family therapy (Benjamin 1977).

The SASB rating scales were developed to parallel exactly the structure and points comprising the SASB model. Benjamin has completed a series of reliability and validity studies over the past decade, and the reader can go directly to those reports for more specific information (Benjamin 1974, 1981, 1982, 1984, 1986 a, in press). These rating scales, called Intrex Questionnaires, can be used to describe raters' feelings toward themselves and relationships with other people in the past or present tense.[1] A typical set of ratings would include a total of 180 items, including 36 items from the introject surface and 72 items from each of the other and self surfaces of the SASB model. For example, the item "She neglects me, my interests,

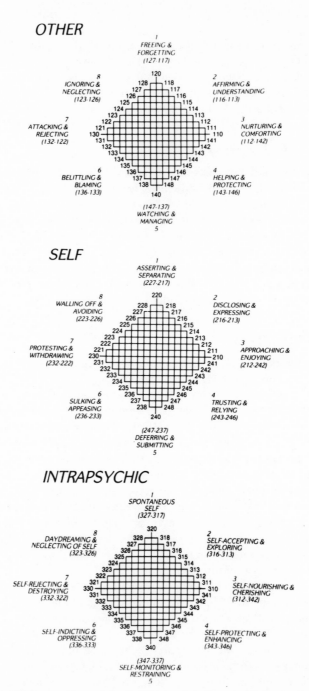

Figure 4.2. Cluster version of L. S. Benjamin's Structural Analysis of Social Behavior (SASB) model. *Source*: Reprinted with permission from Intrex Interpersonal Institute, 1983.

and needs" is focused on other and included in cluster eight, Ignoring and Neglecting. The complementary or parallel item from the self surface is "I wall myself off from her; don't hear; don't react." It is also included in cluster eight called Walling Off and Avoiding on the self surface. The introjected experience of that relationship might be described by the complementary item from the same cluster on surface three, "I neglect myself; don't try to develop my own potential skills, ways of being." All of the items correspond exactly to the points of the SASB model and are rated on a 0 (not at all, never) to 100 (perfectly, always) point scale according to how well they describe the person(s) being rated. Usually, the individual or family rates several significant relationships (e.g., parents or children), and they can be done in their best and worst forms, during ongoing therapy and so forth (Benjamin 1977, 1979 b).

To illustrate the use of the SASB rating scales with clinical populations, consider the findings from a recent study by Benjamin and Wunderlich (1986). They compared SASB ratings of self and each parent for three subtypes of depression among hospitalized patients: (1) major depression; (2) bipolar depression; and (3) depression in borderline personality. Benjamin found that all three subtypes of depressives were submissive to their mothers and perceived their fathers as friendly but controlling. However, only borderlines saw their mothers as actively attacking them and felt strong hostility toward their mothers. In contrast, only major depressives saw their mothers as very affiliative.

SASB Observations

The SASB methodology also includes a behavioral coding system for describing direct interactions among family members, using the same dimensions assessed by the questionnaires (Benjamin et al. in press). A number of recent studies have examined the reliability and validity of the SASB coding schema (Henry, Schacht, and Strupp 1986; Humphrey 1987; Humphrey, Apple, and Kirschenbaum 1986). For example, Henry and his colleagues at Vanderbilt (1986) compared individual psychotherapy process between good versus poor outcome cases using the SASB observational codes. The results showed that therapy outcome was more successful when the therapists were friendly and autonomous (clusters two and four) than when the same therapists were hostile and controlling (cluster six).

In the family area, Humphrey, Apple, and Kirschenbaum (1986) compared the SASB observational system to a well-accepted cognitive-behavioral system in differentiating between families containing a normal versus a bulimic-anorexic daughter. They found that both approaches were equally successful predictors of diagnostic status but that the SASB system was more sensitive to key family processes or styles. To put it another way, the most distinctive interactions were affective and interpersonal exchanges, not the level of cognitive-behavioral skills per se. Therefore, based on Benjamin's research (e.g., 1974, 1979 a) and that of others (e.g., Henry, Schacht, and Strupp 1986; Humphrey, Apple, and Kirschenbaum 1986), it seems that the SASB observational system taps important intra- and interpersonal dimensions that are clinically meaningful.

Keeping such empirical findings in mind, we can now continue with a description of the SASB coding system. Coders work from videotapes and verbatim transcripts of family interactions. They rate each element of speech, and its nonverbal context, for focus, affiliation, and interdependence. Those three judgements then combine to specify the final cluster from SASB that best fits the element of speech. Take, for example, this statement: "I want to be left alone" (said in a sharp, irritated tone of voice). That would be coded as focused on the self and high in both autonomy and hostility. Thus, the statement would best fit cluster self-eight, Walling Off and Avoiding.

The complexity of the SASB coding system ensures that it can capture rich, subtle clinical material, but it also requires fairly extensive experience, either clinically or through training. Several groups of clinically inexperienced, but intelligent and interpersonally astute, coders have now been trained to use the SASB system (Benjamin et al. 1987; Humphrey 1987; Humphrey, Apple, and Kirschenbaum 1986). The results showed that with 60 to 100 hours of intensive training, practice, and feedback, even clinically inexperienced coders can learn to code difficult family material reliably.

Process Versus Content

SASB coding of family interactions requires attention to both the "content" and "process" of the communications. Content is simply what is being discussed in words or the literal meaning of the conversation. Process includes all of the nonverbal and affective nuances that give deeper interpersonal meaning to the words. For example, in a therapy session a patient may openly and affectively express her feelings of being neglected by her father. The process of exploring these feelings could fit cluster self-two, Disclosing and Expressing, or it could be a way of blaming him (other-six, Belittling and Blaming) or both, depending on how she communicates. However, the content of her discussion about how her father treats her best fits cluster other-eight, Ignoring and Neglecting.

Multiple and Complex Communications

Beyond distinguishing between process and content, SASB coding also identifies two types of complicated communications: multiple and complex. Multiple communications combine two distinct messages at once, but they are not necessarily problematic or confusing. A complex message, however is a subtype of multiple communications in which the two (or more) distinct elements imply a kind of simultaneous incompatibility. Complex communications usually are confusing, disorienting, or even "crazy making." Double-binds, of course, are special cases of complex communications wherein the incompatibility involves geometric and psychological opposites located at 180-degree angles on the SASB model. For example:

Mother: You seem worried about something, distracted (other-two, Affirming and Understanding).

Daughter: I can take care of it myself (self-one, Asserting and Separating).

Mother: I could be helpful if you would only open up (other-four, Helping and Protecting, plus other-eight, Ignoring and Neglecting).

This example illustrates a double-bind in which the mother completely ignores (cluster other-eight) her daughter's assertion for independence but makes it seem as though it is for her own good (cluster other-four). Such a negation of the daughter's ability to care for herself, if done chronically, would seriously undermine the daughter's separation from her mother. The fact that her mother combines the negation with pseudo-help would make it all the more difficult for her daughter to perceive realistically, and react to, her mother's true motives and feelings.

The preceding discussion of the SASB methodology shows how it can provide a multitrait– (i.e., different interpersonal approaches) multimethod (i.e., ratings of self and others and direct observations) analysis of individuals and families. These various methods apply equally well to a range of functioning, including both healthy and pathological processes. In fact, one of SASB's greatest strengths is that it has a broad application to a wide array of clinical and empirical questions.

Another strength of the SASB methodology is that it can operationalize important family systems constructs and thereby improve both conceptual clarity and empirical study. For example, in a recent paper Humphrey and Benjamin (in press) chose several central concepts in the family field and used SASB to help make them more concrete and measurable. Among other constructs, they selected Minuchin, Rosman, and Baker's (1978) notion of "enmeshment" and contrasted that with its opposite, healthy differentiation. Minuchin, Rosman, and Baker defined enmeshment as "[e]xcessive togetherness and sharing (that) brings about a lack of privacy. . . . Family members intrude on each others' thoughts and feelings" (p. 30).

In SASB terms, enmeshment can be operationalized as a rigid, complementary pattern of relations characterized by extreme control and submission (cluster other-five, Watching and Managing, complemented by cluster self-five, Deferring and Submitting) at the cost of autonomy giving and taking (clusters other-one, Freeing and Forgetting, and self-one,

Asserting and Separating). The specific items from the SASB rating scales that best illustrate enmeshment are "Believing he or she really knows what is best for the child, tells the child exactly what to do, be, think" (point 148). That intrusive control is complemented by the stance, "Feels, thinks, does, becomes what he or she thinks the other wants" (point 248).

Clearly, enmeshment consists of strong interdependence. It can be friendly and involve cluster four (other and self) or hostile and involve cluster six (other and self). A relationship is enmeshed if it consists almost exclusively of these rigidly interdependent positions. In that paper the authors demonstrated how SASB could codify enmeshment in a family lunch session with Minuchin. Thus, the SASB model and principles can be quite helpful in specifying operationally what our core concepts consist of. This improved definition and specificity may, in turn, refine our ability to measure and examine empirically these important ideas in the family field. For these reasons the SASB approach to family assessment seemed to be the best choice for studying disturbed family patterns in eating disorders. In the subsections that follow, I will present the findings from a recent study of these family processes using SASB.

Methodology of the Present Study

Subjects

As described in the original reports of this study (Humphrey in press), a total of 74 family triads, including father, mother, and teenage daughter, served as subjects. Among these, there were 16 families with a classical restricting anorexic, 16 with a bulimic at normal weight, 18 with a bulimic-anorexic (i.e., met the criteria for anorexia nervosa plus frequent binge eating and self-induced vomiting), and 24 families who had no known psychiatric problems. All three eating disorders groups met the DSM III criteria for their respective disorders according to the consensual judgment of a multidisciplinary treatment team (including a doctoral level clinical psychologist) who were very experienced with these problems. The eating disordered families were recruited through the University of Wisconsin's Eating Disorders Program, where they were new to treatment. Normal families were approached through public high schools in Oregon and McFarland, Wisconsin, or through the Abnormal Psychology Course at the University of Wisconsin. All the families were comparable in terms of annual income levels ($M = \$44,000$), number of children ($M = 3.4$), and daughter's ages ($M = 17.8$ years).

Method

Each family member completed a version of Benjamin's (1974) SASB rating scales, including 36 items from the introject surface, and 144 items from each of the other and self surfaces of the model. The items were rated on a 0 (not at all, never) to 100 (perfectly, always) point scale according to how well they characterized the person being rated. All three family members rated themselves (on all three surfaces) and each other (on the self and other surfaces only) in a total of nine relationships each (e.g., introject; Mother focuses on me; Mother reacts to me; I focus on Mother; I react to Mother; Father focuses on me; Father reacts to me; I focus on Father; I react to Father). These ratings were averaged across all items in a given cluster on each surface to provide an average cluster score. Thus, each family member received a total of 72 average cluster scores (nine surfaces × eight clusters) for the SASB ratings.

In addition to ratings by self and other family members, family interactional patterns were assessed during a ten-minute videotaped discussion of daughter's separation from the family. The families were instructed to role-play their discussion as though they were in their own home and actually confronting the problem. They were also given a similar practice scenario, first to enable them to relax more and get used to being videotaped.

As explained earlier, the observational schema consisted of the 16 SASB interpersonal clusters, coded either singly or in combination. Those cluster names from the other surface are (1) Freeing and Forgetting; (2) Affirming and Understanding; (3) Nurturing and Comforting; (4) Helping and Protecting; (5) Watching and Managing; (6) Belittling and Blaming; (7) Attacking and Rejecting; and (8) Ignoring and Neglecting. The complementary categories from the self surface are (1) Asserting and Separating; (2) Disclosing and Expressing; (3) Approaching and Enjoying; (4) Trusting and Relying; (5) Deferring and Submitting; (6) Sulking and Appeasing; (7) Protesting and Withdrawing; and (8) Walling Off and Avoiding. Both process and content were coded, as well as simple and complex communications, just as described earlier.

The coders were three psychology students; one was an undergraduate senior, one was a recent graduate, and one was a graduate student. They were trained extensively by the author; that is, 100 or more hours of initial training plus ongoing "booster" sessions to prevent criterion drift. At no time during the study did the coders know the group membership of the families or whether a given family's codes would be used for reliability. They did know that different types of families were being examined and that some of them had daughters with eating disorders. Reliabilities were obtained for approximately one third of the families and were based on Cohen's (1968) weighted kappa using a conservative weighting system. These kappas reached acceptable and highly significant levels (cf. Hartmann 1977). For content codes the kappas ranged from .58 to 1.00, with a mean of .79. Kappas for process codes, including a penalty for unmatched complex codes, ranged from .41 to .69, with a mean of .56; excluding the penalty for complex codes, they ranged from .63 to .83 and averaged .74. Thus, the complex codes were less reliable but still acceptable.

Results from Ratings

The results for each dyad's ratings of their relationships will be presented first; then the observational findings will follow. Both sets of data were analyzed using the same basic statistical approach. Initially, the data from each dyad was analyzed using a repeated measure analysis of variance (ANOVA) with eight dependent measures corresponding to each cluster score. Since those ANOVAs were all highly significant, for the group x cluster interactions, they were followed by simple effects tests to determine specifically which clusters differentiated the groups. Subsequently, New-man-Keuls posteriori contrast tests were used to test exactly which of the four groups differed from one another on each cluster. The data from the rating scales involved many dependent measures, so a Bonferroni procedure (Huitema 1980) was also employed to correct the family-wise error rate.

All three eating disorders groups perceived the father–daughter relationship as distressed relative to normal controls, but unique patterns emerged for bulimic as compared to restricting subtypes. Daughters and fathers from the two bulimic groups agreed that their relationships were significantly less friendly and more hostile than were normal controls. More specifically, these bulimic dyads saw their relationship as less Understanding and Disclosing (cluster two), Nurturing and Enjoying (cluster three), and Helping and Trusting (cluster four), and as more Blaming and Sulking (cluster six), Attacking and Withdrawing (cluster seven), and Neglecting and Walling off (cluster 8). The classical restrictors and their fathers viewed their relationships as mostly positive and comparable to controls. In fact, anorexics and their fathers agreed that these daughters were significantly more affectionate toward their fathers (cluster three) than were the bulimic subtypes. The only exception to this general pattern for classical restrictors was that they did perceive their fathers reacting to them in a consistently hostile manner, relative to controls. Figure 4.3 illustrates this set of findings for fathers' ratings of their daughters' reacting to them.

Similar to the findings for the father–daughter dyads, mothers and daughters from the two bulimic subgroups agreed that daughters were more hostile toward their mothers than were their normal counterparts. The bulimic subtypes reported greater Blaming and Sulking (cluster six), Attacking and Withdrawing (cluster seven), and Neglecting and Walling off (cluster eight). However, only the bulimics' mothers saw their daughters as also less friendly—Disclosing (cluster two), Enjoying (cluster three), and Trusting (cluster four)—whereas the daughters themselves did not. As with the fathers, classical anorexics and their mothers were generally more positive and comparable to normal controls. One exception

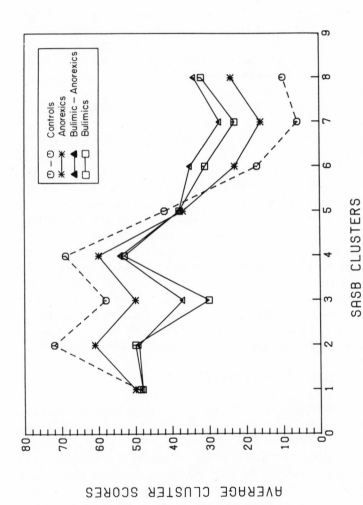

Figure 4.3. SASB cluster scores for all four groups of fathers' ratings of their daughters reacting to them. *Source:* Reprinted from Humphrey, L. L. [in press]. Relationships within subtypes of anorexic, bulimic, and normal families using Structural Analysis of Social Behavior. *Journal of the American Academy of Child and Adolescent Psychiatry.*

to this trend was that anorexics' mothers did perceive their daughters as less Understanding (cluster two) and Trusting (cluster four) than did normal mothers.

Interestingly, only mothers of bulimic-anorexics saw themselves as less friendly and more hostile toward their daughters; neither the bulimics' nor the anorexics' mothers did. The bulimic-anorexic and bulimic daughters themselves, though, both experienced their mothers as more negative toward them than controls. Thus, the bulimic-anorexics concurred with their mothers that they each contributed to the distress in their relationship. In contrast, the bulimics' mothers saw their daughters as the sole problem in their relationship, while daughters disagreed. Figure 4.4 depicts mothers' ratings of their daughters reacting to them.

The findings for the marital dyad were strikingly different from those for the parent–daughter dyads. None of the groups of husbands perceived their wives as more negative or less positive toward them. Further, only the bulimic-anorexic group saw themselves as consistently more hostile toward their wives (clusters six, seven, and eight). In contrast with all the parent–daughter findings, here it was the restricting anorexic subtype that was most distressed among mothers. More specifically, only the mothers of restricting anorexics perceived their husbands as consistently less friendly (clusters, two, three and four) and more hostile (clusters six, seven, and eight) relative to normal controls. The two bulimic subtypes reported some distress in their marital relationships, but not nearly as consistently as the anorexics' parents.

Based on the introject ratings, only daughters from all three eating disorders groups were significantly more disturbed than normal controls; parents were not consistently so. Daughters with all three subtypes of eating disorders were significantly less Self-Accepting (two), Self-Nourishing (three), and Self-Protecting (four) and were more Self-Oppressing (six), Self-Rejecting (seven), and Self-Neglecting (eight) (see Figure 4.5).

To summarize the results from the ratings, all three subtypes of eating disorders experienced significant distress in both parent–daughter dyads. However, the two bulimic subtypes were consistently more negative and less positive compared to normal families, whereas classical restricting anorexics and their parents were generally more favorable about their relationships. Interestingly, classical anorexics reported greater affection toward their fathers, and fathers concurred, than did the two bulimic subtypes. The greatest tension in the restricting anorexic families occurred in the mothers' ratings of the marital relationship, but their husbands did not agree. In fact, these anorexics' mothers were more negative and less positive than either of the bulimic subtypes relative to normal controls. The introject ratings suggested that only the daughters with eating disorders experienced significant deficits in self-care and self-acceptance, along with self-destructiveness; their parents did not.

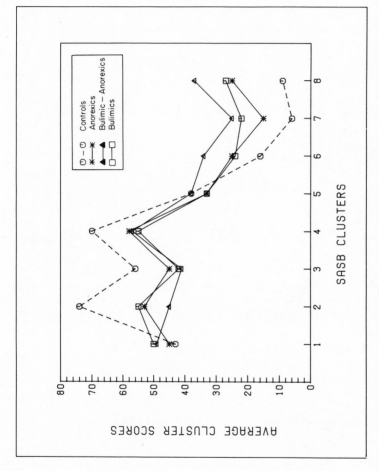

Figure 4.4. SASB cluster scores for all four groups of mothers' ratings of their daughters reacting to them. *Source:* Reprinted from Humphrey, L. L. [in-press]. Relationships within subtypes of anorexic, bulimic, and normal families using Structural Analysis of Social Behavior. *Journal of the American Academy of Child and Adolescent Psychiatry.*

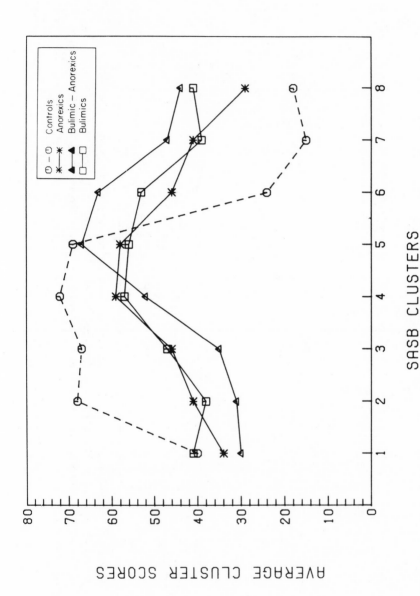

Figure 4.5. SASB cluster scores for all four groups of daughters rating their Introjects. *Source:* Reprinted from Humphrey, L. L. [in press]. Relationships within subtypes of anorexic, bulimic, and normal families using Structural Analysis of Social Behavior. *Journal of the American Academy of Child and Adolescent Psychiatry.*

Results from Observations

Paralleling the findings from ratings, the observational data also suggested that family relationships are quite distressed in eating disorders and that there are different patterns of interaction among subtypes. The most significant findings were based on process codes from the family interactions. Results from the post-hoc analyses of the process data are presented in Table 4.2. These results showed that fathers of all three subtypes of eating disorders were more Watching and Managing (other-five) and Belittling and Blaming (other-six), but also less Helping and Protecting (other-four) and Trusting and Relying (self-four) with their daughters than were normal controls' fathers.[3] However, only the fathers of classical restrictors also conveyed both greater Nurturing and Comforting (other-three) and Ignoring and Neglecting (other-eight) toward their daughter than did either controls or the two bulimic subtypes.

This pattern of results suggests that fathers of the bulimic subtypes are hostilely enmeshed (clusters five and six) with their daughters and are not genuinely supportive or trusting toward them (cluster four), whereas the style of interacting among fathers of classical anorexics seems to be more "pseudo-mutual" (cf. Bateson et al. 1956), as operationalized in SASB (Humphrey and Benjamin in press). More specifically, the fathers of restrictors communicated interpersonal control (other-five) and negation (other-eight), as well as "pseudo" affection and warmth (other-three), in a way that is contradictory and confusing (cf. Humphrey and Benjamin in press).

Similarly, the daughters' styles of relating to their fathers were distinct among subtypes. Only the classical anorexics were significantly more Deferring and Submitting (self-five) than either controls or the two bulimic subtypes. All three eating disorders groups were less Helping and Protecting (other-four) and Trusting and Relying (self-four) and more Sulking and Appeasing (self-six), relative to normal daughters.

Related, but somewhat different, patterns emerged for the mother–daughter dyads. Mothers of bulimics at normal weight, as compared to controls, were significantly more Belittling and Blaming (other-six), Sulking and Appeasing (self-six) and Ignoring and Neglecting (other-eight), and also less Helping and Protecting (other-four) and Approaching and Enjoying (self-three) toward their daughters. Mothers of bulimic anorexics were similarly more Ignoring and Neglecting (other-eight) and less Helpful (other-four) or Approaching (self-three) toward their daughters, but they were not as hostilely controlling or submissive (cluster six) as the bulimics' mothers were. Much like their husbands, the mothers of classical anorexics were more Nurturing and Comforting (other-three) but also Ignoring and Neglecting (other-eight) toward their daughters as compared to controls and/or the bulimic subtypes. Restrictors' mothers were less assertive (self-one) toward their daughters than were any of the other groups as well.

Table 4.2.
Summary of Significant Newman-Keuls from Observational Analyses

SASB Clusters	Mother:Daughter	Daughter:Mother	Father:Daughter	Daughter:Father
Focus on other				
(1) Free & forget	—	—	—	—
(2) Affirm & understand	AB,A,B C / A C	—	AB,A,B C / A AB,B,C	—
(3) Nurture & comfort	C AB,A,B	C AB,A,B	C AB,A,B	C AB,A,B
(4) Help & protect	B AB,A,C	—	AB,A,B C	—
(5) Watch & manage	—	B C	AB,A,B C	—
(6) Belittle & blame	—	—	AB,A,B C	—
(7) Attack & reject	—	—	—	—
(8) Ignore & neglect	A AB,B,C / B C	—	A AB,B,C	—
Focus on self:				
(1) Assert & separate	AB,B,C A	—	—	—
(2) Disclose & express	—	—	—	—
(3) Approach & enjoy	C AB,A,B	C AB,A,B	C AB,A,B	—
(4) Trust & rely	—	C AB,A,B / A AB,B,C	—	C AB,A,B
(5) Defer & submit	B C	—	—	A AB,B,C
(6) Sulk & appease	—	—	—	AB,A,B C
(7) Protest & withdraw	—	—	—	—
(8) Wall off & avoid	—	—	—	—
Total complex	AB,A,B C / A AB	AB,A,B C	AB,A,B C / A,B AB	AB,A,B C / A,B AB

Note: AB = bulimic-anorexics; A = anorexics; B = bulimics; C = controls. All of the group differences indicated are significant at the $p < .05$ level or beyond.
Source: Compiled by the author.

The mothers' styles of interacting with their daughters were also unique for the subtypes of eating disorders and comparable to their husbands in many respects. Mothers of bulimics at normal weight were, like their husbands, hostilely enmeshed with their daughters and not truly supportive of them. Classical anorexics' mothers were also similar to their husbands, and different from bulimics' mothers, in combining pseudo-affection with neglect or negation of their daughters. However, the mothers of bulimic-anorexics did not evidence the hostile enmeshment with their daughters that their husbands did, although they were instead neglectful toward their daughters.

Daughters' interactions with their mothers generally paralleled those toward their fathers, with several exceptions. Bulimics, at normal weight only, Belittled and Blamed (other-six) their mothers significantly more than controls, whereas this was not true with their fathers or among any other groups. In contrast, all three subtypes showed greater Sulking and Appeasing (self-six) toward their fathers, relative to controls, while with mothers this trend did not quite reach significance. Process data for the marital dyad were also examined, but with minimal results. This is probably due to the low base rates of interactions between husband and wife among all four groups (i.e., 7% of the total).

All of the observational findings thus far have been based on analyses of simple process codes; however, the data on complex codes were also important. Complex codes combine simultaneously incompatible messages and are usually disorienting and disturbing for the recipient. All three family members from the eating disorders groups used significantly greater percentages of complex communications than did their normal counterparts. In addition, both the classical anorexics and the bulimics at normal weight, along with their fathers, used greater percentages of complex statements than did bulimic-anorexics and their fathers. Also, the fathers of classical restrictors combined the opposite clusters of Nurturing (other-three) and Managing (other-five); Managing (other-five) and Ignoring (other-eight); and Helping (other-four) and Ignoring (other-eight) in their complex codes, as compared to normal fathers.

This suggests that the classical anorexics' fathers were significantly more pseudo-mutual (cf. Humphrey and Benjamin in press) toward their daughters, in simultaneously combining affection, control, and negation. This was not true for the bulimic subtypes, however; they used a different type of complex code. Fathers of both bulimic subtypes were significantly greater than controls in their complex use of Affirming (other-two) and Managing (other-five) their daughters.

The daughters, in turn, also mirrored their fathers' complex communications. All three subtypes of eating disorders were significantly greater than normal daughters in their complex combination of Asserting (self-one) plus Sulking (self-six) toward their fathers. Only the classical restrictors, however, were also using more complex combinations of Disclosing (self-two) and Submitting (self-five) with their fathers than any of the other groups.

Beyond analyzing both the simple and complex process codes for the observational data, the content and amount of total speech were also examined. Interestingly, though, virtually none of the eating disordered groups differed from controls on these measures for any family members. Thus, it was not how much each family member spoke or what they said that mattered; it was more the way they said it that differentiated among families with eating disorders and normal ones.

Discussion

The results from both the ratings and behavioral observations converged in suggesting that families with eating disorders are significantly distressed, relative to controls, and that there are unique patterns among subtypes. The fact that such differences among family subtypes emerged suggests that these patterns of disturbed relations in bulimia and anorexia are not merely the result of having a sick child. Rather, there do seem to be characteristic and unique styles of disturbed family interactions in these disorders.

Based on data from the ratings, the two bulimic subgroups and their parents experienced greater Blaming and Sulking, Attacking and Withdrawing, and Neglecting and Walling off among family members and less Understanding and Disclosing, Nurturing and Enjoying, and Helping and Trusting between them. The classical restrictors and their parents generally perceived their relationships as more positive and similar to controls. In fact, both the anorexics and their fathers agreed that they are even more affectionate toward their fathers than normal daughters are. It was the mothers of these restrictors who reported substantial dissatisfaction with their marital relationships, and this was quite unusual among the eating disorders. The patterns found among daughters' introject ratings mirrored these disturbed family relationships overall but did not differentiate among subtypes of eating disorders. All three groups were extremely hostile and destructive toward themselves and were much less self-accepting and self-caring, as compared to normal controls. There were few signs of distress, however, among their parents' introject ratings.

The observational data also reflected this high level of distress among families with eating disorders. While all three groups showed disturbed patterns of interacting with each other, again the families of classical anorexics consistently differed from the two bulimic subtypes. The parents of the anorexics, especially fathers, were more pseudo-mutual toward their daughters in that they combined affection (cluster three) with simultaneous negation (cluster eight) and/or control (cluster five). This was found in the process transactions for both simple and complex codes. The parents of the two bulimic subgroups were more hostile and enmeshed (clusters five and six) or neglectful (cluster eight) toward their daughters and were not affectionate or supportive either. It was interesting that the ratings also reflected greater nurturance and affection (cluster three) in anorexic families, but there it was from daughter to father instead of from parents to daughter, as it was in the interactions.

The overall findings for daughters reflected a related pattern. All three eating disordered groups were ambivalently enmeshed and hostile toward their parents. They were also less trusting and helpful than normal daughters. However, only the classical anorexics were more totally submissive (cluster five) toward both parents, and only the bulimics at normal weight were more blaming (cluster six) of their mothers, as compared to controls.

These findings are generally supportive of existing evidence from self-report data. Prior studies have repeatedly shown that families of bulimics and bulimic-anorexics are more conflictive (Johnson and Flach, in press; Ordman and Kirschenbaum 1986) and isolated and detached (Humphrey 1986a) and are less involved, supportive, and cohesive (Humphrey 1986a; Ordman and Kirschenbaum 1986; Strober 1981) as compared to restrictor anorexics and/or normal controls. The present findings were also consistent with those from earlier studies by Strober et al. (1982) and Garner, Garfinkel, and O'Shaughnessy (1983) that showed that bulimic-anorexics' families reported greater overall distress and dissatisfaction on a number of affective and relational dimensions, as compared to families of restrictors.

The observational results from the present study, however, clarify the nature of the disturbed family relationships in classical anorexia, as opposed to other eating disorders. This seems important, because much of the extant self-report data suggest that families of classical restrictors are relatively healthy by comparison to the bulimic subtypes. Observational results here suggested that the restrictors' families are communicating in very subtle and complex ways that may be extremely difficult to perceive and respond to. The parents are even more affectionate than those of controls' but in the same breath are controlling and/or negating their daughter.

According to Bateson and his colleagues (1956), this type of "pseudo" relating is what drives people crazy, precisely because it is impossible to unravel and "metacommunicate" about. It stands to reason, then, that these anorexics and their parents would not report so much tension between them and instead would perceive relatively positive relationships. However, the anorexic daughters do seem to be introjecting the hostility and control that is not unequivocally expressed among the family members.

In sharp contrast to the classical anorexics, the two bulimic subtypes perceived more consistent hostility and neglect among family members and less affection and support. Their perceptions were also very parallel to the data from actual observations of interactions between them. These findings provide further support for the hypothesized family-wide distress and dysregulation and relatedly for the binge–purge metaphor of family relations in bulimia. More specifically, the data from this study showed that bulimics' families are less understanding and nurturing toward one another than are normal families; this is consistent with the nurturance (food) hypothesis of the binge–purge metaphor. In addition, fathers of bulimics were also more controlling of their daughters than were normal fathers. That finding was expected from the interpersonal restriction hypothesis (diet). Both the ratings and observational data supported the purge or expelling of hostility hypothesis. The two bulimic groups, but particularly those at normal weight, were significantly more Belittling and Blaming, and Sulking and Appeasing in their family relationships than were normal controls, whereas restrictors were not. Thus, the bulimic families were less able to effectively modulate, focus, or resolve negative affect and interpersonal conflict.

The results from this study also suggest that Benjamin's SASB model and methodology are extremely promising approaches to family assessment. SASB's complexity and comprehensiveness provided a rich and meaningful description of subtle, elusive family processes and even distinguished among disturbed groups. Further, its multimethod approach captured some potentially pathognomonic discrepancies between family members' perceptions of their relationships versus their actual behavior toward one another.

CONCLUSIONS

Emerging evidence from clinical and empirical studies suggests that bulimia is more than a chronic, intractable pattern of binge eating and purging. It is, instead, a pervasive, multifacted problem of dyregulation that extends beyond eating habits and weight to broader areas of emotionality, self-esteem, work performance, and interpersonal relationships. There is also growing evidence that bulimia reflects family-wide transgenerational distress and poor self-regulation. In fact, the binge–purge cycle itself is a fitting metaphor for the family-wide inability to regulate vital resources, affect, and interpersonal conflict. However, empirical examination of these family processes has been minimal, probably because of a limited array of sound, but clinically relevant, assessment procedures.

A new approach to family assessment, using Benjamin's (1974) model of Structural Analysis of Social Behavior, was applied to the study of family-wide distress in bulimia. Based on parallel ratings and direct observations of family interactions, the findings showed consistently that bulimic families are deficient in mutual understanding, nurturance, and support. They are also excessive in their reciprocal blaming and neglect, and they do not communicate clearly and directly about their feelings. Bulimia, in the broader sense, does seem to reflect a family legacy of disturbed interpersonal relations and poor self-regulation of affect and behavior.

The findings are only the first step in understanding the connection between bulimia and poor family relationships. Thus far, we have established only that certain unique patterns of disturbed interactions differentiate among bulimic, anorexic, and normal families. We have not yet demonstrated that such patterns actually precede and cause or exacerbate the development of eating disorders. It may be that the opposite is true; bulimia and anorexia could cause family relationships to deteriorate. In either case, though, it may be that optimal interventions involve changing family interaction patterns. Even if family communication and relationships are not etiologically significant, they may prevent growth or change on the part of the client and therefore sustain eating problems.

Another important area for future research is the similarity between bulimia and chemical addictions. It may be that young drug abusers and their families show the same problems with generalized dysregulation and impaired self-care seen in bulimia. Other family factors have already been implicated in the maintenance, if not one of the causes, of chemical addictions (e.g., Nathan et al. 1985; Billings and Moos 1983). Utilizing the SASB methodology, researchers could further examine family dynamics in chemical dependence, much as my colleagues and I have done with bulimia. Potentially, these findings could then be used to predict the patient's response to treatment and even to establish goals for individual and family therapy. With the SASB approach, specific excesses and deficits in family relationships, such as hostility or nurturance (respectively), suggest specific treatment interventions. Future studies should take advantage of SASB's promise to help unravel the complex causes of, and determine the best treatments for, disturbed family processes in all addictive disorders.

NOTES

1. For research and teaching purposes, the SASB rating scales are available through Intrex Interpersonal Institute, Inc., P.O. Box 55218, Madison, Wisconsin 53705. Computer software programs for scoring and analyzing data from the rating scales are also available at cost through Intrex.

2. Benjamin has developed computer software packages to describe interactions among family members (or other people) and to perform sequential analyses, including Markov Chains. If used for research, these are also available at cost through Intrex.

3. Both parents of daughters with eating disorders were also more Affirming and Understanding (cluster two) toward their daughters than were controls. However, that finding is due to the fact that this cluster occurred significantly more often as part of a complex (i.e., disturbed) communication from parents of daughters with eating disorders than it did for normal parents.

REFERENCES

American Psychiatric Association (1980). *Diagnostic and statistical manual of mental disorders*. Washington, D.C.: American Psychiatric Association.

Bateson, J.; D. D. Jackson; J. Haley; and J. Weakland. (1956). Toward a theory of schizophrenia. *Behavioral Science*, 1:251–64.

Benjamin, L. S. (1974). Structural Analysis of Social Behavior. *Psychological Review*, 81:392–425.

Benjamin, L. S. (1977). Structural Analysis of a family in therapy. *Journal of Consulting and Clinical Psychology*, 45:391–406.

Benjamin, L. S. (1979a). Structural Analysis of differentiation failure. *Psychiatry*, 42:1–23.

Benjamin, L. S. (1979b). Use of Structural Analysis of Social Behavior and Markov Chains to study dyadic interactions. *Journal of Abnormal Psychology*, 88:303–19.

Benjamin, L. S. (1981). A psychosocial competence classification system. In *Social competence*, eds. J. D. Wine and M. D. Smye. New York: Guilford Press.

Benjamin, L. S. (1982). Use of Structural Analysis of Social Behavior (SASB) to guide interventions in psychotherapy. In *Handbook of interpersonal psychotherapy*, eds. D. Kiesler and J. Anchin. New York: Pergamon Press.

Benjamin, L. S. (1984). Principles of prediction using Structural Analysis of Social Behavior (SASB). In *Personality and the prediction of behavior*, eds. R. A. Zucker, J. Aronoff, and A. J. Rabin. New York: Academic Press.

Benjamin, L. S. (in press). *Interpersonal diagnosis and treatment: The SASB approach*. New York: Guilford Press.

Benjamin, L. S.; S. W. Foster; L. Giat-Roberto; and S. E. Estroff. (1987). Breaking the family code: Analyzing videotapes of family interactions by Structural Analysis of Social Behavior. In *Psychotherapeutic process: A research handbook*, eds. L. S. Greenberg and W. M. Pinsoff. New York: Guilford Press.

Benjamin, L. S., and S. Wunderlich. (1986). Using social variables to differentiate among DSM-III diagnostic groups: Major depression, bipolar depression, and borderline personality. Unpublished manuscript, University of Wisconsin.

Billings, A. G., and R. H. Moos. (1983). Psychosocial processes of recovery among alcoholics and their families: Implications for clinicians and program evaluators. *Addictive Behaviors*, 8:205–18.

Blatt, S. J.; C. McDonald; A. Sugarman; and C. Wilber. (1984). Psychodynamic theories of opiate addiction: New directions for research. *Clinical Psychology Review*, 4:159–89.

Brisman, J., and M. Siegel. (1984). Bulimia and alcoholism: Two sides of the same coin? *Journal of Substance Abuse Treatment*, 1:113–18.

Campbell, D. T., and D. W. Fiske. (1959). Convergent and discriminant validation by the multitrait-multimethod matrix. *Psychological Bulletin*, 56:81–105.

Carroll, K., and G. R.Leon. (1981). The bulimia-vomiting disorder within a generalized substance abuse pattern. Paper presented at the annual meeting for the Association for the Advancement of Behavior Therapy, Toronto, November 1981.

Cohen, J. (1968). Weighted kappas: Nominal scale agreement with provision for scaled disagreement or partial credit. *Psychological Bulletin*, 70:213–20.

Frank, G. (1965). The role of the family in the development of psychopathology. *Psychological Bulletin*, 64:191–205.

Garner, D. M.; P. E. Garfinkel; and M. O'Shaughnessy. (1983). Clinical and psychometric comparisons between bulimia in anorexia and bulimia in normal weight women. In *Understanding anorexia nervosa and bulimia: Report of the fourth Ross conference on medical research*. Columbus, Ohio: Ross Laboratories.

Goodsitt, A. (1983). Self-regulatory disturbances in eating disorders. *International Journal of Eating Disorders*, 2:51–60.

Gurman, A. S., and D. P. Kniskern. (1981). *Handbook of family therapy*. New York: Brunner/Mazel.

Halmi, K. A.; J. R. Falk; and E. Schwartz. (1981). Binge-eating and vomiting: A survey of a college population. *Psychological Medicine*, 11:697–706.

Hartmann, D. P. (1977). Considerations in the choice of interobserver reliability estimates. *Journal of Applied Behavior Analysis*, 10:103–16.

Henry, W. P.; T. E. Schacht; and H. H. Strupp. (1986). Structural Analysis of Social Behavior: Application to a study of interpersonal process in differential psychotherapeutic outcome. *Journal of Consulting and Clinical Psychology*, 54:27–31.

Hudson, J. I.; H. G. Pope; J. M. Jonas; and D. Yurgelum-Todd. (1983). Family history study of anorexia nervosa and bulimia. *British Journal of Psychiatry*, 142:133–38.

Huitema, B. E. (1980). *The analysis of covariance and alternatives*. New York: Wiley.

Humphrey, L. L. (1986a). Family dynamics in bulimia. *Annals of adolescent psychiatry*, vol. 13, eds. S. C. Feinstein, A. H. Esman, J. G. Looney, A. Z. Schwartzberg, A. D. Sovoski, and M. Sugar. Chicago: University of Chicago Press.

Humphrey, L. L. (1986b). Structural Analysis of parent-child relationships in eating disorders. *Journal of Abnormal Psychology*, 95:395–402.

Humphrey, L. L. (1987). A comparison of bulimic-anorexic and nondistressed family processes using Structural Analysis of Social Behavior. *Journal of the American Academy of Child and Adolescent Psychiatry*, 26:248–55.

Humphrey, L. L. (in press). Relationships within subtypes of anorexic, bulimic, and normal families using Structural Analysis of Social Behavior. *Journal of the American Academy of Child and Adolescent Psychiatry*, under revision.

Humphrey, L. L.; R. F. Apple; and D. S. Kirschenbaum. (1986). Differentiating bulimic-anorexic from normal families using an interpersonal and a behavioral observation system. *Journal of Consulting and Clinical Psychology*, 54:190–195.

Humphrey, L. L., and L. S. Benjamin (in press). Structural Analysis of Social Behavior: A multimethod assessment of families. In *Techniques of family assessment: Methods and clinical applications*, ed. O. A. Barbarin. New York: Guilford Press.

Johnson, C., and R. A. Flach. (1985). Family characteristics of bulimic and normal women: A comparative study. *American Journal of Psychiatry*, 142:1321–4.

Johnson, C., and R. Larson. (1982). Bulimia: An analysis of moods and behavior. *Psychosomatic Medicine*, 44:333–45.

Johnson, C., and K. L. Maddi. (1986). The etiology of bulimia: A bio-psycho-social perspective. In *Annals of adolescent psychiatry*, vol. 13, ed. S. C. Feinstein. Chicago: University of Chicago Press.

Johnson, C.; M. K. Stuckey; L. D. Lewis; and D. Schwartz. (1982). Bulimia: A descriptive survey of 316 cases. *International Journal of Eating Disorders*, 2:3–18.

Katzman, M. A., and S. A. Wolchick. (1984). Bulimia and binge-eating in college women: A comparison of personality and behavioral characteristics. *Journal of Consulting and Clinical Psychology*, 52:423–28.

Khantzian, E. (1981). Some treatment implications of the ego and self disturbances in alcoholism. *Dynamic approaches to the understanding and treatment of alcoholism*. New York: The Free Press.

Kohut, H. (1977). Preface in *Psychodynamics of drug dependence*. Research Monographs, vol. 12. Rockville, Md.: National Institute on Drug Abuse.

Leary, T. (1959). *Interpersonal diagnosis of personality: A functional theory and methodology for personality evaluation*. New York: Ronald Press.

Mahler, M. S. (1968). *On human symbiosis and the vicissitudes of individuation*. Infantile Psychosis, vol. 1. New York: International Universities Press.

Minuchin, S.; B. L. Rosman; and L. Baker. (1978). *Psychosomatic families: Anorexia nervosa in context*. Cambridge, Mass.: Harvard University Press.

Mitchell, J. E., and R. L. Pyle. (1982). The bulimic syndrome in normal weight individuals: A review. *International Journal of Eating Disorders*, 1:61–73.

Mitchell, J. E.; R. L. Pyle; and E. D. Eckert. (1981). Binge eating behavior in patients with bulimia. *American Journal of Psychiatry*, 138:835–36.

Moos, R., and B. S. Moos. (1980). *Family environment scale manual*. Palo Alto, Calif.: Consulting Psychologists Press.

Murray, H. A. (1938). *Explorations in personality*. New York: Oxford University Press.

Nathan, P. E.; R. F. Sullivan; W. M. Hay; and K. Cocco. (1985). Asymmetry of influence effects on interaction dominance. *Journal of Marital and Family Therapy*, 11:300–410.

Olson, D. H.; R. Bell; and J. Portner. (1978). *Family adaptibility and cohesion evaluation scale*. St. Paul, Minn.: Family Social Science, University of Minnesota.

Ordman, A. M., and D. S. Kirschenbaum. (1986). Bulimia: Assessment of eating, psychological adjustment and familial characteristics. *International Journal of Eating Disorders*, 5:865–78.

Pyle, R. L.; J. E. Mitchell; and E. D. Eckert. (1981). Bulimia: A report of 34 cases. *Journal of Clinical Psychiatry*, 42:60–64.

Schaefer, E. S. (1965). A configurational analysis of children's reports of parent behavior. *Journal of Consulting Psychology*, 29:552–57.

Schlesier-Stropp, B. (1984). Bulimia: A review of the literature. *Psychological Bulletin*, 95:247–57.

Skinner, H. A.; J. Santa-Barbara; and D. D. Steinhauer. (1983). The family assessment measure. *Canadian Journal of Community Mental Health*, 2:91–105.

Stimmel, B. (1983). Dependency on mood altering drugs: The need for a holistic approach. *Advances in Alcohol and Substance Abuse*, 2:1–8.

Strangler, R.S., and A. M. Printz. (1980). DSM III: Psychiatric diagnosis in a university population. *American Journal of Psychiatry*, 137:937–40.

Strober, M. (1981). The significance of bulimia in juvenile anorexia nervosa: An explanation of possible etiological factors. *International Journal of Eating Disorders*, 1:28–43.

Strober, M.; B. Salkin; J. Burroughs; and W. Morrell. (1982). Validity of the bulimia-restrictor distinction in anorexia nervosa. *The Journal of Nervous and Mental Disease*, 170:345–51.

Sullivan, H. S. (1953). *The interpersonal theory of psychiatry*. New York: Norton.

Weidman, A. (1983). Adolescent substance abuse: Family dynamics. *Family Therapy*, 10:47–55.

Winnicott, D. W. (1965). *The maturational processes and the facilitating environment*. New York: International Universities Press.

Part II

Treatment

5

DELAYING SMOKING RELAPSE WITH EXTENDED TREATMENT

Thomas H. Brandon,
Diane C. Zelman, and
Timothy B. Baker

Smoking treatment programs now exist that reliably produce high initial rates of abstinence, usually via aversion therapy. Such programs continue to be plagued, however, with poor long-term success rates. Across treatment methods, only around 30% of subjects who reach abstinence during treatment are likely to be nonsmokers three months later (Danaher 1977; Hunt and Bespalec 1974). A major challenge to researchers is to prolong the effects of cessation treatments. In this regard two general strategies have emerged. In the multicomponent approach a number of treatment components are included in a smoking cessation package to increase the probability of treatment effects generalizing beyond treatment termination. This approach has been heavily researched, and the best of these treatments have produced long-term abstinence rates in the 40% to 70% range (Erickson et al. 1983; Hall et al. 1984; Tiffany, Martin, and Baker 1986). The second approach, the maintenance session approach, has been less adequately investigated. In this approach clients are exposed to therapy procedures after the termination of the formal cessation treatment. These procedures generally extend well into the follow-up period and are designed to extend, rather than produce, abstinence.

This study was supported by National Heart, Lung, and Blood Institute Grant 28519–03, awarded to Timothy B. Baker.

(Although some have distinguished between maintenance and cessation treatments on the basis that only the former has as a focus the production of prolonged abstinence, it is clear that all smoking treatments have that as a principal goal.)

A simple maintenance strategy, extended therapist contact per se, generally has been unsuccessful (Bernstein 1970; Colletti and Supnick 1980; Schmahl, Lichtenstein, and Harris 1972; Shipley 1981). Booster sessions (aversive smoking trials administered during the follow-up period) have also been tried unsuccessfully (Best 1975; Elliott and Denney 1978; Relinger et al. 1977). Likewise, maintenance interventions based on social support/pressure generally have been unable to improve long-term abstinence rates (Colletti and Kopel 1979; Colletti and Stern 1980; Karol and Richards 1981). Hamilton and Bornstein (1979) successfully improved six-month outcome by adding to their rapid smoking and behavioral counseling treatment a social support maintenance component that included a "buddy system" whereby group members maintained supportive telephone contact for 20 weeks posttreatment. However, the maintenance conditions produced six-month abstinence rates that were only in the 30% range.

Perhaps the most work on the effects of maintenance sessions has been done by Lando and his associates, with varied results (Lando 1977, 1978, 1981, 1982; Lando and McCullough 1978; Lando and McGovern 1982). These studies supplemented aversive smoking therapy with maintenance sessions comprising a form of coping response training, contingency contracting, and booster sessions and have yielded six-month abstinence rates ranging from 28% to 76% with a mean of 55%. This is comparable to the best results achieved with multicomponent, nonmaintenance treatment packages that include coping response training (Erickson et al. 1983; Hall et al. 1984; Tiffany, Martin, and Baker 1986).

In summary, attempts to maintain nonsmoking via maintenance treatments have largely been unsuccessful. In the rare cases in which abstinence rates have increased with maintenance contact, the benefits generally have evaporated by a later follow-up period. Moreover, the best results are no better than those of the best cessation treatments without maintenance contact. It is clear that the effects of maintenance treatments must be evaluated with respect to the nature of the cessation treatment. The single study that produced increased long-term abstinence rates via maintenance sessions employed only a single treatment strategy during cessation (aversive smoking) and then provided additional treatment elements (including coping response training) during follow-up (Lando 1977). Unfortunately, this research strategy reveals little more than the fact that multicomponent programs tend to be more effective than single-element treatments (e.g., Elliott and Denney 1978; Erickson et al. 1983; Hall et al. 1984; Tiffany, Martin, and Baker 1986). Thus, currently there are no unassailable data showing that maintenance treatments can enhance the long-term effects of a successful multicomponent cessation program. Moreover, there are no data showing that any treatment exerts greater effects when delivered after, rather than during, cessation treatment.

The principal objective of the current study was to improve the long-term outcome of an effective, multicomponent cessation treatment—namely, rapid smoking combined with behavioral counseling emphasizing coping response training (Erickson et al. 1983; Tiffany, Martin, and Baker 1986). To this treatment were added maintenance procedures constructed on theoretical and empirical bases—a maintenance coping response treatment targeted explicitly at relapse prevention and an exposure treatment based on Pavlovian principles of extinction.

Coping response training was based on the hypothesis that clients and therapists could anticipate situations or conditions posing an increased risk of relapse and that the execution of particular types of coping responses would decrease relapse risk (Marlatt 1982). Identification of relapse risk situations was based on three sources of information: published studies characterizing relapse contexts (Brandon, Tiffany, and Baker 1986; Chaney, Roszell, and Cummings 1982; Lichtenstein, Antonuccio, and Rainwater 1977; Marlatt and Gordon 1980; Shiffman 1982), the clients' previous relapse history, and the clients' appraisal of high-risk situations (Condiotte and Lichtenstein 1981). Clients were trained to respond to high-risk situations with coping responses that were selected on the basis of their apparent utility in cessation treatments (Chaney, O'Leary, and Marlatt 1978; Erickson et al. 1983; Hall et al. 1984; Jones and Lanyon 1981; Tiffany, Martin, and Baker 1986). They were trained to use both behavioral and cognitive coping strategies in response to urges and in response to situations and problems hypothesized to give rise to urges (Shiffman 1982, 1984).

The second treatment strategy, exposure therapy, was based on the notion that drug urges reflect, at least in part, Pavlovian conditioned responses elicited by drug- or withdrawal-associated cues (Ludwig, Wikler, and Stark 1974; O'Brien 1976; Siegel 1983). This hypothesis is consistent with observations that such cues can elicit both the self-report of urges and withdrawal signs. (Baker, Sherman, and Morse 1987; Poulos, Hinson, and Siegel 1981; Siegel 1983).

If drug urges are produced by conditioned responses elicited by drug-paired cues, this suggests that such urges could be extinguished through repeated exposure to environmental cues and emotional states associated with drugs (Ludwig, Wikler, and Stark 1974; O'Brien and Ng 1979; Poulos, Hinson, and Siegel 1981; Siegel 1983). Innocuous exposure to drinking cues and alcohol has successfully been used to treat alcoholics (Blakey and Baker 1980; Hodgson and Rankin 1976). However, such studies have been uncontrolled and have contained few subjects. Cue exposure by itself has not been found to be successful as a cessation treatment with smokers (Raw and Russell 1980). The exposure treatment in the present study included planned exposures to emotional and environmental contexts that subjects' recollections and self-monitoring records indicated were associated with smoking, urges to smoke, and relapse in previous quitting attempts.

Cessation treatment in the present study consisted of two weeks of rapid smoking and behavioral counseling, a multicomponent treatment previously shown to produce high abstinence rates (Erickson et al. 1983; Tiffany, Martin, and Baker 1986). This was followed by one of three follow-up conditions. Nonmaintenance Control (NMC) groups met only once during the follow-up period, at three-months posttreatment, for assessment. Counseling Only Maintenance (COM) groups met four times over three months for maintenance sessions consisting of coping response training and Pavlovian exposure treatment. Another maintenance condition was included as an in-study replication of any maintenance effects and to test the efficacy of an additional exposure technique. Counseling plus Puffing Maintenance (CPM) groups received the same counseling as COM groups but also were exposed to the sight, feel, smell, and taste of cigarettes through rapid puffing (without inhaling) extinction trials. Previous studies have found booster aversive smoking sessions to be unsuccessful (e.g., Elliot and Denney 1978), but this could have been due to the fact that receipt of nicotine, so long after subjects had quit smoking, "primed" urges for more nicotine (see Stewart, de Wit, and Eikelboom 1984). We hypothesized that rapid puffing would produce a variety of therapeutic effects (e.g., extinction of urges elicited by cigarettes and the pairing of cigarettes with mild aversive effects) without subjects receiving a large nicotine bolus that might stimulate urges (see Tiffany, Martin, and Baker 1986). We made one a priori prediction with respect to outcome: both maintenance conditions would be superior to the control condition in producing long-term maintenance of nonsmoking. We were undecided about whether rapid puffing would cause the two maintenance conditions to be differentially effective.

An additional goal of this study was to explore the relationship between pre- and posttreatment variables and long-term follow-up status. Variables were selected for inclusion if they permitted replication of previous studies or if they were theoretically related to the maintenance process.

METHOD

Subjects

Sixty-five smokers (27 males and 38 females) were recruited from the community via radio and newspaper advertisements, posters, and referral from physicians and exclients. Subjects were between the ages of 16 and 40, smoked a minimum of one pack of cigarettes per day for at least one year, and were in good general health. After contacting the clinic, subjects were assigned to treatment cohorts ranging in size from three to seven people. Counterbalanced for order of treatment, the cohorts were randomly assigned to either one of the two maintenance conditions or to the control condition. Two subjects dropped out during the cessation treatment, and six others failed to achieve complete abstinence by the second and final week of the cessation treatment. To ensure a fair comparison between the postcessation conditions, only the remaining 57 (25 males and 32 females) "maintenance-eligible" subjects were included in analyses. Consequently, 19 subjects were included in the Nonmaintenance Control (NMC) condition, 20 in the Counseling Only Maintenance (COM) condition, and 18 in the Counseling plus Puffing Maintenance (CPM) condition. Among these subjects, mean age was 31.30, mean years as a smoker was 13.50, and mean self-reported pretreatment smoking rate was 27.32 cigarettes per day.

Therapists

Two therapists led each treatment cohort. The principal therapist was always one of the three primary investigators. One was a clinical psychologist on the faculty of the Department of Psychology, University of Wisconsin, Madison. The other two were advanced graduate students in clinical psychology. All three had extensive experience leading smoking groups prior to this study. The principal therapists were either paired together or with other advanced clinical psychology graduate students. Assignment of the three principal therapists was counterbalanced across experimental conditions and over time.

Orientation Meetings

All cohorts met for a 45-minute orientation meeting two weeks prior to the start of cessation treatment. During these meetings, subjects were provided with information about the counseling and rapid smoking treatments. They were told of the medical risks involved in the rapid smoking procedure and were told to obtain physicians' signed approval before beginning rapid smoking.

Therapists told subjects to begin self-monitoring their daily smoking rates the week before treatment began. Subjects were to smoke at their normal rate during the week prior to treatment, reduce their smoking to half their normal rate on the two days prior to the first treatment meeting, and refrain from smoking on the day of the first meeting.

All subjects paid $50 and were told that $35 would be returned to them contingent on their attendance at treatment and assessment sessions and completion of the various assessment inventories. Subjects provided the names of two "collaterals" who could independently confirm their smoking status during fullow-up.

Cessation Treatment

The cessation treatment was virtually identical to that used by Tiffany, Martin, and Baker (1986) in their Full Scale Rapid Smoking with Full Counseling condition. Cohorts met in the evening six times over a two week period: Monday, Tuesday, Wednesday, and Friday of the first week; Monday and Thursday of the second week. Each meeting was divided into 90 minutes of counseling and 30 to 45 minutes of rapid smoking.

Counseling

The counseling consisted primarily of coping response training, as well as informational and supportive counseling. Each session was structured around subjects individually reviewing the previous intersession interval with respect to withdrawal symptoms, problematic urges to smoke, stressful situations, or smoking-related events. Therapists informed subjects of the nature of nicotine withdrawal in terms of expected symptomatology and timecourse. They encouraged subjects to deal with withdrawal by using behavioral and cognitive coping responses (e.g., chewing gum or reminding oneself of the time-limited nature of withdrawal). In addition, subjects were given a model of postwithdrawal urges and relapse crises. They were taught to recognize, anticipate, and prepare for situational (e.g., smoking-related activities), cognitive (e.g., wanting to "test" oneself with just one cigarette), and affective (e.g., depression) concomitants and/or precursors to smoking urges. Therapists stressed the use of both cognitive (e.g., telling oneself "smoking is not an option") and behavioral (e.g., leaving the smoking situation) coping responses.

Therapists emphasized the need for absolute abstinence during treatment (aside from cigarettes smoked during the rapid smoking sessions), yet warned against the "Abstinence Violation Effect" (Marlatt and Gordon 1980) should subjects experience an initial relapse. Additionally, subjects completed both daily and long-term behavioral contracts specifying rewards and punishments contingent on their smoking status.

Rapid Smoking

Subjects were instructed to inhale deeply on a *More*[R] cigarette at the sound of a tone, which occurred at six-second intervals. They were told to concentrate on the unpleasant effects of smoking. Subjects inhaled at this rate until they felt too ill to continue smoking or until they consumed three cigarettes, whichever occurred first. At this point, they left the room and completed a Smoking Aversion Questionnaire (Tiffany, Martin, and Baker 1986) in which they rated on a seven-point scale the intensity of a number of negative sensations associated with aversive smoking (burning mouth, headache, nausea, pounding heart, dizziness, negative emotion, numbness, eye irritation). After a five-minute rest period, subjects repeated this procedure twice more, for a total of three rapid smoking trials per session.

Maintenance Procedures

Counseling Only Maintenance (COM)

Subjects assigned to the COM maintenance condition met for one-and-a-half hour sessions at 2, 4, 8, and 12 weeks posttreatment. They gave breath samples for alveolar carbon monoxide (COa) analysis at each session and were refunded $5 for attending. All subjects who had successfully completed the cessation treatment phase were encouraged to attend the maintenance sessions. Subjects attended sessions in the same cohort with whom they underwent cessation treatment. As in cessation treatment meetings, subjects reviewed the previous intersession interval, and therapists continued to offer encouragement and support for the subjects' efforts to maintain abstinence. However, most emphasis was placed on the coping response training and exposure treatment.

At the first maintenance meeting, the therapists explained the rationale underlying the maintenance treatments. Since coping response training had been discussed during cessation treatment, it was necessary only to emphasize that subjects use coping response skills during the follow-up period. Subjects were encouraged to continue to anticipate potential situations that could produce urges to smoke and to use coping responses in the presence of strong urges. To assist in the identification of both urge-inducing situations and urge-alleviating responses, subjects were given pocket-sized "Personal Exsmoker Diaries." They were instructed to self-monitor their urges and record physical, cognitive, and behavioral information associated with each serious urge, including any coping responses used. The diaries also included lists of common problematic behavioral and cognitive cues to smoke, with space to add individualized cues to the lists. Lists of behavioral and cognitive coping responses were also included in the diaries with space for individual additions. Time was spent during the session developing individual problematic situations and coping responses for each subject. Therapists stressed the importance of self-monitoring urges to enable subjects to recognize patterns of urge-eliciting situations and to identify coping responses that successfully counter urges. The diaries included urge graphs on which subjects could plot the decline of daily urges over the three-month maintenance period.

The therapists explained the exposure treatment by telling subjects that they form associations between cues associated with drug intake and the drug effect. Such associations are experienced as unpleasant urges for drug. If the urge is followed by drug intake, the association becomes stronger. The only way to rid oneself of urges is to break the association between drug cues and drug intake. This "extinction" is accomplished by exposure to the drug cues, experiencing urges, but not taking the drug.

Thus, subjects were told to expect that initial exposures to previous smoking situations would be difficult or aversive—especially the first few times the situations are encountered after quitting. They were reminded that emotional states and cognitions could also serve as cues to smoke. Therapists told subjects to interpret smoking urges positively, as signs of extinction. Only time and continued exposure to smoking cues without smoking would diminish the urges. Together therapists and subjects planned intersession "exposure homework." Subjects were to expose themselves to affects and stimuli that they expected would produce urges to smoke (e.g., drinking at a bar; being with other smokers) and to be prepared to utilize specific coping responses. They were encouraged to increase gradually the potential urge severity of the exposure sessions as their confidence and coping skills increased.

At the remaining three maintenance meetings, therapists reviewed the coping response and exposure training rationales and methods. Subjects discussed their exposure sessions and coping responses and updated the individualized sections of their diaries. Problems encountered since the previous session were discussed, and therapists emphasized self-attributions of success. Subjects who had relapsed were encouraged to attempt to quit again immediately, before dependence redeveloped.

Counseling plus Puffing Maintenance (CPM)

Subjects in this maintenance condition received exactly the same intervention as those in the COM condition, with the addition of a rapid puffing session following each maintenance meeting. Rapid puffing sessions were the same as the rapid smoking sessions of the cessation treatment except that subjects did not inhale cigarette smoke. The therapists provided the rationale that the rapid puffing constituted an exposure treatment.

Nonmaintenance Control (NMC)

Subjects assigned to the control condition met only once during the postcessation period, 12 weeks after the cessation treatment. Although this meeting was presented to subjects as a "maintenance session," it was included as an opportunity to administer questionnaires and take COa readings to verify smoking status. Subjects reported their smoking status and were encouraged to remain abstinent. They each were rebated $20 for attendance.

Assessment

Subjects were administered a range of assessments that served four primary functions: to monitor clients' smoking status, to evaluate the impact of the cessation treatment, to assess the nicotine withdrawal syndrome, and to investigate potential predictors of long-term smoking status.

Smoking Status

Breath samples were taken from subjects and analyzed for COa level using an Ecolyzer[R] made by Energetics Science. COa samples were taken at each treatment and maintenance session and at the psychophysiological assessment sessions. Subjects also self-monitored daily smoking beginning the week prior to the cessation treatment and continuing through the last day of the cessation treatment.

Responses to Cigarettes

As in previous studies (Erickson et al. 1983; Tiffany, Martin, and Baker 1986), psychophysiological, attitudinal, and behavioral measures were collected in order to evaluate the impact of the cessation treatment. These data were collected during one pretreatment and two posttreatment (weeks one and three) assessment sessions. Responses on these measures will be discussed in a future paper.

Nicotine Withdrawal Symptoms

Two questionnaires were used to investigate the nature of nicotine withdrawal. Subjects completed withdrawal rating forms twice per day (at 9:00 AM and 2:00 PM) for ten days, beginning two days before treatment. The 27-item Likert-type (7-point scale) form was a modified version of a questionnaire developed by Shiffman and Jarvik (1976) to assess nicotine withdrawal symptoms during the first two weeks of abstinence. Scales assessed depression, confidence, cognitive distortions, craving, psychological discomfort, stimulation, physical symptoms, and appetite.

The Profile of Mood States (POMS; McNair, Lorr, and Droppleman 1971), was included to assess further withdrawal symptomatology. The POMS is a mood adjective checklist that has been shown to measure changes in affect during smoking withdrawal (Hall et al. 1983). Subjects completed the POMS at pretreatment, at each cessation treatment meeting, at assessment sessions, and at maintenance meetings.

Predictor Variables

Several variables were measured as potential predictors of long-term outcome. Prior to treatment, subjects completed the Self-Control Schedule (SCS; Rosenbaum 1980), the Depression Proneness Inventory (DPI; Abramson and Metalsky 1983), and the Social Support for Nonsmoking questionnaire (SSN).

The SCS is a 36-item Likert-type measure of self-control behaviors that was included to test the hypothesis that relapse is due to a breakdown of self-regulation (Kirschenbaum and Tomarken 1982). Individuals with greater self-regulatory tendencies, as measured by the SCS, should be more likely to employ coping responses and thus be more successful at maintaining abstinence (Katz and Singh 1986).

The DPI was included to investigate the relationship between negative affective states and relapse that has been reported in retrospective studies (Brandon, Tiffany, and Baker 1986); Marlatt and Gordon 1980; Shiffman 1982). The DPI is a face valid, ten-item Linkert-type measure of diathesis for depression. Its reliability and validity has been demonstrated by recent research (Tabachnik et al. 1986).

The SSN was included to measure subjects' anticipated social support for quitting smoking. It assessed subjects' degree of exposure to smokers and nonsmokers at home and at work, as well as their perceived level of smoking-specific social support. Social support is believed to attenuate the effects of stress on a variety of physical and psychological symptoms (Cobb 1976; Cohen and Hoberman 1983; Dean and Lin 1977) and has been related to rate of smoking (Billings and Moos 1983) and to successful maintenance of nonsmoking (Coppotelli and Orleans 1985; Horwitz, Hindi-Alexander and Wagner 1985; Mermelstein, Cohen, and Lichtenstein 1983; Mermelstein, Lichtenstein, and McIntyre 1983).

Two confidence measures were taken the week preceding treatment and the week following treatment. On the Confidence Questionnaire (Condiotte and Lichtenstein 1981), subjects rated their confidence in resisting urges to smoke in 48 different smoking situations during the following year. On the second confidence measure, subjects were asked to rate on a five-point scale their global confidence in remaining abstinent for one year. This global measure was the single best predictor of outcome in a previous study (Tiffany, Martin, and Baker 1986).

Other questionnaire measures included a structured smoking history interview administered pretreatment and a stress questionnaire. Topics covered by the interview included rate and duration of smoking, history of other drug use or abuse, history of psychiatric treatment, current satisfaction with smoking, estimate of difficulty to quit smoking, previous attempts to quit, withdrawal symptoms and severity of previous quit attempts, previous relapse situations, reasons for quitting, and confidence that subject would still be a nonsmoker after one year. At the three-month posttreatment meeting subjects completed the Social Readjustment Scale (SRS; Holmes and Rahe 1967). Subjects were instructed to endorse any of the 41 life stressors (e.g., sexual difficulty, being fired from work) they had experienced since the start of treatment. Relapse often occurs during times of stress (Brandon, Tiffany, and Baker 1986; Marlatt and Gordon 1980; Shiffman 1982), and measures of stress have been related to outcome (Glasgow et al. 1985; Mermelstein, Cohen, and Lichtenstein 1983; Gunn 1983).

Follow-up

In addition to information and COa analyses obtained at the maintenance meetings, follow-up smoking status was determined via telephone contact with subjects by a nontherapist experimenter. Attempts were made to contact all subjects at 1, 2, 3, 4, 6, 8, 10, and 12 months posttreatment. During each follow-up interview, the subject's smoking status was determined, and if the subject had smoked at all since the last contact, a detailed description of the relapse episode and information on the smoking pattern over that interval was collected. In addition, all subjects were questioned about any problem situations they had encountered since the previous follow-up call.

Collaterals, who could provide information about subjects' smoking, were contacted at 3, 6, and 12 months posttreatment. Attempts were made to contact two collaterals for each subject.

RESULTS

Subject Characteristics

Of the 65 subjects entering treatment, 2 dropped out during the cessation treatment and 6 failed to reach abstinence by the second week of treatment. All of these "maintenance-ineligible" subjects initially had been assigned to maintenance conditions—7 to CPM, 1 to COM. Five of the CPM subjects who did not achieve abstinence were members of the same cohort. Subjects were aware of the time of cessation treatment that they had been assigned to a maintenance condition but did not know the specific condition. The maintenance conditions were combined and compared against the NMC condition to test for a difference in failure rates. Fisher's exact test revealed that the difference did not reach statistical significance ($p = .09$). Although this difference was not significant by conventional standards, the trend suggests that the provision of a prolonged treatment may result in smokers feeling less urgency to quit in the short term.

All further results are based on data from the 57 "maintenance-eligible" subjects only.

Table 5.1 summarizes the pretreatment subject characteristics. One-way analyses of variance of the continous variables and chi-square analyses of the nominal variables revealed no significant group differences with the exception of subject age ($F(2, 54) = 3.34$; $p < .05$). Post hoc Tukey comparisons revealed that COM subjects were older than CPM subjects ($p < .05$).

Table 5.1.
Pretreatment Characteristics of Maintenance-Eligible Subjects

	Maintenance Condition		
Variable	COM	CPM	NMC
n	20	18	19
Age	33.35	28.56	31.73 *
Male/Female	8/12	7/11	10/9
Years of schooling	15.45	15.28	14.74
Estimated cigarettes per day	29.55	24.22	27.89
Baseline cigarettes per day	24.35	20.74	26.29
Pretreatment COa	30.50	30.39	31.67
Years smoking	15.15	11.19	13.95
Maximum cigarettes regularly smoked per day	38.50	34.50	35.79
Motivation (0–100 scale)	78.00	74.17	80.00
Estimated quitting difficulty (0–100 scale)	73.25	71.39	67.89
Past serious quit attempts (in last 5 years)	4.00	3.44	1.95
Length of last abstinence (days)	35.95	43.61	58.32
Unpleasantness of previous withdrawal (0–100)	62.75	69.11	55.29
Pretreatment confidence (1–5 scale)	3.75	3.36	4.00
Self-Control Scale	29.50	21.94	17.75
Depression Proneness Inventory	30.00	34.12	32.85
Pretreatment Confidence Questionnaire	43.52	46.08	48.15
Percent Ss with Drug Abuse History	15.00	38.88	15.79
Percent Ss with Psychiatric Treatment History	45.00	72.22	63.16
Percent Ss married or cohabitating	35.00	16.67	36.84

Note: COM = counseling only maintenance; CPM = counseling plus puffing maintenance; NMC = nonmaintenance control; * $p < .05$.

Source: Compiled by the authors.

Cessation Treatment

No significant differences across the three experimental conditions were found for any of the variables collected during the cessation treatment per se. Collapsing across groups and sessions, subjects rapid smoked an average of 15.4 minutes per session, consumed 4.0 cigarettes, and produced a mean postsmoking COa level of 34.9. Rapid smoking aversion ratings were averaged over the six treatment sessions. There were no significant differences across conditions for any of the eight symptoms on the Smoking Aversion Questionnaire.

Summing over the ten-day cessation treatment period (not including day one), subjects smoked an average of 0.16 cigarettes outside of treatment. Ratings made after the cessation treatment showed no group differences on the five-point scale of perceived treatment effectiveness, with a mean rating of 4.44.

Profile of Mood States

POMS data were reduced to means of four time intervals: POMS gathered pretreatment, cessation treatment meetings one to three, meetings four to six, and short-term posttreatment (the three-week period comprising both posttreatment assessments and the two-week maintenance meeting, if applicable). POMS scales include tension-anxiety, depression-dejection, anger-hostility, vigor, fatigue, and confusion-bewilderment. Data were analyzed using separate mixed design analyses of variance for each scale, with experimental condition as the between factor and time-point as the repeated factor. No significant differences between conditions or interactions were found on any of the scales. Table 5.2 shows the change in scores over time for the six scales. Every scale showed significant change over time (all F's(3, 150) > 5.00; p's < .005). Mood states were most negative during the first three days of treatment, probably reflecting the effects of withdrawal, and then improved through short-term posttreatment.

Withdrawal Rating Forms

These data were reduced to means of four time intervals: pretreatment (when subjects reduced their smoking rate by half), days one to four of cessation, days five to seven, and days eight to ten. Again, a mixed design analysis of variance was used to analyze the data. No differences across experimental conditions were found on any of the eight scales. Table 5.3 lists the means of the eight scales over the four time intervals. Significant changes over time were found on the scales of craving, lack of confidence, psychological discomfort, depression, physical symptoms, and appetite.

Table 5.2
Profile of Mood States Scores over Time

	Assessment Period			
Scale	T1	T2	T3	T4
Tension-Anxiety	9.0	13.2	9.5	6.2 ***
Depression-Dejection	5.6	8.7	6.7	4.7 ***
Anger-Hostility	5.2	10.1	7.7	4.2 ***
Vigor	16.1	11.2	13.7	14.6 ***
Fatigue	5.9	7.5	6.1	5.2 **
Confusion-Bewilderment	5.9	9.2	7.1	5.2 ***

Note: T1 = pretreatment; T2 = cessation treatment meetings 1, 2, and 3; T3 = cessation treatment meetings 4, 5, and 6; T4 = weeks 1 through 3 posttreatment; ** $p < .005$; *** $p < .0001$.
Source: Compiled by the authors.

Table 5.3.
Withdrawal Rating Form Scores over Time

	Assessment Period			
Scale	T1	T2	T3	T4
Craving	4.75	4.88	4.33	4.16 ***
Lack of Confidence	3.18	2.73	2.56	2.46 ***
Psychological Discomfort	4.05	4.47	4.15	4.01 **
Depression	2.96	3.45	3.47	3.21 **
Sedation	4.72	4.57	4.68	4.69
Physical Symptoms	2.47	2.80	2.67	2.57 *
Appetite	3.87	3.99	4.11	4.11 *
Cognitive Distortions	1.76	1.64	1.68	1.60

Note: Scales range from 1 (no symptoms) to 7 (severe symptoms). T1 = 1 and 2 days pretreatment; T2 = cessation days 1, 2, 3, and 4; T3 = cessation days 5, 6, and 7; T4 = cessation days 8, 9, and 10; * $p < .05$; ** $p < .001$; *** $p < .0001$.
Source: Compiled by the authors.

Whereas confidence increased from pretreatment on, the other scales indicated that withdrawal symptoms peaked during the first four days of treatment and decreased thereafter.

Maintenance Session Compliance

Subject attendance in the two maintenance conditions was comparable. Of the four maintenance meetings, COM subjects attended a mean of 3.25 meetings, and CPM subjects attended a mean of 3.39. Eight of the 18 CPM subjects refused to rapid puff on at least one occasion, and several others expressed reluctance to puff. Five of the CPM subjects did not attend the final maintenance meeting, but one came in individually, to complete the questionnaires and give a breath sample for COa analysis. Six COM subjects also missed the last meeting, but two of these came in individually. Only two NMC subjects missed their 12-week meeting. Subjects did not self-monitor urges and coping responses in their exsmoker diaries.

Follow-Up

Over the first twelve months of follow-up, subjects were contacted a mean of 7.77 times, with 4.88 collateral contacts. In two cases collaterals' reports of smoking contradicted subjects' self-reports of abstinence. For data analyses these subjects were recorded as smoking. In every case COa analyses at the 12-week meeting supported subjects' self-reported abstinence status (ten parts per million [ppm] was considered the cutoff between smoking and nonsmoking COa levels). All ten subjects who missed the 12-week meeting/assessment were smoking, according to their follow-up self-reports.

Six indexes of smoking status were analyzed: percentage of subjects abstinent per condition, percentage of pretreatment smoking, mean number of days abstinent during the follow-up period, mean number of days to first cigarette, mean number of days to daily smoking (defined as the first of at least three consecutive days of smoking), and mean lapse–relapse latency (defined as the difference between the previous two variables for subjects who had smoked). Subjects were considered abstinent at a given follow-up time point if they had not used any tobacco product during the seven days prior to and including the time point.

Table 5.4 summarizes the follow-up results. Means are also included for all 65 subjects who entered the program (i.e., the 2 who dropped out of treatment, and the 6 who failed to achieve abstinence during treatment, as well as for the 57 maintenance-eligible subjects). These values are provided to permit cross-study comparisons of treatment effectiveness.

The following orthogonal contrasts were tested: COM versus CPM, and then NMC versus COM and CPM. Comparisons performed for all

Table 5.4.
Outcome Measures Through 12 Months Posttreatment

Outcome Measures	All Subjects	Maintenance-Eligible Subjects			
		NMC	COM	CPM	COM +CPM
n	65	19	20	18	38
Ss Abstinent (%)					
At treatment completion	88	100	100	100	100
At 28 days (4 weeks)	69	74	85	78	82
At 56 days (8 weeks)	54	47	70	67	68
At 84 days (12 weeks)	51	37	65	67	66 *
At 120 days (4 months)	55	42	65	67	66 +
At 180 days (6 months)	40	37	50	44	47
At 360 days (12 months)	39	37	40	50	45
Percent of Pretreatment Smoking					
At 28 days	10.7	7.8	.3	5.2	2.6
At 56 days	17.4	16.9	3.9	15.3	9.3
At 84 days	27.8	33.6	14.4	22.0	18.0
At 120 days	32.6	44.2	17.4	27.3	22.1 *
At 180 days	45.1	52.8	25.6	50.5	37.4
At 360 days	50.4	57.4	36.7	47.8	42.0
Mean number of days abstinent					
At 28 days	23.7	24.7	27.5	25.4	26.5
At 56 days	44.3	43.5	51.0	49.7	50.4 +
At 84 days	61.8	57.9	72.7	70.1	71.4 *
At 120 days	83.4	75.9	98.7	95.1	97.0 +
At 180 days	114.8	103.6	135.4	130.7	133.2
At 360 days	193.9	170.4	222.2	223.8	223.0
Mean number of days to first cigarette at 360 days	133.7	108.2	171.5	175.9	173.6
Mean number of days to daily smoking at 360 days	185.8	174.7	228.3	199.7	214.8
Mean lapse-relapse latency at 360 days	72.1	84.2	87.5	38.9	65.2

Note: NMC = minimum contact control; COM = counseling only maintenance; CPM = counseling plus puffing maintenance. Daily smoking is defined as at least three consecutive days of smoking. Lapse-relapse latency is defined as the number of days between the first cigarette and daily smoking in subjects who smoked at least one cigarette during the follow-up period. * $p < .05$ comparing NMC against combined maintenance groups (COM + CPM); + $p < .10$.

Source: From Brandon, H. T.; D. C. Zelman; and T. B. Baker. Effects of maintenance sessions on smoking relapse: Delaying the inevitable. *Journal of Consulting and Clinical Psychology*, 1987, 55:780–82. Copyright 1987 by the American Psychological Association. Adapted by permission.

follow-up variables at each time point yielded no significant differences between COM and CPM conditions.

As seen in Table 5.4, maintenance subjects performed consistently better than nonmaintenance subjects at each timepoint, on each outcome variable. The differences only reached significance, however, at three and four months posttreatment. Figure 5.1 shows that the two maintenance conditions have virtually identical relapse curves but that during the first three months posttreatment the nonmaintenance condition had a much steeper relapse curve compared to the two maintenance conditions. By 12 weeks, 66% of the maintenance subjects were abstinent compared to only 37% of the nonmaintenance subjects ($\chi^2(1, N = 57) = 4.31; p < .05$).

By four months posttreatment, nonmaintenance subjects were smoking at 44.2% of their pretreatment rate, twice as much as were the maintenance subjects. An analysis of covariance, with pretreatment smoking rate as the covariate, proved this difference significant ($F(3, 53) = 2.97; p < .05$). At 12 weeks, maintenance subjects had been abstinent an average of 71.4 of the possible 84 days, while control subjects had spent only 57.9 days abstinent ($F(1, 55) = 4.24; p < .05$).

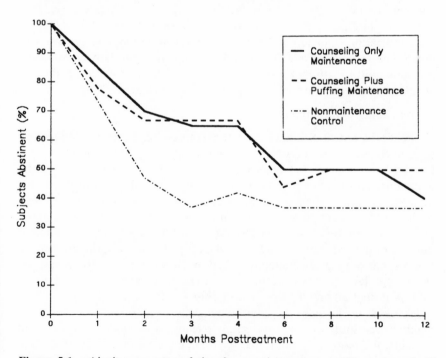

Figure 5.1. Abstinence rates of the three maintenance conditions through 12 months posttreatment. *Source*: Compiled by the authors.

No significant differences were found between conditions for the latency from treatment end to subjects' first cigarette, for the latency to daily smoking, or for the lapse–relapse latency.

Relationships Between Predictor and Outcome Variables

Three different outcome variables were examined as dependent measures. The first, number of days of abstinence during the first year posttreatment, utilized all 57 maintenance-eligible subjects. The other two variables relied on truncated subject pools. The number of days from the end of treatment to subjects' first cigarette was used for the 39 subjects who smoked during the first year. The number of days from the end of treatment to subjects' return to daily smoking was used for the 32 subjects who returned to daily smoking within the first year. Special attention was given to variables with different prediction patterns for the maintenance versus the nonmaintenance subjects.

Smoking History

The number of previous quitting attempts was related to number of days abstinent ($r(55) = .284; p < .05$), number of days to first cigarette ($r(37) = .691; p < .001$), and number of days to daily smoking ($r(30) = .422; p < .05$), indicating that numerous previous quitting attempts are related to greater cessation success. The length of abstinence following subjects' previous quitting attempt was inversely related to the number of days of abstinence in their current attempt ($r(55) = -.405; p < .01$).

Pretreatment Questionnaires

The Self-Control Schedule and the Depression Proneness Inventory were uncorrelated with outcome measures, although there was a tendency for DPI scores to be associated with earlier relapse among the nonmaintenance subjects only ($r(8) = -.498; p < .10$). From the Social Support for Nonsmoking questionnaire, two items were related to outcome of the entire subject pool. The percentage of the day subjects spent in the presence of smokers (the mean estimate was 39%) was inversely related to number of days abstinent ($r(52) = -.445; p < .001$). Also, the greater the control that subjects estimated they had over their work environment, the shorter the length of time before their first cigarette ($r(33) = -.423; p < .05$). A potentially interesting relationship was found between number of nonsmokers in the subjects' environment and days to daily smoking. For maintenance subjects, no significant correlation was obtained; for control subjects, the number of nonsmokers at home correlated .598 with days to daily smoking, whereas the number of nonsmokers at work correlated $-.710$ with the same dependent measure, a significant difference ($t(7) = 7.65; p < .001$).

Two demographic variables were related to outcome. Years of education was correlated with number of days abstinent ($r(55) = .366$; $p < .01$). Subjects with a psychiatric treatment history (i.e., those who had ever been treated by a mental health professional) tended to relapse earlier than subjects without such a history ($r(55) = -.270$; $p < .05$). Sixty percent of subjects had a history of psychiatric treatment. (Of these, 39% had entered therapy for depression, 29% for relationship problems, and 18% for drug or alcohol abuse. The mean length of therapy was 47 weeks.)

Withdrawal Measures

None of the POMS scales was related to outcome; however, several of the scores from the withdrawal rating form were. The greater the total withdrawal reported during the first week of treatment, the fewer the number of days of abstinence ($r(52) = -.322$; $p < .05$). The mean craving score during the entire treatment also was negatively correlated with days of abstinence ($r(52) = -.335$; $p < .05$). Unexpectedly, the mean depression score was positively correlated with days to first cigarette ($r(35) = .352$; $p < .05$).

Social Readjustment Questionnaire (SRQ)

There was no significant difference across experimental conditions on this measure of life stressors experienced during the first three months posttreatment. Out of a possible 41 stressors, subjects endorsed a mean of 4.44. The experience of life stressors was associated with an earlier return to daily smoking among the maintenance subjects ($r(14) = -.574$; $p < .05$) but not with the NMC subjects ($r(9) = .271$; ns). This difference is significant ($z = 2.073$; $p < .05$).

To test the notion that social support acts as a buffer for life stressors, the interaction between social support and stressors was examined for its contribution to outcome. Number of nonsmokers at home was taken as a measure of social support; score on the SRQ as the index of life stressors; and number of days to first cigarette as the dependent variable. The interaction was statistically significant ($sR^2 = .119$; $F(1,28) = 4.49$; $p < .05$). The form of the interaction was such that as stress level increased the protective effect of living with nonsmokers also increased. Further inspection of this interaction revealed that it was significant for only the maintenance subjects ($sR^2 = .223$; $F(1,15) = 5.22$; $p < .05$) and not the NMC subjects.

Confidence Questionnaires

Total self-efficacy scores were obtained by averaging the 0 to 100 ratings of confidence in the 44 separate smoking situations. No differences were found across experimental conditions. The mean score at pretreatment was 45.87 and at posttreatment, 82.38. Posttreatment scores predicted days to first cigarette ($r(37) = .352$; $p < .05$) and days to daily smoking ($r(30) = .390$; $p < .05$).

Experimental conditions did not differ on the single five-point rating of confidence taken posttreatment—the mean rating was 3.97. As was found by Erickson et al. (1983) and Tiffany, Martin, and Baker (1986), this rating was the single best predictor of outcome. It predicted number of days of abstinence ($r(51) = .474$; $p < .001$), days until first cigarette ($r(34) = .395$; $p < .05$), and days until daily smoking ($r(28) = .480$; $p < .01$). Across all three outcome measures, confidence ratings were more predictive of nonmaintenance subjects' success than of maintenance subjects'. The difference only reached significance, however, in the prediction of days to daily smoking: confidence was highly predictive for nonmaintenance subjects ($r(10) = .837$; $p < .001$), but not for maintenance subjects ($r(16) = .104$; ns.), a significant difference ($z = 2.625$; $p < .01$). Pretreatment confidence ratings were not predictive of outcome.

Regression Analyses

Multiple regression was used to assess the independent contributions to outcome of the various predictor variables. Number of days of abstinence was regressed on the variables discussed above that had produced significant zero-order correlations. A stepwise regression analysis showed that three variables accounted for 41% of the outcome variance: posttreatment global confidence rating ($sR^2 = .225$; $F(1,49) = 14.22$; $p < .001$); percent of day spent in the presence of smokers ($sR^2 = .133$; $F(1,48) = 9.93$; $p < .01$); and psychiatric treatment history ($sR^2 = .054$; $F(1,47) = 4.28$; $p < .05$).

As confidence ratings consistently appear to be powerful predictors of relapse across a number of studies (Condiotte and Lichtenstein 1981; Erickson et al. 1983; Tiffany, Martin, and Baker 1986), we attempted to identify the variables that influenced posttreatment confidence. Two variables significantly predicted confidence: magnitude of withdrawal reported during the first week of treatment ($r(49) = -.433$; $p < .005$) and pretreatment smoking rate ($r(51) = -.308$; $p < .05$). Multiple regression analysis revealed that the latter variable was redundant with the former. Since confidence questions contributed to the overall withdrawal scores, we recalculated withdrawal scores with confidence questions removed. This purer withdrawal measure remained significantly correlated with posttreatment confidence ratings ($r(49) = -.377$; $p < .01$). Posttreatment confidence continued to predict days of abstinence even after both pretreatment confidence and withdrawal variance were removed through partial correlations using multiple regression ($sR^2 = .149$; $F(1,47) = 9.36$; $p < .01$). This indicates that treatment-related variables other than withdrawal severity affect posttreatment confidence and, in turn, influence long-term outcome.

Finally, we examined the various subject variables for their ability to predict the interval between the first posttreatment cigarette and return to daily smoking (i.e., lapse–relapse latency). An analysis of covariance revealed that psychiatric treatment history was associated with a quicker return to daily smoking, with days to first cigarette as the covariate ($pr = -.424$; $F(1, 36) = 7.89$; $p < .01$).

DISCUSSION

The two maintenance conditions performed nearly identically on follow-up outcome measures. No effect was found from including rapid puffing trials in the maintenance sessions. This is consistent with previous findings concerning booster sessions (Best 1975; Elliott and Denney 1978; Lando 1982; Relinger et al. 1977). Apparently, restricting nicotine intake and administering the trials in an exposure treatment context did not alter the effectiveness of booster sessions. Subjects' dissatisfaction with the rapid puffing maintenance procedure is an additional argument against its use in the maintenance period.

Compared to the nonmaintenance control condition, maintenance sessions appeared to retard the relapse process, but only during the maintenance period. By 12 weeks posttreatment, maintenance subjects were almost twice as likely to be abstinent than were nonmaintenance subjects. Beyond three months, after maintenance meetings terminated, the outcome differences diminished. This is consistent with previous research. Of the few studies that have produced any positive maintenance effect, none has reported significant differences beyond 6 months posttreatment, and most have reported a loss of significant group differences by 6 or 12 months (Colletti and Supnick 1980; Lando 1976; Lando 1982).

Even though maintenance sessions only delayed and did not prevent relapse, it might aid the design of effective maintenance procedures if we could identify the constituents of maintenance treatments responsible for this temporary effect. Among the potential condidates are the provision of coping response training, exposure treatment, self-monitoring, social support afforded through therapist contact and group meetings, and the in-group verification of smoking status. The fact that subjects rarely self-monitored their urges or their coping responses suggests that formal self-monitoring was not responsible for any palliative effect of maintenance. Therapist contact per se is also probably not responsible for improved performance as continued therapist contact was not associated with improved performance in the majority of maintenance studies reviewed above. Moreover, although subjects receiving coping response training tend to do better than those who do not (Hall et al. 1984; Tiffany, Martin, and Baker 1986), there is little evidence in this study that extending coping response training into the posttreatment period yields superior outcomes. Presumably, if such training inculcated new skills, or higher skill levels, maintenance subjects would have continued to outperform controls after the maintenance period ended. Such are the findings when coping response training is added to cessation treatments (Hall et al. 1984; Tiffany, Martin, and Baker 1986). It may be that subjects achieved near maximal coping skill levels during the cessation treatment program.

Although maintenance treatments delayed relapse to smoking, there was little evidence that this was due to the provision of theoretically derived treatments (i.e., coping response or exposure training). Indeed, many subjects were unwilling to cooperate with major aspects of such treatments. For example, subjects who were abstinent and confident of their success found self-monitoring and exposure to be unnecessary and superfluous. Subjects who were having a more difficult time found any reminder of smoking to be tempting and disturbing. The principal motivation of most group members appeared to be social. This was very different from the cessation group meetings in which subjects were primarily interested in dealing with smoking urges.

Although it is impossible to identify unequivocally the prepotent features of the maintenance treatment, previous research and some of our predictor variables suggest that the social support provided by the group was important. First, few studies have fostered group cohesiveness to the degree that the present study did by retaining group membership from the cessation period into the maintenance period. It is noteworthy that Lando's poorest outcome occurred in his only maintenance study in which subjects were randomly reassigned to groups at each stage of the treatment (Lando 1978). Moreover, by explicitly manipulating social support and social pressure factors, Hamilton and Bornstein (1979) were able to increment follow-up abstinence rates. Etringer, Gregory, and Lando (1984) found that encouraging group cohesiveness during cessation led to enhanced abstinence rates during the maintenance period. Finally, subjects in the present study often stated during meetings or follow-up phone calls that one reason they did not smoke was they they knew that they would have to face their group later.

One seemingly anomalous finding of this research is that stressor incidence was related to outcome only among maintenance subjects. It seemed incongruous that maintenance sessions would render subjects more vulnerable to the deleterious effects of stress. Subjects reported the occurrence of stressors at the three-month postcessation meeting, and many nonmaintenance subjects relapsed in the first month after treatment. We believe that the lack of relationship between stress level and outcome in nonmaintenance subjects is due to the fact that many of the stressors they reported occurred after their relapse. There was a significant relationship between stress incidence and relapse among maintenance subjects because these subjects remained abstinent long enough to encounter significant stressors.

One reason for doing this study was to gain insight into ways that maintenance treatments influence relapse incidence and the relapse process. Our analysis of the relationship between stress level and outcome suggests that nonmaintenance subjects frequently relapsed in response to events that occurred relatively soon after cessation and that were not related to reported life stress events. We cannot conclusively identify the factors that led to faster relapse among NMC as opposed to maintenance subjects, but results show that subjects with low confidence were more likely to relapse quickly in the NMC condition. Also, there was a trend (p < .10) for psychiatric history and depression proneness to account for more variance in outcome among NMC subjects than among maintenance subjects. These relationships suggest that unconfident individuals who are prone to psychological disturbances are especially aided by maintenance sessions.

Our results also suggest an area to be targeted in future addiction maintenance research. About 33% of variance in return to daily smoking by maintenance subjects was accounted for by reported life stressor incidence. Therefore, while maintenance sessions were effective in helping subjects surmount short-term threats to their abstinence, such sessions did not innoculate subjects adequately against life stress events. A potential resource to be used in the development of stress innoculation treatments is extratherapeutic social support. Among maintenance subjects, stressor incidence was significantly less deleterious if subjects lived with a number of nonsmokers. Living with nonsmokers may benefit the exsmoker in several ways: the exsmoker is not likely to be exposed to other smokers and smoking cues at home; cigarettes are not readily available; the exsmoker may feel social pressure to remain abstinent; and the exsmoker may receive social support for remaining abstinent in times of stress.

If social support were indeed an important determinant of the effects of maintenance treatment, and if high levels of extratreatment social support helped maintenance subjects cope with stressors, it would augment other evidence of the interdependence of social and drug motivational systems. Naturally evolving addiction maintenance treatments (e.g., Alcoholics Anonymous) all emphasize the provision of continued social support as an important treatment element. Moreover, recent research suggests a direct link between social affiliation and drug use. Panksepp and his colleagues have shown that addictive drugs, such as morphine and nicotine, have in common the fact that both effectively quell social separation distress in animals (Panksepp, Siviy, and Normansell 1985). Panksepp, Siviy, and

Normansell present evidence that drugs opportunistically activate neural systems that are associated with the control of social affect. Perhaps social support is used by addicts as a motivational substitute for drug.

Two global measures that may reflect "personal resources" were predictive of outcome: education level and psychiatric treatment history. Psychiatric history was the only variable that predicted lapse–relapse latency. Some subjects may lack the ability to utilize the strategies learned during treatment or the social resources available to them. We originally decided to assess psychiatric history after observing that smoking clients who appeared to have psychiatric problems did more poorly in treatment. In the present study 60% of subjects had a history of psychiatric treatment. Although we did not collect this information in previous studies, we suspect that our treatment population has shifted over the years, and that a higher proportion of subjects in the present study had serious psychiatric histories. We believe that this may account for the somewhat poorer outcome in the present study compared to our previous studies using similar treatments (Erickson et al. 1983; Tiffany, Martin, and Baker 1986).

As found in the earlier studies, posttreatment confidence was the best predictor of long-term outcome. Confidence was related to overall withdrawal severity. This may in part reflect lower confidence and poorer outcome in the more dependent smoker; however, expectancies of self-efficacy may itself be an individual difference variable that mediates response to treatment and is open to manipulation (Bandura 1977). If the discomfort of nicotine withdrawal discourages subjects, treatments that ameliorate withdrawal—such as nicotine gum (Schneider, Jarvik, and Forsythe 1984) and, to some extent, rapid smoking (Erickson et al. 1983)—may succeed in part by improving subjects' sense of self-efficacy. That severity of withdrawal symptoms and craving during treatment was related to successful long-term outcome extends Gunn's (1986) finding of the same relationship with short-term outcome.

An unexpected finding was the negative correlation between degree of control over one's work environment and number of days to first cigarette. We had predicted that subjects who were able to structure their work environment so as to minimize exposure to smoking cues would fare better than those who were unable to do so. In the light of the results, however, it appears that subjects who had the "freedom" to smoke at work were likely to avail themselves of that opportunity. Along with data revealing that most subjects deliberately acquire their first posttreatment cigarette (Brandon, Tiffany, and Baker 1986), a picture is developing of relapse as more of an active, purposeful behavior than had been previously thought.

Finally, this study lent support for a new dependent measure of smoking treatment outcome—number of days from treatment end to onset of daily smoking. Despite the truncated sample size associated with this measure, it was significantly correlated with subject variables more often than any other outcome measure used. More importantly, it appears to represent variance in outcome that is unique from that embraced by the traditional outcome variables. It is a meaningful measure given Marlatt's (1982) distinction between a "lapse" and "relapse." The motivational processes that lead to additional smoking after the first lapse may be different from the processes that led to the initial lapse. The first cigarette may initiate the "Abstinence Violation Effect" (Marlatt and Gordon 1980) or "prime" the smoker for future drug use (Stewart, de Wit, and Eikelboom 1984). Given that over 90% of smokers who lapse eventually relapse (Brandon et al. in press), a focus on relapse *survival* as an intervention would appear warranted.

ACKNOWLEDGMENT

The authors thank Bob Hodes, Eric Howland, Dave Kosson, Julie McGivern, Sharon Nichols, Jack Sherman, and Mike Zinser, for serving as cotherapists. We thank Karen Obremski, Tim Sielaff, and Steve Sutton for assisting in data collection.

REFERENCES

Abramson, L. Y., and G. I. Metalsky. (1983). The depression proneness inventory. Unpublished manuscript, University of Wisconsin, Madison.

Baker, T. B.; J. E. Sherman; and E. Morse. (1987). The urge as affect. In *The Nebraska Symposium on Motivation: Alcohol use and abuse*, ed. C. Rivers. Lincoln: University of Nebraska Press.

Bandura, A. (1977). Self-efficacy: Toward a unifying hypothesis. *Psychological Review*, 84:191–215.

Bernstein, D. A. (1970). The modification of smoking behavior: A search for effective variables. *Behaviour Research and Therapy*, 8:133–46.

Best, A. J. (1975). Tailoring smoking withdrawal procedures to personality and motivational differences. *Journal of Consulting and Clinical Psychology*, 43:1–8.

Billings, A. G., and R. H. Moos. (1983). Social-environmental factors among light and heavy cigarette smokers: A controlled comparison with nonsmokers. *Addictive Behaviors*, 8:381–91.

Blakey, R., and R. Baker. (1980). An exposure approach to alcohol abuse. *Behavior Research and Therapy*, 18:319–25.

Brandon, T. H.; S. T. Tiffany; and T. B. Baker. (1986). The process of smoking relapse. In *Relapse and recovery in drug abuse*, eds. F. Tims and C. Leukfeld. National Institute of Drug Abuse Research Monograph. Washington, D.C.: U.S. Government Printing Office.

Chaney, E. F.; M. R. O'Leary; and G. A. Marlatt. (1978). Skill training with alcoholics. *Journal of Consulting and Clinical Psychology* 46:1092–1104.

Chaney, E. F.; D. K. Roszell; and C. Cummings. (1982). Relapse in opiate addicts: A behavioral analysis. *Addictive Behaviors*, 7:291–97.

Cobb, S. (1976). Social support as a moderator of life stress. *Psychosomatic Medicine,* 38:300–14.

Cohen, S., and H. M. Hoberman. (1983). Positive events and social supports as buffers of life change stress. *Journal of Applied Social Psychology,* 13:99–125.

Colletti, G., and S. A. Kopel. (1979). Maintaining behavior change: An investigation of three maintenance strategies and the relationship of self-attribution to the long-term reduction of cigarette smoking. *Journal of Consulting and Clinical Psychology,* 47:614–17.

Colletti, G., and L. Stern. (1980). Two-year follow-up of a nonaversive treatment for cigarette smoking. *Journal of Consulting and Clinical Psychology,* 48:292–93.

Colletti, G., and J. A. Supnick. (1980). Continued therapist contact as a maintenance strategy for smoking reduction. *Journal of Consulting and Clinical Psychology,* 49:665–67.

Condiotte, M. M., and E. Lichtenstein. (1981). Self-efficacy and relapse in smoking cessation programs. *Journal of Consulting and Clinical Psychology,* 49:648–58.

Coppotelli, H. C., and C. T. Orleans. (1985). Partner support and other determinants of smoking cessation maintenance among women. *Journal of Consulting and Clinical Psychology,* 53:455–60.

Danaher, B. G. (1977). Research on rapid smoking: Interim summary and recommendations. *Addictive Behaviors,* 2:151–66.

Dean, A. and N. Lin. (1977). The stress-buffering role of social support. *The Journal of Nervous and Mental Disease,* 165:403–17.

Elliott, C. H., and D. R. Denney. (1978). A multiple-component treatment approach to smoking reduction. *Journal of Consulting and Clinical Psychology,* 46:1330–39.

Erickson, L. M.; S. T. Tiffany; E. M. Martin; and T. B. Baker (1983). Aversive smoking therapies: A conditioning analysis of therapeutic effectiveness. *Behavior Research and Therapy,* 21:595–611.

Etringer, B. D.; V. R. Gregory; and H. A. Lando. (1984). Influence of group cohesion on the behavioral treatment of smoking. *Journal of Consulting and Clinical Psychology,* 52:1080–86.

Glasgow, R. E.; R. C. Klesges; J. S. Mizes; and T. F. Pechacek. (1985). Quitting smoking: Strategies used and variables associated with success in a stop-smoking contest. *Journal of Consulting and Clinical Psychology,* 53:905–12.

Gunn, R. C. (1983). Smoking clinic failures and recent life stress. *Addictive Behaviors,* 8:83–87.

Gunn, R. C. (1986). Reactions to withdrawal symptoms and success in smoking cessation clinics. *Addictive Behaviors,* 11:49–53.

Hall, S. M.; J. Bachman; J. B. Henderson; R. Barstow; and R. T. Jones. (1983). Smoking cessation in patients with cardiopulmonary disease: An initial study. *Addictive Behaviors,* 8:33–42.

Hall, S. M.; D. Rugg; C. Tunstall; and R. T. Jones. (1984). Preventing relapse to cigarette smoking by behavioral skill training. *Journal of Consulting and Clinical Psychology,* 52:372–82.

Hamilton, S. B., and P. H. Bornstein. (1979). Broad-spectrum behavioral approach to smoking cessation: Effects of social support and paraprofessional training on the maintenance of treatment effects. *Journal of Consulting and Clinical Psychology*, 47:598–600.

Hodgson, R. J., and H. J. Rankin. (1976). Modification of excessive drinking by cue exposure. *Behaviour Research and Therapy*, 14:305–07.

Holmes, T. H., and R. H. Rahe. (1967). The Social Readjustment Rating Scale. *Journal of Psychosomatic Research*, 11:213–18.

Horwitz, M. B.; M. Hindi-Alexander; and T. J. Wagner. (1985). Psychosocial mediators of abstinence, relapse, and continued smoking: A one-year follow-up of a minimal intervention. *Addictive Behaviors*, 10:29–39.

Hunt, W. A., and D. A. Bespalec. (1974). An evaluation of current methods of modifying smoking behavior. *Journal of Clinical Psychology*, 30:431–38.

Jones, S. L., and R. I. Lanyon. (1981). Relationship between adaptive skills and outcome of alcoholism treatment. *Journal of Studies on Alcohol*, 42:521–25.

Karol, R. L., and C. S. Richards. (1981). Cognitive maintenance strategies for smoking reduction. *JSAS Catalog of Selected Documents in Psychology*, 11:15 (Ms. No. 2204).

Katz, R. C., and N. Singh. (1986). A comparison of current smokers and self-cured quitters on Rosenbaum's Self Control Schedule. *Addictive Behaviors*, 11:63–65.

Kirschenbaum, D. S., and A. J. Tomarken. (1982). On facing the generalization problem: The study of self-regulatory failure. In *Advances in cognitive-behavioral research and therapy*, vol. 1, ed. P. C. Kendell, pp. 119–200. New York: Academic Press.

Lando, H. A. (1976). Aversive conditioning and contingency management in the treatment of smoking. *Journal of Consulting and Clinical Psychology*, 44:312.

Lando, H. A. (1977). Successful treatment of smokers with a broad-spectrum behavioral approach. *Journal of Consulting and Clinical Psychology* 45:361–66.

Lando, H. A. (1978). Stimulus control, rapid smoking, and contractual management in the maintenance of nonsmoking. *Behavior Therapy*, 9:962–63.

Lando, H. A. (1981). Effects of preparation, experimenter contact, and a maintained reduction alternative on a broad-spectrum program for eliminating smoking. *Addictive Behaviors*, 6:123–33.

Lando, H. A. (1982). A factorial analysis of preparation, aversion, and maintenance in the elimination of smoking. *Addictive Behaviors*, 7:143–54.

Lando, H. A., and J. A. McCullough. (1978). Clinical application of a broad-spectrum behavioral approach to chronic smokers. *Journal of Consulting and Clinical Psychology*, 46:1583–85.

Lando, H. A., and P. G. McGovern. (1982). Three-year data on behavioral treatment for smoking: A follow-up note. *Addictive Behaviors*, 7:177–81.

Lichtenstein, E.; D. O. Antonuccio; and G. Rainwater. (1977). Unkicking the habit: The resumption of cigarette smoking. Paper presented at the meeting of the Western Psychological Association, April, 1977. Seattle, Wash.

Ludwig, A. M.; A. Wikler; and L. H. Stark. (1974). The first drink:

Psychobiological aspects of craving. *Archives of General Psychiatry*, 30:539–47.

Marlatt, G. A. (1982). Relapse prevention: A self-control program for the treatment of addictive behaviors. In *Adherence, compliance, and generalization in behavioral medicine*, ed. R. B. Stuart, pp. 329–78. New York: Brunner/Mazel.

Marlatt, G. A., and J. R. Gordon. (1980). Determinants of relapse: Implications for the maintenance of behavior change. In *Behavioral medicine: Changing health lifestyle*, eds. P. O. Davidson and S. M. Davidson, pp. 410–52. New York: Brunner/Mazel.

McNair, D. M.; M. Lorr; and L. F. Droppleman. (1971). *Manual for the profile of mood states*. San Diego: Educational and Industrial Testing Service.

Mermelstein, R.; S. Cohen; and E. Lichtenstein. (1983). Psychosocial stress, social support, and smoking cessation and maintenance. Paper presented at the meeting of the American Psychological Association, August, 1983, Anaheim, Calif.

Mermelstein, R.; E. Lichtenstein; and K. McIntyre. (1983). Partner support and relapse in smoking-cessation programs. *Journal of Consulting and Clinical Psychology*, 51:465–66.

O'Brien, C. P. (1976). Experimental analysis of conditioning factors in human narcotic addiction. *Pharmacological Reviews*, 27:533–43.

O'Brien, C. P., and L. K. Y. Ng. (1979). Innovative treatments for drug addiction. In *Handbook on drug abuse*, eds. R. I. Dupont, A. Goldstein, and J. O'Donnell, pp. 193–201. Washington, D.C.: U.S. Government Printing Office.

Panksepp, J.; S. M. Siviy; and L. A. Normansell. (1985). Brain opioids and social emotions. In *The psychobiology of attachment and separation*, eds. M. Reite and T. Field, pp. 3–49. New York: Academic Press.

Poulos, C. X.; R. E. Hinson; and S. Siegel. (1981). The role of Pavlovian processes in drug tolerance and dependence: Implications for treatment. *Addictive Behaviors*, 6:205–11.

Raw, M., and M. A. H. Russell. (1980). Rapid smoking, cue exposure, and support in the modification of smoking. *Behaviour Research and Therapy*, 18:363–72.

Relinger, H.; P. H. Bornstein; I. D. Bugge; T. P. Carmody; and C. J. Zohn. (1977). Utilization of adverse rapid smoking in groups: Efficacy of treatment and maintenance procedures. *Journal of Consulting and Clinical Psychology*, 45:245–49.

Rosenbaum, M. (1980). A schedule for assessing self-control behaviors: Preliminary findings. *Behavior Therapy*, 11:109–21.

Schmahl, D. P.; E. Lichtenstein; and D. E. Harris. (1972). Successful treatment of habitual smokers with warm, smoky, air and rapid smoking. *Journal of Consulting and Clinical Psychology*, 38:105–11.

Schneider, N. G.; M. E. Jarvik; and A. B. Forsythe. (1984). Nicotine vs. placebo gum in the alleviation of withdrawal during smoking cessation. *Addictive Behaviors*, 9:149–56.

Shiffman, S. (1982). Relapse following smoking cessation: A situational analysis. *Journal of Consulting and Clinical Psychology*, 50:71–86.

Shiffman, S. (1984). Coping with temptations to smoke. *Journal of Consulting and Clinical Psychology*, 52:261–67.

Shiffman, S. M., and M. E. Jarvik. (1976). Smoking withdrawal symptoms in two weeks of abstinence. *Psychopharmacology*, 50:35–39.

Shipley, R. H. (1981). Maintenance of smoking cessation: Effect of follow-up letters, smoking motivation, muscle tension, and health locus of control. *Journal of Consulting and Clinical Psychology*, 49:982–84.

Siegel, S. (1983). Classical conditioning, drug tolerance, and drug dependence. In *Research advances in alcohol and drug problems*, vol. 7, eds. R. G. Smart, F. B. Glaser, Y. Israel, H. Kalant, R. E. Popham, and W. Schmidt, pp. 207–46. New York: Plenum.

Stewart, J.; H. de Wit; and R. Eikelboom. (1984). Role of unconditioned and conditioned drug effects in the self-administration of opiates and stimulants. *Psychological Review*, 91:251–68.

Tabachnik, N.; L. B. Alloy; D. Romer; and J. Crocker. (1988). Predicting depressive reactions in the classroom: A test of a cognitive diathesis-stress theory of depression using causal modeling techniques. Manuscript submitted for publication.

Tiffany, S. T.; E. M. Martin; and T. B. Baker. (1986). Treatments for cigarette smoking: An evaluation of the contributions of aversion and counseling procedures. *Behaviour Research and Therapy*, 24:437–52.

6

DEVELOPMENT AND DIFFUSION OF A SKILLS-TRAINING INTERVENTION

Sharon M. Hall, James L. Sorensen, and Peter C. Loeb

Treatment of heroin addiction must be multifocal. Removing the physical addiction is important. However, even proponents of biomedical models of addiction agree that psychosocial rehabilitation is a major task. Rehabilitation strategies may include psychotherapy (Woody et al. 1983), family therapy (Stanton, Todd, and Associates 1982), or training in specific coping skills.

Among the most important sets of skills are those that are concerned with finding and keeping a job. Heroin addiction can be a full-time career for many users (Preble and Casey 1969; Rubington 1967). Giving up opiates means loss of a daily schedule of activities, of friends, and of a certain status. Unless another career replaces the addict career, the void that is left may encourage relapse. It is not surprising that for drug treatment clients paid employment is seen as a milestone in rehabilitation (Brown, Dupont, and Glendinning 1972; Gearing 1972) and is a replicable correlate of continued abstinence (e.g., Balsam et al. 1973), whether employment is in the private sector or through a supported work program (Manpower Demonstration Research Corporation 1980).

Preparation of this manuscript and the research described in it were funded in part by Grants Number 5 K02 00065, IH8 DA01978, and 1 R81 DA03058, from the National Institute on Drug Abuse.

Despite the positive relationship between employment and treatment success, there has not been much work on the development of methods for increasing career success in drug treatment clients. Little work has been reported on methods to increase career placement in any population. The exception to this is the work of Azrin and his colleagues (Jones and Azrin 1973; Azrin, Flores, and Kaplan 1975), who developed a comprehensive job-finding program that emphasized group support, role playing, resume writing, increased family support, and telephone contacts. In a sample recruited from several sources, Azrin, Flores, and Kaplan reported a 92% employment rate at three months for participants in the intervention, as compared to 60% for controls.

This chapter describes the development of the Job Seeker's Workshop, a behaviorally based skill-training program designed to help ex-heroin addicts to improve their job-interviewing and job-finding skills. Following this overview, we describe the three clinical trials that evaluated the workshop, and the evolution of the intervention throughout those trials. Two of the trials were with methadone maintenance clients. The third was with probationers and parolees who had heroin abuse histories. Differences in methods to suit these different samples and changes that came about because of experience are described. The next section describes the way in which we disseminated the workshop to drug treatment programs and an experiment designed to test different strategies of dissemination. A final section describes the content of the workshop in detail so that others who would like to replicate our work or use the workshop clinically can do so.

Altogether, the Job Seeker's Workshop is an example of how behavioral skill training can be used in treatment programs for addictive disorders and how such an intervention can be developed, tested, cross-validated, and disseminated to the treatment community.

The workshop was developed from a straightforward behavioral rehearsal model. It was based on the premise that all other things being equal, the best presentation of history, skills, and self would increase the chances of employment. We further assumed that presentation would be improved by accurate information about job interviewers' perception of interviewees and practice in "good" interview behaviors. Videotape feedback supplemented guided interview practice. We also assumed that preparation before an interview was essential and that this preparation could best be accomplished by guiding clients to take small steps toward the goal and by reinforcing these steps.

The activities included in the workshop came from our observations of the problem characteristics drug treatment clients showed in interview situations, as well as in their general job-seeking strategies. These included (1) *poor work histories*, especially few jobs or many short-lived jobs, long gaps in work history, or repeated firings; (2) *criminal records*; (3) *lack of knowledge about effective behaviors in an interview situation*, including ineffective, masochistic honesty or poorly formulated lies, use of addict slang, distracting mannerisms, or inappropriate dress; and (4) *lack of knowledge of informal job-seeking resources*, such as telephone books and friends.

In its final form the workshop had three major components. Most of the time in the workshop was spent on the first component—job interview training. This included first becoming desensitized to seeing oneself on videotape. Early taped interviews included practice in desirable entrance and exit behaviors, and feedback about distracting behaviors or expressions. A positive presentation of self was gradually shaped. Much of the behavior change came about when participants observed themselves on videotape. Leaders and other participants also provided verbal feedback about the interview. The difficulty level of the interview was gradually increased. Difficulty was defined by the number of questions directed at the clients' weak spots, the attitude of the interviewer, and the length and thoroughness of the interview. The second component was completion of job application forms. Preparing crucial personal information, such as social security numbers and license numbers, was taught, as well as how to describe difficult parts of one's history, such as drug use and arrests. Clients also learned how to emphasize positive aspects of job history briefly, in forms appropriate for application materials. The third component of the program was learning job-search procedures. This included setting up informal networks within workshops to share job leads, learning how to use friends and relatives as resources, and how to use resources in the environment, such as the job interviewer, the telephone, telephone books, and the newspaper to find job leads.

EVALUATIONS OF THE JOB SEEKER'S WORKSHOP

Pilot Study

The first project (Hall et al. 1977) had three specific aims: (1) to determine whether the workshop would be attractive to drug treatment clients; (2) to test the hypothesis that subjects receiving the workshop would be superior to controls on ratings of employability or training acceptability; and (3) to test the hypothesis that subjects receiving the workshop would be more likely than controls to find vocational placement.

The study included methadone maintenance treatment subjects from four methadone clinics run by the City of San Francisco. Subjects participated for two reasons: 34 subjects were seeking jobs, and another 15 were interested in participating in a competitive skill-training program. A competitive skill-training program was a publicly supported work or training program that demanded an application procedure and an admission interview and only accepted a certain percentage of applicants.

Most of the subjects (57%) were Caucasian, 27% were black, and 16% were of Hispanic descent; 34 subjects were men, and 15 were women. The mean number of months in treatment at the current treatment clinic was slightly under 11. Subjects were in their early thirties or late twenties. About half had completed high school.

Subjects were randomly assigned to receive the Job Seeker's Workshop or to a minimal contact control condition. Both experimental and control subjects attended a first meeting during which the director of vocational rehabilitation services for the four clinics gave all subjects information about training programs and resources open to them. The director explained the assessment interview and told subjects of their condition assignment. Control subjects were dismissed at that point. They were scheduled for an assessment interview to occur at the same time as the experimental subjects.

An afternoon session outlined the format of the workshop. At this point, the content of the workshop included a discussion of vocational aspirations followed by a brief relaxation training session. Subjects then role played short segments of a job interview and the final component of the interview. At the end of the second day, subjects discussed difficulties involving completing job application forms. Subjects received a form to complete before the next session. They also formulated a next step in the placement process, which they were to have completed in the free day that followed. Following the free day, subjects met for a half-day session. They discussed the difficulties encountered and ways of handling these difficulties. The remainder of the session concerned written application forms.

The rest of the workshop practiced the complete interviews. Subjects role played interviews in progressively more difficult situations. The interviewer acted cold, hostile, or distracted. Subjects also took the interviewer role with other subjects and proved to be difficult interviewers, indeed, usually by drawing from their own experiences. A detailed description of the conduct of a workshop is described later in the chapter.

Five two-week workshops were held over a six-month period with three to six individuals participating in each workshop. During each week of the workshop, subjects met on two days for about five hours and one for three hours.

At the end of the workshop, all subjects participated in a simulated interview. A single interviewer, blind to experimental condition, rated subjects on a global scale tapping employability/acceptability as a trainee. Three months after the end of the assessment interview, project staff reached subjects, asking them to indicate whether they had found a job, the date of the placement, and the number of job interviews attended since the end of the workshop. Project staff verified the place of employment and date of placement by checking with subjects' counselors.

The results from this first study were promising. Only four of the experimental subjects dropped out of the workshop. This attrition rate indicated that the workshop seemed attractive to clients. Participation in the experimental condition resulted in significant increases in ratings by interviewers and in vocational placement. Subjects who participated in the workshop were rated superior to controls on both interview performance and written applications. Of greater importance, at follow-up, 50% of the experimental subjects had been placed in a job, as compared with 14% of the controls.

Later Trials of the Job Seeker's Workshop

This study led to two companion studies, both of which examined the effect of the Job Seeker's Workshop on job finding.

Criminal Justice Cross-Validation

This study tested a revised version of the Job Seeker's Workshop with ex-heroin addicts drawn from the criminal justice system (Hall et al. 1981b). Subjects were 55 parolees or probationers who had documented histories of heroin abuse. They were referred to the project from either county probation officers or state parole officers. Again, we ruled out only subjects who were psychotic, illiterate, or who anticipated serving jail time within three months. Most of the subjects (62%) were black. Most of the rest (34% of the total sample) were Caucasian. Most participants were in their mid-thirties. About half had high school diplomas. There was a greater proportion of men than in our previous study (85%), but as in our first study, about one half had completed high school. Many subjects had spent significant amounts of time within the last five years in jail or the penitentiary.

Once again, a treatment/no-treatment design tested the effectiveness of the workshop. Treatment content was streamlined to the three components of job-interview training, instruction in completion of application forms, and job-search procedures. The amount of time spent on job-interview training and on completion of application forms was increased. The job-search procedures were modeled after the work of Azrin and his colleagues (Azrin, Flores, and Kaplan 1975; Azrin and Philips 1979). They included sharing of job leads and learning how to obtain them from friends, relatives, job interviewers, newspapers, and telephone books. Subjects also practiced making telephone calls, with coaching and suggestions by the leaders.

This study, and the next, eliminated the free day activity and relaxation training. The free day activity was omitted because subjects in the first study failed to follow through with these activities, viewing them as unimportant make work tasks. Relaxation training was omitted because anxiety was not a problem for most subjects. For those for whom it was a problem, knowledge of interviewing skills seemed to be more potent in reducing anxiety than relaxation training. A more sophisticated assessment device, a factor-based instrument called the Interview Rating Survey (IRS), was used. It included two scales, the first of which might best be characterized as a general, primarily verbal competency factor. The second scale taped specific nonverbal behaviors.

At a mock assessment interview, subjects were rated on this scale by interviewers who were blind to treatment conditions and blind to the content of the experimental intervention. Interviewers were volunteers from the personnel departments of large corporations or were employed in vocational rehabilitation positions in local agencies. Following treatment, the project contacted subjects once a month for three months to obtain information about the day of their hiring and the amount earned. Again, we verified employment whenever possible. At the end of three months, 86% of the experimental subjects had found employment as compared to 54% of the controls. The statistically significant difference between the conditions appeared as early as one week posttreatment and remained significant throughout the three-month period.

Besides having higher placement rates, the experimental subjects differed significantly from the controls on the IRS scale measuring specific, nonverbal behaviors.

We were surprised at the high general rate of employment in both experimental and control conditions in this study. We had selected this population for replication because we thought they would provide a stringent test of the effectiveness of the intervention, since subjects had both recent prison histories *and* a history of heroin abuse. Several factors may explain the reason for the differences between this condition and the methadone sample, including prevailing employment rates, differences in leaders, and differences in subjects' abilities and degree of addiction. A final hypothesis is that these differences were the results of a potent contingency. Many of these subjects faced a return to prison if they did not find jobs rapidly.

Methadone Maintenance Replication

In the final study, we returned to methadone maintenance clinics. The sample was similar to that in the first methadone maintenance sample. Using a random assignment, no treatment control design, 60 job-seeking methadone maintenance clients received either the Job Seeker's Workshop or were assigned to an information-only condition. In this study, the workshop occurred over four days, with the assessment interview on the final fifth day. However, the content was the same as that used with the criminal justice sample. A comparison for all experimental subjects with controls indicated differences that narrowly failed to reach conventional levels of statistical significance, although they were in the expected direction. Of the experimental subjects, 52% were employed, as compared with 30% of the controls. Four experimental subjects left immediately following the information presentation and therefore never received the experimental treatment. If they are excluded, along with their matched controls, the employment differences reach statistical significance. In interview behaviors, as rated by blind interviewers, we found that participation in the workshop increased scores on the general competency scale of the IRS but not on the specific behavior scale.

DISSEMINATION OF THE WORKSHOP

Although the three studies yielded an effective intervention for job seeking, diffusion throughout the treatment community was by no means automatic. In a final step we collaborated with Drs. Edward Glaser and Paul Greenberg of the Human Interaction Research Institute of Los Angeles (HIRI) to develop and test strategies for disseminating the Job Seeker's Workshop to drug treatment programs.

Early behavioral interventions were designed in part to provide "front line" staff, such as nurses and psychiatric technicians, with effective, simple tools for changing behavior. Despite this avowed goal, we could find no systematic studies on how to encourage use of these techniques in clinical settings.

The literature on disseminating new treatment techniques in general, and encouraging their use, is small. There have been few experimental evaluations of alternative diffusion methods of *any* intervention. Glaser et al. (1967) evaluated the efficacy of successive "increments of communication" to facilitate the spread of a sheltered workshop program for mentally retarded young adults. The increments of communication were (1) printed materials describing the innovative training program; (2) a subset of training programs at diverse institutions also sent representatives to a conference that included observation of the innovation; and (3) a subset of the programs whose representatives observed the innovation also received consultation at their home sites from a representative of the innovative program. Representatives from each group of workshops were interviewed to assess whether any features of the innovative program that they may have adopted were linked to the communications that they had received. The results indicated that facilities receiving the printed materials were more likely to report adopting innovations as a result of that intervention than were the controls who received no information from the "increments of communication" study but who could have learned about the successful program from published information or word of mouth.

Similarly, a smaller proportion of programs receiving just the printed materials adopted innovations than did those that received one or both of the additional communication increments. However, the findings are ambiguous because the facilities were not randomly assigned to the second and third increments of communication. An alternative interpretation of the findings is that those agencies that were more motivated to change were more likely to volunteer for the more extensive communication increments.

Larsen, Aruntunian, and Finley (1974) compared the effectiveness of (1) written materials; (2) visits by participants to other sites; and (3) consultant visits, in facilitating the diffusion of participant-selected innovations. Centers were randomly assigned to one of four conditions: (1) a no-information control; (2) printed materials only; (3) printed materials and expense-paid visits by center staff to other programs; and (4) printed materials, site visits, and consultant visit to participating centers. The criterion for evaluating the effectiveness of the different diffusion techniques was the number of innovations considered by each center. No significant differences were found. Information on which programs were implemented was not available.

Fairweather and colleagues (Fairweather, Sanders, and Tornatzky 1974; Fairweather 1980) conducted a series of experiments in an effort to disseminate a successful innovation, the Community Lodge society, to other mental hospitals. In the first study three diffusion techniques were evaluated: (1) written materials; (2) on-site workshops; and (3) demonstration wards. Hospitals were more likely to agree to accept the written materials or sponsor a workshop than they were to have a demonstration ward but were more likely to make a decision to adopt the lodge if they had agreed to establish the demonstration ward. Again, self-selection of hospitals to experimental conditions suggests caution in interpreting the findings.

In a second phase, programs that decided to adopt the lodge program were randomly assigned to receive either a written manual or three visits by a team of consultants. The results showed a significant difference favoring the consultant intervention. The outcome measure, however, was not adoption but "progress toward adoption" (e.g., ratings of accomplishment in such tasks as acquiring a facility and funding).

In a third phase of the study, the investigators examined the extent to which unplanned diffusion of the lodge to other programs took place. Unplanned adoption of lodges did not occur in any hospitals that had not already adopted the lodge.

Tornatzky et al. (1980) studied the effect of consultation alone with consultation plus organizational development activities as a means to facilitate adoption of the lodge. While hospitals in the two experimental conditions did not differ on a "degree of implementation index" at initial follow-up, those that received organizational development as part of consultation had greater change scores at later follow-ups.

Another experiment in this series was designed to determine whether receiving a newsletter about the lodge program would significantly affect the likelihood of adopting the program. The intent of the newsletter was to foster communication between innovators and those who might be interested in innovation. The results revealed no significant differences between hospitals that received the newsletter and a no-newsletter control group on a number of measures, including interest in implementing a lodge or in receiving consultations or workshops. In a final experiment adoption rates were compared for a one-day workshop condition and a condition that included the workshop plus site visit by a hospital staff member to a lodge. The results revealed no significant differences between the two experimental conditions. The site visit had little effect on adoption.

Fergus (1979) tested the effectiveness of telephone consultation to supplement workshops on milieu therapy for geriatric programs. Health organizations were randomly assigned to one of three conditions: no consultation, one person, or three persons receiving telephone consultation at the site. No significant differences among the three groups were found in "initiation of change" scores.

Stevens and Tornatzky (1980) used a two by two factorial design to study the adoption of program evaluation methodology in substance abuse agencies. The results indicated that on-site consultations produced more change than telephone consultations. Group consultations were more effective than private consultations.

Of the studies reviewed, few confirmed their hypotheses or used actual adoption of the innovation as an outcome. Only one study (Stevens and Tornatzky 1980) employed random assignment to all treatment conditions and used adoption as an outcome measure. Despite the methodologic flaws, the converging evidence of these studies is that the most promising interventions for facilitating adoption involve face-to-face contact.

The research project to disseminate the Job Seeker's Workshop was designed in part to increase use of the workshop in drug treatment programs. It was also seen as a methodological advance, designed to move research in the dissemination area one step further. Programs were randomly assigned to intervention conditions. Adoption of the workshop, or adoption of elements of it, were used as the outcome measure. Degree of adoption, and its presence or absence, were confirmed by research staff.

Aims and Hypotheses

Our hypotheses were the following: (1) Drug treatment programs exposed to experimental diffusion techniques would be more likely to adopt the Job Seeker's Workshop than similar drug treatment programs that did not receive an intervention. (2) Programs assigned to active diffusion interventions that include face-to-face contact would be more likely to adopt the Job Seeker's Workshop than programs receiving information only.

The subjects were 172 drug treatment programs in the states of California, Washington, Oregon, Illinois, Michigan, and Indiana, randomly assigned to one of four experimental conditions.

The experimental conditions were the following:

- *Printed materials only*: Programs assigned to this condition received a 20-page booklet that introduced the Job Seeker's Workshop and a 52-page *Leader's Manual*.

- *Technical assistance site visit*: Programs assigned to this condition received the printed materials plus one-day training in the Job Seeker's Workshop at their program site. The training included a one-hour demonstration videotape of an actual Job Seeker's Workshop, training in the use of the videotape equipment, and an implementation planning discussion. Clinic representatives at workshops varied. We urged that as a minimum, the programs director and primary counseling staff attend. However, as many staff as possible were encouraged to attend. Attendees sometimes included physicians, nurses, and clerical staff.

- *Training Conference*: Programs assigned to this condition received the printed materials and were each invited to send one representative to a two-day conference with expenses paid by the reseach project. Each conference was attended by one representative from each of five to eight programs. Representatives were either the program director, vocational specialist, or senior counselor to the conference. The conferences included a review of the purpose of the project, a summary of the research that had led up to it, small group activity to help group development, the demonstration videotape with discussion, extensive Job Seeker's Workshop leadership training via videotaped role-play practice, and an implementation planning discussion in which participants developed a specific plan for the implementation of the Job Seeker's Workshop at their home programs.

- *Control*: Programs assigned to this condition received a letter informing them of their assignment to this condition and indicating they would receive the printed materials after the follow-up period.

Results

The principal outcome measure was the rate at which drug treatment programs adopted the Job Seeker's Workshop. The criterion used for classifying a program as having adopted the workshop was their use of role-play interview practice with or without videotape feedback. At three-month follow-up, the highest adoption rates were in the site visit condition (28.1%) and the conference condition (19.4%). Only 3.7% of programs in the printed material condition adopted a workshop, and none of the control programs did so. The difference in adoption rate among the four conditions was statistically significant beyond the .001 level.

Since the absence of adoption in the control group contributed to the significance of the differences, rate of adoption among the three intervention conditions alone was assessed. These differences were also statistically significant as was the test of the difference in rate of adoption between the printed material condition (3.7%) and the two face-to-face interventions (23.8%). Although there was a higher proportion of adoptions in the site visit condition (28.1%) than in the conference condition (19.4%), the difference in the rate of adoption between these two active interventions was not statistically significant.

As noted above, the criterion for classifying a program as having completed a workshop was the use of role-play interview practice. Though some programs did not adopt the use of role play, they adopted other elements of the workshop, such as training in completing job applications, making telephone calls, or finding job leads. Since they did not adopt the role-play interview practice, they were technically classified as nonadopters. To better understand the impact of the interventions, we also compared the differences among the four experimental conditions using a broader definition of adoption, one in which "adopters" included those programs that either had implemented the workshop or had adopted elements of it. Rates for elements of adoption were the following: Site visit, 31.3%; conference, 25.8%; printed material, 5.6%; control, 0.0%.

A subsample of clinics ($N = 93$) was also followed-up at nine months. Some adoption occurred between three and nine months. For example, collapsing across the four conditions, when conduct of the workshop is the measure of adoption, the increase was 11.8% for all conditions at month three to 20.4% at nine months. Thus, rate of adoption almost doubled from three to nine month follow-up. The relative rankings of the treatment conditions remained the same. These data are consistent with findings reported by others (Larsen 1981) that mental health organizations receiving consultation reported higher degrees of problem solving after eight months than after four months.

An analysis of the relationship between rate of adoption and primary drug treatment modality indicated that residential treatment programs were more likely to adopt the workshop than were outpatient drug free or methadone maintenance programs.

Adopters gave several reports of favorable results ("We placed all 20 clients from the workshops in jobs within two months") and reports of having obtained additional funds for vocational services. When asked to identify which part of the project was most significant in helping to implement the workshop, the most frequently mentioned aspect was the use of videotape either in the role plays or in the demonstration tape. When asked to indicate what factor other than the project had been most significant in facilitating adoption of the Job Seeker's Workshop, the most frequent responses were that clients need this type of help or had specifically requested help in obtaining employment.

For the most part, drug treatment staff responded positively to the Job Seeker's Workshop approach. They recognized the need and saw the workshop as appropriate. Seeing the demonstration videotape of an actual workshop was perhaps the most effective part of the site visits and conferences in terms of persuasion attempts. Several counselors expressed the view that they liked the idea of having a specific, concrete focus for counseling rather than passing the time reviewing past events or trying to get clients to express feelings or take responsibility for themselves.

Most of the concerns expressed were about limitations of time, staff, or funds. Many programs felt that the requirements of providing units of service would not take into account the time involved in offering the workshop, that is, conducting a group with several clients for several hours would be recorded as one hour of service for each client or would not meet requirements for units of service at all. When counselors saw the workshop as an addition to their normal duties, it was presented as a more effective *alternative* to regular counseling for some clients. The cost of the videotape equipment was a stumbling block for many programs. The value of the workshop role-playing activities even without video feedback was stressed, along with exploring ways of acquiring the equipment through fund raising, grant writing, soliciting equipment donations from service clubs, or sharing equipment with other agencies.

Several programs emphasized the need for dissemination efforts to include higher levels of the drug treatment system. They felt it was important to incorporate the state agency and the county coordinating agency, rather than approach the individual drug treatment programs as though they were autonomous. Program directors stated that they respond to pressure and support, especially funding priorities, from the agencies that coordinate them.

In general, the results of the study generally confirmed the major hypotheses: (1) Drug treatment programs exposed to the three experimental diffusion efforts were more likely to adopt the Job Seeker's Workshop. (2) Programs assigned to receive a diffusion effort that included face-to-face training (site visit or conference) were much more likely to adopt the workshop than programs that received printed materials only.

This investigation demonstrated that specially designed diffusion efforts can be conceived, delivered, and evaluated within a systematic research framework and that such efforts are likely to be significantly more effective than conventional dissemination techniques, such as publications in professional journals and technical research reports. The study demonstrated that small service programs can implement an innovation such as the Job Seeker's Workshop with minimal technical assistance. However, care must be taken to match skills of program staff to the technique disseminated. It was our clinical impression that some programs failed to adopt the workshop because staff did not understand behavioral principles well enough to effectively use the technique. Such techniques as use of positive reinforcement rather than punishment, shaping, and modeling are not in the therapeutic repertoire of some drug treatment counselors whose primary qualifications for a counseling job may be an exaddict status. We do not yet have enough data to specify which technique may be more effectively disseminated with face-to-face procedures rather than through printed materials or through the research literature alone.

This study incorporated methodological features that have not been present in most previous diffusion research. For example, it employed random assignment without self-selection to any experimental condition and used adoption of the innovation (rather than some oblique measure such as intent to adopt or progress toward adoption) as the primary measure of outcome.

CONDUCTING A WORKSHOP

Those of us involved in the development and evaluation of the workshop have long felt that the scientific articles describing the workshop are of limited value to the clinician who wants to provide drug treatment clients with this service. In our combined experience, treatment research rarely, if ever, proceeds along the neat lines described in journal articles, and the expertise and clinical sophistication needed to run the intervention is assumed to lie somewhere within the skin of the reader. In this section, we give information to the practitioner about the background of the workshop, how to conduct interviews, how to help clients complete job applications, and how to develop job leads.

Background

The Job Seeker's Workshop was designed to increase job-seeking skills, not to motivate participants to get a job or to sell the work ethic.

The format is unstructured by necessity, as some clients may resist anything more than minimal structure. Clients may arrive or leave meetings at different times, they may move around the room, attending or not attending as they choose during the meetings. Willingness to offer the workshop with minimal structure is an important factor in preventing attrition.

It is important to be clear with clients that the workshop is not psychotherapy, which many clients actively dislike. The dislike often stems from past experience with enforced therapy while in prison.

Our experience with methadone maintenance clients indicated that they often lack interpersonal skills and therefore do not coalesce easily as a group. However, in a more structured program, such as a therapeutic community, the workshop can be more tightly organized.

Some themes weave themselves throughout the workshop. One is transparency. Because part of their clients' background (street life) is so obviously deviant to them, participants often assume that it is equally apparent to "normal" people. Participants often say that they know an "exhype" instantly. In applying for a job, their approach is to be completely honest because they are so convinced that their identity as an exaddict is visible to all. "Being honest" is defined as revealing all the negative information that might affect the interviewer's decision to hire.

A second theme is use of rationalizations about inability to get a job, such as "I can't get a job because of my jail time ... because I'm on methadone ... because I haven't had a job before ... because I was fired from all the jobs I've had for using dope." This often culminates with further complaints about prejudices against addicts, excons, and so forth. The workshop leaders acknowledge the reality of much of these complaints but counter with three points:

1. An employer is not interested in a *victim* but in someone who presents himself or herself in a positive, motivated way.
2. The workshop cannot change one's background or wider social conditions, but it can teach some skills to help counteract such disadvantages.
3. Decisions about hiring are based primarily on a positive presentation of self.

The last theme is self-confidence about work. Many drug treatment clients have little confidence about work, although they may be confident in their abilities as street people. In their view, asking them to emphasize positive traits to a job interviewer is asking them to lie. It is often difficult for them to think of any qualities they have that would be desirable to a prospective employer. The only options they see are either to lie or to tell *all* negative information. Therefore, building self-confidence and helping them to develop positive presentations of themselves are important.

Typically, on the first day of a workshop participants arrive at different times. As people arrive, the leaders repeat these introductory comments, emphasizing that they are not there to force anyone to work, but to teach skills that are useful for getting a job. Furthermore, they point out that developing these skills is not difficult and can be fun and that the atmosphere will be relaxed, casual, and informal.

As people arrive, the videotape is running, which provides an opportunity to explain how and why it will be used and to allow participants to become familiar with and somewhat desensitized to an anxiety-provoking experience.

Job Interviews

First Videotape Experience

During the first day, participants try a first interview. This is not a job interview but an opportunity for participants to see how they present themselves. The first interview is nondirective and conversational, with neutral questions about personal interests, job history, background, and what they want from the workshop. This five to ten minute segment is immediately played back. The playback is stopped at a few appropriate times for the leader to solicit comments from the interviewee. Others are asked to withhold comments until after the interviewee has had an opportunity to react. Usually, the interviewee makes spontaneous observations, such as, "I didn't know my hair looked like that," or "I have a funny way of talking." The participants may be self-critical, apologetic, or embarrassed. The leader's comments are supportive: "You look good doing that," "You are able to express yourself," "You make good eye contact," or "It took courage to be videotaped."

Usually interviewees have some ideas about how to improve their presentations and are given an opportunity to express them before others comment. There are usually some obvious points that can be made about posture, tone of voice, or not being clear about specific information.

The leader stresses the novelty of the experience and that harsh criticism is unfair and inappropriate. Confrontation is discouraged.

These first interviews give the leader information about job interests, background, appropriateness of career goals, and potential problem areas. This information forms the basis for later interviews.

First Job Interview

The first videotaped job interview should be informal yet realistic. The interviewee knocks, enters, introduces him or herself, and continues as if in an interview. This segment is replayed without much comment from the leader or others. The interview should be saved, for replay and comparison with later interviews at the end of the workshop.

During this first replay, the interviewee has the first opportunity to react to the tape. The leader then supports, expands, or suggests alternate ways of handling difficult areas. Other group members also contribute. Negative comments will be offered by the interviewee and others. The leader can strive to make negative feedback specific to the behavior performed.

Later Job Interviews

In the later practice interview sessions the leaders use the completed applications as the basis for the interviews, which become increasingly realistic. When the application is first used, the leaders can help the interviewees in talking about the information on the form. In the video playback the interviewees have an opportunity to see how various attitudes and explanations come across. Later interviews can then focus on sensitive areas as the interviewees develop more confidence in their new self-presentation. The interviewees also begin to shift the focus of the interviews to their strong points.

As more information is gathered about a particular person's interests, skills, and weak areas, the interviews can be tailored to provide practice in important areas. Discussions about dress, posture, eye contact, and use of slang follow naturally at this point. Participants also learn how it feels to be saying different things about themselves and their job interests and can reflect on what type of job seems most appropriate for them.

Participants practice entering, shaking hands firmly, sitting down, getting comfortable, taking a breath or two, and then presenting themselves: "I'm interested in the job I saw advertised in the paper, and I'd like to know some more about it." Exits are also practiced in the same way, with a firm handshake and a clear agreement of what is to happen next.

The leader can indicate ways that interviewers shunt people out of the office, and participants practice recognizing this and avoiding it. Rather than accepting, "We'll let you know," and leaving, they learn to make assertive comments, such as, "Can I call you?" "Can I come back on Thursday?" "When can I expect your call?" "When will you be making a decision?" Thus, they leave the interviewer with a strong impression that they are responsible and assertive.

Participants also learn to influence the direction of an interview if it is not going well. They learn to redirect the interview by saying, for example, "I'm nervous because I really want this job and there are some things that I wanted to say."

Final Interviews

The interviews gradually become more difficult and stressful with more focus, detail, and practice on specific effective behaviors. The participants may bring up situations that are particularly difficult. These often include times the interviewer is bored, distracted, or frequently interrupted by phone calls or coworkers. These situations are then played out. The interviewees practice returning the focus of the interview to themselves and their strong points.

As part of this effort to gradually increase the complexity, realism, and successful outcome of the interviews, the participants take turns playing the role of interviewer. This role also gives them a better opportunity to appreciate the demands on the interviewer. They enjoy playing this role and can do it "with a vengeance," introducing realism from their own experience with cold, indifferent, or hostile interviewers. They may be very good at giving someone the "brush-off." In one workshop the client-interviewer was pressuring the interviewee by saying, "We only have janitorial work." When the interviewee responded that he was not interested in that type of work, the interviewer shot back, "Do you think you're too good for janitorial work? You ever heard the saying 'you have to crawl before you walk'?" The interviewee calmly pointed out that he was looking for a position with some room to develop. If this exchange had taken place at the beginning of the workshop, the response undoubtedly would have been less appropriate.

The leader encourages and reinforces clients whenever possible, but often other participants are first to be supportive. Spontaneous applause may occur at the completion of an interview when someone has presented him or herself well, was not "blown away" by the interviewer, has closed firmly, and has a concrete commitment from the interviewer about the next contact.

Issues During Job Interview Practice

Two issues frequently arise early in role playing. One is performance anxiety. The second is descriptions of past work experience. About the former, participants are often nervous and have difficulty answering some questions. The leader can give concrete suggestions of what to say but encourages the interviewees to use their own words as much as possible.

About the latter, some participants may have trouble describing past work experience. They may have been in prison during the last several years. Some may not present themselves as working people because their street identities may be strong. The response to a question about previous job experience may be, "I rob people," or "I'm a criminal." The leader can use this as an opportunity to explain that total disclosure of negative information is not necessary. Presenting facts in their most positive light without lying is appropriate.

The first job interview often sets the stage for two new issues. These are the choice of which job to seek and how best to present information about sensitive or potentially damaging areas.

The interviewees may have trouble thinking of jobs they can apply for. The leader may respond with reassurance that they are not committed to this job interest for the rest of the workshop and may encourage them to try a specific job interview.

The most important concept that the leader must communicate about the interview is that *everyone* looking for work should present himself or herself in the best possible light in a job interview. The problem for drug treatment clients is not fundamentally different. Participants are not encouraged to lie or falsify information but to emphasize their strong points or skills that would be attractive to a potential employer. They should avoid discussing negative information. A useful technique is to have interviewees think of three things about themselves that would make a favorable impression and that they believe to be true. If they cannot do so, the leader can remind them that some of the skills they have learned on the street are also valued in the working world, such as the ability to "hustle," or to work with people. Participants usually find a few things they can say with conviction, such as, "I learn quickly," "I'm punctual," "I like to take responsibility," "I like working with people." For example, one client gave incidental information that he had been married for eight years and had one child and another on the way. It was pointed out to him that this suggested stability, responsibility, and ability to meet commitments. In future interviews he found a way to inject into the conversation his desire to work because he had a family to care for.

In response to questions about their interests, participants sometimes say "I'll do anything; I just want a job." However, when they see the playback, they see that this response is unlikely to make a favorable impression on an interviewer and learn to express specific job interests.

Participants are dissuaded from trying to "hustle" their way into a job. A job obtained through misrepresentation is not likely to be stable. Frequently, workshop participants ask, "What if they find out about ... (history, drug use, being fired, criminal convictions) after the interview?" This can be answered with two points: (1) It is unlikely that this information will be discovered, as most businesses do not check thoroughly (except for jobs where the worker is bonded). (2) If this information is discovered, it will result in the job being lost, and the end result is the same—no job. The point is emphasized that full disclosure of damaging information is not necessary so long as the applicant does not lie.

For many clients the question of whether to lie or tell the truth about their background is central. An interviewer usually can detect lying. An effective approach in the workshop is to ask the interviewee to try the interview first one way, then the other—that is, to lie, see the playback, then do a truthful interview, and compare the two. The weakness of the false interview will be apparent in the video feedback, which is often more effective than the leader's advice.

In dealing with negative or difficult information, participants learn to give themselves an opportunity to stress positive attitudes and information. If the interviewer is dwelling on a prison record, for example, the interviewee might emphasize recent efforts at rehabilitation with remarks such as, "The past is behind me, and I'm interested in making a future for myself," or, "I've been in some rehabilitation programs (*name*), and I'm ready to work."

In the interview practice participants are helped to develop "standard" responses to direct questions about previous employment and criminal convictions. If a client has been fired from a previous job and there is no way of avoiding that fact, the interviewee practices giving a brief and honest explanation of what happened and stressing something positive to put the focus back on the the present, such as, "That's not me now—I learned my lesson." Participants who have been fired learn to avoid "badmouthing" a previous employer and to resist placing blame either on others or on themselves. The workshop leader can learn the details of the circumstances under which interviewees were fired and work with them to develop an explanation that is true but that does not excessively emphasize the story's most negative aspects.

In discussing their criminal records, participants talk about the *convictions*, rather than arrests, and avoid the use of street slang, legal terms, or other jargon. Clients learn to avoid loaded words or phrases such as "narcotic" or "armed robbery." Other ideas for saying the same things are tried until all participants have better ways to describe their experiences; for example, "using narcotics" may become "I had some past involvement with drugs," and "armed robbery" may become "I stole some things." Another suggestion is to offer the names of people who will give personal or character references: "That was some time ago, but I learned my lesson, and I'm a different person now. I'm interested in starting on my career. If you would like to contact Reverend Smith, I'm sure he would provide a good reference."

The job interviewers are generally less interested in discovering specific offenses than in determining the individual's *present* attitude. They want to learn whether the applicant can be trusted, whether he or she is honest and willing to explain problem areas without getting defensive. By practicing answering these difficult questions, the interviewee can develop the confidence and assurance that the interviewer is looking for. Although taking some initiative in the interview is recommended, clients are cautioned against verbal "overkill." Many of them attempt to cover up or obscure by talking too much. One way the leader can deal with this is by stopping the interviewees after they have answered the interviewer's question. The leader may also point out that interviewers are generally in a hurry. It is important for the interviewee to get to the point quickly and effectively.

Job Applications

During the workshop, the leader passes out lengthy and detailed job application forms, which clients are asked to complete. Sometimes the reaction is, "Oh, no, not those. I hate them. I can't do that." The leader responds that the job application is a distasteful but important part of the job seeking process and is used as a screening device to determine who gets into an interview.

We emphasize the potential of the various items of information on the application for creating a favorable impression on the interviewers and giving them material to work with in the interview. For instance, one client did not fill out a section that inquired about hobbies and interests, because he had not been involved in any for several years. Upon further questioning, he mentioned that he used to hunt and fish frequently. Then he listed this information, giving an interviewer the opportunity to discuss these interests or related ones and thereby providing a basis for establishing rapport between them.

To complete everything on the application, the participants learn to have current information readily available—such as social security number, driver's license, address, phone number, references, dates, and places—and to write this information down ahead of time if it is difficult to remember.

Many clients may take a long time to complete the application and need help with spelling or understanding certain items. They learn that sometimes it is acceptable to ask for an application form to take home.

Participants answer all questions and write "NA" if an item is not applicable to them. This helps the person who scans the completed application to have an adequate picture of the applicant and also gives an impression of thoroughness. Clients are encouraged to list any skills they have that may possibly be relevant to the job—for example, the ability to speak other languages or to operate office machines or other equipment, such as photocopiers, power tools, or electronic equipment.

Regarding acceptable salary, participants are told that it may be appropriate, if possible, to discuss this item with the prospective employer to establish what might be a reasonable salary for the job. Participants are advised that it is usually better to overstate than understate their salary requirements.

Completing job applications can be viewed as a way of reviewing and organizing one's history in chronological order. It may be difficult for some people to remember dates, names of employers, and other basic information. The application pinpoints many of the problem areas that the person will have to deal with in a real job interview.

The most difficult sections of the application are the parts that ask about previous job history and criminal convictions. In the workshop this is a natural lead-in to discussions about how to explain gaps in work history, reasons for leaving jobs, and convictions.

If the form asks about prior convictions, rather than simply answer "yes," we suggest clients write, "I would like to discuss this with you in an interview." In this way the person creates an opportunity to deal with this subject in the best way possible. It is pointed out that people have been fired from jobs because they lied on their applications, even though the information they lied about, such as a criminal record, would probably not have been held against them had they been truthful. Most participants have spotty work records because of having been fired for drug use or time spent in jail. No one is encouraged to develop a complicated cover story, but clients are discouraged from revealing unrequested information. They learn to explain gaps in work history and reasons for leaving previous jobs.

In reviewing the application, the leader tries to offer reinforcement for good points with comments such as, "That sounds really good," "That would make a good impression on the interviewer," or "That's what they like to see." For negative points the leader may say, "Can you think of any other way to say that?" Applications are checked for neatness, spelling, and accuracy and are returned to be redone if necessary.

Developing Job Leads

This component of the workshop helps people to identify a job interest and find a suitable job, rather than limiting the person to a job available or easily attainable. The interview practice defines appropriate job interests, and the job lead portion of the workshop is directed toward learning how to discover specific job openings that relate to that interest.

Participants who turn up job leads that do not interest them share these with others in the workshop. The leader also points out that a great many jobs are found through information given by friends and relatives. It is important to let them know of one's job interest and to remind them from time to time.

The job interview, even if it does not result in a job offer, is also a potential source of job leads. Interviewers can be asked if they are aware of any similar or related job openings and, if so, whether their name may be used as a referral source.

Copies of the want-ad section of a newspaper are distributed for review as a source of job leads. The leader can discuss what job categories and other information may be contained in the want ads and which jobs are likely to be found by this means. One drawback of using the ads is that in a tight job market the person may be competing with many other applicants. However, the ads may be useful for information about what firms are hiring. Participants are asked to circle those ads that seem appropriate and also to include ads that are not what they had in mind. It may be necessary to help some clients look for ads if the task seems overwhelming. The process of looking over the ads may also stimulate discussion about job interests or skills that had not yet come to light in the workshop.

The telephone is another tool in developing information about jobs. The phone book is also introduced as an important information source. The yellow pages are cited as a list of businesses that may suggest potential employers. Clients are asked to find business headings that reflect their job interests (additional ones can be suggested) and to list firm names, addresses, and phone numbers. They are then asked to make exploratory phone calls. Through such calls a client may discover that an employer has a job opening but has not done anything about it yet and may turn up a job lead for which there is no competition. Even if there is no opening, the person contacted may know of other firms that are hiring or other ways to develop job leads. By calling specific businesses, the callers can focus on the job that they want and get information about openings in that field.

This procedure is low cost in energy, time, and money and yields a high information return. Furthermore, callers can get information without being under pressure to present themselves well.

In using the telephone, participants are cautioned that they may get many misses before they hit, but when a hit is scored, they are not competing with many other applicants. One workshop participant got a job on his first phone call, because he had relevant experience and understood the job. Clients seek a variety of jobs. Most have training in some trade but are not able to target the types of firms that might employ them. The leader can encourage them to be imaginative and remind them that many firms employ individuals in trades outside the product or service offered by the company. For example, a large trucking concern might employ a computer programmer to maintain program computing payrolls, work schedules, and delivery routes.

Each participant makes at least one phone call in the workshop. The choice of whom to call can be arrived at in discussion. Some clients may need the moral support or coaching of the leader at their side as they call. Others may be self-conscious and prefer to be alone. Some may be unsure about talking on the phone. In that case it is important for the leader to review specifically what they will ask and to give them concrete things to say. For example, one workshop client initially could not say more than "hello" and would instantly hang up with relief if she got a busy signal. However, with practice she was gradually able to ask questions.

After each call there is discussion about what happened, with reinforcement for positive behavior. Suggestions for alternate ways of handling situations can be made, and callers can try again if they are ready.

The payoff from using the telephone in job seeking has been illustrated dramatically in the workshops. Many clients assumed certain things about working conditions, job availability, or their qualifications but learned on the phone that their assumptions were false. One woman, for example, had ruled out the possibility of starting as a day care substitute teacher because she lacked the license that was required where she had previously lived. When she made a telephone inquiry, she discovered that there was an immediate need for teachers, with no licensing requirement. Another client had been a printer but thought he would have to pay a large sum in back union dues to resume his trade. One call to the union revealed that he did not have to pay more than a small reinstatement fee, and he was working as a printer the following week. Another man was interested in becoming a draftsman. He called an engineering firm and spent half an hour talking with a chatty employee who gave him much information about positions in the drafting field and how to get them.

In addition to the sources of job leads previously discussed, the workshop staff should develop a resource guide to employment (and related) services. Such a guide might list the name, address, telephone number, services offered, and eligibility requirements for various agencies in the community that provide employment assistance, vocational training, and allied services.

Closing

The workshop ends with a brief summary, the objective of which is to reinforce the skills that have been developed, to instill a further measure of confidence, and to provide closure to the workshop experience.

For closing the leader can briefly review what has been learned in the workshop and specifically point to skills that individuals have developed, reemphasizing improvement in problem areas. It may be appropriate to replay brief segments of first and last interviews to illustrate dramatic changes, to recall particularly successful interview segments or telephone conversations, or to compare first and final job applications.

SUMMARY

The Job Seeker's Workshop is a treatment based directly on skill-training principles. It incorporates visual feedback, shaping, modeling and social reinforcement in a successful replicable treatment program. It offers a major rehabilitative service that may well be adaptable with few changes to other populations, including alcohol treatment clients, disadvantaged youth, and clients with criminal justice histories. Of even greater importance, perhaps, it can be used by treatment programs. Drug treatment programs usually include few professional staff. Implementation of the program would probably be easier in programs with more staff trained in behavioral principles. Even so, in the dissemination study a good proportion of the programs adopted the workshop, and even more incorporated some parts of it into their vocational services. Although treatment outcome studies conducted by highly trained staff are of interest in the early stages of an intervention, its promise cannot be considered fulfilled until it is used in the wider treatment community. The series of studies of the Job Seeker's Workshop indicates we are well along that path. The next step is to establish that implementation of the workshop by program staff actually increases the effectiveness of programs.

REFERENCES

Azrin, N. H.; T. Flores; and S. J. Kaplan. (1975). Job-finding club: A group-assisted program for obtaining employment. *Behaviour Research and Therapy*, 13:17–27.

Azrin, N. H., and R. A. Philips. (1979). The job club method for the handicapped: A comparative outcome study. *Rehabilitation Counseling Bulletin*, 23:144–55.

Balsam, M.; J. Centrangal; R. Horn; J. Randell; and H. Robinson. (1973). Work: What difference does it make? In *Proceedings of the fifth national conference on methadone treatment*, pp. 1253–58. New York: National Association for the Prevention of Addiction to Narcotics.

Brown, B.S.; R. L. Dupont; and S. T. Glendinning. (1972). Narcotics treatment and behavioral change. In *Proceedings of the fourth national conference on methadone treatment*, pp. 157–58. New York: National Association for the Prevention of Addiction to Narcotics.

Fairweather, G. W., ed. (1980). *The Fairweather Lodge: A twenty-five year retrospective*. San Francisco: Jossey-Bass.

Fairweather, G. W.; D. H. Sanders; and L. G. Tornatzky. (1974). *Creating change in mental health organizations*. New York: Pergamon.

Fergus, E. O. (1979). Telephone change agentry in the diffusion of a program for the elderly. *Journal of Community Psychology*, 7:270–77.

Gearing, F. A. (1972). A road back from heroin addiction. *Proceedings of the fourth national conference on methadone treatment*, pp. 150–56. New York: National Association for the Prevention of Addiction to Narcotics.

Glaser, E. M.; H. S. Coffey; J. B. Manka; and I. B. Sarason. (1967). *Utilization of applicable research and demonstration results*. Los Angeles: Human Interaction Research Institute.

Hall, S. M.; P. Loeb; J. Norton; and R. Yang. (1977). Improving vocational placement in drug treatment clients: A pilot study. *Addictive Behaviors*, 15:438–41.

Hall, S.M.; P. Loeb; K. Coyne; and J. Cooper. (1981a). Increasing employment in ex-heroin addicts I: Criminal justice sample. *Behavior Therapy*, 12:443–52.

Hall, S. M.; P. Loeb; M. LeVois; and J. Cooper. (1981b). Increasing employment in ex-heroin addicts II: Methadone maintenance sample. *Behavior Therapy*, 12:453–60.

Jones, R. H., and N. H. Azrin. (1973). An experimental application of social reinforcement approach to the problem of job finding. *Journal of Applied Behavioral Analysis*, 6:345–53.

Larsen, J. K. (1981). Technical assistance consultation. Unpublished manuscript. (Available from author, Cognos Associates, 111 Main Street, Suite 5, Los Altos, Calif. 94022.)

Larsen, J. K.; C. A. Aruntunian; and C. J. Finley. (1974). *Diffusion of innovations among community mental health centers*. Palo Alto, Calif.: American Institutes for Research.

Manpower Demonstration Research Corporation (1980). *Summary and findings of the national supported work demonstration*. Cambridge, Mass.: Ballinger.

Preble, E., and J. J. Casey. (1969). Taking care of business: The heroin user's life on the street. *International Journal of the Addictions*, 4:11–24.

Rubington, E. (1967). Drug addiction as a deviant career. *International Journal of the Addictions*, 3:1–20.

Stanton, M. D.; T. Todd; and Associates. (1982). *The family therapy of drug abuse and drug addiction*. New York: Guilford.

Stevens, W. F., and L. G. Tornatzky. (1980). The dissemination of evaluation: An experiment. *Evaluation Review*, 4:339–54.

Tornatzky, L. G.; E. O. Fergus; J. W. Avellar; and G. W. Fairweather. (1980). *Innovation and social process*. New York: Pergamon.

Woody, G. E.; L. Luborsky; T. McLellan; C. P. O'Brien; A. T. Beck; J. Blaine; I. Herman; and A. Hole. (1983). Psychotherapy for opiate addicts: Does it help? *Archives of General Psychiatry*, 40:639–45.

7

ALCOHOL AVERSION THERAPY: RELATIONSHIP BETWEEN STRENGTH OF AVERSION AND ABSTINENCE

Dale S. Cannon, Timothy B. Baker, Antonio Gino, and Peter E. Nathan

Emetic aversion therapy consists of the pairing of a target flavor (e.g., an alcoholic beverage) with illness. Emetic aversion therapy has been used in the treatment of alcoholism since 1935 (Shadel 1940; Smith 1982), and in 1984 there were 24 inpatient alcoholism hospitals in which emetic aversion therapy was a principal component of treatment (DeBoer, personal communication). Despite its long history, emetic aversion therapy is a controversial treatment and is not widely used outside of private hospitals dedicated to its use. This treatment is controversial because of concern regarding its efficacy and safety (e.g., *The Alcoholism Report* 1982), and at least one third-party reimburser of medical expenses for alcoholism treatment has specifically excluded coverage for aversion therapy (*Federal Register* 1982). Although it is typically considered a behavior therapy technique, behavior therapists often deemphasize its use (e.g., Miller 1978; Pomerleau 1982). Since completion of this research, the corporation that owns the hospital in which this research was conducted has discontinued the use of aversion therapy in all 21 of its hospitals to improve its ability to recruit patients.

While emetic aversion therapy has definite drawbacks (e.g., unpleasantness, some health risk), data generated by both basic and applied research

This research was supported by the Veterans Administration.

support its use. Basic research on taste aversion learning in numerous animal species shows that pairing a flavor with toxicosis (poisoning) reliably produces strong flavor aversion as inferred from animals' avoidance of the target flavor. Animals can acquire strong aversions even to flavors that are initially highly preferred (Berman and Cannon 1974) or are very familiar (Elkins 1974). Not only are strong taste aversions acquired rapidly (often in one flavor-illness pairing), but there appears to be an intrinsic tendency to associate flavors with toxicosis. Most species learn an association between a flavor and toxicosis more rapidly than associations between a flavor and an external consequence (e.g., shock) and more rapidly than associations between an external context and toxicosis (Garcia and Ervin 1968; Garcia, Hankins, and Rusiniak 1974; cf. Berk and Miller 1978; Sherman et al. 1980).

Recent research (Baker and Cannon 1979; Cannon and Baker 1981) suggests that emetic aversion therapy procedures produce conditioned aversions to the taste of alcohol. The former study, using a single subject design, demonstrated changes in heart rate and skin conductance responses to alcoholic flavors as a function of the flavor–toxicosis contingency. In the latter study, subjects receiving an emetic unconditioned stimulus (US) showed pre- to posttreatment changes in heart rate response to alcohol, alcohol consumption, and subjective ratings of alcoholic beverages relative both to control subjects' responses to alcoholic beverages and to their own responses to nonalcoholic beverages. They also evidenced more overt behavioral signs of alcohol aversions, such as gagging when trying to swallow alcohol. Subjects receiving electric shock as the US demonstrated no such evidence of conditioned alcohol aversions. This latter finding is consistent with animal studies previously cited that report greater associability of tastes with toxicosis and with the failure of Hallam, Rachman, and Falkowski (1972) to find conditioned heart rate and skin conductance responses to alcohol among alcoholics who received electrical aversion therapy.

Follow-up data for emetic aversion therapy are encouraging but inconclusive. Clinical reports of the use of emetic aversion therapy for alcoholics report one-year abstinence rates of 50 to 70% (e.g., Kant 1945; Lemere and Voegtlin 1950; Neuberger et al. 1980; O'Hollaren and Lemere 1948; Thimann 1943, 1949; Voegtlin et al. 1941; Wiens et al. 1976; Wiens and Menustik 1983). However, because no experimental controls were included in these studies, it is difficult to determine the extent to which this high success rate is due to aversion therapy rather than to other treatment components or to patient variables (cf. Franks 1966; Pattison, Coe, and Rhodes 1969; Nathan and Briddell 1977; Rachman and Teasdale 1969). Patient variables are of particular importance in view of the high socioeconomic status (SES) typical of patients in the private alcoholism hospitals in which these studies were conducted (Pattison, Coe, and

Rhodes 1969) and the reported positive relationship between SES and outcome within these facilities (Neuberger et al. 1980; Wiens and Menustik 1983).

Boland, Mellor, and Revusky (1978), in a controlled study with lower SES alcoholics in a Canadian provincial hospital, found that 35% of alcoholics who received lithium chloride paired with alcohol were abstinent six months after treatment while only 12% of a comparison group were. When only those emetic aversion patients who became ill during conditioning sessions are included in the data analysis, the disparity in the six-month follow-up data is even greater: 47% of treated subjects who actually became ill stayed sober for six months. This research suggests that emetic aversion therapy may be clinically effective, but it provides little information on the mechanisms responsible for its efficacy.

In an investigation of the follow-up performance of subjects in the Cannon and Baker (1981) study previously cited, Cannon, Baker, and Wehl (1981) found that emetic therapy subjects differed from control and shock subjects combined on number of abstinent days at the six-month follow-up mark. At the one-year follow-up mark the emetic and control groups did not differ, but both were abstinent a greater number of days than the shock group. Emetic aversion subjects showed greater posttreatment heart rate responses to alcohol than other subjects, and such responses were significantly related to follow-up performance across all three groups at the one-year follow-up mark. Cannon, Baker, and Wehl (1981) argued that heart rate response reflects aversion acquisition and that aversion magnitude is positively related to duration of posttreatment abstinence. However, the small sample size (total $n = 20$) and the lack of a difference between emetic and control subjects at the one-year follow-up limit the generalizability and significance of these findings.

The thesis that emetic aversion therapy is effective due to an associative mechanism rather than to some other process, such as guilt expiation, dissonance reduction, or expectancy (cf. Hallam, Rachman, and Falkowski 1972), requires the demonstration of two propositions: (1) emetic aversion therapy conditions alcohol aversions; and (2) posttreatment abstinence rate is related to magnitude of conditioned alcohol aversion. As reviewed previously, the evidence for the first proposition is stronger than that for the second. The present research had two major goals. The first was to replicate with a larger sample of subjects our previous findings that emetic aversion procedures produce conditioned alcohol aversions (Baker and Cannon 1979; Cannon and Baker 1981). The second major aim was to gather additional data on the relationship between conditioned alcohol aversion and posttreatment drinking status. Secondary aims of the research included a controlled comparison of two emetic techniques in current use and analyses of the relationship among conditionability, patient variables, and postdischarge abstinence. The two emetic techniques differ in terms of medical risk and subjective discomfort, and we were interested in whether the two procedures would produce different levels of conditioned aversion or outcome.

METHOD

Subjects

Sixty volunteer subjects were recruited from a private alcoholism facility that offered emetic alcohol aversion therapy as a principal (but not the sole) treatment modality. Thus, all potential subjects had already agreed to undergo aversion therapy when they entered the hospital.

Patients met the following criteria before being asked to participate in the study: (1) They were between 21 and 60 years of age. (2) They had no medical contraindication to emetic therapy, such as cardiovascular disease, renal disease, cirrhosis, hiatal or inguinal hernia, esophageal varices, psychosis, major affective disorder, organic brain syndrome, recent hematemesis, active ulcers, or pregnancy. (3) They intended to reside within the catchment area of this study. (4) They had no polydrug abuse history. (5) They provided the name of at least one individual able and willing to provide follow-up data. (6) They had never received aversion therapy previously.

Table 7.1 presents the number of patients admitted to the hospital during the recruitment phase of the study (October 1981 through January 1983) who were eliminated by each of these criteria (criteria four to six are grouped together as "miscellaneous study criteria"). As these criteria are successive screens, subjects disqualified by earlier criteria also may have failed to meet a later criterion. Table 7.1 also reports the number of patients not recruited for other reasons, the number of who declined to participate, and the number of volunteers. While only 10% of all patients admitted to the hospital volunteered for the study, 58% of those asked to volunteer did so. Of the 74 subjects who volunteered for the study, 2 left the hospital against medical advice (AMA) after recruitment, 7 chose to withdraw from the study prior to discharge (usually because they did not want to complete the follow-up), 5 regular subjects who were to receive full-strength emetic therapy had to be switched to "SSS" (swish, swallow, spit) emetic therapy for medical reasons, and 60 completed the inpatient phase of the study. All subjects who completed the inpatient phase were included in the follow-up phase.

Recent papers have called attention to potential sources of bias in the recruitment of alcoholic volunteers that may limit the generalizability of research results (Nathan and Lansky 1978; Taylor, Obitz, and Reich 1982). In comparison with all the hospital's patients, study subjects were by selection criteria somewhat restricted in age range, had fewer medical and

Table 7.1
Disposition of Patients Admitted During the Subject Recruitment Period

Disposition	N	%
Left hospital AMA prior to recruitment	41	6
Failed to meet screening criteria	(449)	(63)
Age under 21 or over 60	121	17
Medical/psychiatric contraindication	211	29
Lived out of catchment area	40	6
Miscellaneous study criteria	77	11
Not recruited	(101)	(14)
Administrative discharge	21	3
Not contacted by recruiter	80	11
Recruited	(127)	(17)
Declined to participate	53	7
Volunteered	74	10
Total	718	100

Source: Compiled by the authors.

psychiatric problems, were less likely to be transient or loners, and were less likely to be polydrug abusers. To assess directly the comparability of research subjects along other dimensions, the 60 subjects who completed the inpatient phase were compared with the patients who declined to participate and for whom data were available ($N = 47$) and a random sample of 30 patients not recruited because of one or more of the exclusion criteria previously described. The results, shown in Table 7.2, indicate that research subjects were younger, had higher incomes, and had been in fewer treatment programs previously than had nonsubjects. Wiens and Menustik (1983) report that for patients at another alcoholism hospital that used aversion therapy, age was positively related to posttreatment abstinence but that occupational status, occupational type, and prior treatment history did not predict outcome. On the other hand, Neuberger et al. (1980) report a higher abstinence rate among employed patients at yet another aversion therapy facility, a finding consistent with the relationship usually observed in other treatment settings (e.g., Armor, Polich, and Stambul 1978). Subjects in the present study were comparable on other demographic variables (e.g., marital status, education) to patients at other aversion therapy hospitals (e.g., Wiens and Menustik 1983; Neuberger et al. 1980). It should be noted that the median income of subjects was comparable to the median income in the Dallas metropolitan area at the time of the study ($18,827; Department of Commerce).

Table 7.2
Comparison of Subjects ($N = 60$), Patients Who Declined to Participate ($N = 47$), and Nonrecruited Patients $N = 30$) on Demographic Variables

Variable	Subjects ($N = 60$)	Decliners ($N = 47$)	Nonrecruits ($N = 30$)	F(2,134)
Age (years)	34.6	39.7	44.6	9.11[b]
Sex (% female)	15	28	17	n.s.
Income (median/1000)	20	12	15	[a]
Marital status				n.s.
Married (%)	65	68	83	
Divorced (%)	15	15	10	
Single (%)	15	13	0	
Widowed (%)	5	4	7	
Education (years)	13.5	13.3	12.2	n.s.
Age of first drink (years)	16.3	16.5	15.8	n.s.
Duration of drinking problems (years)	6.8	5.9	9.3	n.s.
Number of prior treatments	.17	.49	1.20	6.92[b]

[a]Kruskal-Wallis one-way analysis of variance, $H = 10.69$, $p < .02$.
[b]$p = .01$
Source: From Cannon, D. S.; T.B. Baker; A. Gino; and P. E. Nathan. (1986). Alcohol-aversion therapy: Relation between strength of aversion and abstinence. *Journal of Consulting and Clinical Psychology*, 54:826. Copyright 1986 by the American Psychological Association. Reprinted with permission.

To assess further the representativeness of the study subjects, they were compared with a random sample of 60 nonvolunteers on the Alcohol Use Inventory (AUI), a questionnaire that characterizes alcoholics in terms of drinking patterns, benefits derived from drinking, and negative consequences of drinking (Wanberg and Horn 1983). The AUI revealed that subjects had more pathological scores than nonsubjects on the following scales: Loss of Control, Social Role Maladaptation, Nonalcoholic Drug Use, Drinking Following Marital Problems, Drinking Provokes Marital Conflict, and Self-Enhancing Drinking (Fs[1,118] ≥ 3.98; $p < .05$).

In summary, the subjects in this study do not differ from nonsubject hospital patients in ways that would consistently bias outcome. Subjects are younger, which would predict less abstinence (Wiens and Menustik 1983) but have higher incomes, which would predict greater abstinence (Neuberger et al. 1980). They have more pathological scores on a number of AUI subscales, but on most demographic variables assessed, subjects do not differ from nonsubjects.

Procedure

Recruitment

Prospective subjects were asked to volunteer for a project evaluating the effectiveness of alcohol aversion therapy. The aversion tests, random assignment to one of two routinely used emetic techniques, and follow-up procedures were explained.

Aversion Tests

Aversion tests were conducted at the Dallas Veterans Administration Medical Center prior to the first and following the fourth aversion therapy session. The measures employed have been shown to reflect the effects of emetic aversion therapy procedures (Baker and Cannon 1979; Cannon and Baker 1981) and are similar to measures shown to reflect accurately degree of cigarette aversion and predict abstinence following smoking cessation treatment (Baker and Tiffany 1983; Baker et al. 1984; Erickson et al. 1983). The alcohol aversion measures include psychophysiological response, consumption during a taste test, subjective taste ratings, and overt manifestations of aversion.

Psychophysiological assessments were conducted in a 2.13 by 2.16 by 1.96 meter sound attenuated, electrically shielded booth with the subject seated in a reclining chair. A 60-decibel white noise was presented continuously over headphones. All recording equipment was located outside the booth. Psychophysiological signals were amplified by a Grass Model 7B polygraph and were then digitized through an analog/digital (A/D) converter and recorded on line by a DEC LSI 11/03 microprocessor. The electromyograph (EMG) signal was integrated by a Grass Model 7P10E integrator prior to A/D conversion. The conductance medium was a 5% saline-Unibase solution, and Ag/AgCl electrodes were used.

Psychophysiological measures included skin conductance (SC), cardiac response (CR), and EMG. SC recording sites were the middle phalanx of the second and third fingers of the right hand, CR sites were the right forearm and left ankle (Lead II), and EMG was obtained from the buccinator muscles of the cheek.

At the beginning of the first psychophysiological test, subjects were informed that the purpose of the test was "to measure your body's response to flavors" and were assured that they would not be shocked through the recording electrodes. After electrodes were attached, subjects were given ten minutes to habituate to the laboratory. Then, on each of the three trials subjects were given two-milliliter samples of each of two alcohol flavors (vodka and their preferred drink) and one nonalcohol flavor (a soft drink) presented in random order. Flavors were squirted into a subject's mouth with a syringe. This presentation method obviates the need for subject movement, which would interfere with psychophysiological recording, and it also affords the experimenter control over such stimulus parameters as onset and magnitude of flavor exposure. Finally, to measure cardiac orienting response, subjects were exposed to a series of 70-decibel complex tones of one second duration at the end of the second psychophysiological test. Tones were presented on a variable interval schedule (mean interval = 30 seconds) through the headphones. Unfortunately, because of recording problems, psychophysiological response to tones was obtained for only 32 subjects.

The taste test, conducted in an adjoining room, was modeled after the technique of Miller and Hersen (Miller and Hersen 1972; Miller et al. 1974; Miller, Hersen, and Hemphill 1973). Subjects were asked to smell, taste, and rate six different beverages. Four of the drinks contained alcohol: two mixed spirits (20 milliliters of distilled liquor in 40 milliliters of water), 60 milliliters of wine, and 60 milliliters of beer. The nonalcoholic drinks were 60 milliliters each of two soft drinks. Fourteen adjectives (alarming, unpleasant, dangerous, pleasant, relaxing, repulsive, distasteful, appetizing, safe, bad, tasty, harmless, good, harmful) were each rated on a four-point Likert scale for each beverage. Subjects were given the following instructions: "This is a taste experiment. We want you to judge each beverage on the attitude dimensions (e.g., good, bad) listed on these sheets. Some of the drinks are alcoholic and some are nonalcoholic. Taste as little or as much as you want of each beverage in making your judgments. The important thing is that your ratings be as accurate as possible" (Miller et al. 1974, p. 75). Subjects were then left alone in the taste rating room. The amount of beverage each subject consumed in making flavor ratings was determined immediately after each taste test session. Taste tests were videotaped and rated later by independent observers for overt manifestations of alcohol aversions.

Treatments

Subjects were randomly assigned to one of two emetic aversion techniques then in routine use at the hospital. Full-strength or "regular" (REG) therapy is ordinarily used with patients who have none of the medical conditions described above as exclusion criteria for this study. "Smell, swish, and spit" (SSS) therapy is a modified technique ordinarily used only with patients who have some medical contraindication to REG therapy. Both techniques consist of five treatments, administered at 48-hour intervals, in which the smell and taste of alcoholic beverages are paired with toxicosis. In REG therapy beverages are swallowed and then regurgitated, and subjects receive a maximal emetine dose. In SSS therapy

Table 7.3
Mean Drug Dosage (mg) by Treatment Session and Group

		Session				
Drug	Group	1	2	3	4	5
Emetine, IM	REG	51.6	64.4	70.1	75.0	75.0
	SSS	52.0	63.3	70.4	75.0	75.0
Emetine, oral	REG	75.0	75.0	75.0	75.0	75.0
	SSS	37.7	44.7	51.7	58.7	65.7
Pilocarpine	REG	8.8	8.9	12.0	14.8	17.4
	SSS	9.0	9.0	12.0	14.8	18.0
Ephedrine	REG	22.0	24.2	37.0	47.0	54.2
	SSS	23.0	24.2	40.0	47.2	58.0

Source: Compiled by the authors.

drinks are smelled, swished in the mouth, and spit out without being swallowed, and subjects receive a lower oral emetine dose. Patients receiving SSS therapy normally have no emeses during treatment sessions.

Three drugs were administered at the beginning of each session in both treatments. The emetic, emetine hydrochloride, was given both orally and intramuscularly (IM). Pilocarpine was given to close the pyloric sphincter and thus retard alcohol absorption during treatment. Ephedrine was used to prevent shock and to induce diaphoresis and mild tachycardia. The mean dosage of each drug for each session and treatment is shown in Table 7.3. With the exception of oral emetine, there were no significant differences between groups in drug dosage. There was a significant group by session interaction for oral emetine ($F[4,116] = 89.9; p < .01$). As can be seen from Table 7.3, this interaction is due to the fact that the REG subjects were given the same high dose of oral emetine daily while the dosage for SSS subjects increased from a low to high level across sessions.

Approximately five minutes after drug administration, subjects began drinking (or smelling, swishing, and spitting) a variety of alcoholic beverages. The mean latency to onset of self-reported nausea, as recorded by the treatment nurse, was 8.9 minutes. There was no significant intergroup difference on this measure. Following the session, which lasted approximately 20 minutes, subjects were sent to bed for three to four hours to recover. REG subjects were given orally an additional nauseant (24 milligrams potassium antimony tartrate in 60 milliliters of beer) following 52% of treatment sessions to prolong nausea. (Potassium antimony tartrate was given only if REG subjects reported little malaise following treatment). The probability of receiving the potassium antimony tartrate first increased and then decreased across sessions (session 1 = 0.00, session 2 = 0.77, session 3 = 0.80, session 4 = 0.63, and session 5 = 0.40; $F[4,116]$ = 23.0; $p < 01$). When given, potassium antimony tartrate was administered a mean of 46.5 minutes following the patients' return to their rooms. No SSS subject received the additional nauseant.

Subjects were asked to indicate the presence or absence of 15 symptoms (nausea, vomiting, sweating, heart pounding, heart racing, chills, fever, weakness, tremulousness, blurred vision, headache, aches, sore muscles, faintness, and cramps) 20 to 30 minutes following treatment. They also were asked to rate the severity of illness on a four-point Likert scale at 30-minute intervals for three hours following treatment.

All subjects participated in all other rehabilitative components of the hospital's program (e.g., individual counseling, alcohol education) and were encouraged to participate in the hospital's after-care program.

Follow-up

All subjects agreed to participate in a one-year follow-up when they volunteered for the study. Contact was maintained with 57 of the 60 subjects throughout follow-up. They or their collaterals were interviewed monthly by phone or in person. To obtain an estimate of the reliability of follow-up reports, on 22 occasions both the subject and his or her collateral were interviewed independently regarding the same follow-up periods with 100% agreement on whether the subject had been drinking. This finding is consistent with previous research reporting general agreement between alcoholics' self-reports and reports of collateral informants regarding the drinking status of the alcoholic informants during the follow-up period (e.g., Maisto, Sobell, and Sobell 1979). All follow-up interviews were conducted by individuals aware of subject's treatment condition but blind to results of the aversion tests. To enhance the likelihood of veridical reports, subjects were made aware that information obtained in follow-up interviews would not be disclosed to clinical staff.

RESULTS

Treatment Comparisons

Overall, the results indicate that SSS treatment is more benign than REG treatment but that the treatments do not differ in efficacy. In this study all subjects had to meet the fairly strict medical criteria for REG treatment; but even so, five REG subjects had to be switched to the SSS intervention due to the development of medical problems. One subject developed chest wall contusions from the emeses, two were unable to induce emesis, one developed headaches, and one had hematemesis. These five subjects were dropped from the study. No SSS subjects had to

Table 7.4
Mean Illness Severity Rating Following Treatment

Treatment	Interval (minutes)					
	30	60	90	120	150	180
REG	3.3	3.4	3.1	2.8	2.4	2.2
SSS	3.9	3.6	3.0	2.6	2.2	2.0

discontinue treatment. Thus, there was a significant difference between the treatments in the incidence of medical complications ($p = .039$, one-tailed Fisher Exact Test).

There was no difference between treatments in the incidence of any of the 15 physical symptoms (e.g., nausea, vomiting, sweating) rated 20 to 30 minutes after sessions. There was a significant treatment by interval effect for the illness severity ratings made at 30-minute intervals following each session ($F[5,250] = 4.24$; $p < .05$), but none of the simple effects tests yielded significant F tests. Mean illness ratings per interval are shown in Table 7.4. As can be seen, REG subjects rated themselves somewhat less ill during the first hour following treatment but as slightly more ill from two to three hours following treatment. It is possible that REG patients feel better immediately following treatment because they regurgitated more of the oral emetine during treatment but feel worse later because of the potassium antimony tartrate. There were no other drug dosage differences that might account for this treatment by interval interaction. Just prior to discharge, subjects were asked whether aversion therapy was "more unpleasant than going to the dentist." Ninety percent of REG subjects said yes compared to 60% of SSS subjects ($F[1,50] = 7.96$; $p < .01$). In sum, SSS treatment is associated with fewer medical complications and is perceived as being less unpleasant than REG treatment.

Because there were no group differences on any of the aversion or follow-up measures, the aversion and follow-up data reported below are combined across groups.

Aversion Measures

The basic design for the statistical analyses of aversion measures included two repeated measures: day (pre- and posttreatment) and flavor (favorite drink, vodka, and one soft drink for the psychophysiological assessments, plus wine, beer, and second soft drink for the consumption and attitude measures). Two additional repeated measures (trial and block for heart rate, and trial and interval for EMG) were included in some

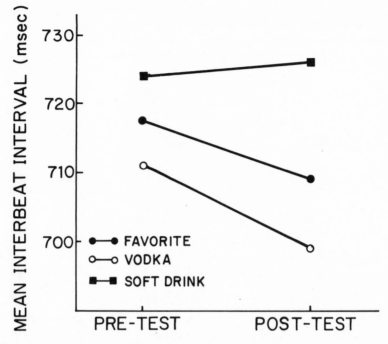

Figure 7.1.   Mean pretest and posttest cardiac interbeat intervals (msec) following favorite alcoholic drink, vodka, and soft drink presentation. *Source*: From Cannon, D. S.; T. B. Baker; A. Gino; and P. E. Nathan. (1986). Alcohol-aversion therapy: Relation between strength of aversion and abstinence. *Journal of Consulting and Clinical Psychology*. 54:827. Copyright 1986 by the American Psychological Association. Reprinted with permission.

analyses. Alpha level was $p = .05$, unless otherwise indicated. Electrodermal measures did not reveal any significant changes from pre- to posttreatment and will not be discussed further.

Heart Rate Measure

Mean pre- and posttest interbeat intervals (IBIs) across trials following presentation of the favorite alcohol flavor, vodka, and soft drinks are displayed in Figure 7.1, and mean pre- and posttest weighted second-by-second heart rate (beats per minute) during alcohol and soft drink trials is shown in Figure 7.2. As these figures demonstrate, there was an accelerated CR to alcohol and a decelerated CR to soft drinks on the posttest. Statistical analyses confirmed the reliability of this observation. For these analyses the IBI was averaged for five blocks of five IBIs: one prestimulus (baseline) block and four poststimulus blocks. The residual mean poststimulus IBI was then computed for each of the four poststimulus blocks, using the baseline mean as a covariate to partial out any variance in poststimulus IBIs attributable to prestimulus differences. This residual IBI was used in subsequent analyses. There was a significant day by flavor by block interaction ($F[6,336] = 4.95$; data were lost from three subjects because of equipment problems). Simple effects tests showed significant day by flavor interactions for the third ($F[2,112] = 5.64$) and fourth ($F[2,112] = 4.27$) blocks of IBIs. These interactions were the result of a significant increase in CR from pre- to posttreatment for both favorite alcoholic drink and vodka on the third block ($F[1,56] \geqslant 4.73$) and a decrease in CR pre- to posttreatment for cola on the fourth block ($F[1,56] = 11.64$).

Inspection of CR to tones revealed that the tones elicited orienting responses; that is, tones elicited marked decelerations in CR. Only the first

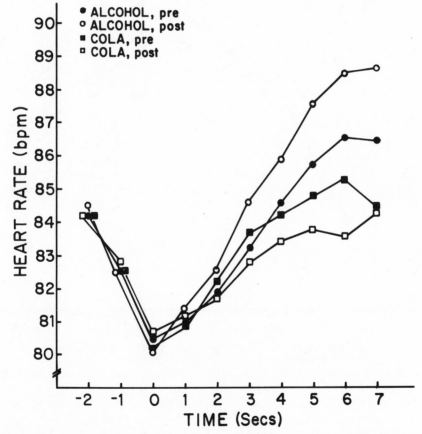

Figure 7.2. Mean pretest and posttest heart rate (weighted second-by-second bpm) elicited by alcohol flavors (favorite and vodka) and soft drinks.

two tone presentations were used in this analysis since subjects had habituated to the tone after that point. The mean values for the three pretone IBIs averaged over subjects were 786.5, 788.8, 804.3 milliseconds, while values for the five posttone IBIs were 813.9, 808.5, 794.2, 810.9, and 823.0 milliseconds.

EMG Measure

The slope (beta) of the integrated EMG signal was computed for each of five five-second intervals (one prestimulus and four poststimulus intervals). Mean pre- and posttest betas per interval for the favorite alcoholic flavor, vodka, and soft drink are shown in Figure 7.3. As can be seen, there

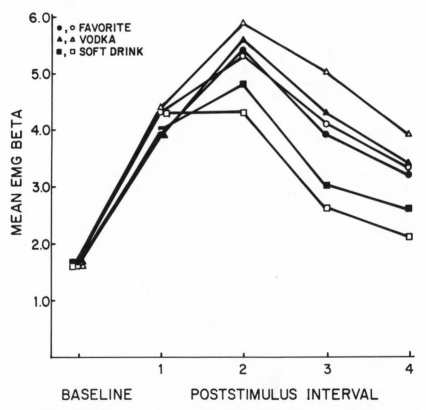

Figure 7.3.   Mean pretest and posttest EMG (beta over five-second intervals of an integrated EMG signal) elicited by favorite alcoholic drink, vodka, and soft drink trials. Pretest values are represented by closed symbols; posttest values by open symbols. *Source*: From Cannon, D. S.; T. B. Baker; A. Gino; and P. E. Nathan. (1986). Alcohol-aversion therapy: Relation between strength of aversion and abstinence. *Journal of Consulting and Clinical Psychology,* 54:827. Copyright 1986 by the American Psychological Association. Reprinted with permission.

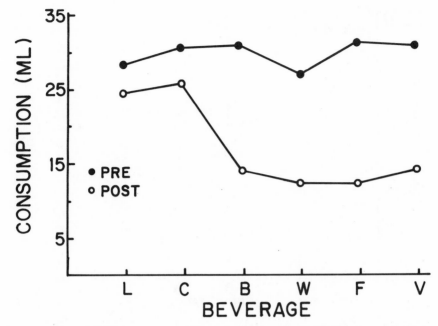

Figure 7.4. Mean pretest and posttest consumption (ml) of lemon-lime soft drink (L), cola (C), beer (B), wine (W), favorite alcoholic beverage (F), and vodka (V).

was an increase in EMG for both alcoholic and nonalcoholic flavors in the first five seconds poststimulus, probably due to facial movements associated with stimulus delivery and swallowing. During the remaining 15 seconds, there was a greater EMG activity for alcohol than soda on both tests, but this difference was greater on the posttest. For data analyses, residual EMG response (EMGR) was computed as for the cardiac measure; that is, the baseline was used as a covariate for each of the four post-stimulus slopes. The response to alcohol increased from the first to third intervals, while the response to soda declined, resulting in a day by flavor by interval interaction ($F[6,354] = 2.26$). Simple effects tests showed significant day by flavor interactions for the second ($F[2,118] = 4.55$), third ($F[2,118] = 7.15$), and fourth ($F[2,118] = 7.56$) intervals. The day by flavor interactions reflected a significant increase in EMG response from pre- to posttreatment to vodka on the third interval ($F[1,56] = 7.55$) and significant decreases in response to soda on both the third ($F[1,59] = 7.55$) and fourth ($F[1,59] = 10.91$) intervals.

Consumption Measure

Mean consumption (in milliliters) of each of the six beverages presented during the taste tests is shown in Figure 7.4. As may be seen in Figure 7.4,

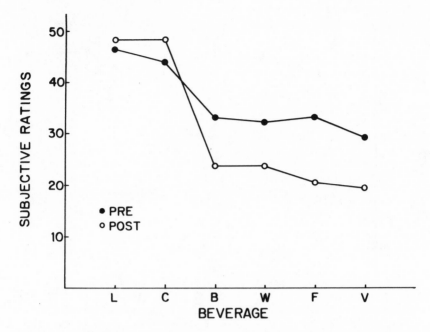

Figure 7.5.   Mean pretest and posttest subjective ratings of lemon-lime soft drink (L), cola (C), beer (B), wine (W), favorite alcoholic beverage (F), and vodka (V). A higher rating indicates a more positive evaluation of the beverage.

consumption of alcoholic drinks decreased from the first to the second test, while consumption of nonalcoholic drinks remained unchanged (day by flavor interaction; $F[5,295] = 11.17$). Simple main effects tests confirmed the reliability of the change in consumption of alcoholic drinks ($F\mathrm{s}[1,59] \geq 28.41$) and the lack of changes for nonalcoholic drinks.

Attitude Rating Measure

A positive taste rating score was determined for each of the six drinks sampled during the consumption tests by reversing the rating scale of negative adjectives (e.g., "bad") and adding the resulting scores to the positive adjective ratings. The mean ratings are shown in Figure 7.5. As may be seen in Figure 7.5, the ratings mirror the consumption data: the lower the consumption, the less positive the rating, and vice versa. The statistical analysis revealed a significant day by flavor interaction $F[5,295] = 36.82$) and significant simple effects for cola ($F[1,59] = 8.79$) and the four alcoholic drinks ($F\mathrm{s}[1,59] \geq 31.83$). As Figure 7.5 reveals, cola consumption increased from pre- to posttreatment, while alcoholic beverage consumption declined.

Videotape Rating Measure

The videotapes of the taste tests were rated by two independent raters for overt manifestations of acquired aversion (e.g., grimaces, shuddering, exclamations). The order of viewing of taste tests was randomized, and an attempt was made to hide taste test identity (pre- versus posttreatment) and the identity of the beverages. For each taste test the raters decided whether an aversion had been acquired to each of the six drinks. Interobserver reliability was high (kappa coefficient = .70). The average ratings for alcohol and soft drinks for both taste tests are shown in Figure 7.6. On the second day subjects were more likely to be judged as displaying aversions to alcohol flavors, but not cola (day by flavor $F[1,58] = 14.93$).

Relationships Among Aversion Measures

For each response domain (CR, EMGR, consumption, attitude rating, and videotape rating) an index of alcohol aversion learning was derived

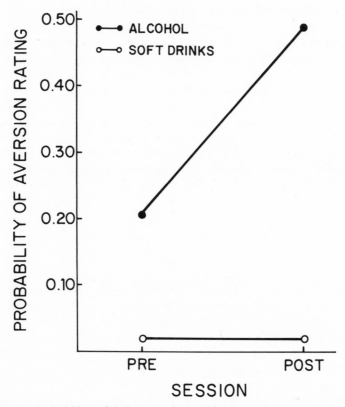

Figure 7.6. Probability of being rated by videotape observers as having an aversion to alcoholic and nonalcoholic drinks on the pretest and posttest.

Table 7.5
Correlation Matrix of Residual Posttest Aversion Measures

	CR	EMGR	Consumption	Attitude
EMGR	−.13	—	—	—
Consumption	.25[a]	.03	—	—
Attitude	.48[b]	−.15	.36[b]	—
Videotape	−.04	.06	−.16	−.12

[a]$p < .06$.
[b]$p < .05$

that is statistically independent of the effects of repeated measurement per se (e.g., habituation) and intersubject variability in response set, pretreatment alcohol preference, and so forth. This index was computed for each dependent measure by regressing the posttreatment response to alcohol (with *prestimulus* baseline values removed through partial regressions) on the *pretreatment* response to alcohol (residualized *poststimulus* responses) and the *pre-* and *posttreatment* responses to soda. The correlations between these residuals are reported in Table 7.5. As can be seen, there is a modest correlation between the CR, consumption, and attitude measures, while neither EMGR nor tape ratings correlated with any other measure.

Thus, CR, EMGR, consumption, subjective ratings, and overt behavior (videotape ratings) all reflect response changes to alcohol flavors in predicted directions from pre- to posttreatment relative to responses to nonalcohol flavors. Although these response changes are all consistent with the proposition that subjects acquired alcohol aversions, regression analyses revealed that the various measures were not highly interrelated.

Follow-up

Relapse Rate

Of the 60 subjects, complete follow-up data were available on 58. Subjects lost to follow-up were counted as drinking from the date of the last contact. Over the entire year, 45% of the subjects remained completely abstinent. The percentage of abstinent subjects as a function of time since discharge is shown in Figure 7.7. Abstinence percentage is a very conservative measure of the drinking adjustment of these subjects: a single "slip" would remove a subject from the abstinent category even if the subject were abstinent most of the time. As Figure 7.8 demonstrates, for the first six months of follow-up most subjects were in fact abstinent most of the time.

The number of days of abstinence during the year preceding treatment was estimated using a "follow-back" procedure that has been shown to be reliable (Cooper et al. 1981). A comparison of the number of days of abstinence during the six months periods prior to and following treatment did indicate a significant decrease in drinking following treatment ($F[1,41] = 306.5$).

Wiens and Menustik (1983) reported that abstinence was a positive function of the number of outpatient aversion therapy "recap" treatments. A similar relationship was observed in our sample: the correlation between number of recaps and days to relapse was .64 ($p < .01$) across all subjects. It is not possible to conclude that recaps enhanced abstinence, since continued abstinence is a prerequisite for receiving further recaps.

Relationship Between Aversion and Relapse

The question of paramount importance in this study is whether measures of alcohol aversion are predictive of clinical outcome. The previous analyses suggest that emetic therapy produces alcohol aversions and that subjects decreased their drinking from pre- to posttreatment. We now

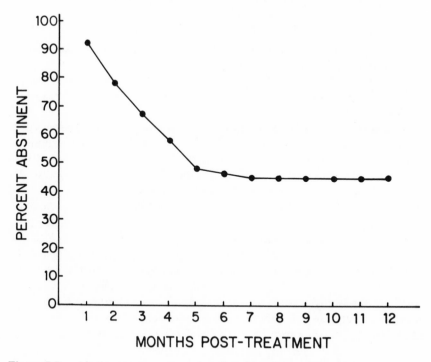

Figure 7.7.   Abstinence percentage as a function of time since discharge over the one-year follow-up period.

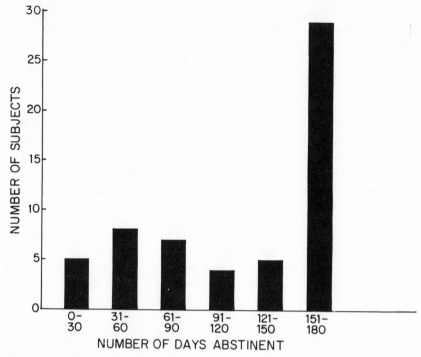

Figure 7.8. The distribution of days of abstinence accumulated by subjects across the first six months after treatment.

address the issue of whether the measures of aversion predict follow-up drinking status.

For both the 6- and 12-month follow-up data the posttest aversion scores previously described were correlated with two outcome variables: number of days between treatment and the first drink (i.e., latency to first drink) and total number of days of abstinence. Nonrelapsers were assigned scores of 180 and 360 for the 6- and 12-month analyses, respectively, on both variables. Over all 57 subjects for whom complete data were available, none of the aversion measures predicted either latency to relapse or days abstinent at either of the follow-up intervals.

There was a strong predictive relationship between residual posttreatment CR and relapse latency among subjects who drank during the first 6 months ($r = -.56$; $p < .01$). (Since only one subject relapsed the second 6 months, this analysis was not repeated for the 12-month data.) The negative correlation indicates that the greater the posttreatment heart rate acceleration (i.e., the shorter the IBI) to alcohol, the greater the latency to relapse. Figure 7.9 presents a scatterplot of the relationship between CR and days to relapse across all 57 subjects, as well as the regression line for the relationship for relapsers only.

None of the zero-order correlations for relapsers only between the other posttest aversion scores and relapse latency was significant. When all aversion measures were entered simultaneously in a multiple regression analysis with relapse latency as the dependent variable, CR independently accounted for 34% of the variance in drinking outcome ($sR^2 = .34$; $F[1,22] = 10.86$). Collectively, the other variables accounted for less than 2% of the drinking outcome variance.

In order to assess the nature of the cardiac effects reported in this chapter, we examined the relationship between CR to tones and the

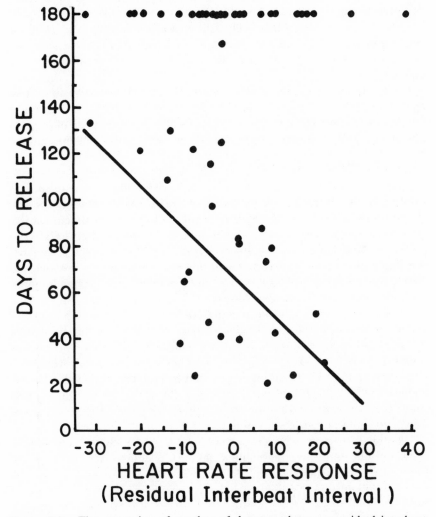

Figure 7.9. The regression of number of days to relapse on residual interbeat interval for subjects who drank in the first six months of posttreatment.

following two variables: CR to alcohol and follow-up performance over the first six months posttreatment. CR to tones was determined by residualizing the mean of the five posttone IBIs on the mean of the three pretone IBIs over the first two tone presentations. Zero-order correlations revealed that CR to tones and the residual posttest CR to alcohol were negatively correlated; $r = -.28$ for all subjects, and $r = -.52$ for relapsers only. The relationship between CRs to tones and alcohol is even more striking if CR to tones is regressed on the raw posttreatment CR to alcohol; $r = -.30$ across all subjects and $r = -.74$ among just the relapsers. Just as with CR responses to alcohol, CR to tones was not significantly predictive of relapse latency when all subjects were considered ($r = .17$). The correlation was somewhat larger for relapsers ($r = .32$). Multiple regression analyses revealed that CR to tones did not enhance the prediction of follow-up status by CR to alcohol, either for relapsers or all subjects.

No posttest aversion score was predictive of total days of abstinence at the six-month mark when data from relapsers only were analyzed. (Although not significant, the sR^2 between CR and number of days of abstinence [.09] was larger than that of any other aversion measure.)

Independence of CR and Subject Variables

Since the experimental design of this study does not include a nontreatment control group, the observed relationship between CR and days to relapse among relapsers may simply reflect a pretreatment subject difference related to outcome rather than a treatment effect related to outcome. To evaluate this possibility, subject variables (e.g., age, income, marital status) that have been shown in other research (e.g., Wiens and Menustik 1983) to predict relapse were entered into a simultaneous multiple regression equation. Across all subjects, both age ($sR^2 = .05$; $F[1,53] = 3.29$; $p < .07$) and income ($sR^2 = .09$; $F[1,53] = 5.44$) were found to be positively associated with days to relapse, while amount of leisure time spent reading was inversely related to number of days of abstinence ($sR^2 = .10$; $F[1,53] = 6.24$). These three variables were then entered with CR into a multiple regression equation across relapsers only. Income ($sR^2 = .25$; $F[1,25] = 13.28$) and CR ($sR^2 = .15$; $F[1,25] = 7.98$) made independent contributions to the prediction of days to relapse, and only CR was associated with number of days of abstinence ($sR^2 = .14$; $F[1,25] = 3.98$; $p = .056$). These analyses suggest that the relationship between CR and posttreatment drinking is not related to assessed demographic variables.

Comparison of Relapsers and Abstainers

As can be seen in Figure 7.9, relapsers and abstainers did not differ in CR magnitude. Contrasts of relapsers and abstainers on a number of demographic variables suggest that relapsers had less social stability. Relapsers were younger (32.4 versus 37.2 years; $t[56] = 2.12$; $p < .05$), a finding consistent with the report of Wiens and Menustik (1983) that age is positively related to outcome in an alcohol aversion therapy program. Relapsers were also somewhat more transient prior to treatment. On a five-point scale used to indicate length of stay at one's most recent residence prior to treatment, relapsers' mean response was 2.3 (three months to one year) while abstainers' mean response was 3.8 (one to two years) ($t[56] = 5.10$). Relapsers reported more drinking among neighbors prior to treatment (means = 3.4 and 2.5, respectively, on a five-point scale; $t[37] = 2.74$). Further, there was a difference in median income the year prior to treatment: relapsers earned a median of $15,000, while nonrelapsers earned a median of $20,000 ($H = 1.46$; $p < .05$). There were no differences between relapsers and abstainers on any of the AUI scales.

DISCUSSION

Conditioned Aversion

The pre- to posttreatment changes in response to alcohol (i.e., increased CR, decreased consumption, less positive subjective evaluation, and increased overt behavioral indicants of aversion) observed in the present study are consistent with the findings of our previous research with alcoholics and smokers (Baker and Cannon 1979; Cannon and Baker 1981; Cannon, Baker, and Wehl 1981; Erickson et al. 1983). Together, these studies support the hypothesis that pairing the flavor of an addictive substance with toxicosis results in conditioned aversions to the ingestion of that substance.

Cardiac Response and Clinical Outcome

This study provides the strongest evidence to date that the magnitude of conditioned alcohol aversion affects clinical outcome. As in the Cannon, Baker and Wehl (1981) study, CR predicted posttreatment abstinence, but the effect size among relapsers was greater in the present study. Indeed, CR accounted for over 30% of the variance in relapse latency among patients who drank posttreatment, and 15% of the variance in relapse latency among relapsers was independently predicted by CR if income, age, and frequency of avocational reading were also entered into the regression equation. We believe these effects are sufficiently substantial to be clinically relevant. That CR predicts posttreatment abstinence is consistent with the report by Erickson et al. (1983) of a significant relationship between posttreatment CR to cigarette smoke and number of days of cigarette abstinence.

The absence of a randomized control group in the present study makes it possible that the observed relationship between CR and relapse latency is simply an artifact of some other subject or treatment variables responsible for clinical outcome. The following arguments can be marshaled against such a possibility: (1) CR was not significantly correlated with any demographic variable; (2) CR made a significant independent contribution to the prediction of outcome when entered simultaneously with demographic variables; and (3) the correlation replicates the findings of previous research on alcohol and smoking aversion therapy, which did include randomized control conditions (Cannon, Baker, and Wehl 1981; Baker and Tiffany 1983; Erickson et al. 1983). Thus, we conclude that CR is a measure of a potent treatment effect.

Although the magnitude of CR is related to posttreatment functioning among some patients (i.e., relapsers), it is not significantly related to outcome among all patients. There are two possible explanations for the failure to observe a relationship between CR and relapse latency across all subjects. One is that the failure is due to restriction of range of the follow-up variable; approximately half the subjects remained abstinent throughout the follow-up period. However, for the observed correlation for relapsers to hold for all subjects over a longer follow-up interval (during which more subjects would relapse), the CR of subjects who were still abstinent at the end of one year would have to be greater than that of subjects who had already relapsed. Since there was no such difference in CR, it seems more likely that relapsers and abstainers differ in some way that interacts with the relationship between strength of aversion and clinical outcome. For instance, compared to relapsers, abstainers were older, less transient, reported less drinking by associates, and tended to have higher incomes. Because of their relative lack of social stability or support, relapsers may have been more dependent on aversion acquisition to remain abstinent.

Abstinence Rate and Its Relationship to Demographic Variables

The 45% abstinence rate found over a one-year follow-up interval compares favorably to many estimates of one-year posttreatment abstinence rates (e.g., Armor, Polich, and Stambul 1978) but is lower than the 65 to 70% reported in previous follow-up studies of patients in private alcoholism hospitals employing emetic aversion therapy (e.g., Lemere and Voegtlin 1950; Wiens and Menustik 1983). Since the patient population and treatment technique in the present study are comparable to those of other emetic aversion therapy studies, the lower abstinence rate we observed may be due to our follow-up methodology. We made more use of collateral interviews to verify subjects' self-reports, and we interviewed subjects at more frequent intervals. Both these procedural differences would be expected to increase self-reports of drinking.

Previous follow-up studies of patients in private alcoholism hospitals employing emetic aversion therapy have found a positive relationship between SES variables and abstinence, which is consistent with the pattern of differences found between relapsers and abstainers in the present study. These patient characteristics predict favorable outcome following any type of alcohol treatment (e.g., Armor, Polich, and Stambul 1978), though, and so it cannot be concluded that aversion therapy is more helpful for higher SES alcoholics. As suggested previously, the opposite may be true. Additional research is needed to identify patient variables that could serve as differential indicators for aversion therapy.

Comparison of REG and SSS Treatments

The two treatments studied (REG and SSS) produced equivalent alcohol aversions, and subjects undergoing the two treatments had comparable abstinence rates. Basic taste aversion learning research with animals suggests that magnitude of learned taste aversion is positively related to US magnitude (e.g., dose of emetic drug; Elkins 1984) and to actual swallowing of the CS (Domjan 1980; Domjan and Wilson 1972). The dosages and number of CS–US pairings used in these two treatments may exceed the asymptote for these variables to exert an effect. Inspection of Table 7.3 shows that the two therapies were actually quite similar in drug dosage and illness severity ratings. The frequent tasting of alcoholic flavors by SSS subjects may obscure any effect due to lack of beverage ingestion.

The comparison of the two treatments is of clinical significance as many of the medical risks posed by emetic aversion therapy are due to the production of repeated emeses. Avoiding the need for emesis would permit the use of fewer drugs and lower dose levels. Also, if the treatment did not require emesis, it should be less of a threat to patients with hernias or esophageal varices.

Psychophysiological Basis of the Cardiac Response

It is of theoretical interest to speculate about the particular psychophysiological processes that may subserve the portion of CR variance related to clinical outcome (cf. Baker et al. 1984, for additional discussion of this topic). Phasic accelerative CRs may be placed into two major categories: (1) somatically coupled CRs that are secondary to, or preparatory for, motor acts; and (2) accelerations that are independent of motor acts.

Motor acts, even subtle ones, can result in sizable accelerative CRs (e.g., Freyschuss 1970; Obrist 1968, 1976; cf. Lang 1983a), which may be even greater than necessitated by metabolic requirements (e.g., Obrist et al. 1974; Sherwood, Brener, and Moncur 1983). There is ample evidence that these somatically coupled heart rate responses (HRRs) can be associatively elicited and vary as a function of motor requirements of the signaled task (e.g., Chase, Graham, and Graham 1968). Obrist et al. (1974) have found that in humans such somatically mediated cardiac accelerations tend to be mediated by the parasympathetic nervous system (PNS) through a decrease in vagal tone (cf. Obrist 1976).

There appear to be two major classes of situations that lead to nonsomatically mediated cardiac accelerations. The first is the receipt of an appetitive reward or incentive (Fowles 1980; Fowles, Fisher, and Tranel 1982; Crook and Lipsitt 1976), and the second is active avoidance responding. Although motor components of response execution can, no doubt, produce somatically mediated increases in heart rate, Obrist has shown that humans responding to avoid shock in a reaction time task show phasic cardiac accelerations that cannot be attributed to motor responding per se (Obrist et al. 1974). Such motor responses appear to be mediated via the sympathetic nervous system (SNS) and appear to be due to cognitive activity related to the avoidance contingency. That such accelerations are not due to receipt of aversive stimulation is demonstrated by the fact that cues for inescapable shock often elicit very moderate accelerations, or decelerations (Elliott 1969; Hallam and Rachman 1976; Obrist 1976) and magnitude of acceleration appears to be dependent on the difficulty of the avoidance response requirement. Avoidance response requirements that are either too easy or too difficult do not result in cardiac responses that are as great as those produced by a requirement of moderate difficulty that keeps subjects engaged (Obrist 1976). Based on such data, Obrist concluded that cardiac accelerations elicited in appropriate active avoidance contexts reflect cognitive activity, which he has labeled "active coping."

At present we do not have sufficient information to characterize definitively the nature of the phasic HRRs observed in this research. However, the data of this study and others (Baker et al. 1984) suggest some possible explanations. The significant correlations among CR, attitudinal, and consumption measures clearly indicate that the CR cannot be attributed to an increase in the appetitive valence or liking of alcohol. Rather, it appears the taste of alcohol was more repugnant following treatment. Either increased motor activity (e.g., bracing, shuddering, grimacing) or active coping information processing could conceivably be components of a conditioned response supported by an aversive US. That subjects were largely motionless during psychophysiological sessions and the EMG measure was uncorrelated with the HR aversion score are inconsistent with a somatic coupling explanation, but this evidence certainly does not rule out a somatic coupling explanation. It seems important to explore each of these explanations in future research since they may have very different implications for treatment. For example, if active coping were critical, one might want to teach cognitive coping strategies as a part of treatment.

Non-Cardiac Aversion Measures and Clinical Outcome

As in our previous aversion therapy research (Cannon, Baker, and Wehl 1981; Baker and Tiffany 1983; Erickson et al. 1983), no aversion measure other than CR was predictive of outcome. The lack of correlation of taste-test alcohol consumption with follow-up measures may appear to be an especially incongruous outcome. Certainly it is logical that aversion acquisition should influence flavor intake, and numerous animal research studies have shown that consumption measures reliably index the development of conditioned flavor aversions (e.g., Barker, Best, and Domjan 1977). As used in our research, taste-test consumption may not be a sensitive aversion index for one or more of the following reasons: (1) Taste-test procedures place an artificial ceiling on alcohol intake. Although greater access to alcohol might permit a more valid assay of aversion, the potential validity of this strategy would have to be weighed against ethical/therapeutic concerns. (2) Experimenter demand effects may influence both consumption and attitudinal ratings in taste tests. Even though subjects rarely guess that experimenters measure their consumption, some subjects are aware that their behavior is being observed. Moreover, it is difficult to characterize the nature of such demand effects. While some subjects undoubtedly sample little alcohol or cigarettes to please the experimenters, others report consuming all of the available drug in order to rate the flavor as accurately as possible, a duty they undertake out of an obligation to treatment program personnel. This bias is not so great as to mask the differential impact of aversive and nonaversive treatments on taste-test measures (e.g., Cannon and Baker 1981; Erickson et al. 1983), but it may be sufficient to attenuate correlations with outcome. (3) It is possible that taste-test measures are simply less sensitive measures than CR of cognitive/physiological processes critically related to the effectiveness of aversion techniques. For example, it may be that alcohol consumption or flavor ratings in the taste tests are largely a function of hedonic valence, while CR reflects avoidance or coping information processing that may be more highly determinant of outcome. There is copious evidence that individuals are unreliable assessors of their own emotions and visceral activity (Lang 1983b; Mandler et al. 1961), and it is possible that aversion therapy exerts critical effects on processes beyond a subject's purview.

Like taste-test measures, skin conductance (SC) has consistently been a poor predictor of outcome (Baker and Tiffany 1983; Cannon, Baker and Wehl 1981; Erickson et al. 1983). Unlike taste-test measures, SC was probably not affected by an artificial ceiling or demand effects. There are two reasons that SC may lack predictive efficacy. First, SC simply may be a less reliable measure than CR. Alternatively, as with taste-test measures, SC may not reflect cognitive/physiological processes related to therapeutic effects of aversion therapy. Fowles (1980) has observed that phasic SC increases may reflect activity of the Behavioral Inhibition System (see Gray 1982) and therefore should be reliably elicited by stimuli previously associated with punishment. However, as opposed to cardiac response, SC is a poor index of either somatic activation or active avoidance and therefore may not tap processes critical to therapeutic success.

Cardiac Response to Alcohol and Tones

Relapsers showed a significant negative correlation between CR to alcohol and CR to tones; that is, subjects showing the greatest cardiac accelerations to alcohol showed the smallest decelerations to tones. This negative correlation was highest when nonspecific variance (HRR to soft drinks and pretreatment HRR to alcohol) was not removed through partial regression from posttreatment HRR to alcohol. This sort of response stereotype is well precedented in psychophysiological research (e.g., Lacey and Lacey 1958). In a recent study Bunnell (1982) compared the cardiac performance of subjects engaged in tasks designed to produce tachycardia (i.e., "stimulus rejection" tasks: mental arithmetic, word formation) and bradycardia ("stimulus intake" tasks: reaction task to tones and lights). Bunnell found that those individuals displaying the largest cardiac accelerations during "stimulus rejection" tasks displayed either accelerations or the smallest decelerations during the "stimulus intake" tasks. Based on analyses of heart rate and pulse transit time (Obrist et al. 1974), Bunnell concluded that the consistent cardiac patterns evident across the diverse tasks reflected relative SNS and PNS activation. For instance, individuals who responded with relatively high CRs across tasks appeared to show evidence of both SNS overreactivity as well as PNS (vagal) hyporeactivity. It is important to note that such differences in autonomic nervous system (ANS) activity in Bunnell's research were not due to any conditioning procedure, but rather reflected individual differences.

Within the relapser group, CRs to alcohol were negatively correlated with magnitude of orienting (bradycardic) responses to tones. This suggests that those subjects showing the greatest CRs to alcohol might display ANS activity characterized by SNS hyperactivity and PNS hypoactivity. Thus, there is the possibility that individual differences may have moderated the effectiveness of aversion therapy. Support for this hypothesis comes from research by Hodes, Cook, and Lang (1984), who used cluster analyses to identify groups of subjects who responded to aversive noises with primary patterns of cardiac acceleration or deceleration. These authors found that "accelerators" and "decelerators" differed on the following basis: (1) only accelerators acquired conditioned cardiac acceleratory responses following conditioning with an aversive US; (2) Accelerators showed more persistent conditioned electrodermal responses; (3) accelerators rated their emotional responses to the conditioned stimuli as less appetitive and dominant than did decelerators. Hodes, Cook, and Lang suggested that "accelerators" may constitute a special population that is likely to acquire defensive responses following exposure to aversive stimuli, and such defensive responses are likely to be accompanied by strong affective changes (e.g., fear, distress).

Taken together, Bunnell's research, along with that of Hodes, Cook, and Lang, suggests that among relapsers, subjects remaining abstinent for the longest period of time posttreatment may have predisposed to respond to a range of stimuli with cardiac patterns emphasizing acceleration and deemphasizing deceleration and may also have been predisposed to acquire negative emotional reactions to stimuli paired with aversive events. It is possible that a substrate of this predisposition is an ANS characterized by SNS hyperactivity and PNS hypoactivity. More research will have to be done to explore individual differences in aversion conditioning before any firm conclusions can be drawn.

Summary and Conclusions

Subjects showed predicted changes in response to alcohol from pre- to posttreatment: more negative attitudinal ratings, decreased consumption, increased EMGRs, and increased CRs. Posttreatment cardiac response to alcohol predicted relapse latency among subjects who relapsed. The correlation between CR and days to relapse was a semipartial correlation with variance attributable to pretreatment responses to alcoholic and nonalcoholic flavors and posttreatment response to nonalcoholic flavors removed. Thus, it is unlikely that the observed relationships were due to pretreatment subject differences or to nonspecific intratreatment changes. The effect of aversion therapy on CR was sufficiently sizable so as to be clinically relevant; it independently accounted for over 30% of the variance in relapse latency among patients who drank posttreatment (15% of the variance if we enter income, age, and reading into the regression equation). We hypothesize that aversion therapy results in the acquisition of a CR to alcohol that is important to the long-term effectiveness of emetic aversion therapy. The CR may reflect one or both of the following: (1) engagement in, or preparation for, motor responding; or (2) active coping, or active avoidance information processing. Whatever the nature of the associative relationship, the finding of a relationship between a treatment process variable and clinical outcome is extremely rare in the alcoholism treatment literature. This study, however, is by no means conclusive with respect to the clinical efficacy of emetic alcohol aversion therapy, and it says nothing about the relative efficacy of aversion therapy and other treatment techniques.

ACKNOWLEDGMENTS

The authors gratefully acknowledge the assistance with data collection of Laura Carrell, Suzanne Drabeck, Grace Puente, Jody Rubenstein, and Steven Whiteman.

REFERENCES

The Alcoholism Report, March 16, 1982, *10*:1–8.

Armor, D. L.; J. M. Polich; and H. B. Stambul. (1978). *Alcoholism and treatment.* New York: John Wiley and Sons.

Baker, T. B., and D. S. Cannon. (1979). Taste aversion therapy with alcoholics: Techniques and evidence of a conditioned response. *Behavior Research and Therapy,* 17:229–42.

Baker, T. B.; D. S.Cannon; S. T. Tiffany; and A. Gino. (1984). Cardiac response as an index of the effect of aversion therapy. *Behavior Research and Therapy,* 22:403–11.

Baker, T. B., and S. T. Tiffany. (1983). Role of aversion learning in the treatment of cigarette addiction. Paper presented at the Ninety-first Annual Convention of the American Psychological Association, Anaheim, Calif.

Barker, L. M.; M. R. Best; and M. Domjan. (1977). *Learning mechanisms in food selection.* Waco, Tex.: Baylor University Press.

Berk, A. M., and R. R. Miller. (1978). LiCl-induced aversions to audiovisual cues as a function of response measure and CS–UCS interval. *Behavioral Biology,* 24:185–208.

Berman, R. F., and D. S. Cannon. (1974). The effect of prior ethanol experience on ethanol-induced saccharin. *Physiology & Behavior,* 12:1041–44.

Boland, F. J.; C. S. Mellor; and S. Revusky. (1978). Chemical aversion treatment of alcoholism: Lithium as the aversive agent. *Behavior Research and Therapy,* 16:401–09.

Bunnell, D. E. (1982). Autonomic myocardial influences as a factor determining inter-task consistency of heart rate reactivity. *Psychophysiology,* 19:442–48.

Cannon, D. S., and T. B. Baker. (1981). Emetic and electric shock alcohol aversion therapy: Assessment of conditioning. *Journal of Consulting and Clinical Psychology,* 49:20–23.

Cannon, D. S.; T. B. Baker; and C. K. Wehl. (1981). Emetic and electric shock alcohol aversion therapy: Six- and twelve-month follow-up. *Journal of Consulting and Clinical Psychology,* 49:360–68.

Chase, W. G.; F. K. Graham; and D. E. Graham. (1968). Components of HR response in anticipation of reaction times and exercise tasks. *Journal of Experimental Psychology,* 76:642–48.

Cooper, A. M.; M. B. Sobell; L. C. Sobell; and S. A. Maisto. (1981). Validity of alcoholics' self-reports: Duration data. *The International Journal of the Addictions,* 16:401–06.

Crook, C. K., and L. P. Lipsitt. (1976). Neonatal sucking: Effects of quantity of the response-contingent fluid upon sucking rhythm and heart rate. *Journal of Experimental Child Psychology,* 21:539–48.

DeBoer, D. (1983). Personal communication.

Domjan, M. (1980). Ingestional aversion learning: Unique and general processes. In *Advances in the study of behavior*, eds. J. S. Rosenblatt, R. A. Hinde, L. Beer, and M. C. Busnel. New York: Academic Press.

Domjan, M., and N. E. Wilson. (1972). Contribution of ingestive behaviors to taste-aversion learning in the rat. *Journal of Comparative and Physiological Psychology*, 80:403–12.

Elkins, R. L. (1974). Conditioned flavor aversions to familiar tap water in rats: An adjustment with implications for aversion therapy treatment of alcoholism and obesity. *Journal of Abnormal Psychology*, 83:411–17.

Elkins, R. L. (1984). Taste-aversion retention: An animal experiment with implications for consummatory-aversion alcoholism treatments. *Behavior Research and Therapy*, 22:179–86.

Elliott, R. (1969). Tonic heart rate: Experiments on the effects of collative variables lead to a hypothesis about its motivational significance. *Journal of Personality and Social Psychology*, 12:211–28.

Erickson, L. M.; S. T.Tiffany; E. Martin; and T. B. Baker. (1983). Aversive smoking therapies: A conditioning analysis of therapeutic effectiveness. *Behavior Research and Therapy*, 21:595–611.

Federal Register, September 15, 1982, vol. 47, no. 179, 40648.

Fowles, D. C. (1980). The three-arousal model: Implications of Gray's two factor learning theory for heart rate, electrodermal activity, and psychopathy. *Psychophysiology*, 17:87–104.

Fowles, D. C.; A. E. Fisher; and D. T. Tranel. (1982). The heart beats to reward: The effect of monetary incentive on heart rate. *Psychophysiology*, 19:506–13.

Franks, C. M. (1966). Conditioning and conditioned aversion therapies in the treatment of the alcoholic. *International Journal of Addiction*, 1:61–98.

Freyschuss, V. (1970). Cardiovascular adjustments to somatomotor activation: The elicitation of increments in heart rate, aortic pressure and venomotor tone with initiation of motor contraction. *Acta Physiologica Scandinavia Supplement*, 342:1–63.

Garcia, J., and F. R. Ervin. (1968). Gustatory-visceral and telereceptor-cutaneous conditioning-adaptation in internal and external milieus. *Communications in Behavioral Biology*, 1:389–415.

Garcia, J.; W. Hankins; and K. Rusiniak. (1974). Behavioral regulation of the *mileau interne* of man and rat. *Science*, 185:824–31.

Gray, J. A. (1982). *The neuropsychology of anxiety: An enquiry into the functions of the septo-hippocampal system*. Oxford, England: Oxford University Press.

Hallam, R.S., and S.Rachman. (1976). Current status of aversion therapy. In *Progress in behavior modification*, eds. M. Hersen, R. M. Eisler, and P. M. Miller. New York: Academic Press.

Hallam, R.; S. Rachman; and W. Falkowski. (1972). Subjective, attitudinal and physiological effects of electrical aversion therapy. *Behavior Research and Therapy*, 10:1–13.

Hodes, R. L.; E. W. Cook; and P. J. Lang. (1985). Individual differences in autonomic response: Conditioned association or conditioned fear. *Psychophysiology*, 22:545–57.

Kant, F. (1945). The use of the conditioned-reflex in the treatment of alcohol addicts. *Wisconsin Medical Journal*, 44:217–21.

Lacey, J. I., and B. C. Lacey. (1958). Verification and extension of the principle of autonomic response stereotype. *American Journal of Psychology*, 71:50–73.

Lang, P. J. (1983a). Cognition in emotion: Concept and action. In *Emotion, cognition, and behavior*, eds. C. Izard, J. Kagan, and R. Zajonc. New York: Cambridge University Press.

Lang, P. J. (1983b). The cognitive psychophysiology of emotion: Fear and anxiety. Paper presented at the NIMH Conference on Anxiety and Anxiety Disorders, September 12–14, 1983, Sterling Forest Conference Center, Tuxedo, New York.

Lemere, F., and W. L. Voegtlin. (1950). An evaluation of the aversion treatment of alcoholism. *Quarterly Journal of Studies on Alcohol*, 11:199–204.

Maisto, S. A.; L. C. Sobell; and M. B. Sobell. (1979). Comparison of alcoholics' self-reports of drinking behavior with reports from collateral informants. *Journal of Consulting and Clinical Psychology*, 47:106–12.

Mandler, G.; J. M. Mandler; J. Kremen; and R. Sholition. (1961). *The response of threat: Relations among verbal and physiological indices.* Psychological Monographs, vol. 75, whole no. 13.

Miller, P. M. (1978). Behavior therapy in the treatment of alcoholism. In *Behavioral Approaches to Alcoholism*, eds. G. A. Marlatt and P. E. Nathan. New Brunswick, N.J.: Publications Division, Rutgers Center of Alcohol Studies.

Miller, P. M., and M. Hersen. (1972). Quantitative changes in alcohol consumption as a function of electrical aversive conditioning. *Journal of Clinical Psychology*, 28:590–93.

Miller, P. M.; M. Hersen; R. M. Eisler; and T. E. Elkin. (1974). A retrospective analysis of alcohol consumption on laboratory tasks as related to therapeutic outcome. *Behavior Research and Therapy*, 12:73–76.

Miller, P. M.; M. Hersen; R. M. Eisler; and D. P. Hemphill. (1973). Electrical aversion therapy with alcoholics: An analogue study. *Behavior Research and Therapy*, 11:491–97.

Nathan, P. E., and D. W. Briddell. (1977). Behavioral assessment and treatment of alcoholism. In *Treatment and rehabilitation of the chronic alcoholic*, eds. B. Kissen and H. Begleiter. The Biology of Alcoholism, vol. 5. New York: Plenum.

Nathan, P. E., and D. Lansky. (1978). Common methodological problems in research on the addictions. *Journal of Consulting and Clinical Psychology*, 40:713–26.

Neuberger, O. W.; J. D. Matarazzo; R. E. Schmitz; and H. H. Pratt. (1980). One year follow-up of total abstinence in chronic alcoholic patients following emetic counter conditioning. *Alcoholism: Clinical and Experimental Research*, 4:306–12.

Obrist, P. A. (1968). Heart rate and somatic-motor coupling during classical aversive conditioning in humans. *Journal of Experimental Psychology*, 77:180–93.

Obrist, P. A. (1976). The cardiovascular-behavioral interaction—as it appears today. *Psychophysiology*, 13:95–107.

Obrist, P. A.; J. E. Lawler; J. L. Howard; K. W. Smithson; P. L. Martin; and J. Manning. (1974). Sympathetic influences on cardiac rate and contractility during acute stress in humans. *Psychophysiology* 11:405–27.

O'Hollaren, P., and F. Lemere. (1948). Conditioned reflex treatment of chronic alcoholism. Results obtained in 2323 net cases from 3125 admissions over a period of ten and a half years. *New England Journal of Medicine*, 239:331–33.

Pattison, E. M.; R. Coe; and R. J. Rhodes. (1969). Evaluation of alcoholism treatment: A comparison of three facilities. *Archives of General Psychiatry*, 20:478–88.

Pomerleau, O. F. (1982). Current behavioral therapies in the treatment of alcoholism. In *Encyclopedic handbook of alcoholism*, eds. E. M. Pattison and E. Kaufman. New York: Gardner Press.

Rachman, S. J., and J. Teasdale. (1969). *Aversion therapy and behavior disorders: An analysis*. Coral Gables, Fla.: University of Miami Press.

Shadel, C. A. (1940). Aversion treatment of alcohol addiction. *Quarterly Journal of Studies on Alcohol*, 5:216.

Sherman, J. E.; C. Pickman; H. Rice; J. C. Liebeskind; and E. W. Holman. (1980). Rewarding and aversive effects of morphine: Temporal and pharmacological properties. *Pharmacology Biochemistry & Behavior*, 13:501–05.

Sherwood, A.; J. Brener; and D. Moncur. (1983). Information and states of motor readiness: Their effects on the covariation of heart rate and energy expenditure. *Psychophysiology*, 20:513–29.

Smith, J. W. (1982). Treatment of alcoholism in aversion conditioning hospitals. In *Encylopedic handbook of alcoholism*, eds. E. M. Pattison and E. Kaufman. New York: Gardner Press.

Taylor, W. C.; F. W. Obitz; and J. W. Reich. (1982). Experimental bias resulting from using volunteers in alcoholism research. *Journal of Studies on Alcohol*, 43:240–51.

Thimann, J. (1943). The conditioned reflex as a treatment for abnormal drinking: Its principle, technic and success. *New England Journal of Medicine*, 228:333–35.

Thimann, J. (1949). Conditioned-reflex treatment of alcoholism, I. Its rational and technic. *The New England Journal of Medicine*, 241:368–409.

Voegtlin, W. L.; F. Lemere; W. R. Broz; and P. O'Hollaren. (1941). Conditioned reflex therapy of chronic alcoholism: IV. A preliminary report on the value of reinforcement. *Quarterly Journal of Studies on Alcohol*, 2:505–11.

Wanberg, K. W., and J. L. Horn. (1983). Assessment of alcohol use with multidimensional concepts and measures. *American Psychologist*, 38:1055–69.

Wiens, A. N., and C. E. Menustik. (1983). Treatment outcome and patient characteristics in an aversion therapy program for alcoholism. *Journal of the American Psychological Association*, 38:1089–96.

Wiens, A. N.; J. R. Montague; T. S. Manaugh; and C. J. English. (1976). Pharmacological aversive counterconditioning to alcohol in a private hospital: One-year follow-up. *Journal of Studies on Alcohol*, 37:1320–24.

8

THE ROLE OF AVERSION AND COUNSELING STRATEGIES IN TREATMENTS FOR CIGARETTE SMOKING

Stephen T. Tiffany and
Timothy B. Baker

The problems created by cigarette smoking continue to bedevil both researchers and the general public. Despite decades of research, the essential social, psychological, and pharmacological contributors to the initiation and maintenance of smoking remain elusive. Furthermore, in the face of diverse smoking cessation treatments, smoking remains highly prevalent and intractable.

Reviews of intensive individual or group treatments for smoking cessation paint a fairly dismal picture of the success of these interventions. For instance, Raw (1978) reviewed the success of smoking clinics and found that on the average, of those who started out in the clinics, only 15 to 20% were abstinent at six months to one year after treatment was completed. Controlled studies with interventions, such as hypnosis or drug therapies, tend to produce comparable outcome (Raw 1978; Bernstein and McAlister 1976; Kozlowski 1981). With few exceptions behavioral interventions or social-learning approaches fare no better. A number of reviews examining a variety of behavioral techniques for smoking treatment (e.g., contingency contracting, stimulus control, electrical aversion, covert aversion, systematic desensitization, and so forth) have concluded that treatment is better than no treatment, yet treatment rarely

The research in this chapter was supported, in part, by a National Heart, Lung, and Blood Institute Award (No. 28519–03), awarded to T. B. Baker.

produces more than 30% abstinence at six months to one year (e.g., Bernstein and McAlister 1976; Hunt and Bespalec 1974; Levanthal and Cleary 1980; Lichtenstein 1982; Lichtenstein and Danaher 1976; McFall and Hammen 1971; Raw 1978). Perhaps the greatest contribution of the behavioral or social-learning approach to smoking cessation has been the use of a sophisticated evaluation methodology that has unambiguously demonstrated the disappointing impact of smoking treatments.

In an overview of the extant literature on smoking treatments, Lichtenstein (1982) concluded: "Review of the literature indicates that at six months or one year after follow-up, the average participant has a 15 to 20% chance of being abstinent. More successful programs report abstinence rates of 30 to 40%. Anything better than that is very good indeed" (p. 806).

One treatment approach that exhibited initial promise as being "very good indeed" was the aversive treatment of rapid smoking. Although Lublin and Joslyn introduced this procedure in 1968, it was Lichtenstein and his colleagues at the University of Oregon who first examined rapid smoking systematically in a series of studies published in the early 1970s. In their first report, Schmahl, Lichtenstein, and Harris (1972) had smokers smoke rapidly, inhaling once every six seconds until they could not tolerate another puff. After a few minutes rest, the subject began another trial and this procedure continued until the subject was unable to tolerate another cigarette. The subjects were admonished not to smoke between sessions. If their desire for a cigarette became overpowering, subjects were instructed to contact the experimenters for an impromptu session any time day or night.

After an average of eight treatment sessions all subjects were abstinent from cigarettes, and at six months 57% were still abstinent. These very impressive findings were essentially replicated in three additional studies by Lichtenstein and his colleagues. In four studies employing rapid smoking in eight different conditions (Harris and Lichtenstein 1971; Lichtenstein et al. 1973; Schmahl, Lichtenstein, and Harris 1972; Weinrobe and Lichtenstein 1975), Lichtenstein and his group produced 100% abstinence at treatment termination in seven of the eight conditions and 90% abstinence in the eighth condition. Across all of these studies a little over half of the subjects were abstinent at long-term follow-up (i.e., three to six months posttreatment).

Some subsequent evaluations of the rapid smoking treatment have produced results that are less encouraging. Danaher (1976) reviewed the rapid smoking literature and found that of the studies that allowed comparison with an appropriate control condition, rapid smoking produced relatively greater abstinence in all but a few studies, but none of these differences was found to be statistically significant. If the investigations by Lichtenstein and his colleagues are excluded from the studies reviewed by Danaher, the end-of-treatment abstinent rate averaged across all conditions employing some form of rapid smoking was 64% and the long-term abstinence rate was 32%. This is a sizable decline from the abstinence rates reported in the early rapid smoking studies conducted by Lichtenstein and his associates. Studies conducted subsequent to the Danaher review have continued to show mixed results, with a few producing impressive outcomes (e.g., Best, Owen, and Trentadue 1978; Hall, Sachs, and Hall, 1979) and others reporting discouraging findings (e.g., Norton and Barske 1977; Raw and Russell 1980).

An overall evaluation of the rapid smoking literature suggests that rapid smoking, in comparison to nonaversive cessation treatments, produces a substantially superior short-term and modestly superior long-term outcome, but its present success rate rarely achieves the levels reported in the initial studies. This conclusion must be qualified, however, by the fact that it is difficult to evaluate the effectiveness of rapid smoking per se in many recent studies as it is generally embedded in multicomponent programs that include self-management and self-control strategies (e.g., Best, Owen, and Trentadue 1978; Tongas 1979; Youngren and Parker 1977).

Some reviewers have argued that multicomponent programs that include rapid smoking should be more effective than rapid smoking alone (Bernstein and McAlister 1976; Danaher 1977a; Lando 1975; Lichtenstein and Brown 1980; Pechacek and Danaher 1979). While this approach is intuitively appealing, there is little evidence that adding specific treatment components to rapid smoking increases the latter's effectiveness. Elliott and Denney (1978) reported that self-control procedures marginally enhanced the effectiveness of rapid smoking, but the majority of studies have failed to demonstrate an incremental effect due to adjunct interventions (Danaher 1977a; Glasgow 1978; Merbaum, Avimier, and Goldberg 1979; Pechacek 1977; Poole, Sanson-Fisher, and German 1981; Sutherland et al. 1975). There is some indication that self-management techniques may add to the effectiveness of satiation, an aversive smoking procedure similar to rapid smoking (Lando 1977), but these results have not been replicated consistently (Lando 1978).

Although considerable evidence suggests that rapid smoking produces treatment effects that are marginally superior to other interventions, there has been little systematic theorizing and less research on the mechanisms that account for the effectiveness of this treatment. Rapid smoking is generally considered an aversive conditioning procedure in which excessive smoke is the aversive stimulus. The aversion effect has been viewed in terms of a punishment paradigm as well as Pavlovian conditioning (e.g., Danaher 1977b; Danaher and Lichtenstein 1974). In an effort to evaluate this hypothesis, several investigators have attempted to determine whether a relationship exists between the magnitude or intensity of the unconditioned stimulus (aversive effects) and therapeutic efficacy. Russell et al.

(1978), for instance, found that postsession smoking (at one day posttreatment) and self-reported desire to smoke were not related to levels of COHb (carboxyhemoglobin) or plasma nicotine obtained during rapid smoking.

Thus, there appeared to be no dose-response relationship—something that would be expected if the therapeutic effects of rapid smoking were due to aversion learning. Merbaum, Avimier, and Goldberg (1979) related aversive smoking success (six-month abstinence) to the number of emeses subjects produced during aversive smoking sessions. They obtained a U-shaped function; a moderate number of emeses (three to four) was associated with better outcomes than fewer or higher number of emeses. Finally, other investigators have related subject self-reports of rapid smoking malaise to clinical outcome. For instance, Glasgow et al. (1981) examined the relationship between negative symptoms and sensations produced by normal-paced or rapid smoking, and subjects' ratings of their aversion to cigarettes and their follow-up performance. Results showed that subjects' aversion ratings were significantly related to the number of negative symptoms reported but that there was no relationship between negative symptoms, or aversion ratings, and smoking rates at posttreatment or follow-up.

It should not be surprising that there is little relationship between measures of smoking severity and clinical outcome. Measures like COHb and serum nicotine do reflect magnitude of self-administered dose, but they do not index interindividual variations in thresholds for malaise, nor do they reflect differences in learning rates. Likewise, self-ratings of aversive smoking symptoms have often been dichotomous, of unknown reliability, and not indicative of variance in aversion learning rate. Moreover, because the nicotine in rapid smoking is self-administered, any dose-outcome relationships are inextricably confounded with a host of other variables (e.g., motivational variables, such as feelings on the part of the subjects that they "need" a great deal of rapid smoking).

Some researchers have attempted to explore the role of aversion learning in rapid smoking by manipulating the level of malaise produced by the smoking treatment. These studies have produced mixed results. For instance, Norton and Barske (1977) used treatments that were intended to produce two different levels of aversiveness. Although there were no differences between the groups in abstinence rate or percent of baseline smoking at treatment termination or at the six-month follow-up, there was an indication that in the "mild" aversion group relapsed subjects returned to baseline levels of smoking more rapidly across the follow-up period than did the relapsed subjects in the "high" aversion group. Similarly, Merbaum, Avimier, and Goldberg (1979) compared a group receiving "mild" aversion (rapid smoking) with treatments consisting, in part, of "strong" aversion training. The "mild" aversion subjects were smoking significantly more cigarettes than the "strong" aversion subjects at the end of treatment and at the two-month follow-up, but there were no differences at six months following treatment. Unfortunately, because the aversion manipulation in this study consisted of the addition of a completely different intervention (i.e., covert sensitization) to the rapid smoking procedure, it is impossible to attribute the outcome solely to differences in level of aversion.

Because little relationship has been observed between smoking session severity and outcome in either correlational or experimental investigations, the success of rapid smoking has been attributed to a variety of factors other than aversion conditioning per se: for example, satiation, local irritation of the oral cavity, habituation to smoking cues, cognitive rehearsal of the smoking-induced malaise (Bandura 1969; Danaher 1977b; Leventhal and Cleary 1980). With the exception of one unpublished study that indicated that rapid smoking might be more successful if smokers are encouraged to engage in active cognitive rehearsal of the unpleasant experiences between trials (McAlister 1975), none of these hypotheses has been systematically investigated. Some researchers have suggested that the contribution of the aversive component of rapid smoking to the overall outcome of this treatment is small at best (e.g., Raw 1978; Raw and Russell 1980) and instead claim that "nonspecific" factors, such as motivation, structure, support, and encouragement, account for the majority of the success of the intervention (McFall and Hammen 1971; Raw 1978; Raw and Russell 1980). The difficulty in obtaining rates of success comparable to the outstanding outcomes of the early rapid smoking studies suggests the importance of nonspecific factors and precludes a theoretical examination of the mechanisms underlying the successful application of the treatment.

Even among those who may consider aversion learning to be a necessary element in the success of rapid smoking, there has been little consensus about the learning paradigm that should be used to conceptualize the procedure (e.g., Berecz 1973; 1974; Danaher and Lichtenstein 1974). In a related vein, there has been continuing controversy in the aversion treatment literature regarding the type of noxious stimulus to be employed in order to produce the greatest aversion learning. For instance, Rachman and Teasdale (1969) argued that electric shock may be the preferred aversive stimulus in aversion therapies because of its ease of application and the precise control that can be obtained over its intensity, onset, and duration. In contrast, Wilson and Davison (1969) suggested that aversive stimuli that bear some topographical similarity to the target behavior (e.g., excessive smoke for the treatment of cigarette smokers) may be maximally effective in the production of conditioned aversions (see also Danaher and Lichtenstein 1974; Lublin 1969). The resolution of these issues has been hampered by the paucity of data on conditioned responses to target stimuli following aversion therapy (Hallam and Rachman 1976).

TASTE-MEDIATED LEARNING AND RAPID SMOKING

Basic research indicates that the pairing of gustatory cues with aversive internal consequences produces long-lasting flavor aversions that are acquired rapidly and are more robust than are external environment-illness associations (Baker and Cannon 1982; Garcia, Hankins, and Rusiniak 1974). It is well established that humans readily acquire taste aversions when flavors are paired with central malaise, such as nausea (e.g., Bernstein 1978; Cannon et al. 1983; Logue, Ophir, and Strauss 1981). The procedures of rapid smoking conform to the taste-aversion learning paradigm, as this treatment involves the pairing of the smell and flavor of cigarettes with aversive internal consequences (e.g., nausea). Thus, rapid smoking could be viewed as producing an aversion to the flavor of cigarettes that contributes to an avoidance of smoking (i.e., abstinence). A similar formulation has been applied in an examination of emetic therapy for alcoholism. Baker and Cannon showed that pairing the flavor of alcohol with drug-induced illness resulted in the acquisition of a conditioned response to alcohol as assessed by behavioral, attitudinal, and psychophysiological measures (Baker and Cannon 1979; Cannon and Baker 1981). Subsequently, Cannon, Baker and Wehl (1981) and Cannon et al. (this volume) demonstrated that relapse latency posttreatment was positively associated with the magnitude of posttreatment cardiac acceleration to the taste of alcohol.

In the remaining sections of this chapter we will present the results of two treatment studies that provide data relevant to the hypothesis outlined above; namely, that taste aversion learning is an important component in the success of rapid smoking. If this hypothesis is valid, then it should be possible to manipulate the level of central malaise induced by aversion treatments and observe corresponding differences in measures of aversion (conditioned responses), as well as differences in long-term outcome. Furthermore, the magnitude of conditioned responses should be associated with long-term success in maintaining abstinence. The absence of such a relationship would suggest that although rapid smoking may produce apparent conditioned responses to cigarettes, these responses are not essential features of the clinical efficacy of this treatment.

A shortcoming in previous aversive smoking research has been the paucity of detailed information regarding responses of subjects to cigarettes after undergoing smoking treatments. The data collected tend to be global self-report measures that rarely show any systematic correlation

Table 8.1
Experimental Design for Study 1

Group	N	Treatment
Rapid Smoking (RS)	10	Rapid Smoking + Behavioral Counseling
Rapid Puffing (RP)	9	Rapid Puffing + Behavioral Counseling
Behavioral Counseling (BC)	7	Behavioral Counseling

Source: Reprinted with permission from Erickson, L. M.; S. T. Tiffany; E. M. Martin; and T. B. Baker. (1983). Aversive smoking therapies: A conditioning analysis of therapeutic effectiveness. *Behavioral Research and Therapy*, 21:595–611. Copyright 1983, Pergamon Journals, Ltd.

with long-term outcome indexes (Danaher 1977b). In our studies we use a "three-systems" approach in assessing the impact of treatments. With this strategy, borrowed from research on anxiety disorders (Lang 1978), we sampled across behavioral, attitudinal, and psychophysiological domains in order to determine subjects' reactions to cigarettes. This allowed a fine-grained analysis of potential conditioned aversions to cigarettes and made it possible for us to explore interrelationships among variables in order to illuminate processes contributing to the long-term maintenance of abstinence.

Study 1

In our first study (Erickson et al. 1983), 26 subjects were randomly assigned to one of three treatments: rapid smoking with behavioral counseling, rapid puffing with behavioral counseling, and behavioral counseling alone (see Table 8.1). The two aversion treatments were combined with the behavioral counseling program in order to determine if either of these packages were more effective clinically than behavioral counseling alone. Treatment, which was conducted in small groups, took place in six sessions over the course of two weeks.

The rapid smoking procedures were similar to those used in other successful rapid smoking treatments (e.g., Hall, Sachs, and Hall 1979) but with some modifications intended to maximize taste aversion learning. Medically screened smokers were required to reduce their smoking substantially for several days prior to the start of treatment and not smoke at all on the day of the first session. This was intended to enhance the salience of cigarettes, the putative conditioned stimulus (CS), and to decrease tolerance to the aversive consequences of smoking, that is, increase the magnitude of the unconditioned stimulus (UCS). Animal research indicates that withholding a flavor and increasing UCS magnitude result in greater taste aversion learning (Cannon et al. 1975; Elkins and Hobbs 1979). Subjects were also asked to abstain from eating or drinking for several hours prior to each session. This was intended to decrease flavor cues that might compete with cigarettes for association with malaise (Kalat and Rozin 1971).

Sessions were conducted so as to produce intense, long-lasting malaise. For each session subjects sat in a small room and inhaled deeply on a cigarette every six seconds, while concentrating on the unpleasant effects. They continued smoking until they had consumed three cigarettes or until they felt unable to continue smoking. The therapists repeatedly encouraged the subjects to smoke until they became ill but to stop short of emesis. (We observed that emesis frequently reduced the duration of the malaise.) After subjects completed their first trial of rapid smoking, they left the smoking room for five minutes during which they completed ratings of the unpleasant sensations they were experiencing. Following this, subjects returned to the smoking room and went through the sequence two more times. During the breaks between trials, the therapists advised the subjects to use their memory of the unpleasant sensations they were currently experiencing to combat cravings for cigarettes between sessions. Subjects were asked to link their revulsion and disgust following rapid smoking to cigarette smoking and to contrast their present negative feelings toward smoking with their typically strong desire for a cigarette prior to the session.

The rapid smoking treatment was compared with a less aversive rapid puffing procedure that was identical to the rapid smoking treatment except that subjects were instructed to puff, but not inhale cigarettes during the aversion sessions. These subjects were told that smoking in this manner would make cigarettes aversive and they should avoid inhaling since this would prolong withdrawal and produce pleasurable effects that would attenuate the aversion. Rapid puffing was chosen because it was procedurally similar to rapid smoking (e.g., subjects went through the same smoking ritual at a fixed pace and were exposed to the taste and smell of cigarettes) and resulted in comparable levels of peripheral discomfort (e.g., burning mouth) but *less* central malaise. The inclusion of this treatment was important for practical as well as theoretical reasons. Rapid smoking may constitute a health risk, particularly for individuals with cardiovascular or pulmonary disease (e.g., Hall, Sachs, and Hall 1979; Poole et al. 1980). If intense central malaise is not crucial to the effectiveness of aversion treatments for smoking, then these treatments could be implemented using procedures that involve little or no smoke inhalation (e.g., Tori 1978).

The behavioral counseling received by all groups (and the sole intervention used in the behavioral counseling condition) consisted, in part, of features borrowed from smoking treatments emphasizing social learning approaches and included such elements as contingency contracting for abstinence, self-monitoring of urges and smoking, lists of suggestions on how to manage urges and cravings for cigarettes, and relaxation training. These were incorporated into an addiction model of smoking that emphasized both psychological and physiological processes in the maintenance of the disorder. This approach covered the following components: (1) the nature and management of nicotine withdrawal; (2) an associative model of drug craving; (3) the management of drug urges; and (4) the maintenance of long-term abstinence. We tended to conceptualize our general treatment approach as emphasizing coping response training.

In the early phase of treatment subjects were prepared for the physiological, affective, and cognitive symptoms of the nicotine withdrawal syndrome that they might encounter as their abstinence proceeded (e.g., Shiffman and Jarvik 1976). It was stressed that withdrawal is highly variable from person to person in terms of symptoms, intensity, and duration. Although the subjects have little control over the course of the withdrawal syndrome, we emphasized the time-limited nature of withdrawal and the importance of continued abstinence so as not to prolong the withdrawal phase.

In order to provide subjects with a conceptual model of their cravings and urges for cigarettes, we attributed these phenomena to the operation of two processes. First, persistent cravings are a common feature of nicotine withdrawal, and second, certain situations are so frequently associated with smoking that they come to elicit urges for cigarettes. Subjects were trained to identify and anticipate urge-eliciting situations and then plan strategies to deal with these situations. Problem situations were identified by subjects' self-reports of situations they anticipated or experienced as most difficult, as well as by examining urge-rating forms on which subjects recorded the time, intensity, setting, and affective state associated with urges to smoke. Coping strategies were suggested by the therapists and other group members, and subjects were helped to generate their own set of coping responses.

Both cognitive and behavioral coping strategies were advocated. For example, it was suggested that subjects avoid urge-eliciting situations (behavioral) or generate a list of the benefits of quitting smoking (cognitive). It was stressed repeatedly that subjects attempt to use coping strategies rather than "wait out" an urge as the latter approach tended to exhaust their emotional resources and did not give them a chance to practice their coping skills. Subjects were told that they would minimize or avoid urges to the extent that they employed coping strategies. Alternatively, it was emphasized that urges would escalate if they began to entertain the possibility of smoking or allowed smoking to remain as a possible option for dealing with future problematic situations.

In preparing subjects for the long-term maintenance of abstinence, such topics as the abstinence violation effect (Marlatt and Gordon 1980) and cognitive precursors to relapse were discussed. We emphasized the importance of continuing to engage in active coping strategies whenever subjects experienced urges to smoke and talked about situations, cognitions, and affective states commonly associated with relapse (e.g., Marlatt and Gordon 1980; Shiffman 1982, 1984). It was noted that self-arguments about the value of quitting smoking or such statements as "I am a non-smoker so one cigarette will not hurt me" were best identified as insidious cognitive urges (see Table 8.2 for other common cognitive precursors). We engaged in a step-by-step debunking of such rationalizations and instructed subjects to utilize their coping strategies when they encountered these cognitive precursors to relapse. Throughout treatment subjects received a considerable amount of support and encouragement for abstinence and were strongly admonished not to smoke between sessions.

Subjects also participated in assessment sessions before and after the treatment phase of the study. These sessions included psychophysiological assessments of responses to cigarettes and taste-test measures intended to assess subjects' attitudinal and behavioral responses to cigarettes. During the psychophysiological assessments, the subject was given several presentations of either a lit cigarette or a small syringe of fresh water in a randomized order. If the subjects saw the syringe, they were to open their mouths and the experimenter squirted water into their mouths. If the subjects saw the lit cigarette, they were to take it from the experimenter, puff on it (but not inhale), exhale the smoke, and hand the cigarette back to the experimenter. Heart rate and skin conductance were monitored during this session, and responses were determined by calculating maximum response within 20 seconds after stimulus presentation and expressing these as changes from the baseline data collected just prior to stimulus onset.

During the taste-test assessment, modeled after taste tests used in alcoholism research (e.g., Baker and Cannon 1979; Miller et al. 1973), subjects were asked to smoke cigarettes and drink fluids while rating the flavors on bipolar adjective checklists. Unbeknownst to the subjects, they were being observed during the taste test and several consumption measures were being recorded—for example, how much time they spent

Table 8.2
Examples of Cognitive Precursors to Urges and Relapse

1. "When I used to smoke all the time I always wanted to quit smoking and I hardly ever enjoyed smoking. Now that I have quit smoking I want a cigarette all the time and can't remember the reasons for wanting to quit. If I have just one or two cigarettes I'll rekindle my desire to quit."

2. "It's been so long since I've wanted to smoke that I really must not be hooked anymore. I'm really over the addiction. Therefore, I can have just one cigarette and it won't hurt."

3. "If I have just one puff it will help me get over this tremendous urge to smoke. If I don't reduce this urge pretty soon I'll relapse completely."

4. "I'm just not going to make it. I'm going to relapse eventually. What's the use? If I'm going to relapse eventually, why delay the inevitable? It doesn't matter whether I relapse now or next week."

5. "I never really wanted to quit smoking. I was only doing it for my wife and kids. However, they haven't been treating me very considerately lately. Besides, they think that my smoking progblem is over since I haven't had a cigarette in three weeks. They shouldn't take me for granted like that. They should appreciate what I'm doing for them."

6. "I don't want to return to full time smoking. However, I know this friend who smokes periodically--like at parties. That's all I want to do. Why not?"

7. "I don't really want to get the nicotine--I don't really have a strong 'drug urge'--I just want to see what one would taste like."

Source: Compiled by the authors.

smoking each cigarette. (No subject guessed that these measures were being collected.)

Outcome

On the basis of data collected during the smoking sessions, there was evidence that the rapid smoking subjects experienced a greater level of malaise than the rapid puffing subjects. Across treatment sessions the rapid smoking subjects reported significantly more negative symptoms following aversive smoking than did the rapid puffing subjects. In particular, the two symptoms presumably most indicative of central malaise, "feeling sick in the stomach" and "nausea," significantly differentiated the two treatments.

Figure 8.1 shows the average number of cigarettes smoked outside of the treatment sessions for each group. All subjects in the rapid smoking and rapid puffing groups were abstinent at treatment termination. These

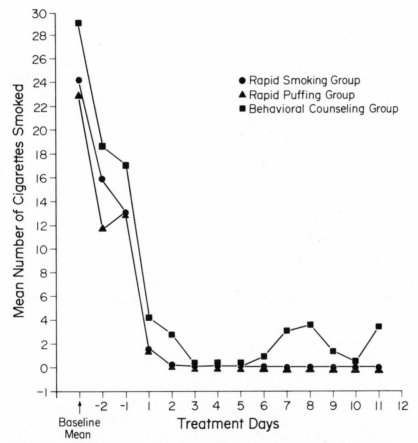

Figure 8.1. Mean number of cigarettes smoked outside of treatment sessions by rapid smoking (●), rapid puffing (▲), and behavioral counseling (■) subjects. Data reflect smoking over a two-week baseline period (baseline mean) and daily means starting two days before treatment and extending until the last treatment session. *Source*: Reprinted with permission from Erickson, L. M.; S. T. Tiffany; E. M. Martin; and T. B. Baker. [1983]. Aversive smoking therapies: A conditioning analysis of therapeutic effectiveness. *Behaviour Research and Therapy*, 21:595–611. Copyright 1983, Pergamon Journals, Ltd.

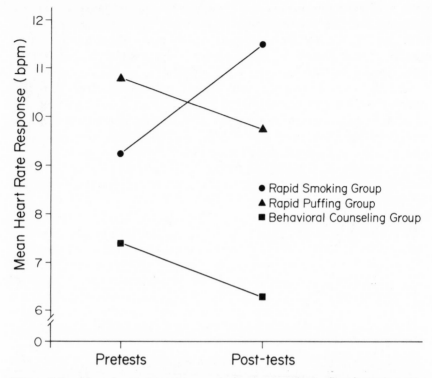

Figure 8.2. Mean heart rate response in beats per minute (bpm) to cigarettes averaged over the two pretreatment psychophysiological sessions (pretests) and the two posttreatment psychophysiological sessions (posttests) for rapid smoking (●), rapid puffing (▲), and behavioral counseling (■) subjects. *Source*: Reprinted with permission from Erickson, L. M.; S. T. Tiffany; E. M. Martin; and T. B. Baker. [1983]. Aversive smoking therapies: A conditioning analysis of therapeutic effectiveness. *Behaviour Research and Therapy*, 21:595–611. Copyright 1983, Pergamon Journals, Ltd.

subjects achieved uninterrupted abstinence by the second day of treatment. Although the behavioral counseling subjects drastically reduced their smoking, only a third were abstinent at the end of treatment. This difference between the two aversion groups and the behavioral counseling treatment was significant. Thus, aversion treatments appeared to increment the short-term success rate of the behavioral counseling.

Analysis of the psychophysiological data revealed no systematic significant posttreatment differences among groups on the skin conductance measures. The mean heart rate response to cigarettes for each of the three treatment groups is depicted in Figure 8.2. Although there are notable pretreatment group differences, it was clear that the rapid puffing and behavioral counseling groups showed a parallel decline in responsiveness from pre- to postassessments, while the rapid smoking group showed an increase. Our analysis on posttreatment scores indicated that the contrast between the rapid smoking group and the other two treatments was significant. Similar analyses of heart rate response to water revealed that there were no significant group differences on this measure.

The only taste-test variable that clearly differentiated the groups was time spent smoking during the rating of the cigarettes. There was a significant decline in this measure in the two aversion groups from pre- to postassessment but no change in the behavioral counseling group. No other taste-test measures revealed significant group differences. Nor were there any significant differences in ratings of treatment effectiveness. We did find that subjects in both of the two aversion groups rated themselves as significantly more confident that they would be abstinent from cigarettes one year after treatment than did the behavioral counseling subjects. Finally, our analyses of the number of urges to smoke reported by subjects across the treatment phase of the study showed that the rapid smoking subjects had significantly fewer strong smoking urges than subjects in the other two treatments.

To summarize the short-term effects of these treatments: The two aversion therapy treatments produced greater short-term abstinence, less time smoking in posttreatment taste tests, and higher ratings of confidence of long-term abstinence than did the behavioral counseling treatment with no aversion component. In addition, the rapid smoking treatment was associated with fewer urges to smoke across treatment and an increase from pre- to posttreatment assessments in heart rate responsiveness to cigarettes.

Table 8.3 shows the outcome measures for each treatment group at treatment termination, six months, and one year. These follow-up data were confirmed by reports of collaterals. At six months we found that the rapid smoking group achieved significantly greater abstinence than the behavioral counseling group, whereas the rapid puffing group did not differ significantly from either of the other treatments. At one year the abstinence levels of the rapid smoking and behavioral counseling groups did not change, but an additional rapid puffing subject relapsed. Comparisons of rapid smoking to behavioral counseling and to a combination of behavioral counseling and rapid puffing were both significant. It should be noted that the 70% abstinence rate of the rapid smoking subjects is comparable to the best results ever reported in the rapid smoking literature, whereas the 14% abstinence of the behavioral counseling subjects is comparable to the typical outcome of most smoking interventions. Table 8.3 also shows the mean number of days of abstinence for each group. At 6 and 12 months both the rapid smoking and rapid puffing treatments resulted in significantly more abstinent days than did behavioral counseling alone.

Table 8.3
Outcome Measures by Treatment Groups

Statistic	Treatment Group		
	Rapid smoking	Rapid puffing	Behavioral counseling
Subjects abstinent (%)			
At treatment completion	100	100	28.6
At six months	70	44.4	14.3
At one year	70	33.3	14.3
Mean number of days abstinent			
At treatment completion	10	10	6.3
At six months	140.5	103.4	32.3
At one year	270	165.7	58.7

Source: Reprinted with permission from Erickson, L. M.; S. T. Tiffany; E. M. Martin; and T. B. Baker. 1983. Aversive smoking therapies: A conditioning analysis of therapeutic effectiveness. *Behavioral Research and Therapy*, 21:595–611. Copyright 1983, Pergamon Journals, Ltd.

We conducted a number of correlational and regression analyses in an attempt to isolate factors associated with long-term abstinence. Several treatment variables—for example, confidence rating, rating of treatment effectiveness, amount smoked during treatment, and heart rate response to cigarettes—were significantly correlated with outcome. Confidence rating showed the strongest relationship to outcome with correlations of .76 and .70 with days abstinent at 6 and 12 months, respectively. Regression analysis revealed that two factors, number of cigarettes smoked during treatment and amount of time spent smoking during posttreatment taste tests, accounted for significant portions of the confidence rating variance. It is important to note that these two variables were significantly affected by aversion therapy. Thus, it appears that both aversion therapies produced cigarette aversions that resulted in rapid cessation of smoking during treatment and decreased smoking during taste tests. Furthermore, these effects were related to subjects' judgments of the confidence of remaining abstinent. Confidence ratings, in turn, were highly predictive of outcome.

Heart rate response to cigarettes, both pre- and posttreatment, was also significantly correlated with clinical outcome in this study. The correlation between number of days abstinent and posttreatment heart rate response was even larger (i.e., .50) when an analysis was performed on data from subjects who had relapsed. (This was done to avoid problems of restriction of range in the dependent variable.) In fact, for subjects who had relapsed, heart rate response to cigarettes accounted for 18% of the variance in days abstinent even *after* pretreatment heart rate responsiveness was covaried out of the outcome data. This finding suggests that heart rate response reflects a conditioned aversion to cigarettes, which accounts, at least in part, for the success of rapid smoking.

Heart rate responsiveness must reflect other processes in addition to aversion conditioning, as there was also a relationship between pretreatment heart rate and outcome. This relationship may arise because low levels of heart rate reactivity might be indicative of global, long-term severity of a subject's smoking problem, which in turn is negatively related to outcome. We found that four variables showed a significant negative correlation with pretreatment heart rate response to cigarettes: age, estimates of daily cigarette consumption, years smoking at present level, and years of regular smoking. Thus, an older subject who has been a regular, heavy smoker for a number of years would display an attenuated cardiac response when presented with a cigarette and also be less likely to succeed in our treatment program.

Overall, this study supported several conclusions regarding the impact of aversion therapy on cigarette smoking. First, aversion treatment in combination with behavioral counseling produced superior short- and long-term outcome in comparison with the behavioral counseling alone. Second, there was some indication that the treatment designed to maximize taste-aversion learning (i.e., rapid smoking) was associated with better long-term outcome than an aversive treatment that supposedly minimized such learning. Third, only the more aversive smoking procedure produced evidence of a conditioned cardiac response and, finally, cardiac response to cigarettes was predictive of long-term outcome across all treatments.

Study 2

Recently we have completed a second treatment outcome investigation (Tiffany, Martin, and Baker 1986) that was intended as a replication and extension of the Erickson et al. (1983) study. One purpose of this research was to overcome several shortcomings present in our first study. For instance, the number of subjects in that study was relatively small, which compromised that study's internal and external validity and precluded correlational analysis at a group level. Furthermore, the two aversive smoking procedures in that study may have been too similar to test adequately the importance of central malaise to the clinical effectiveness of rapid smoking. For example, the rapid puffing procedure may have been too aversive. There was no limit placed on the length of time rapid puffing subjects could spend in the aversive smoking trials, and consequently, these subjects were given a prolonged exposure to a great deal of ambient smoke. (Rapid smoking entailed a time limit as well as a cigarette limit. This, along with our inability to ensure that subjects were not inhaling, may have resulted in a substantial degree of central malaise in the rapid puffing group.)

Finally, the absence of an aversive nonsmoking stimulus in the psychophysiological sessions meant that we could not rule out the possibility that rapid smoking subjects show greater posttreatment heart rate responsiveness to aversive stimuli in general and are not displaying *specific* conditioned responses to cigarettes. This same argument can be extended to the association between heart rate responsivity and clinical outcome. If rapid smoking produces an aversion to cigarettes that is indexed by heart rate response, then we should find that heart rate response to cigarettes, but not to aversive noise blasts, is predictive of clinical success.

Our second study was designed with several questions and goals in mind. First, could we clearly manipulate the levels of central malaise produced by our aversion treatments and produce corresponding differences in levels of aversion, as well as differences in clinical outcome? Three aversion treatments, designed to induce three distinct aversive physical states, were combined with our behavioral counseling program. Full-scale rapid smoking, intended to produce substantial central malaise, was compared with two less aversive interventions, rapid puffing and truncated rapid smoking (see Table 8.4). Animal research indicates that illness or central malaise provides the most efficacious UCS for the production of taste aversion learning (e.g., Garcia and Ervin 1968; Garcia, Hankins and Rusiniak 1974). Thus, to the extent that taste aversion learning contributes to the success of rapid smoking, treatment outcome should be positively associated with the intensity and duration of the central malaise paired with smoking. (It is difficult, however, to specify the central toxic effects responsible for aversion acquisition; Goudie et al. 1982; Ionescu and Buresova 1977).

The procedures for rapid smoking were identical to the ones we used in our first study. The rapid puffing treatment was similar to the rapid puffing procedure used in Erickson et al. (1983) except that steps were taken to reduce the level of central malaise produced by the treatment. In this investigation the same time limit placed on rapid smoking trials was used for rapid puffing, the "smoking" room was well ventilated, and carbon

Table 8.4
Experimental Design for Study 2

Group	N	Treatment
Full-Scale Rapid Smoking	22	Rapid Smoking + Behavioral Counseling
Truncated Rapid Smoking	20	Truncated Rapid Smoking + Behavioral Counseling
Rapid Puffing	20	Rapid Puffing + Behavioral Counseling
Reduced Counseling	23	Rapid Smoking + Reduced Behavioral Counseling

Source: Reprinted with permission from Tiffany, S. T.; E. M. Martin; and T. B. Baker. (1986). Treatments for cigarette smoking: An evaluation of the contributions of aversion counseling procedures. *Behaviour Research and Therapy*, 24:437–52. Copyright 1986, Pergamon Journals, Ltd.

monoxide levels were obtained from each subject after aversion sessions to ensure subjects were not inhaling.

The truncated rapid smoking treatment was intended to produce levels of central malaise intermediate to the other two treatments. Although these subjects inhaled during smoking trials, they were given one trial of rapid smoking during each aversive smoking session instead of three. Thus, these subjects experienced less prolonged central malaise than subjects receiving full-scale rapid smoking. There is considerable evidence that the magnitude of taste aversion learning is determined, in part, by the duration of the effects of the illness-inducing agent (Cappell and LeBlanc 1977; Goudie and Dickens 1978; Goudie, Dickens, and Thornton 1978).

A second goal of this study was to examine the impact of our behavioral counseling treatment on the outcome of rapid smoking. In our first study we showed that rapid smoking substantially incremented the success of our behavioral counseling, but as already noted, there are no data clearly demonstrating that behavioral counseling is beneficial to the rapid smoking treatment.

It was our belief that the prepotent element in our behavioral counseling was coping response training. If true, the elimination of this training from a treatment combining counseling with rapid smoking should attenuate the clinical success of this package. In order to evaluate this hypothesis, we included a fourth treatment consisting of the full-scale rapid smoking intervention combined with a reduced behavioral counseling program (see Table 8.4). In this counseling condition we administered the nonspecific features of the full counseling program—for example, strong support and encouragement for abstinence and admonishments not to smoke between sessions. For the first 30 minutes of each session these subjects were given an opportunity to discuss the problems they encountered while quitting. In addition, these subjects received many of the specific treatment elements used in our full-scale behavioral counseling treatments. They completed long-term and short-term contracts, were given a list of suggestions on how to combat urges, and received relaxation training to help manage tension and control urges while quitting smoking. Subjects in this condition were informed about the various withdrawal signs and symptoms they might experience while quitting, the time-limited nature of withdrawal and urges, and the importance of maintaining abstinence as the most effective strategy for the long-term management of withdrawal and urges. These subjects also completed urge-rating forms and smoking-record forms, and were given access to a 24-hour smokers' hotline.

In general, our reduced counseling treatment was similar to many other package approaches to smoking cessation (e.g., Lando 1977; Poole et al. 1981; Sutherland et al. 1975), but the coping response training used in our full-scale behavioral counseling was not induced. Therefore, subjects receiving reduced counseling were *not* trained to anticipate danger situations—situations likely to lead to urges or relapse. In addition, they were not trained to identify cognitive precursors to urges/relapse, and they were not given training in coping response selection and execution.

The only treatment component incorporated into behavioral counseling in this study that was not used in Erickson et al. (1983) was the addition of a smokers' hotline service. At treatment completion subjects were given the hotline number so they could contact the therapists if they felt their urges to smoke were overpowering and they were at high risk for relapse or if they had already relapsed and wanted help to avoid the resumption of regular smoking. These calls were routed to therapists through a 24-hour beeper service, and callers were given support and were counseled to use the problem-solving strategies they had learned during treatment.

Very few subjects made use of the smoker's hotline service. The majority of those who did call had already relapsed (smoked one or more cigarettes) and wanted to return to total abstinence. In examining the follow-up data from these subjects, we found that most of them ultimately resumed regular smoking. Although the availability of the hotline service may have some therapeutic benefits (e.g., subjects may view it as a potential last coping strategy when all else fails and consequently not feel helpless when faced with strong urges), it was not helpful for those who actually called.

The general assessment strategy used in this study was similar to that employed in the Erickson et al. (1983) investigation with a few modifications, particularly in the psychophysiological assessments. In order to have more precise temporal control over the onset of the stimuli during the psychophysiological assessments, we had subjects sit with their eyes closed and open them only after a brief tone was presented over the headphones they were wearing. When they opened their eyes they either saw a syringe containing water (three trials) or a lit cigarette (six trials). At this point they received a squirt of water or puffed on the cigarette. After this they again closed their eyes. With these procedures subjects were unable to anticipate when or what kind of stimulus they were receiving, and we were able to use the tone onset to demarcate more accurately the beginning of a stimulus trial.

Following the cigarette and water trials subjects were administered four loud noise blasts over their headphones, consisting of white noise and square and sine waves of frequency varying between 400 and 500 hertz (500 milliseconds, 100 decibels). The subjects uniformly described these blasts as extremely unpleasant. The blasts were used for two reasons. First, we wanted to evaluate the specificity of any intergroup differences in posttreatment heart rate response. Second, we wondered whether individual differences in psychophysiological responding (response stereotypes) might be related to aversion acquisition. Presumably, the elicitation of cardiac defensive responses might serve as an index of such individual differences (e.g., Baker et al. 1984). Skin conductance, EKG, and respiration were continuously monitored throughout the psychophysiological sessions. Interbeat intervals from the EKG were stored by computer and later transformed into second-by-second heart rate data for an analysis of phasic heart rate responsiveness.

While taste-test assessments were essentially the same as used in our first study, some additional assessments were included. For instance, we administered a Confidence Questionnaire (Condiotte and Lichtenstein 1981) that required subjects to rate their confidence of resisting the urge to smoke in 48 separate smoking situations. In addition, in order to provide independent verification of smoking, carbon monoxide (CO) levels determined from breath samples were collected twice during each assessment session (before and after the psychophysiological session) and twice during each treatment session (before and after the aversive smoking trials). CO levels sampled after the aversive smoking trials were used primarily to ensure that the rapid puffing subjects were not inhaling. (While running our first subjects in the study, we discovered that they were very interested in their presession CO levels and pleased to see these levels decline over the course of treatment. Consequently, this feedback was incorporated formally into the treatment package for all groups.)

A total of 85 volunteers (49 women and 36 men) were randomly assigned to one of the four treatment conditions. As with our first study, treatment was carried out in small groups with each group meeting for six treatment sessions over the course of two weeks. The treatment conditions were equated on all major pretreatment variables. Mean age was 31.1, mean years as a smoker was 12.9, mean self-report baseline smoking was 24.3 cigarettes a day, and mean previous attempts to quit smoking was 3.4. Attrition was quite low in this study; only three subjects dropped out from treatment, all from the full-scale rapid smoking group with reduced counseling.

Outcome

Table 8.5 presents data gathered in the six aversion sessions, averaged across the sessions for each treatment group. As this table reveals, rapid puffing subjects spent more time smoking and smoked more cigarettes during the aversive smoking sessions than the other groups. In fact, only a few rapid puffing subjects used less than the full 20 minutes allotted for aversive smoking during each treatment session. In contrast, subjects in the two groups receiving full-scale rapid smoking, with either full counseling or reduced counseling, rarely were able to make it to the 20-minute time limit and smoked significantly fewer cigarettes during the aversive smoking trials than the rapid puffing subjects. The two full-scale rapid smoking groups were similar in terms of both time spent in aversive smoking and number of cigarettes consumed. The truncated rapid smoking subjects averaged considerably less time smoking and smoked fewer cigarettes than the other treatments.

As we had hoped, our three types of aversive smoking treatments produced three distinct levels of smoke inhalation during treatment sessions. Table 8.5 shows the CO levels collected after the last aversion smoking trial averaged across treatment sessions for each treatment condition. The two groups receiving full-scale rapid smoking had the highest CO levels, and the rapid puffing group had the lowest level. The truncated rapid smoking group had an intermediate CO level. (All these group differences were significant.)

The differences in CO levels were paralleled by subjects' symptom ratings following aversive smoking trials. These ratings indicated that the rapid smoking treatments produced greater levels of central malaise than did the rapid puffing treatment. Table 8.5 lists the eight symptoms rated by subjects following each aversive smoking trial averaged across all treatment sessions. Comparisons of group differences on each symptom showed that subjects receiving some form of rapid smoking rated

Table 8.5
Group Means of Aversion Session Measures

	Group			
	Full-Scale Rapid Smoking	Truncated Rapid Smoking	Rapid Puffing	Reduced Counseling
Minutes spent smoking	15.9	7.8	19.8	15.9
Cigarettes smoked	4.2	2.3	6.4	4.2
Post-session CO level[a]	41.2	28.8	10.4	47.5
Aversion Session Symptoms[b]				
Burning mouth/throat	5.0	5.1	6.0	5.3
Headache	2.9	2.5	3.0	3.3
Nausea/sick to stomach	5.3	4.9	3.4	4.9
Heart/blood pounding	4.8	5.4	3.2	4.8
Dizziness/spinning sensation	5.7	5.7	3.4	5.7
Negative emotion/sad/anxious	4.5	4.7	3.6	4.6
Tingling sensations/numbness	5.0	5.3	2.9	5.3
Tearing eyes/eye irritation	3.2	3.3	3.9	3.0

[a]In parts per million.
[b]Each symptom was rated on a 7-point scale; 1 = none, 7 = extremely.
Source: Reprinted with permission from Tiffany, S. T.; E. M. Martin; and T. B. Baker. (1986). Treatments for cigarette smoking: An evaluation of the contributions of aversion counseling procedures. *Behaviour Research and Therapy*, 24:442. Copyright 1986. Pergamon Journals, Ltd.

themselves as significantly higher than rapid puffing subjects on the symptoms of nausea/sick to stomach, heart/blood pounding, dizziness/spinning sensation, negative emotion/sad/anxious, and tingling sensations/numbness. These symptoms most likely reflect central malaise produced primarily by nicotine toxicosis (Taylor 1980).

In contrast, rapid puffing subjects produced significantly higher ratings on the burning mouth/throat and tearing eyes/eye irritation items than did rapid smoking subjects. There were no group differences on the rating of headache. Although the self-ratings of the truncated rapid smoking group did not differ from the full-scale rapid smoking groups, it is likely that the former subjects experienced rated symptoms for a shorter period of time. After all, truncated rapid smoking subjects had lower postsession CO levels, spent less time in aversive smoking sessions, and smoked fewer cigarettes than subjects in the two full-scale rapid smoking treatments. Overall, cigarette consumption data, postsession CO data, and ratings of aversion session symptoms indicate that our treatment manipulations were successful in producing three different levels of smoke inhalation that were paralled by three distinct levels or durations of central malaise.

Short-term Outcome

Subjects receiving behavioral counseling with either full-scale rapid smoking or truncated rapid smoking rapidly achieved total abstinence during treatment. While both the rapid puffing and reduced counseling subjects achieved substantial short-term abstinence rates, these rates were not as impressive as those achieved by the other two groups. After the first treatment session, 91% of the full-scale rapid smoking subjects with full counseling, 90% of the truncated rapid smoking subjects, 70% of the rapid puffing subjects, and 60% of the reduced counseling subjects remained completely abstinent from cigarettes across treatment days.[1] Our analyses of the proportion of abstinent subjects in each group showed that both the full-scale rapid smoking group with full counseling and the truncated rapid smoking group had significantly more subjects abstinent than the reduced counseling group. Furthermore, all full-scale rapid smoking subjects with full counseling and truncated rapid smoking subjects were completely abstinent during the week of treatment, whereas only 80% of the rapid puffing subjects and 70% of the reduced counseling subjects were abstinent over the same period.

The CO levels determined for each subject just prior to each aversive smoking session declined over treatment sessions, with an average across all treatments of 12.4 parts per million (ppm) at the first session (all subjects had been instructed to abstain from cigarettes the day of the first session) to 6.6 ppm at the last session. Although there were group differences in cigarette abstinence during treatment, there were no group differences in CO levels. This is not surprising as, among the subjects who smoked outside of sessions during the treatment phase, the median number of cigarettes consumed on any smoking day was one—an amount too low to have a marked effect on CO levels assessed one to ten hours later (Ringold et al. 1962). An evaluation of the CO levels collected during the posttreatment assessment sessions indicated that the groups continued to maintain low CO levels, with no differences among the treatments.

Across all treatments, subjects reported a declining number of strong urges to smoke during the treatment phase. On the day following the first session, subjects reported an average of 2.3 strong urges, and this declined to an average of .5 strong urges by the last day of treatment. We did not find, in contrast to our previous study, that groups differed in the number of smoking urges they reported. This is probably because we did not insist that subjects rigorously keep a record of all strong smoking urges in the present study and, indeed, subjects reported substantially fewer smoking urges in this study than in our first investigation. Our decision to deemphasize these records was based on pragmatic concerns. We have found that as we increase the demands for self-recording from the subjects, the data we receive in return seem to decline in quality and quantity. Since subjects were also asked to fill out a detailed withdrawal questionnaire several times a day during treatment, we decided to make the use of urge-recording forms optional. These forms were not eliminated from the study because some subjects routinely used them as a strategy to deal with urges. They often said that by the time they filled out the form the intensity of their urge declined.

Taste Test Assessments

In general, the posttreatment taste-test measures for cigarettes or beverages did not differentiate the treatment groups. Subjects in all the groups except for rapid puffing treatment decreased the amount of time they spent smoking during the posttreatment assessment (as compared to the pretreatment taste test). Similarly, subjects across all groups rated the flavor of cigarettes more negatively and less positively from pre- to posttreatment taste tests, but there were no group differences on any of these measures. Although it would be reasonable to expect that our manipulations of level of taste aversion learning across the three types of aversive interventions would be reflected in consumption measures or flavor ratings of cigarettes following treatment, this was not the case. The taste-test assessments as used in our studies may be more sensitive to the presence or absence of any type of aversive intervention rather than the development of specific taste aversions to the flavor of cigarettes. If we had employed a treatment without an aversive component as in our first study (see also Cannon and Baker 1981), group differences on these measures might have emerged. Furthermore, it has been suggested (Briddell et al. 1979) that the highly structured nature of the taste test so constrains subjects that it reflects factors unrelated to disposition or desire to smoke (e.g., motivation to make accurate judgments).

Subjects in all groups rated the perceived overall effectiveness of their treatment as fairly effective with no substantial significant differences among groups. On global ratings of confidence in remaining abstinent, all but the reduced counseling group displayed an increase in self-efficacy estimates from pretreatment to posttreatment, but there were no significant group differences. On the Confidence Questionnaire, which required subjects to estimate their probability of resisting the urge to smoke in each of 48 smoking situations, subjects across all treatments

Table 8.6
Covariate Adjusted Mean SCR to Posttreatment Presentations of Stimuli

	Group			
Stimulus	Full-Scale Rapid Smoking	Rapid Smoking	Truncated Rapid Smoking	Reduced Counseling
Cigarettes	1.04	.83	.55	.82
Water stimuli	.43	.30	.16	.31
Noise blasts	1.56	1.07	1.04	1.27

Note: SCR = skin conductance response. Pretreatment SCR used as covariate. SCR is expressed in umhos.
Source: Compiled by the authors.

displayed a substantial increase in their confidence in their ability to resist urges in these diverse situations. Based on the cluster analysis of the Confidence Questionnaire by Condiotte and Lichtenstein (1981), seven cluster scores representing distinct groups of smoking situations were obtained from each subject and subjected to analysis in order to explore group differences. In accord with the global confidence rating, this detailed evaluation of self-efficacy across a variety of smoking situations did not discriminate treatment groups.

Psychophysiological Assessments

Skin Conductance Response.   Table 8.6 shows the covariate adjusted skin conductance response (SCR) means (using pretreatment response as a covariate) for each group in response to the various stimuli presented during posttreatment psychophysiological assessments. This table suggests that full-scale rapid smoking subjects with full counseling displayed the greatest skin conductance response to cigarettes following aversive conditioning and that rapid puffing subjects displayed the lowest SCR. However, our analysis showed that there were no significant group differences on this measure. The same group patterns emerged for SCRs to water stimuli and noise blasts, but again, none of these differences was significant. Thus, in this study, as in Erickson et al. (1983), SCRs to cigarettes or nonsmoking stimuli were not strongly related to type of aversion training employed during treatment.

Heart Rate Response. Among the various posttreatment aversion measures only heart-rate response to cigarettes clearly discriminated among the treatment groups. Figure 8.3 shows the second-by-second heart rate response to cigarettes for 50 seconds after the cigarette presentation for the full-scale rapid smoking group with full counseling. These data are expressed as deviations from the prestimulus baseline (i.e., the average of five seconds prior to the tone signaling subjects to open their eyes) in beats per minute. An examination of the average pretreatment response shows that from seconds one through six there is an initial acceleration followed by a deceleration back to baseline. (This portion of the heart rate response corresponds to the period when the subject is puffing on the cigarette.) Following this there is another acceleration that peaks above the initial acceleration and then decelerates to baseline within approximately 20 seconds. During the posttreatment assessments, the same wave form is again observed, but now the second acceleration is higher than in pretreatment, and although there is some deceleration, the heart rate remains elevated throughout the interval.

In comparison, the heart rate wave form response to cigarettes for the rapid puffing group is shown in Figure 8.4. Again, there is a two-component wave form for both pre- and posttreatment response, but in this group there is no difference in peak response, and although during the posttreatment assessment the heart rate remains elevated over baseline throughout the assessment period, this elevation is not of the same magnitude observed in the full-scale rapid smoking with full counseling treatment.

The posttreatment peak heart rate response to cigarettes for each group is depicted in Figure 8.5. These are covariate adjusted means representing the maximum acceleration within 20 seconds of stimulus onset determined for each cigarette presentation across the two posttreatment assessments. (The average of seconds 7 through 20 of the pretreatment response was selected as the covariate for all heart rate analysis of responses to cigarettes, as analyses of pilot data indicated that this component was the most representative of pretreatment heart rate responsiveness to cigarettes.) It can be seen that the two groups receiving full-scale rapid smoking, that is, with either full or reduced counseling, exhibit a greater elevation in peak heart rate than the two groups that had a lower level of aversive conditioning during treatment, that is, truncated rapid smoking and rapid puffing. Our analysis showed that the two full-scale rapid smoking groups had significantly elevated peak heart rate in comparison to the truncated rapid smoking and rapid puffing groups. These data replicate the findings of Erickson et al. (1983) with aversive treatments designed to produce substantial levels of central malaise eliciting greater heart rate acceleration in response to cigarettes than treatments utilizing a lower level of aversion.

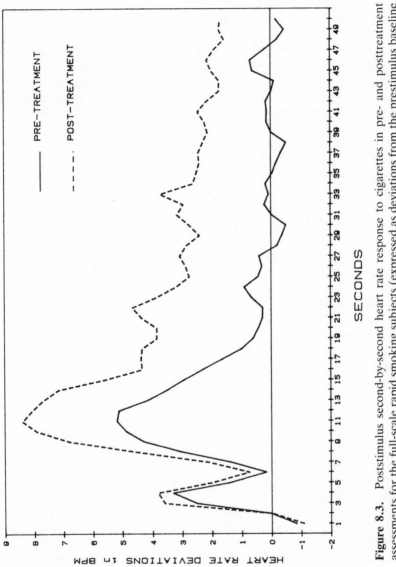

Figure 8.3. Poststimulus second-by-second heart rate response to cigarettes in pre- and posttreatment assessments for the full-scale rapid smoking subjects (expressed as deviations from the prestimulus baseline in bpm). *Source:* Reprinted with permission from Tiffany, S. T.; E. M. Martin; and T. B. Baker. (1986). Treatments for cigarette smoking: An evaluation of the contributions of aversion and counseling procedures. *Behaviour Research and Therapy*, 24:437–52. Copyright 1986, Pergamon Journals, Ltd.

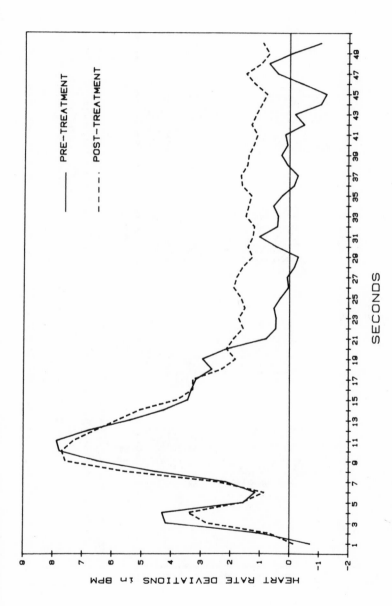

Figure 8.4. Poststimulus second-by-second heart rate response to cigarettes in pre- and posttreatment assessments for the rapid puffing subjects (expressed as deviations from the prestimulus baseline in bpm). *Source:* Reprinted with permission from Tiffany, S. T., E. M. Martin; and T. B. Baker. (1986). Treatments for cigarette smoking: An evaluation of the contributions of aversion and counseling procedures. *Behaviour Research and. Therapy,* 24:437–52. Copyright 1986; Pergamon Journals, Ltd.

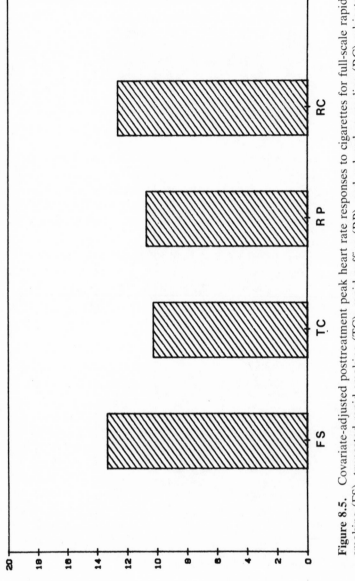

Figure 8.5. Covariate-adjusted posttreatment peak heart rate responses to cigarettes for full-scale rapid smoking (FS), truncated rapid smoking (TC), rapid puffing (RP), and reduced counseling (RC) subjects (expressed as maximum deviations from the prestimulus baselines in bpm. Pretreatment response used as covariate. *Source:* Reprinted with permission from Tiffany, S. T.; E. M. Martin; and T. B. Baker. (1986). Treatments for cigarette smoking: An evaluation of the contributions of aversion and counseling procedures. *Behaviour Research and Therapy*, 24:437–52. Copyright 1986, Pergamon Journals, Ltd.

In an analysis of the phasic heart rate responses to cigarettes, the wave form was averaged across five separate time blocks. These segments, second 1 to 6, 7 to 20, 21 to 30, 31 to 40, and 41 to 50, capture the essential components of the phasic heart rate data. Figure 8.6 shows that the covariate adjusted averages for each of the five components from the heart rate responses of rapid puffing subjects are lower than those of subjects receiving other treatments. At seconds 21 through 30 the full-scale rapid smoking group with full counseling remains elevated while the rapid puffing and reduced counseling groups have declined considerably. The truncated rapid smoking group is intermediate in level. At seconds 31 and 40, and 41 and 50, the same pattern continues, with the full-scale rapid smoking with full counseling group elevated over both the rapid puffing and reduced counseling treatments. The truncated rapid smoking remains intermediate to these groups.

Across all time blocks the rapid puffing group was significantly lower than the full-scale rapid smoking group with full counseling. We conducted analyses at each time block comparing the two full-scale rapid smoking groups. At seconds 1 to 6 and 7 to 20 these groups did not differ, but the reduced counseling group was significantly lower than the full counseling group at the 21 to 30, 31 to 40, and 40 to 50 second intervals.

In general, these heart rate data appear to reflect the manipulations of level of central malaise in our study and also the impact of counseling. Overall, a treatment designed to produce maximum levels of central malaise (i.e., full-scale rapid smoking), produces greater heart rate acceleration in response to cigarettes than does a treatment yielding substantially reduced malaise. Furthermore, heart rate elevations produced by full-scale rapid smoking are sustained for up to 50 seconds following cigarette presentation only if full counseling is provided.

Although it is impossible to identify definitively the mechanisms that subserve the cardiac accelerations to cigarettes, there is substantial information that they are associative in nature—that is, conditioned. For instance, group differences in cardiac response were specific to cigarettes, the stimuli paired with malaise. Analysis of posttreatment heart rate response to water stimuli revealed no significant effect due to treatment groups on peak response or average response over the 50 seconds of poststimulus sampling. Similar analyses on posttreatment heart rate response to noise blasts also did not discriminate treatment groups. Thus, these data replicate the findings of our first study in which only the full-scale rapid smoking group showed an increase in heart rate response to cigarettes from pre- to postassessments.

There is additional evidence that the enhanced cardiac accelerations to cigarettes are associative in nature. Intergroup differences were not dependent on pretreatment influences on heart rate reactivity; that is, intergroup differences in posttreatment cardiac response persisted even when pretreatment response was removed through partial regressions from posttreatment scores. Further, the fact that significantly elevated cigarette-elicited cardiac accelerations were found only among high-aversion (full-scale rapid smoking) subjects suggests that such accelerations cannot be attributed to general or nonspecific treatment characteristics, such as positive set or experimenter demand. In general, the pattern of results provides evidence of a conditioned aversion to cigarettes produced by the rapid smoking technique with the conditioned response being best reflected in posttreatment heart rate response to cigarettes. This conclusion is in accord with other investigations of taste-aversion treatments for addictive disorders that have shown that cardiac responsiveness to target stimuli serves as a reliable index of aversion therapy (Baker and Cannon 1979; Cannon and Baker 1981; Cannon, Baker, and Wehl 1981, Cannon et al. 1983).

Follow-up

The follow-up results suggest that both full-strength aversion and full-scale counseling were necessary to produce the best outcome. Table 8.7 shows the four indexes of smoking status analyzed for this study: number of subjects abstinent per group, percentage of baseline smoking, number of days abstinent per group, and number of days to first relapse. It can be seen that type of aversive smoking strategy did affect long-term outcome. At each interval during the six months of follow-up, the full-scale rapid smoking group with full counseling had a higher percentage of abstinent subjects than any other group. Thus, while truncated rapid smoking and rapid puffing produced fairly high levels of immediate cessation, subjects in these groups tended to relapse more quickly than subjects receiving maximum aversion with full counseling. This was particularly true for subjects receiving truncated rapid smoking, who exhibited high abstinence rates at treatment termination and in the early phase of follow-up but declined considerably as the follow-up progressed. At 180 days these subjects had a significantly earlier first relapse and a higher percentage of baseline smoking than the full-scale rapid smoking subjects with full counseling. These data are consistent with basic research showing a strong positive relationship between the dose of an illness-producing drug (i.e., the unconditioned stimulus) and taste aversion retention (Elkins 1984).

Rapid puffing subjects, who received an aversive treatment that minimized the production of central malaise, had a significantly lower abstinence rate than full-scale smoking subjects with full counseling at an early stage of follow-up (i.e., 45 days) but were not significantly different from any other treatment on any other outcome measure. This outcome is similar to that reported by Erickson et al. (1983) in which rapid puffing enhanced the effects of behavioral counseling but did not produce

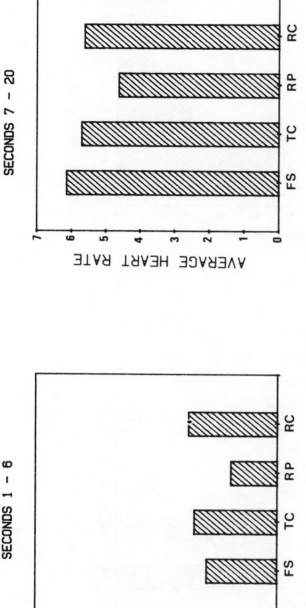

Figure 8.6. Posttreatment heart rate response to cigarettes (covariate-adjusted means) averaged for each of five time intervals across 50 second poststimulus presentations for the full-scale rapid smoking (FS), truncated rapid smoking (TC), rapid puffing (RP), and reduced counseling (RC) subjects (expressed in bpm; pretreatment response used as covariate). *Source:* Reprinted with permission from Tiffany, S. T.; E. M. Martin; and T. B. Baker. (1986). Treatments for cigarette smoking: An evaluation of the contributions of aversion and counseling procedures. *Behaviour Research and Therapy*, 24:437–52. Copyright 1986, Pergamon Journals, Ltd.

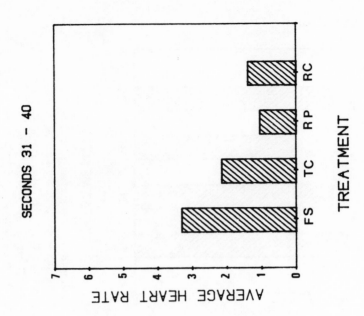

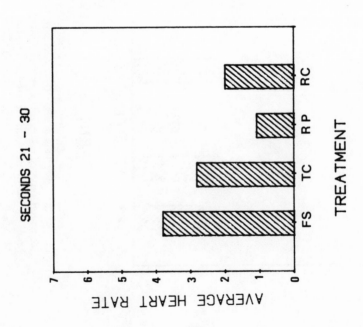

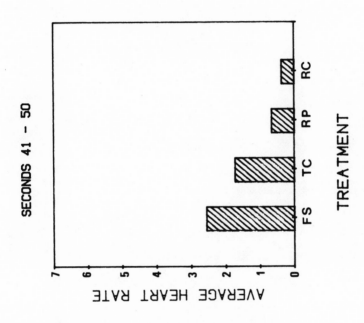

Figure 8.6. (continued)

Table 8.7
Outcome Measures by Treatment Groups

	Treatment Group			
Outcome Measures	Full-Scale Rapid Smoking	Truncated Rapid Smoking	Rapid Puffing	Reduced Counseling
Ss abstinent (%)				
At treatment completion	100	100	80	70
At 45 days	91	80	65	50
At 90 days	73	70	60	45
At 135 days	68	40	60	35
At 180 days	59	35	55	35
% of baseline smoking				
At 90 days	13.0	20.0	20.0	30.1
At 180 days	18.0	46.5	26.7	44.7
Mean number of days abstinent				
At 90 days	77.6	67.3	66.1	54.9
At 180 days	137.9	103.3	119.5	85.8
Mean number of days to first relapse at 180 days	111.6	69.1	90.2	46.2

Source: Reprinted with permission from Tiffany, S.T.; E. M. Martin; and T. B. Baker. (1986). Treatments for cigarette smoking: An evaluation of the contributions of aversion counseling procedures. *Behaviour Research and Therapy*, 24:447. Copyright 1986, Pergamon Journals, Ltd.

outcomes as good as those produced by rapid smoking. Together, the present results and those of Erickson et al. (1983) suggest that even though aversive interventions that induce mild or moderate levels of malaise may increment the effectiveness of smoking counseling treatments, the best results would be expected with aversive treatment in which high levels of central malaise are associated with smoking. Our finding that the best long-term results are associated with a treatment based on taste aversion learning is in accord with findings of Cannon et al. (1981, 1983), who reported that chemical, but not shock, aversion therapy enhanced the effectiveness of an alcoholism counseling program.

Although the rapid puffing treatment was not significantly different from any of the other treatments across long-term follow-up, the abstinence rate of 55% at six months for subjects receiving this intervention is notable. (Even the six-month abstinence rate of 44% produced by the rapid puffing treatment in our first study exceeds the typical outcome reported for most behavioral interventions.) Some authors have advocated a rapid puffing procedure for reasons of safety and practicality (e.g., Russell et al. 1978; Tori 1978). Others have noted that given proper precautions, rapid smoking may be a relatively safe procedure for smokers with even moderate cardiopulmonary disease (Hall et al. 1984). Our data suggest that rapid puffing may be a promising alternative for smokers for whom the safety of rapid smoking has not been established. Leventhal and Cleary (1980) have proposed that rapid puffing may be effective because the nonreinforced exposure to smoking cues should extinguish conditioned compensatory drug responses. It has been hypothesized that such responses contribute to relapse among drug addicts (e.g., Poulos, Hinson, and Siegel 1981; Solomon 1980; although cf. Baker and Tiffany 1985).

Across the various long-term outcome indexes, the full-scale rapid smoking treatment combined with full counseling produced an outcome superior to that of a treatment using full rapid smoking but employing reduced counseling. The full-scale rapid smoking subjects were significantly different from the reduced counseling subjects on percentage of baseline smoking at 180 days, number of days abstinent at 90 and 180 days, and days to first relapse at 180 days. The abstinence rates of the full-scale rapid smoking treatment were significantly higher than the reduced counseling treatment at 45 and 135 days and approached significance at 90 days. Overall, these data strongly support the conclusion that our full counseling procedures clearly incremented the short-term and long-term success of the rapid smoking treatment.

The abstinence rates of the full-scale rapid smoking treatment with full counseling replicate the outcome of Erickson et al. (1983) and are comparable to the early rapid smoking studies. In Erickson et al. we showed that full-scale rapid smoking substantially incremented the clinical impact of behavioral counseling procedures. Those results, along with the present findings that counseling enhances the rapid smoking treatment, suggest that the combination of full counseling and full-scale rapid smoking accounts for the success of our smoking treatment package. Neither component alone is sufficient; both are necessary for the best short- and long-term outcome.

The counseling effect observed in the present study is unusual in smoking research (see Lichtenstein 1982 for a review of the impact of various counseling interventions on long-term outcome). It must be noted that we have no conclusive proof that (1) we actually said different things to the different groups; or (2) that the content of the full counseling was crucial, as opposed to the duration of therapist contact per se. However, the difference in clinical outcome between the full counseling and reduced counseling treatments cannot be readily attributed to discrepancies in nonspecific elements or treatment credibility. The reduced counseling program was specifically designed to contain the nonspecific elements of the full counseling package (e.g., strong support and encouragement for abstinence, self-monitoring of cigarette consumption) and also included a variety of interventions that have been widely advocated for the treatment of cigarette smoking—for example, relaxation training, monitoring of urges to smoke, contracting, general suggestions for quitting, access to a smokers' hotline. These elements combined to form a treatment package that was credible, comparable to many other smoking treatment approaches, and rated as no less effective than the full-scale counseling treatment by its participants. Moreover, the end-of-treatment abstinence rate of 70% in the reduced counseling treatment is consistent with treatment termination abstinence rates produced by most rapid smoking packages (Danaher 1977b) and superior to the short-term impact of many other smoking cessation programs (e.g., McFall and Hammen 1971; Raw 1978). The six-month abstinence rate of 35% is comparable to most other rapid smoking studies (Danaher 1977b). Nevertheless, the addition of certain counseling components to this basic package clearly enhanced the impact of the treatment.

In addition to the elements presented in the reduced counseling, the full-scale counseling included training in anticipating problem situations and engaging in coping strategies to manage urges; presentation of a model of cigarette addiction that acknowledged physiological and psychological processes in the disorder, as well as the interaction of those processes in the maintenance of the addiction; and attention to the maintenance of abstinence by preparing subjects for cognitive, affective, behavioral, and situational precursors to relapse. Our data do not allow us to determine which component or set of components in the coping response training contributed most to the incremental effect of the full counseling package, but the outcome measures suggest that the specific content of behavioral counseling is an important factor in the impact of treatment packages for smoking cessation. We did not include an assessment of the content or process of the therapeutic interactions during counseling, nor did we evaluate subjects' detailed perceptions of the therapeutic interventions. A careful examination of such variables in future research may amplify the crucial differences between our two counseling packages and suggest the features essential to a positive clinical outcome.

Recently Hall and her associates (Hall et al. 1984) investigated the impact of "skills training" on the long-term abstinence produced by aversive smoking treatments. The skills training utilized by these researchers consisted of three components: relaxation training, enhancement of commitment to quitting by a review of the costs of smoking, and relapse-prevention skill training. The relapse-prevention portion of the skills training contained some elements similar to the coping-response training employed in our full-scale behavioral counseling program. Subjects were first trained to anticipate scenarios likely to promote relapse and then encouraged to generate responses (e.g., through role playing) to deal more effectively with the high-risk situations. Their results showed that smokers administered skill training in combination with one of two forms of aversive smoking evidenced significantly more abstinence across one year of follow-up than subjects given the aversive smoking treatments combined with a control intervention in which problems associated with smoking cessation were discussed in an unstructured format. The design of this study did not allow for a determination of the active ingredients of the skill-training intervention, but our data would suggest that the most potent element was the relapse-prevention skill training. The two aversive smoking treatments used in this research were rapid smoking, limited to one trial per treatment session (i.e., comparable to our truncated rapid smoking treatment), and a slower-paced smoking procedure in which subjects inhaled once every 30 seconds. Interestingly, the outcome data indicated that there was no difference in abstinence rates produced by these two aversive treatments. This would be consistent with the results of our studies, which show that rapid smoking is maximally effective only when very high sustained levels of malaise are produced by the aversion treatments.

Relationships Between Treatment and Outcome Variables

Relationships between treatment measures and outcome were examined to elucidate further factors that potentially differentiated treatments, identify variables that predicted long-term outcome, and evaluate hypotheses regarding the impact of aversion treatments. Table 8.8 reveals the zero-order correlations between the pre-, intra-, and posttreatment measures with two indexes of outcome: days to first relapse and days abstinent at 180 days for all subjects across the groups. Four types of variables appear to be significantly related to outcome. The variables most highly associated with long-term outcome are confidence ratings of remaining abstinent from cigarettes and ratings of treatment effectiveness. Both the global rating of confidence and the more detailed confidence questionnaire were positively correlated with long-term outcome, particularly posttreatment confidence measures. The second set of variables represents cigarette consumption before, during, and after treatment as indicated by actual cigarette consumption and CO measures. For instance, estimates of pretreatment smoking rate, pretreatment baseline consumption of cigarettes, reduction in smoking just prior to the onset of treatment, cigarettes smoked outside of treatment sessions, presession CO levels, and posttreatment CO levels were negatively correlated with outcome. The third set of predictor variables is associated with the flavor ratings of cigarettes. Subjects rating the flavor of cigarettes more negatively following treatment had a better long-term outcome. Finally, posttreatment peak heart rate response to water presentations was positively correlated with outcome.

In a further examination of the relationship of treatment variables with long-term outcome (i.e., through 180 days), we regressed days to first relapse and days abstinent on the variables depicted in Table 8.8. This analysis utilized a stepwise multiple regression by which variables were entered into the regression equation in descending order of their zero-order correlation with the criterion measure. Three variables emerged as significant predictors of days to first relapse among all subjects: posttreatment global confidence rating ($sR^2 = .1637$; $F[1,80] = 15.66$; $p < .0001$), average rating of peripheral irritation following aversive smoking session ($sR^2 = .0438$; $F[1,79] = 4.37$; $p < .05$), and previous attempts to quit smoking ($sR^2 = .0708$; $F[1,78] = 7.65$; $p < .01$). Confidence rating was positively related to outcome, while postsession ratings of peripheral irritation and previous attempts to quit smoking were negatively related to outcome. (It is of interest to note that higher levels of peripheral irritation are associated with poorer outcome across various types of aversive treatments, a relationship not supportive of the hypothesis that peripheral irritation contributes to the success of rapid smoking; e.g., Danaher 1977b.) A similar analysis of days abstinent at 180 days showed that three variables were predictive of this measure: posttreatment global confidence rating ($sR^2 = .2349$; $F[1,80] = 24.57$; $p < .0001$), pretreatment baseline cigarettes ($sR^2 = .1009$; $F[1,79] = 123.00$; $p < .001$), and the gender of the subjects ($sR^2 = .386$; $F[1,78] = 4.81$; $p < .05$). Global confidence rating was again positively related to outcome, while pretreatment baseline cigarette consumption was negatively related. Females tended to have fewer abstinent days than males.

Across both outcome indexes, posttreatment ratings of global confidence were the best predictors of long-term performance. Similarly, this measure was found to be the best predictor of long-term outcome in Erickson et al. (1983). Apparently, this relationship is quite reliable, as other researchers have found that self-efficacy appraisals are reliably associated with success in smoking treatment programs (e.g., Condiotte and Lichtenstein 1981; McIntyre, Lichtenstein, and Mermelstein 1983;

Table 8.8
Correlations Between Outcome Measures at 180 Days and Treatment Variables

Outcome Measure	Age	Gender[a]	Estimated Cigarettes/day	Baseline Cigarettes/day	Years Smoking	Previous Quit Attempts	Current Satisfaction with smoking[b]	Anticipated difficulty quitting[b]
First relapse	-.04	-.17	-.20	-.19	-.13	-.10	.07	-.06
Days abstinent	.03	-.22*	-.33**	-.42**	-.01	-.03	.05	-.09

Heart rate response

	Cigarettes				Water				Noise Blasts			
	Pre peak	Post peak	Pre average	Post average	Pre peak	Post peak	Pre average	Post average	Pre peak	Post peak	Pre average	Post average
First relapse	.16	.07	.21	.13	.15	.23*	.09	.09	.00	.00	.18	.03
Days abstinent	.08	.04	.16	.11	.10	.25*	.06	.12	-.02	-.04	-.11	.02

Table 8.8
(continued)

| | Skin conductance response | | | | | | Confidence ratings | | | | Treatment Effectiveness[c] |
| | Cigarettes | | Water | | Noise Blasts | | Global[c] | | Questionnaire[b] | | |
	Pre	Post	Pre	Post	Pre	Post	Pre	Post	Pre	Post	
First relapse	-.09	-.10	-.13	-.10	.01	-.04	.17	.40**	.13	.32**	.37**
Days abstinent	-.03	-.16	-.06	-.11	.00	-.12	.09	.48**	.28**	.42**	.46**

| | CO levels | | | | Aversion session ratings[d] | | | | Reduction smoking | Treatment smoking |
	Pre treatment	Post treatment	Pre session	Post session	Urges	Central malaise	Peripheral irritation	Headache		
First relapse	-.03	-.29**	-.22*	-.16	-.01	-.11	-.13	-.16	-.41**	-.15
Days abstinent	-.17	-.40**	-.27*	-.14	-.08	-.10	-.06	-.13	-.22*	-.22*

278

Cigarette taste test measures

| | Adjective ratings[e] | | | | Consumption Measures | | | |
| | Positive | | Negative | | Puffs | | Time Smoking | |
	Pre	Post	Pre	Post	Pre	Post	Pre	Post
First relapse	-.11	-.23*	.03	.27*	-.03	-.02	.08	-.16
Days abstinent	-.22*	.00	.18	.00	.02	.04	.15	-.09

Note: Correlations are for all subjects ($n = 82$). Heart rate response, peak = maximum acceleration after stimulus presentation; heart rate response, average = average over 50 seconds after stimulus presentations; confidence ratings, global = subjects' ratings of their confidence in remaining abstinent; questionnaire = subjects' ratings of their confidence of resisting urge to smoke in smoking situations; treatment effectiveness = posttreatment ratings of overall treatment effectiveness; urges = average number of strong urges reported by subjects during treatment aversion session ratings; central malaise = average of five ratings reflecting central malaise across aversion trials; peripheral irritation = average of two ratings reflecting peripheral irritation across aversion trials; headache = average rating of headache rating across aversion trials; reduction smoking = cigarettes smoked over three days of reduced smoking just prior to treatment; treatment smoking = cigarettes smoked after treatment began; adjective ratings, positive = average across the positive adjective ratings of flavors; negative = average across the negative adjective ratings of flavors.

[a]Female scored 1, male scored 0
[b]Rated on a scale from 0 to 100%
[c]Rated on a scale from 1 (not at all) to 5 (extremely)
[d]Rated on a scale from 1 (none) to 7 (extremely)
[e]Rated on a scale from 1 (not at all) to 4 (extremely)
*$p < .05$
**$p < .01$
Source: Compiled by the authors.

Owen et al. 1982). Bandura (1977) has posited that expectancies of personal efficacy mediate the initiation and persistence of coping behavior and are based on four major sources of information: performance accomplishments, vicarious experience, verbal persuasion, and emotional arousal. To determine the set of factors most highly related to confidence in the present study, stepwise regression was used to predict posttreatment confidence rating from the other pre-, intra-, and posttreatment variables. (The pre- and posttreatment Confidence Questionnaire was excluded from this analysis because of the conceptual and statistical redundancy of this measure with the global confidence rating.) This analysis revealed that ratings of treatment effectiveness ($sR^2 = .4600$; $F[1,80] = 70.66$; $p < .0001$), cigarettes smoked outside of sessions during the treatment phase ($sR^2 = .0731$; $F[1,79] = 12.61$; $p < .01$), subject estimates of pretreatment cigarette consumption ($sR^2 = .520$; $F[1,78] = 9.99$; $p < .01$), postsession CO levels ($sR^2 = .0483$; $F[1,77] = 10.40$; $p < .01$), and positive flavor ratings of cigarettes in posttreatment taste tests ($sR^2 = .0351$; $F[1,76] = 8.26$; $p < .05$) accounted for significant portions of the variance in confidence ratings. In general, subjects who rated treatment as more effective, smoked less before and during treatment, had lower levels of CO following aversion sessions, and rated cigarette flavors less positively in posttreatment taste tests were the most confident of maintaining long-term abstinence. Ratings of treatment effectiveness alone accounted for 47% of the variance in posttreatment confidence ratings, indicating that subjects who perceive their treatment as ineffective are not likely to be confident of long-term success.

Posttreatment cardiac responses to cigarettes were not significantly related to long-term outcome across all subjects. If heart rate response to cigarettes reflects a conditioned aversion and if the magnitude of this aversion is related to clinical outcome, then posttreatment heart rate response should be predictive of latency to relapse among subjects receiving taste aversion conditioning—that is, rapid smoking subjects. This hypothesis was examined by a stepwise regression analysis on days to first relapse among the full-scale rapid smoking subjects (i.e., FS and RC) using all the pre-, intra-, and posttreatment variables. (This analysis was limited to subjects who had smoked at all during the follow-up [$n = 28$] in order to avoid restriction of range on the dependent variable.) Posttreatment average heart rate response to cigarettes was the only variable significantly predictive of latency to relapse among these subjects ($sR^2 = .2075$; $F[1,26] = 6.81$; $p < .05$). In contrast, an analysis of latency to relapse among subjects who had smoked any cigarettes during follow-up ($N = 28$) in the two low aversion groups (i.e., TC and RP) revealed that posttreatment heart rate response did not enter into the regression equation. Among these subjects, posttreatment confidence rating, postsession CO levels, posttreatment average heart rate response to noise blasts, and posttreatment skin conductance response to noise blasts were significantly related to relapse latency (multiple $R^2 = .54$; $F[4.23] = 6.75$; $p < .001$). Thus, cardiac response to cigarettes was predictive of relapse latency within the full aversion groups but not among subjects receiving an attenuated level of taste aversion conditioning.

In addition to our findings that cardiac response to cigarettes served as an index of aversion conditioning that was predictive of clinical outcome, there were some indications that general heart rate responsiveness was also associated with outcome. Across all subjects, posttreatment heart rate response to water was significantly correlated with days abstinent and days to first relapse. Also, posttreatment heart rate response to noise blasts was significantly predictive of relapse among low-aversion subjects. Similarly, in Erickson et al. (1983) we found that heart rate responses to neutral stimuli and even pretreatment responses to cigarettes were significantly related to outcome. These data suggest that general heart rate reactivity may reflect processes important to posttreatment functioning independent of treatment effects. In the Erickson et al. (1983) study we hypothesized that general heart rate reactivity reflected smoking history severity (e.g., years of smoking, level of cigarette consumption) that was, in turn, negatively correlated with outcome. An examination of the nonphysiological correlates of posttreatment heart rate response to water in our second study supported this, as pretreatment smoking level and years of regular smoking were the two variables most highly correlated with the heart rate measure (r's = $-.32$ and $-.25$, respectively; p's $< .05$). Thus, heart rate response was related to outcome in two principal ways in both of the studies we have described. There is a general (not treatment-specific) relationship between heart rate and outcome such that smoking history severity is associated both with quitting difficulty and with attenuated cardiac responsiveness. However, there is also a treatment-specific cardiac response that predicts long-term abstinence from cigarettes: a phasic cardiac acceleration produced by full-strength rapid smoking treatment.

A number of studies have produced results consistent with our finding that aversion therapy increases heart rate response to target stimuli and, further, that cardiac response predicts posttreatment abstinence (e.g., Cannon and Baker 1981; Cannon et al. 1981, 1983). Baker et al. (1984) have advanced the hypothesis that aversion conditioning increases a subject's fear and repugnance of target stimuli and that such responses are positively related to latency to relapse. They suggest that cardiac accelerations to posttreatment presentations of averted substances reflect defensive responses or stimulus rejection. Particularly noxious stimuli can elicit "defensive responses" that are characterized by large and persistent heart rate accelerations (Graham 1979), are associated with reduced sensitivity to stimulation (Graham 1979; Sokolov 1963), and are slow to extinguish or habituate (Graham 1979). Taste aversion learning may provide a particularly efficacious strategy for enhancing defensive responding to addictive substances that have a distinctive flavor and are administered orally.

In addition to defensive responses, Baker et al. (1984) have speculated that heart rate accelerations may reflect the processing of active-coping response information or the rehearsal of active-avoidance strategies when subjects encounter addictive substances. These two types of processing have been associated with significant phasic cardiac acceleration (e.g., Fowles 1980; Obrist 1976). Furthermore, research on factors related to smoking relapse indicates that subjects who engage in active-coping responses are much more likely to remain abstinent in the face of temptations to smoke (Shiffman 1982; 1984). Therefore, subjects who rehearse active-coping strategies when presented with a cigarette would exhibit heart rate accelerations and, presumably, be less likely to relapse when faced with future smoking situations. Our finding that only the full-scale rapid smoking treatment in combination with full counseling produced a sustained heart rate elevation suggests that this effect may represent a synergistic action between taste aversion conditioning and coping response training. One possibility is that taste aversion learning produces a defensive response that in turn triggers rehearsal of active-coping strategies in those subjects who had received such training during treatment.

SUMMARY AND CONCLUSIONS

The data from the two studies we have described provide support for the following arguments:

1.   The combination of full-aversion therapy with a counseling package that includes our coping response training results in the best short- and long-term outcome. Neither alone is sufficient; both appear to be necessary. With this treatment package we can replicate the high success rate of the early rapid smoking studies.

2.   The taste aversion learning paradigm provides a useful model to conceptualize the effectiveness of the rapid smoking treatment. Apparently, the production of central malaise in association with the flavor of cigarettes is an essential feature of the success of rapid smoking.

3.   There is evidence of a conditioned aversion to cigarettes produced by the rapid smoking technique, and this conditioned response is best indexed by posttreatment heart rate response to cigarettes. Moreover, this heart rate response is predictive of long-term outcome because it reflects aversive conditioning that, in turn, contributes to the maintenance of abstinence.

We view these hypotheses as providing the most parsimonious account of the data we have presented but recognize that further research is needed to replicate the findings and rule out alternative hypotheses. In our research we have apparently recaptured the level of clinical success associated with the initial rapid smoking studies, but the history of this treatment suggests that replications of these levels are difficult to achieve (Danaher 1977b). We believe that we have isolated critical factors that will aid in the replication of our results, and we are optimistic that the excellent outcomes we have found with the rapid smoking treatment can be obtained in other clinical laboratories.

Although we contend that taste aversion learning is an important component in rapid smoking success, we cannot, at present, rule out the influence of other factors that are unique to the rapid smoking procedures. For instance, it would be useful to isolate the taste-mediated learning components of the rapid smoking treatment from the effects of learning that smoking poses a personal health risk. Perhaps rapid smoking is effective because subjects learn in a first-hand manner that nicotine has profound toxic effects, and this renders other health-risk data personally relevant. One strategy for contrasting the taste-mediated learning and the health-risk learning effects would be to compare rapid smoking with a treatment in which cigarettes are paired with an illness-producing drug. To the extent that the principles of taste-mediated learning are operative, then drug-induced aversions should produce conditioning specific to cigarette flavors and promote avoidance of cigarettes (i.e., greater abstinence).

Most smoking treatment research has been of the horse race variety (McFall 1978). That is, treatments of various sorts are compared with one another with the primary aim of determining which treatment produces the best outcome. If successful, this research strategy has substantial clinical utility. Unfortunately, the selection of treatments for studies of this type often tend not to be motivated by explicit theoretical considerations, and the data generated rarely illuminate processes that may subserve treatment effects. In contrast to this approach, we have attempted to focus on the question of why a particular treatment may be effective. To this end, we have drawn from diverse areas of basic psychological research and theory—for example, taste-mediated learning, psychopharmacology, and psychophysiology—in order to understand and evaluate the impact of our treatments for smoking. We hope that this approach will ultimately enhance the effectiveness of our clinical interventions and provide insight into the processes that maintain addictive behavior.

ACKNOWLEDGMENTS

The authors wish to thank their collaborators on the studies described in this chapter: Lynelle Erickson and Eileen Martin. We thank Winnie Rockman for her assistance in manuscript preparation.

NOTE

1. The three dropouts from the full-scale rapid smoking treatment with reduced counseling were not included in the data analyses. Therefore, estimates of any success for this group are overestimates for the actual outcome of those who initiated treatment. The exclusion of these subjects is justified, because it biases the analyses against our hypothesis that the coping response training in the counseling package is a necessary component in the success of the full-scale rapid smoking treatment with full counseling.

REFERENCES

Baker, T. B., and D. S. Cannon. (1979). Taste aversion therapy with alcoholics: Techniques and evidence of a conditioned response. *Behaviour Research and Therapy*, 17:229–42.

Baker,T. B., and D. S. Cannon. (1982). Alcohol and taste mediated learning. *Addictive Behaviors*, 7:211–30.

Baker, T. B.; D. S. Cannon; S. T.Tiffany; and A. Gino. (1984). Cardiac response as an index of the effect of aversion therapy. *Behaviour Research and Therapy*, 22:403–11.

Baker, T. B., and S. T. Tiffany. (1985). Morphine tolerance as habituation. *Psychological Review*, 92:78–108.

Bandura, A. (1969). *Principles of behavior modification*. New York: Holt, Rinehart & Winston.

Bandura, A. (1977). Self-efficacy: Toward a unifying theory of behavioral change. *Psychological Review*, 84:191–215.

Berecz, J. M. (1973). Aversion by fiat: The problem of "face validity" in behavior therapy. *Behavior Therapy*, 4:110–16.

Berecz, J. M. (1974). Punishment, placebos, psychophysiology, and polemics in aversion therapy: A reply to Danaher and Lichtenstein. *Behavior Therapy*, 5:117–22.

Bernstein, D. A., and A. L. McAlister. (1976). The modification of smoking behavior: Progress and problems. *Addictive Behaviors*, 1:89–102.

Bernstein, I. L. (1978). Learned taste aversions in children receiving chemotherapy. *Science*, 200:1302–03.

Best, J. A.; L. E. Owen; and L. Trentadue. (1978). Comparison of satiation and rapid smoking in self-managed smoking cessation. *Addictive Behaviors*, 3:71–78.

Briddell, D. W.; D. C. Rimm; G. R. Caddy; and N. J. Dunn. (1979). Analogue assessment: Affective arousal and the smoking taste test. *Addictive Behaviors*, 4:289–95.

Cannon, D. S., and T. B. Baker. (1981). Emetic and electric shock alcohol aversion therapy: Assessment of conditioning. *Journal of Consulting and Clinical Psychology*, 49:20–33.

Cannon, D. S.; T. B. Baker, A. Gino; and P. E. Nathan. (1983). Chemical aversion therapy: Relationship of measures of aversion to clinical outcome. Paper presented at the annual meeting of the American Psychological Association, August, 1983, Los Angeles, Calif.

Cannon, D. S.; T. B. Baker; and C. K. Wehl. (1981). Emetic and electric shock alcohol aversion therapy: Six- and twelve-month follow-up. *Journal of Consulting and Clinical Pathology*, 49:360–68.

Cannon, D. S.; R. F. Berman; T. B. Baker; and C. A. Atkinson. (1975). Effect of preconditioning unconditioned stimulus experience on learned taste aversions. *Journal of Experimental Psychology: Animal Behavior Processes*, 1:270–84.

Cannon, D.S.; M. R. Best; J. D. Batson; and M. Feldman. (1983). Taste familiarity and apomorphine-induced taste aversions in humans. *Behaviour Research and Therapy*, 21:669–73.

Cappell, H., and A. E. LeBlanc. (1977). Gustatory avoidance conditioning of drugs of abuse: Relationships to general issues in research on drug dependence. In *Food Aversion Learning*, eds. N. W. Milgram, L. Krames, and T. M. Alloway. New York: Plenum.

Condiotte, M. M., and E. Lichtenstein. (1981). Self-efficacy and relapse in smoking cessation programs. *Journal of Consulting and Clinical Psychology*, 49:648–58.

Danaher, B. G. (1977a). Rapid smoking and self-control in the modification of smoking behavior. *Journal of Consulting and Clinical Psychology*, 45:1068–75.

Danaher, B. G. (1977b). Research on rapid smoking: Interim summary and recommendations. *Addictive Behaviors*, 2:151–66.

Danaher, B. G., and E. Lichtenstein. (1974). Aversion therapy issues: A note of clarification. *Behavior Therapy*, 5:112–16.

Elkins, R. L. (1984). Taste-aversion retention: An animal experiment with implications for consummatory-aversion alcoholism treatments. *Behaviour Research and Therapy*, 22:179–86.

Elkins, R. F., and S. H. Hobbs. (1979). Forgetting, preconditioning CS familiarization and taste aversion learning: An animal experiment with implications for alcoholism treatment. *Behaviour Research and Therapy*, 17:567–73.

Elliott, C. H., and D. R. Denney. (1978). A multicomponent treatment approach to smoking reduction. *Journal of Consulting and Clinical Psychology*, 44:1002–07.

Erickson, L. M.; S. T. Tiffany; E. M. Martin; and T. B. Baker. (1983). Aversive smoking therapies: A conditioning analysis of therapeutic effectiveness. *Behaviour Research and Therapy*, 21:595–611.

Fowles, D. C. (1980). The three arousal model: Implications of Gray's two-factor learning theory for heart rate, electrodermal activity, and psychopathy. *Psychophysiology*, 17:87–104.

Garcia, J., and R. R. Ervin. (1968). Gustatory-visceral and teleroceptorcutaneous conditioning adaptation in internal and external mileus. *Communications in Behavioral Biology*, 1:389–415.

Garcia, J.; W. Hankins, and K. Rusiniak. (1974). Behavioral regulation of the milieu interne in men and rats. *Science*, 185:824–31.

Glasgow, R. E. (1978). Effects of a self-control manual, rapid smoking, and amount of therapist contact on smoking reduction. *Journal of Consulting and Clinical Psychology*, 46:1493–97.

Glasgow, R. E.; E. Lichtenstein; C. Beaver; and K. O'Neill. (1981). Subjective reactions to rapid and normal paced aversive smoking. *Addictive Behaviors*, 6:53–59.

Goudie, A. J., and D. W. Dickens. (1978). Nitrous-oxide-induced conditioned taste aversion in rats: The role of duration of drug exposure and its relation to the taste aversion-self-administration "paradox." *Pharmacology, Biochemistry and Behaviour*, 9:587–92.

Goudie, A. J.; D. W. Dickens; and E. W. Thornton. (1978). Cocaine-induced conditioned taste aversions in rats. *Pharmacology, Biochemistry and Behavior*, 8:757–61.

Goudie, A. J.; I. R. Stollerman; C. Demellweek; and G. D. D'Mello. (1982). Does conditioned nausea mediate drug-induced conditioned taste aversion? *Psychopharmacology*, 78:277–81.

Graham, F. K. (1979). Distinguishing among orienting, defense, and startle reflexes. In *The orienting reflex in humans*, eds. H. D. Kimmel, E. H. Von Olst, and J. F. Orlebeke, pp. 137–67. Hillsdale, N.J.: Erlbaum.

Hall, R. G.; D. P. L. Sachs; and S. M. Hall. (1979). Medical risk and therapeutic effectiveness of rapid smoking. *Behavior Therapy*, 10:249–59.

Hall, R. G.; D. P. L. Sachs; S. M. Hall; and N. L. Benowitz. (1984). Two-year efficacy and safety of rapid smoking therapy in patients with cardiac and pulmonary disease. *Journal of Consulting and Clinical Psychology*, 52:574–81.

Hall,S. M.; D. Rugg; C. Tunstall; and R. T. Jones. (1984). Preventing relapse to cigarette smoking by behavioral skill training. *Journal of Consulting and Clinical Psychology*, 52:372–82.

Hallam, R. S., and S. Rachman. (1976). Current status of aversion therapy. In *Progress in behavior modification*, vol. 2, eds. M. Hersen, R. M. Eisler, and P. M. Miller, pp. 179–222. New York: Academic Press.

Harris, D. E., and E. Lichtenstein. (1971). Contribution of nonspecific social variables to a successful, behavioral treatment of smoking. Paper presented at the annual meeting of the Western Psychological Association, April, 1971, San Francisco, Calif.

Hunt, W. A., and D. A. Bespalec. (1974). An elevation of current methods of modifying smoking behavior. *Journal of Clinical Psychology*, 30:431–38.

Ionesecu, E., and O. Buresuva. (1977). Failure to elicit a severe taste aversion by severe poisoning. *Pharmacology, Biochemistry, and Behavior*, 6:251–54.

Kalat, J. W., and P. Rozin. (1971). Role of interference in taste-aversion learning. *Journal of Comparative and Physiological Psychology*, 77:53–58.

Kozlowski, L. T. (1981). Pharmacological approaches to smoking modification. In *Behavioral health: A handbook of health enhancement and disease prevention*, eds. J. D. Matarazzo, S. M. Weiss, J. A. Herd, N. E. Miller, and S. M. Weiss, pp. 713–28. New York: Wiley and Sons.

Lando, H. A. (1975). A comparison of excessive and rapid smoking in the modification of chronic smoking behavior. *Journal of Consulting and Clinical Psychology*, 43:350–55.

Lando, H. A. (1977). Successful treatment of smokers with a broad-spectrum behavioral approach. *Journal of Consulting and Clinical Psychology*, 45:361–66.

Lando, H. A. (1978). Stimulus control, rapid smoking, and contractual management in the maintenance of nonsmoking. *Behavior Therapy*, 9:962–63.

Lang, P. J. (1978). Anxiety: Toward a psychophysiological definition. In *Psychiatric diagnosis: Exploration of biological criteria*, eds. H. S. Akiskal and W. L. Webb, pp. 265–389. New York: Spectrum.

Leventhal, H., and P. D. Cleary. (1980). The smoking problem: A review of the research and theory in behavioral risk modification. *Psychological Bulletin*, 88:370–405.

Lichtenstein, E. (1982). The smoking problem: A behavioral perspective. *Journal of Consulting and Clinical Psychology*, 50:804–19.

Lichtenstein, E., and R. A. Brown. (1980). Smoking cessation methods: Review and recommendations. In *The addictive behaviors: Treatment of alcoholism, drug abuse, smoking, and obesity*, ed. W. R. Miller, pp. 169–206. New York: Pergamon.

Lichtenstein, E., and B. G. Danaher. (1976). Modification of smoking behavior: A critical analysis of theory, research and practice. In *Progress in behavior modification*, vol. 3, eds. M. Hersen, R. M. Eisler, and P. M. Miller, pp. 133–72. New York: Academic Press.

Lichtenstein, E.; D. E. Harris; G. R. Birchler; J. M. Wahl; and D. P. Schmahl. (1973). Comparison of rapid smoking, warm smoky air, and attention placebo in the modification of smoking behavior. *Journal of Consulting and Clinical Psychology*, 40:92–98.

Logue, A. W.; I. Ophir; and K. E. Strauss. (1981). The acquisition of taste aversions in humans. *Behavior Research and Therapy*, 19:319–33.

Lublin, I. (1969). Principles governing the choice of unconditioned stimuli in aversive smoking. In *Advances in Behavior Therapy*, eds. R.D. Rubin and C. M. Franks, pp. 73–81. New York: Academic Press.

Lublin, I., and L. Joslyn. (1968). Aversive conditioning of cigarette addiction. Paper presented at the meeting of the Western Psychological Association, September, 1968, Los Angeles, Calif.

Marlatt, G. A., and J. R. Gordon. (1980). Determinants of relapse: Implications for the maintenance of behavior change. In *Behavioral medicine: Changing health lifestyles*, eds. P. O. Davidson and S. M. Davidson, pp. 410–52. New York: Brunner/Mazel.

McAlister (1975). Revivification of negative imagery as a self-control skill: Maintaining nonsmoking. Unpublished manuscript, Stanford University.

McFall, R. M. (1978). Smoking cessation research. *Journal of Consulting and Clinical Psychology*, 46:703–12.

McFall, R. M., and C. L. Hammen. (1971). Motivation, structure and self-monitoring: Role of nonspecific factors in smoking reduction. *Journal of Consulting and Clinical Psychology*, 37:80–86.

McIntyre, K. O.; E. Lichtenstein; and R. J. Mermelstein. (1983). Self-efficacy and relapse in smoking cessation: A replication and extension. *Journal of Consulting and Clinical Psychology*, 51:632–33.

Merbaum, M.; R. Avimier; and J. Goldberg. (1979). The relationship between aversion, group training and vomiting in the reduction of smoking behavior. *Addictive Behaviors*, 4:279–85.

Miller, P. M.; M. Hersen; R. M. Eisler; and D. P. Elkin. (1973). Electrical aversion therapy with alcoholics: An analogue study. *Behaviour Research and Therapy*, ll:491–97.

Norton, G. R., and B. Barske. (1977). The role of aversion in the rapid-smoking treatment procedure. *Addictive Behaviors*, 2:21–25.

Obrist, P.A. (1976). The cardiovascular-behavioral interaction—as it appears today. *Psychophysiology*, 13:95–107.

Owen, N.; A. Ewins; M. Bullock; and C. Lee. (1982). Adherence and relapse in health-related behaviors. In *Behavioral medicine*, ed. J. Sheppard. Sydney, Australia: Cumberland College.

Pechacek, T. F. (1977). An evaluation of cessation and maintenance strategies in the modification of smoking behavior. (Doctoral dissertation, University of Texas at Austin.) *Dissertation Abstracts International*, 38(5–B), 2380. (University Microfilms No. 77–23, 013.)

Pechacek, T. F., and G. B. Danaher. (1979). How and why people quit smoking: A cognitive-behavioral analysis. In *Cognitive-behavioral interventions: Theory, research, and procedures*, eds. P. C. Kendall and S. D. Hollon, pp. 389–422. New York: Academic Press.

Poole, A. D.; R. W. Sanson-Fisher; and G. A. German. (1981). The rapid-smoking technique: Therapeutic effectiveness. *Behaviour Research and Therapy*, 19: 389–97.

Poole, A. D.; R. W. Sanson-Fisher; G. A. German; and J. Harker. (1980). The rapid-smoking technique: Some physiological effects. *Behaviour Research and Therapy*, 18:581–86.

Poulos, C. X.; R. E. Hinson; and S. Siegel. (1981). The role of Pavlovian processes in drug use: Implications for treatment. *Addictive Behaviors*, 6:205–11.

Rachman, S. J., and J. D. Teasdale. (1969). Aversion therapy: An appraisal. In *Behavior Therapy: Appraisal and Status*, ed. C. M. Franks, pp. 279–320. New York: McGraw-Hill.

Raw, M. (1978). The treatment of cigarette dependence. In *Research advances in alcohol and drug problems*, vol. 4, eds. Y. Israel, F. B. Glaser, H. Kalant, R. E. Popham, W. Schmidt, and R. G. Smart, pp. 441–85. New York: Plenum Press.

Raw, M., and M. A. H. Russell. (1980). Rapid smoking, cue exposure and support in the modification of smoking. *Behaviour Research and Therapy*, 18:363–72.

Ringold, A.; J. R. Goldsmith; H. L. Helwig; R. Finn; and F. Schuette. (1962). Estimating recent carbon monoxide exposure. *Archives of Environmental Health*, 5:308–18.

Russell, M. A. H.; M. Raw; C. Taylor; C. Feyerabend; and Y. Saloojee. (1978). Blood nicotine and carboxyhemoglobin levels after rapid-smoking aversion therapy. *Journal of Consulting and Clinical Psychology*, 46:1423–31.

Schmahl, D. P.; E. Lichtenstein; and D. E. Harris. (1972). Successful treatment of habitual smokers with warm, smoking air and rapid smoking. *Journal of Consulting and Clinical Psychology*, 38:105–11.

Shiffman, S. (1982). Relapse following smoking cessation: A situational analysis. *Journal of Consulting and Clinical Psychology*, 50:71–86.

Shiffman, S. (1984). Coping with temptations to smoke. *Journal of Consulting and Clinical Psychology*, 52:261–67.

Shiffman, S. M., and M. E. Jarvik. (1976). Smoking withdrawal symptoms in two weeks of abstinence. *Psychopharmacology*, 50:35–39.

Siegel, S. (1975). Evidence from rats that morphine tolerance is a learned response. *Journal of Comparative and Physiological Psychology*, 89:498–506.

Sokolov, E. N. (1963). *Perception and conditioned reflex*. New York: Macmillan.

Solomon, R. L. (1980). The opponent-process theory of acquired motivation: The costs of pleasure and the benefits of pain. *American Psychologist*, 35:691–712.

Sutherland, A.; Z. Amit; M. Golden; and Z. Roseberger. (1975). Comparison of three behavioral techniques in the modification of smoking behavior. *Journal of Consulting and Clinical Psychology*, 43:443–47.

Taylor, P. (1980). Ganglionic stimulation and blocking agents. In *The pharmacological basis of therapeutics*, 6th ed., eds. A. G. Gilman, L. S. Goodman, and A. Gilman, pp. 211–19. New York: Macmillan.

Tiffany, S. T.; E. M. Martin; and T. B. Baker (1986). Treatments for cigarette smoking: An evaluation of the contributions of aversion and counseling procedures. *Behaviour Research and Therapy*, 24:437–52.

Tongas, P. N. (1979). The Kaiser-Permanente smoking control program: Its purpose and implications for an HMO. *Professional Psychology*, 10:409–18.

Tori, C. D. (1978). A smoking cessation procedure with reduced medical risk. *Journal of Clinical Psychology*, 34:574–77.

Weinrobe, P. A., and E. Lichtenstein. (1975). The use of urges as termination criterion in a rapid smoking treatment program for habitual smokers. Paper presented at the annual meeting of the Western Psychological Association, April, 1975, Sacramento, Calif.

Wilson, G. T., and G. C. Davison. (1969). Aversion techniques in behavior therapy: Some theoretical and metatheoretical considerations. *Journal of Consulting and Clinical Psychology*, 33:327–29.

Youngren, J. N., and R. A. Parker (1977). The smoking control clinic: A behavioral approach to quitting smoking. *Professional Psychology*, 8:81–87.

INDEX

Norton, G. R., 240, 241
Nunnally, J. C., 9, 34
Nusselt, L., 91

O'Brien, C. P., 153
O'Farrell, T. J., 5
O'Hollaren, P., 206
O'Leary, M. R., 39, 41, 42, 97, 153
O'Leary, S. G., 29
O'Shaughnessy, M., 119
obesity, 29, 44, 47, 65, 119
Obitz, F. W., 208
Obrist, P. A., 229, 230, 232, 282
obsessive-compulsive, 31, 42, 67, 70, 71, 91. 114, 117
Ogborne, A. C., 4
Olsson, G., 41, 44
Ophir, I., 243
Oppenheimer, E., 5
Ordman, A. M., 120, 141
Ordford, J., 5, 88
Orlenas, C. T., 160
Owen, L. E., 240
Owen, N., 280

Panksepp, J., 173
Parker, R. A., 240
Pattison, E. M., 206
Peachy, J. E., 90, 96, 97
Pechecek, T. F., 240
Pennebaker, J. W., 49, 57
Perlmuter, L. C., 62–65
Perri, M. G., 29, 35, 37, 40, 70
Persson, L., 40, 41, 44
Pertschuk, M., 39, 62
Peterson, L., 29, 33, 45, 47, 49
Phillips, J. S., 29
Phillips, R. A., 184
Polich, J. M., 4, 88, 228, 229
Pollak, J. J., 71
Pomerleau, O., 39, 62, 205
Poole, A. D., 240, 246, 256
Portner, J., 117
Postman, L., 55, 60
Poulos, C. X., 153, 273
Prebble, E., 180
Prentice-Dunn, S., 61
Printz, A. M., 114

Prochaska, J. O., 24
program dissemination, 181, 186, 187, 191, 192
psychophysiological assessment, 211, 212, 215, 230, 254, 272, 274, 278
Pryor, J. B., 57
Pyle, R. L., 113, 114, 115, 121
Pyszczynski, T. A., 64

Rachman, S. J., 30, 68, 70, 91, 206, 207, 230, 243
Rahe, R. H., 161
Rainwater, G., 41, 44–47, 50, 153
Rankin, H. J., 153
rapid puffing, 154, 155, 158, 165, 171, 244, 246, 249, 251, 258, 262, 267, 268, 270–82
rapid smoking, 152–57, 163, 243, 246, 248, 249, 251, 254, 258, 262, 267, 268–82
Rapoff, M. A., 30
Rardin, D., 34, 38–40
Raw, M., 154, 238, 239, 242, 274
Raynor, J. O., 60
Rehm, L. P., 36, 41, 47, 49, 50
Reich, J. W., 208
relapse, 3–5, 23, 31, 33, 38–49, 52, 62, 69, 88–90, 95, 96, 101, 104–108, 153, 156, 158, 160, 161, 167–75, 181, 224, 226, 247, 252, 256, 261, 270, 273, 278, 282
Relinger, H., 152, 171
Revusky, S., 207
Rhodes, R. J., 206, 207
Richards, C. S., 29, 35, 37, 40, 49, 70, 152
Rijsmon, J. B., 54
Riley, D. R., 5
Ring, K., 34
Ringold, A., 260
Rist, F., 89, 92
Ritter, B., 91, 92
Roizen, R., 4
Room, R., 4
Rosenbaum, M. C., 160
Rosenberg, S. E., 54
Rosenthal, B. S., 40
Rosman, B. L., 118, 129

ABOUT THE EDITORS AND CONTRIBUTORS

Helen M. Annis: Head, Health Care Systems Research, Addiction Research Foundation, Toronto, Canada

Timothy B. Baker: Professor of Psychology, University of Wisconsin—Madison

Thomas H. Brandon: Department of Psychology, University of Wisconsin—Madison

Dale S. Cannon: Chief, Psychology Service, Dallas Veterans Administration Medical Center

Christine S. Davis: Addiction Research Foundation, Toronto, Canada

Antonio Gino: Psychologist, Psychology Service of the Dallas Veterans Administration Medical Center

Sharon M. Hall: Professor, Medical Psychology, University of California, San Francisco

Laura Lynn Humphrey: Professor, Department of Psychiatry, Northwestern University Medical School

Daniel S. Kirschenbaum: Professor, Department of Psychiatry, Northwestern University Medical School

Hau Lei: Addiction Research Foundation, Toronto, Canada

Peter C. Loeb: Medical Psychology, University of California, San Francisco

Stephen A. Maisto: Professor, Brown University, Butler Hospital, Providence, Rhode Island

Peter E. Nathan: Professor, Department of Psychology, Rutgers University, Busch Campus

Linda C. Sobell: Associate Head, Behavioural Treatment Research, Addiction Research Foundation, Toronto, Canada

Mark B. Sobell: Associate Head, Behavioural Treatment Research, Addiction Research Foundation, Toronto, Canada

James L. Sorensen: Medical Psychology, University of California, San Francisco

Kathy Sykora: Addiction Research Foundation, Toronto, Canada

Stephen T. Tiffany: Assistant Professor, Purdue University

Diane C. Zelman: Department of Psychology, University of Wisconsin—Madison